THE NEW RELIGIOUS
CONSCIOUSNESS

THE NEW RELIGIOUS CONSCIOUSNESS

Edited by CHARLES Y. GLOCK *and* ROBERT N. BELLAH

With contributions by RANDALL H. ALFRED, ROBERT N. BELLAH, CHARLES Y. GLOCK, BARBARA HARGROVE, DONALD HEINZ, GREGORY JOHNSON, RALPH LANE, JR., JEANNE MESSER, RICHARD OFSHE, THOMAS PIAZZA, LINDA K. PRITCHARD, DONALD STONE, ALAN TOBEY, JAMES WOLFE, *and* ROBERT WUTHNOW

Foreword by P.J. PHILIP

UNIVERSITY OF CALIFORNIA PRESS
BERKELEY • LOS ANGELES • LONDON

University of California Press
Berkeley and Los Angeles, California
University of California Press, Ltd.
London, England
Copyright © 1976, by
The Regents of the University of California
ISBN 0-520- 03083-4
Library of Congress Catalog Card Number: 75-17295
Printed in the United States of America

2 3 4 5 6 7 8 9 0

In memory of
THOMAS O'DEA *and* IVAN VALLIER

CONTENTS

FOREWORD

A great deal has been written about the American youth culture of the 1960s and subsequent developments, but not much attention has been paid thus far to their religious dimensions. It is also a fact that most of the writers have based their interpretation of the cultural transformation on their own conjectures and preferences. The present volume has, on the other hand, "chosen religion as the strategic point of entry" into this field "because it is potentially the most profound level of change." The book has grown out of an extensive sociological study of groups and organizations that have contributed most to the youth counterculture. The investigation was centered in the San Francisco Bay Area, whose preeminence as a harbinger of the new consciousness and whose cosmopolitan character proved to be invaluable assets.

The book owes its strength to the able and dedicated research done by a team of advanced graduate students of the University of California and of the Graduate Theological Union, at Berkeley, under the leadership of Professors Robert N. Bellah and Charles Y. Glock. The research brought together two major traditions in the social study of religion, the cultural-historical style represented by Professor Bellah and the quantitative-empirical style represented by Professor Glock. Because of this, a more comprehensive analysis and assessment of the religious situation could be undertaken than would have been possible by one of the approaches alone.

An important finding of the study is that, while belief in a personal God is on the decline, a new self-awareness and spiritual sensitivity are finding expression in the lives of large numbers of people, especially among the young. There is to be seen a quickening of conscience at the continuing violence in national and international affairs, poverty in the midst of plenty, racial strife and oppression, and a host of other problems. The "back to nature" cries we hear, the extraordinary sartorial creations we see, the angry condemnation of technology, the deep and profound involvement with ecology, the growing influence of Eastern religions, and the collective and individual pursuits of cults that promise "inner peace"—all these and many more are powerful reactions to values and ways of living that we have ceased to satisfy, let alone inspire. Separately and together they are speaking in languages we do not at once comprehend, calling for a reorientation of national, social, and personal goals and of the means of reaching them. It is what they are trying to say that constitute the theme of this book. Two chapters, one by Professor Bellah and another by Professor Glock, set our their conclusions about the abiding significance of youth counterculture on the character and shape of American life.

It is immensely gratifying to the Institute for Religion and Social Change that the research that produced the book was done under its auspices. We are happy also to have been able to organize a colloquium on New Religious Consciousness in Changing Societies, to bring together the Berkeley group and members of our Japan group, who are engaged in a similar study in their country. The colloquium, which was attended by other scholars working on the subject of religious consciousness, enabled the research team to share and to discuss their results and to have such discussion taken into account in the final preparation of the manuscripts.

We are particularly glad that the Religious Consciousness project brought the Berkeley team and the institute closer together. Finally, we are deeply indebted to the Ford Foundation for its generous support of the research project as well as of the conference.

Institute for Religion and Social Change   P.J. PHILIP
Honolulu, Hawaii   *Director*

PREFACE

In the middle 1960s Bob Dylan taunted middle-class adults with a song built around the refrain, "Something is happening, and you don't know what it is, do you Mister Jones?" The happening, of course, was the widespread experimentation of youth with cultural alternatives—in dress, in social mores, in living arrangements, in politics, and in values and religion. These changes became enormously visible and prompted responses ranging from violent denunciation to limitless praise. Yet, for those caught up in the changes, whether as participants or observers, their meaning was unclear. "Mister Jones" didn't know what was going on, but when it came right down to it, neither did anyone else.

In retrospect, now that the sixties can be viewed from the perspective of the mid-seventies, the meaning of those events remains a mystery. Was the youth counterculture mainly epiphenomenal—a mere ripple in the stream of history—of momentary but of no permanent significance? Or was it a sign of more profound changes whose course, although more quietly now, continues apace?

The stimulus for this book was curiosity about such questions, curiosity that became activated to the point of generating the project on which the book is based, in the spring of 1971. By 1971 the counterculture had become much less visible than it was in the sixties and certainly less violent. Yet it was evident that the counterculture, though subdued, had not disappeared. Alternative politics was no longer as much the order of the day, but alternative lifestyles were; and substantial numbers of youth continued to be caught up in ways of thinking, living, and acting that were in sharp contrast with their elders and with the generation of youth that had come to adulthood in the early sixties.

Being, all of us, from one vantage point or another, students of religion, our curiosity was whetted especially by the religious dimension still so visible in the 1970s. There is precedent in history for movements that began in a call for political change to be later transformed into movements of religious innovation, although religion played some part even in the early stages of the counter-culture. In an era, however, of what had appeared to be growing secularization, increasing emphasis on religious revitalization seemed hardly in the cards. Yet dozens of new religious and quasi-religious movements, some attracting followers in the hundreds of thousands, have become a significant part of the counterculture's heritage.

Our curiosity about these phenomena led during the academic year 1970–71 to the formation of a bi-weekly discussion group to try to clarify the situation. The group was composed of the two senior authors and a number of graduate students in the Department of Sociology at the University of California, Berkeley, and in the religion and society program of the Graduate Theological Union, Berkeley. In reviewing the literature we found much speculation about what had stimulated these new religious groups, about the character of their appeal, about the alternative states of consciousness they were able to invoke, and about what it all meant for the larger scene. There was little evidence to be found, however, to test the speculations. Even such fundamental questions as how many youth were being attracted to alternative religions and with what degree of commitment could not be answered with the data at hand.

As the extent of our ignorance became more and more evident, the idea arose that we might collectively do something to fill the gap. The suggestion was made almost facetiously at first. There is little precedent for an ad hoc group, such as the one in which these matters were being discussed, to become the vehicle for launching a major research project. The suggestion was so attractive, however, that the discussion turned quickly from debate about what was going on to the formulation of a research project to find out.

The research plan that emerged from our discussion produced, almost miraculously, a research grant, about which we shall have more to say later; and in late 1971 we embarked on a series of investigations which have engaged a substantial portion of our energies since.

Our project has focused largely on the religious dimension of the cultural transformation of young people. This does not mean that we studied only obviously religious phenomena. We also included

ostensibly nonreligious phenomena—for example, youth's involvement in radical politics—where it was evident that participants
were caught up in ideas and activities transcendent of self and out
of harmony, if not in open conflict, with the conventional.

We chose religion as the strategic point of entry into the question
of contemporary cultural transformation because we thought it
potentially the most profound level of change. If investigation
should reveal important changes at this level—changes in the
perceived value and meaning of human existence and how it is
comprehended, then we could be reasonably sure that the changes
were profound, not merely stylistic and epiphenomenal. But we
began with no prior assumption that a major cultural transformation was under way. That is what we set out to determine.

The setting for our investigations was the San Francisco Bay
Area. We judged this an excellent laboratory in which to study the
youth movement, since it is here that much of the youth culture
began (and new trends continue to be born) and it is here that it is
most fully developed. The place to read the future, we reasoned, is
where it is beginning; when it reaches to most of the nation it is no
longer the future. Furthermore, it seemed evident that if we were to
study a wide range of variables and their interconnections in some
depth, our efforts should be concentrated and coordinated. By
restricting the locale, we could achieve that end.

In this setting, our research has involved us in an ethnographic
study of nine groups or movements providing alternatives to conventional forms of consciousness—religious or otherwise—and
appealing especially to youth. We have also looked into how
traditional religion in the Bay Area has been affected by and has
responded to youth counterculture. In addition, a survey of youth
(and their elders) was conducted to learn how much alternative
forms of consciousness have penetrated the general population. Actually, the survey provided a collective focus for much of our work.
Although it was primarily the responsibility of Robert Wuthnow, all
of the staff contributed ideas and there was continuous feedback
between the participant observation work and the survey during the
period when the instrument was being formulated. Finally, our
studies included an examination of the state of religious consciousness in a period of ferment in America's past.

The nine studies were undertaken to learn at first hand what it is
about various alternative approaches to reality that appeal to youth,
what constitutes the alternative states of consciousness they seek to
foster, and what the prospects are for these movements to have a

significant and permanent place in American culture. We followed no rigorous scientific procedure in choosing the nine groups for study. No effort was made, for example, to have them representative of all religious and quasi-religious groups operating in the Bay Area. Within the limits of our resources and the talents and interests of the research team, we sought to include the movements that had attracted the largest number of followers. We also sought in the selections to reflect major variations in existing movements, most especially with respect to the roots from which they stemmed. Thus, we included movements whose inspiration comes from Eastern philosophies, movements that have their roots in Western religious traditions, as well as movements whose origins are essentially old American.

No formula was followed in studying these movements. The nine investigators varied considerably in perspective and in the procedures they followed in their investigations, but on the whole researchers chose groups with which they felt some personal sympathy. This was an only partly conscious outcome of a group consensus to adopt a nonexploitative attitude toward those we studied. We were interested neither in debunking them nor in subjecting them to sensational publicity. Some sought and succeeded in becoming deeply involved in experiencing themselves the alternative state of consciousness that the movement they were studying was able to invoke. Others adopted a more nonparticipant posture in their investigations, relying on observation and depth interviews with leaders and followers to obtain their data. With one exception, no one withheld from the group studied his other identity as a researcher; and the exception, joining the project after his research was already under way, finally adopted the project norm, although late in his research. By and large, our openness in acknowledging what we were about was met with openness in response to our requests to make observations, to conduct interviews, to be given access to records, and where desired by the investigator, to be a participant in a movement's rituals and activities.

The first three parts of this volume are devoted to reports on the results of these studies. Three groups whose roots are in Indian religion—the Healthy-Happy-Holy Organization, the International Society for Krishna Consciousness, and the Divine Light Mission, more popularly known by the name of its leader, Guru Maharaj Ji, are the subjects of the three chapters in Part I. Part II, then, gives attention to three movements that are not explicitly religious but that we see as quasi-religions in nature: the "New Left," the

Human Potential movement, and Synanon. Movements that have their origins in traditional Western religion are the subject of Part III, where separate chapters are devoted to the Christian World Liberation Front (a Bay Area based offshoot of the Jesus movement), Charismatic Renewal in the Roman Catholic church, and Satanism.

The abiding impact of the counterculture is most visible in the movements that are essentially countercultural themselves. In planning the project, however, it was conceived that, though less visible, the broader and more significant import of the counterculture might be its effects on mainline religion. There was potential in the counterculture for undermining mainline religion as well as for revitalizing it. Which course dominated, if either, seemed worth finding out, and the results of three studies undertaken for this purpose are reported in Part IV. Part V is devoted to the results of the survey undertaken to assess the extent to which counterculture religion, life-styles, and values have been diffused to the population at large. Part VI provides historical perspective by means of an essay on the state of religious consciousness during the period of the Second Great Awakening.

There are two concluding chapters to the book, although the two chapters address the same question: What, if anything, is the more abiding meaning and significance of all that we have learned about changing consciousness and today's youth? In keeping with the exploratory character of our project the conclusions are tentative and reflect the different points of view of the senior authors. There is considerable overlap between these two concluding chapters, as the reader will see, but we felt that the remaining differences of perspective should be expressed rather than homogenized in a single concluding chapter. The collaboration of a quantitative empirical sociologist and a qualitative historical sociologist of religion has been rewarding for both of us and apparently for the students as well. The fruitfulness of such collaboration derives from the interplay of different perspectives, not from an effort to attain absolute agreement on all issues.

This volume is a first rather than a full report on the findings of the project. Subsequent volumes and papers will be reporting in more detail on the individual case studies and on the results of the survey. In relation to these more specialized studies, the intention in the present volume is to convey a sense of the whole of our project, and to do so in a way that will interest the general reader as well as the research specialist.

The happy circumstance that made the project, this book, and those to follow possible is that the original research proposal was submitted to the Institute of Religion and Social Change in Honolulu, Hawaii. The proposal struck a responsive chord among the Institute's principals: Dr. P.J. Philip, its director, and Msgr. Daniel J. Dever, its associate director. In part, this was because of the possibilities for comparison with a similar project the institute was supporting in Japan. More important, it was because of the institute's convictions about the significance of religious consciousness, broadly conceived, in shaping the character and quality of social life throughout the world.

The institute did not have sufficient resources of its own to support our project. Its directors, however, managed to persuade the Ford Foundation that our proposal, along with smaller institute proposals, warranted that foundation's support. Thus, most of the funds enabling the project came to us from the Ford Foundation, via the Institute of Religion and Social Change. Once the project was under way, there were things we decided we wanted to do that were not budgeted in the original grant request. Supplementary support was obtained to do these things from the National Endowment for the Humanities, in the form of a postdoctoral fellowship, and from the Tishman Foundation, which tendered a grant to allow the study of the counterculture and identity among Jewish youth. The Ford Foundation, it needs to be remarked, also supplemented its original grant along the way in order to enable the enlargement of the survey sample to encompass adults as well as youth. The Ford Foundation was also the source of support for a conference on the results of the Japanese and American projects, held under the auspices of the Institute for Religion and Social Change at the East-West Center of the University of Hawaii in September 1974.

We are most grateful to these various donors for their support. Most especially, we should like to acknowledge our debts to John Philip and Dan Dever. They are good friends and have given us all the warmth, encouragement, and support which only good friends can give.

We have also been helped by Donald Cutler of the Sterling Lord Academic Division and by Grant Barnes of the University of California Press. They have read drafts of manuscripts and given useful criticisms. Gladys Castor did yeoman service for us in the final editorial process. Karen Muhonen, Emily Harris, Karen Garrett, and Jeanette Roger were serially secretaries to the project over the course of its several years, and we are pleased to recognize and to express our gratitude for their many contributions to all fifteen of us.

The project, and the books, owe most to those who allowed us to study them. To them, all of them, our sincere thanks.

CHARLES Y. GLOCK
ROBERT N. BELLAH

PART I

New Religious Movements in the Asian Tradition

*One of the most striking characteristics of the counterculture and
of the movements growing out of it is the influence of Asian
religions. Of course, Americans have been interested in Asian
religions for over a century, but the present period seems to differ
from earlier ones both quantitatively and qualitatively. Perhaps
never before have themes from Asian religion penetrated mass
culture as they did in the psychedelic explosion of the late 1960s,
particularly rock music, as in the musical* Hair *or the songs of
George Harrison. Popular expositions of Asian beliefs—the books
of Alan Watts or Philip Kapleau—were stuffed in the knapsacks of
thousands of itinerant flower children. But the serious scholarship
in Asian religions that had grown so spectacularly in the period
after World War II itself produced a kind of knowledge explosion
by the late sixties, when translations and serious monographs were
available on a scale never seen before. Most important of all was
the fact that Asian religions were attracting not only the curiosity
of educated youth but also serious devotion and commitment.
Asian religions were no longer merely a new aesthetic delight.
They were also a call to a new intensity of religious devotion that
often involved vegetarianism, pacifism, long hours of strenuous
meditational practice, and, occasionally, the vow of celibacy. It
was the seriousness of the commitment to a score of Asian religious
groups more than anything else that signaled a new stage in the
American response to the East.*

*Although we speak of "new religious movements in the Asian
tradition," that is only partly true. They are new to us, but most of
them have very old roots in their homelands. Nevertheless, even
groups that have kept organizational continuity with old sects in
Asia, the Zen groups begun by Japanese masters, for example,
have had to become new in some sense in order to adapt to*

1

*American conditions. The three groups described in this section
are new in another sense. Though the leader of each of them
comes out of a long Indian tradition, each one—Yogi Bhajan of
the Healthy-Happy-Holy Organization (3HO), Swami Bhaktivedanta of the Hare Krishna movement, and Guru Maharaj Ji of
the Divine Light Mission—has been an entrepreneurial innovator
within his tradition. Even in India their movements in their present form are in a way "new." And it is true of these and several
other movements that their impact in India is a direct result of
their success overseas.*

*The three groups described in this section give a reasonably
good spectrum of movements of Indian origin, although even here
there are important omissions. One of the most successful of all
such movements is Transcendental Meditation, founded by the
Maharishi. This movement is in some respects closer to the
human-growth groups that will be described in the next section,
since it claims to be "not a religion" and emphasizes the value of
its meditational techniques more than any doctrines or beliefs.
Nonetheless, the serious full-time trainers in the movement do
seem to have a religious commitment with a content similar to
other movements of Indian inspiration. The followers of Meher
Baba make up another sizable group with its own distinctive
version of general Indian religiosity.*

*There are two other influential strands of Asian religion that we
have not been able to study: Buddhism and Sufism, the mystical
tradition of Islam. The omission of Zen Buddhism is particularly
regrettable, for its general influence has probably been greater
than any other movement even though the numbers of full-time
devotees is surely smaller than in many others. The cultural
impact of Zen has ranged from painting and poetry to new forms
of psychotherapy. The great Mahayana philosophy of "emptiness"
(Sanskrit: sunyata; Japanese: ku) has provided one of the principal
organizing themes of countercultural thought. If one considers the
fellow travelers of Asian religions, particularly the best educated of
them, no movement has been more important than Zen. Another
significant movement with a growing following among the most
sophisticated followers of Asian religions is Tibetan Buddhism,
which has a major center in Berkeley. Somewhat less evident in
northern California though fairly widespread in southern California are the followers of another group of Japanese Buddhist
inspiration, the Nichiren Shoshu, better known perhaps by the
name of its Japanese lay organization, Soka Gakkai. Though*

vigorous and expansive, Nichiren Shoshu can make no pretense to
the intellectual complexity of Zen or Tibetan Buddhism and draws
largely from a less well educated following.

While Hinduism and Buddhism have provided most of the
impetus for new religious groups in the Asian tradition, Sufism has
not been without some influence. Besides one group of Indonesian
Islamic origin, Subud, there has been the widespread diffusion of
Sufi tales and poetry. One other general source of religious influence that is non-Western though not Asian might also be mentioned here: primitive religion. Although we have not discerned
any movements in the Bay Area that purport to carry on any particular primitive religious tradition (which is not to say that there
is none—we continued to learn of new groups right up to the end
of our study), there has been a great interest particularly in native
American religion. In particular we might note that the writings of
Carlos Castaneda have come to have the centrality in recent years
for the counterculture and its successor groups that the writings of
Kapleau and Watts had in the late sixties.

Turning specifically to the three chapters in this section, we
may note how they exhibit the range of styles pursued by our
researchers. Jeanne Messer is a devoted follower of the Guru
Maharaj Ji, the only one of our researchers who was an adherent
of the group studied. Her chapter, which is one of the most
evocative in the book, is frankly more a view from "inside" than
an analytic study of the movement. Gregory Johnson's chapter
comes close to being a polar opposite to that of Messer. One of the
earliest observers of the birth of the Hare Krishna movement in
San Francisco, Gregory Johnson, who has received his Ph.D. from
Harvard University, was always analytically objective about the
group. Though having considerable empathy for other dimensions
of Asian religion, Johnson remained cool in his assessment of Hare
Krishna. This coolness, combined with an attention to explicit
sociological theory, makes Johnson's chapter an excellent example
of the sociological analysis of a new religious group. Alan Tobey is
in a sense midway between Messer and Johnson. Participating
with considerable inner response in the yogic practices of the
Healthy-Happy-Holy Organization, Tobey always remained in
part the detached observer. In this combination of involvement
and detachment, he is close to the norm for our group of
researchers.

Since we will be returning in Parts V and VII to the common
characteristics of the new religious movements in the Asian tradi-

tion and the ways in which they are similar to and different from other groups that we studied, we will not attempt any summarizing here. But the reader might observe how in each of the three groups there is a stress on charismatic leadership, on direct religious experience, and on a total way of life more or less at odds with the mores of middle America.

1

The Summer Solstice of the Healthy-Happy-Holy Organization

ALAN TOBEY

At a turning of the ages the highest calling is to be ready, to become attuned to the new age, and to lead the way. When one is convinced that the world is beginning to change to something fundamentally better, one must join that change, begin to participate in what the future will bring, and by example manifest the promise of that future to others.

For the members of the Healthy-Happy-Holy Organization (usually called 3HO) the world has entered into just such a period of transition between two great historical ages. Through their experiences and the teachings they have accepted, the members of 3HO have become convinced that we are now seeing the end of the "Piscean age," which has predominated for two thousand years, and that a radically different "Aquarian age" is arising, which will be fully established by early in the next century. The change will be from material to spiritual concerns, from factionalism to a pervasive sense of human unity, from the present dominance of "individual consciousness" to a "group consciousness" and "God consciousness"; in short, we shall see the beginning of a truly spiritual global culture. The dynamic of change is as inevitable as the courses of the stars and planets, whose changing angles forecast the new age; and the force behind it is divine, an impulse in the nature of the Creator.

The Healthy-Happy-Holy Organization sees itself as a family of people who are living and promoting a strong example of the kind of life-style they feel will predominate in the coming age of Aquarius. Founded in this country in 1969 by Harbhajan Singh of India (known to his followers as Yogi Bhajan), 3HO has about a

hundred centers in the United States and several thousand committed members.[1] Its members, who often assume names taken
from the Punjabi language, are even by their appearance, in white
clothing and turbans, set apart from that majority society whose
dominance they see coming to an end.

The roots of 3HO lie in three traditions of northern India: *kundalini* yoga, tantric yoga, and the Sikh religion. Its core of purpose
and action is spiritual, concerned above all with living together in
proper relation to God. 3HO is not for those seeking an escape from
worldly involvement; for marriage, responsible employment, and
social service are normative for all its members. For nearly five years
3HO has been a growing religious and social movement striving to
aid those fundamental changes of personality and society that it
sees as necessary for the transition to the Aquarian age.

Although I studied 3HO as it exists in the San Francisco Bay
Area, through participation in 3HO classes and special intensive
courses, here I will describe 3HO's most important national gathering in order to develop important issues that are not as obvious at
the local level. In order to see in one image what 3HO has become
and is becoming, I will focus on the 1973 Summer Solstice Sadhana,
which I attended. First, however, some background is in order.

BACKGROUND

Yogi Bhajan came to the United States in 1969, not really intending
to found a movement. Then forty, he had spent almost all his life in
spiritual studies and searching and had become a master of several
traditions of yoga and a minister of the Sikh Dharma.[2] Like almost
all Sikhs, he had spent many years in normal worldly life; he is
married and the father of three, has a degree in economics from
Punjab University of Chandigarh, and spent eighteen years as an
officer in the army and the customs service of India. He originally
left India to take up a teaching position in Canada; but when that
unexpectedly fell through, he was brought to the United States

1. The exact size of the movement is difficult to gauge. In December 1973, the
3HO publication *Beads of Truth* listed eighty ashrams and twenty-seven other less
formal "centers" in the United States. One year earlier fifty-three ashrams and
thirty-two centers were listed. Each of these may contain anywhere from two to
more than eighty residents, and each serves as the nucleus of a wider group of nonresident practitioners, yoga students, and fellow travelers of a size impossible to estimate.

2. As used in 3HO, the word *dharma* (literally "path") has a sense somewhere
between "religion" and "way of life."

through the hospitality of people connected with the East-West Center of Los Angeles. There he began teaching classes in kundalini yoga. His first students were mostly middle-aged housewives, but gradually he attracted a small following of a different sort, which gave him a sense of mission—young people of the counter-culture, the "hippies" and "flower children" who were flourishing in Los Angeles at the time. Attracted by the positive and seemingly Sikh-like aspects of their life-style—such as communal living, uncut hair, interest in cosmic harmony, often vegetarian diets—but rejecting the common ground of these experiences in psychedelic drugs, Yogi Bhajan began to create for them the yoga-centered life-style out of which 3HO grew. 3HO was created on American soil out of American and Indian elements; it is not a purely imported movement which groups like Hare Krishna have claimed to be.

Despite its American origins, 3HO is strongly influenced by the Sikh tradition of northern India. Founded in the life experiences of a man named Nanak (1469–1539), Sikhism developed in the context of fierce religious and political contention between Hinduism and Islam. Nanak proclaimed one God common to all faiths, beyond the specific religious expressions and rituals that were being contested, a God whom he claimed could be directly known by meditation on his Name. Over the next two hundred years nine other men became Sikh leaders (known as gurus); their spiritual writings (as well as writings of Muslim and Hundu saints), were collected in a book, the *Siri Guru Granth Sahid* (or *Granth*), which has since been considered the contemporary "living Guru." The ten gurus also developed a strong social focus for Sikhism. They were generally family men, earned their own livings, and were active in organizing charities, community-development projects, and (occasionally) armies, as well as conducting specifically religious work. The Sikhs as a whole have since become a merchant and managerial class, active even today in India's business and government. Sikhs have also worked for social justice, since the time of Nanak opposing such social inequities as India's caste system. Many members of 3HO have formally become Sikhs, finding in the Sikh symbolism and rituals the religious center for an Aquarian life-style with a broader referent.

Since 1969, 3HO has developed into a nationwide network of centers, almost all in urban areas; it has recently begun to establish itself in Europe and Japan as well. These centers, or ashrams, are communal residences where the people most committed to 3HO live together and practice the 3HO life-style; the ashrams also serve as centers from which teachers of kundalini yoga give classes in nearby communities and from which 3HO members may provide such community services as free kitchens and drug-treatment programs. The ashrams are communal in a somewhat restricted sense: Although all residents normally participate together in meals and in the early morning disciplines, most will spend the greater part of the day attending school or working at outside jobs. Usually each resident pays the ashram for room and board rather than sharing all his financial resources with others. Traditional monogamous marriage is the norm, and single persons are expected to remain celibate.

Although most of the focus of 3HO is on developing an individual's life-style, on living together, and on teaching locally, twice each year members of 3HO may attend a national gathering; the major one is the Summer Solstice Sadhana.[3] Held every year in late June in a semiwilderness setting in the western United States, Solstice (as it is usually called) is an opportunity for people from all over the country to come together for ten days to strengthen and perfect what they are as members of 3HO, to live out and enjoy proleptically (in anticipatory fashion) what they feel to be the life-style of the coming age.

A DAY IN THE LIFE

It is 4 A.M. in the Jemez mountains of northern New Mexico, June 1973.[4] At 7,500 feet even summer nights are cold, and frost sparkles on the tents that huddle in a grassy meadow. A guitar and two singing voices make a brave sound in the darkness. The melody is Western, a gentle folk tune, but the words are Punjabi,[5] a verse of Nanak's: *Ad guray namay, jugad guray namay, sat guray namay, siri guru devay namay*—"We bow to the Wisdom (or Word) which was in the beginning, we bow to the Wisdom which has been through the ages, we bow to the Wisdom which is Truth, we bow to the great shining Wisdom." As the musicians walk along the rows of tents, the people inside stir and stretch; some softly call out "Sat Nam," a name for the God who is truth absolute (Sat) and is known also through his manifestation in creation (Nam). God's Name is at the core of 3HO's theology and praxis.

3. *Sadhana* in 3HO means "time for spiritual work."
4. This is a composite account of a typical day, not an exact chronology of one particular day.
5. Punjabi, a derivative of Sanskrit, is the vernacular language of the territory of the Sikhs in northern India.

From the beginning of the wakeup there is an hour for people to arise, dress, perform personal exercises or devotions, and walk to the central meeting area. They come wrapped in blankets or sleeping bags against the cold, the men with their long hair tied up in turbans, the women also with their heads covered. They sit down quietly in front of an outdoor stage and wrap themselves into a bundle of motionless attention, for the reading of the morning prayer has begun. It is a Sikh prayer, one of the many in the *Siri Guru Granth Sahib* extolling the One God. The Punjabi words rise and fall in an intense rhythm.

The prayer ends by 5 A.M. The leader of today's morning sadhana calls the group to attention (it now numbers several hundreds despite the cold and the hour) and leads them, their eyes closed and their palms pressed together at the center of their chests, in the mantra (verse) that opens almost every 3HO session: *Ong Namo / Guru Dev Namo*—*Ong*, the Creator, I bow to him; *Guru Dev*, the wisdom or teacher both within and without, I bow to him. It is a way of "tuning in" to a receptive and centered attitude of mind felt to be essential in the practices to follow. Punjabi words are used because it is said to be a "mantric language," in which words have not only meanings but also specific sound "vibrations" with effective resonances in the body and mind.

Morning sadhana begins with kundalini yoga, a tradition of exercises, chanting, and meditation aimed at gaining conscious control of the processes of the body and the mind. The central image is this: There is one fundamental human energy, called *prana*, which controls the inner quality of human life and whose main channel in the human body corresponds to the spinal column. In the normal state of men this energy is out of conscious control, conceived to be lying dormant as potential energy (kundalini) at a nerve center at the base of the spine. It is expressed unconsciously through the "lower centers" (nerve plexuses or gates for prana at the rectum, sex organs, and navel point), so that greed, lust, and power are normal activities. But through the practice of kundalini yoga, one's energy can be "raised" and then normally expressed consciously through the "higher centers" at the heart, throat, brow, and top of the head. These higher centers are the channel points for love, truth, wisdom, and God realization.

Although conscious control of the body through kundalini yoga brings health and peace, the ultimate goal of raising and controlling this energy is to gain a direct realization of union with God. This "God realization" is the highest potential of a human life. To reach that state is to break the grip of karma on one's life—the limitations

on present activity that are the result of morally improper past activity—and thereby to be liberated from the endless cycle of births
and deaths that keeps men tied to unfulfilling lives on the earth.
The "bliss" of God realization is said to be gradually achievable in
this life through the faithful practice of kundalini yoga; rather than
seeking a life after death, the members of 3HO hope to become
jivan mukt'—liberated while still alive in the world—and thus to
have their individual existence apart from God *end* with this in-
carnation.

This morning's sadhana begins with a few minutes of *prana-
yama*—conscious controlled breathing. Since the breath is directed
both by autonomic nerve processes and by conscious will, it is used
in almost all yoga traditions as a primary means of gaining access to
normally uncontrolled realms. Today, the first exercise is several
minutes of "alternate nostril breathing"—inhaling through the left
nostril and exhaling through the right, then inhaling through the
right nostril and exhaling through the left. In kundalini yoga each
side of the body is said to flow with a different quality of energy: the
right side with warming "sun energy," the left with cooling "moon
energy." By alternate breathing a balance of energy is created—both physical and mental—in tune with the energy rhythms
of the universe. One inhales and mentally repeats "Nam"; even in
this simple exercise one is filled with an awareness of God's nature
in the sun-and-moon rhythms of life. This physical exercise, combined with a spiritual image for mental concentration, is typical of
almost all kundalini yoga exercises in 3HO.

Then there follows three minutes of "breath of fire," a rapid,
energetic breathing technique using the diaphragm as a pump to
push air in and out of the lungs; this "charges up" the entire body
with pranic energy and is felt to be useful in raising the dormant
kundalini. Here kundalini yoga differs from most other yoga
traditions (such as hatha), which stresses peaceful relaxation and
gentle breathing; kundalini yoga adds powerful effort and strong
flows of energy, to eliminate blocks in the body and mind quickly
rather than gradually eroding them.

This difference is even more apparent in the physical exercises.
Unlike the usual image of yoga exercises as gentle stretches or the
maintaining of one position for a long period, most kundalini yoga
exercises are strenuous work. Today there are some warmup exercises for the spine (to "help the energy flow")—catching hold of the
toes with the legs outstretched and bringing the forehead down to
the knees and up in a rapid pumping motion, twisting the spine

from left to right with the hands on the shoulders, flexing the spine forward and back—but most of the session consists of two specific sets of exercises with precisely stated purposes. The first set is designed to "build and cleanse the aura" (a "biomagnetic field" of energy around the body) so that one will be more harmoniously related to the energy field of the whole universe; specific exercises include three minutes of breath-of-fire with the arms held out straight at a sixty-degree angle up from the horizon, a strong sweeping motion of the arms from front to back with deep breathing, and slow side-to-side sweeps. The people then hold their palms a few inches apart, feeling the energy of their auras as a force of attraction between the palms. The second set of exercises is a tone up for the internal organs; it consists of lying on one's back and raising one's legs, for thirty seconds at a time, to six inches from the ground, then twelve inches, then two feet, then to a forty-five-degree angle, then sixty degrees, and finally ninety degrees, all the while maintaining the breath-of-fire. Each precise angle is said to put beneficial pressure on a different set of "nerve channels" and "acupuncture points," "massaging" them and stimulating energy flow. It is a difficult set, very hard on the abdominal rectus muscles, and many cannot make it all the way through. The leader keeps calling out "Keep up! Keep up!"—a phrase all 3HO people come to know well; Yogi Bhajan calls it the "Maha (great) Mantra of the Aquarian age."

Though the sets of kundalini yoga exercises differ from day to day, there is a certain commonality about them. Often they are very strenuous, and what is stressed is not physical strength but strength of will, the ability to "keep up" beyond the point at which you *want* to quit (not, it is emphasized, *have* to quit). The exercises are all related both to physical effects and to possibilities for spiritual concentration. Most are done with a silently held mantra, as a means of keeping full attention on what is happening. All are done with the awareness of their aftereffects; each exercise is followed by a period of deep relaxation with eyes closed, time to *feel* what is happening within.

It is this *feeling* after the exercises (often compared with—though felt to be better than—being high from drugs) that is for many the initial attraction to 3HO. In one's first yoga classes this state is often the connection with one's previous experiences of altered consciousness. What may be first experienced as merely a familiar feeling of being "stoned" becomes with the help of the teacher's interpretation the mark of a more comprehensively related inner convic-

tion—that of being a "cosmic body" (my term), a universally
related being attuned to all of life. This cosmic awareness (or God
consciousness) becomes in turn the source of a new referent image—the universe as one harmonious organism—which provides a
way to understand all natural and social phenomena. Kundalini
yoga, then, is the means by which in 3HO common physical experience becomes the basis of shared spiritual conviction.

Morning sadhana moves on to the chanting and meditation
aspects of the kundalini yoga tradition. The chanting remains the
same from day to day; the mantra is considered absolutely central
to the whole 3HO way of life.[6] It is *Ek Ong Kar Sat Nam Siri Wha
Guru*, usually translated as "One God has created this creation (*Ek
Ong Kar*); Truth is his Name (*Sat Nam*); Great is his indescribable
wisdom (*Siri Wha Guru*)." But the meaning of this mantra is in-
separable from the way in which it is chanted and the resonances its
sounds have in the body. One sits in a stable cross-legged position
and chants in two and a half breaths: (inhale) *EkOooooooooong-
kaaaaaaaaaaaaaaaa*, (inhale) *SatNaaaaaaaaaaaaaaaaaaaaaaamSiri*,
(short inhale) *Wha Guuuruuu*. Each sound has a resonance in a
different place, moving from the base of the spine up to the top of
the head; the chanting becomes a model (and 3HO people say a
means) of directly raising one's consciousness. Yogi Bhajan asserts
that kundalini yoga is a practical and objective technique for
achieving liberation from the personal ego and union with God.

The chanting continues for a full hour without pause; when it
ends there is a glimmer of light in the eastern sky. Now perhaps six
hundred people shake out their stiff legs and fold them again for the
morning meditation, today on "the primal sounds" *Sa-Ta-Na-Ma*
repeated aloud to a four-note-melody for five minutes, whispered
for five minutes, repeated mentally (silently) for ten minutes,
whispered for five minutes, and finally six more minutes aloud. One
should become totally involved in the mantra, so that it shuts all
else out. 3HO has dozens of different meditations, and 3HO
members are encouraged to use whichever meditation seems appropriate at a particular time. After a few minutes of silence at the
end of the session, Yogi Bhajan's wife reads in Punjabi from the
Sikh scriptures, today a composition of Guru Arjun's (1563–1606)
called "Peace Lagoon." People sit and listen, relaxed.

By this time the sun has risen, and the day begins to warm up.
The group gets up, stretches in the sun, then stands for the raising

6. All 3HO techniques and mantra are public; again in contrast to some other
Eastern traditions, there are no secret teachings or private personal mantra.

of two flags: the American flag and the "flag of the Aquarian nation," which has white and yellow diagonal halves, and in the center a large blue Sikh symbol representing "Adi Shakti" (primal energy, the source of all creation). As the flags go up the group sings "God Bless America," and the leader then directs them to send their "energy out to the nation as a whole, so that once again it can become a nation as a whole, so that once again it can become a nation whose trust is in God."

By now it is nearly eight o'clock and after three hours of work and concentration appetites clamor. The members of 3HO, now about a thousand strong, quickly assemble into double lines and sit cross-legged on the ground facing one another. The servers soon bring food up from the kitchen area, a brief blessing is spoken, and the food is served down the lines. The food is abundant, tasty, nutritionally balanced vegetarian fare: each person receives two bananas, two oranges, a bowl of peppery potato-and-onion soup, and a mug of tea with milk and honey. The 3HO diet contains no meat, fish, or eggs.

Now in the morning light the people can finally see each other. Most noticeable is the uniformity of age and race; almost everyone seems to be in his or her early twenties and white. Only here and there is an older face apparent, and only three or four black people are scattered through the group. Most of the several dozen children are infants or toddlers, very few of school age. There is a striking absence of conversation, for a major part of the special discipline of Solstice is a discipline of silence. Everyone present is to speak only spiritual songs and chants or mantra; for daily needs, writing, gestures, and a multitude of variously inflected "Sat Nams" are supposed to do. The effect of the silence is to make the time an even more reflective one; without a chance to verbally share experiences, each person is forced to make his own evaluation of the daily events.

After about an hour of free time after breakfast, parents can take their children to the children's camp for care in small groups during the main hours of the day. By nine-thirty most people are back for the morning class, dressed now even more uniformly in white. Today's class concerns early child rearing in 3HO with emphasis on the Montessori method of education, which Yogi Bhajan has recommended. On other days topics will range from nutrition and cooking to a question session of the Sikh Dharma to a session on the legal aspects of running a 3HO ashram.

The class ends by eleven, and immediately the groups begin

preparing for the day's tantric yoga session. Tantric yoga is normally performed with a partner of the opposite sex, for it consciously works on the "different polarity energy" of male and female. Couples sit down in long, very straight lines facing one another, packed shoulder-to-shoulder in the lines and back-to-back with the next line; across the main area perhaps ten of these double lines are formed, stretching seventy-five feet from the stage. Monitors circulate to assure that the lines are perfectly straight; if they are not, the "magnetic field" of the group will be awry and the energy of the Yoga will not "flow properly."

Tantric yoga is not a daily part of 3HO life. It is taught only by Yogi Bhajan himself, at events like Solstice or in special tantric courses. It is claimed that only one master of tantric yoga can be alive at one time, and that Yogi Bhajan is the "Mahan Tantric of this time." To put it more practically, the techniques are so powerful that they must be tightly controlled; the straightness of the lines and the stress on specific dress are social reinforcements of the special quality of the endeavor. Once the lines are set people begin to settle down, becoming relaxed and centered, and a period of chanting begins—the same mantras as this morning with more easily singable melodies perhaps, plus special chants calling on Guru Ram Das, third of the ten Sikh gurus and Yogi Bhajan's "special protector," for help.

Yogi Bhajan arrives without warning. Though he walks quietly, he is a huge man, six feet four inches tall and weighing 220 pounds, with a massive chest and a big black beard. He wears a turban as always, and today a simple white robe. He seats himself on the stage. The tantric sessions usually begin with a talk, sometimes with a single focus, more often rambling over a range of topics. Today Yogi Bhajan talks directly about the Solstice:

At a solstice you have to break your patterns. You are here to go through certain changes. . . . We are here to prove to ourselves who we are and what we will be. We are practicing here a way of life, we are practicing a strength in us. We are trying to prove to ourselves whether we can relate to soul or not. . . . Either you undertake the responsibility and be what you should be, or you can never break the patterns. . . . It would be very silly of you to come here and not test yourselves. . . . Here you come to build what we have lost. Here we want to build a nation which we have lost. Here we want to lay the foundations of the new future. That is the purpose of us to be here today: to prove to ourselves that we have the spirit to survive through every obstacle.[7]

7. From Yogi Bhajan's address to the tantric yoga class, 18 June 1973.

His tone is exhortatory, challenging; his words are practical; he is laying out a vision of the possible to his followers. He goes on to talk about the goal of tantric yoga:

Ego is a beautiful thing, and one must have ego, but you cannot use your ego to block you. Your subconscious mind must not make you to live in fear, and it must not negate you. . . . This is a problem of every individual, and in our life we suffer through it. Damage to the personality of the individual is sometimes far great [sic], and it takes sometimes few years to get out of it. . . . There should be no sacrifice that should be costlier than building a new beautiful creative nation. So all the dirt that is stuck in the subconscious mind has to be cleaned out. . . . It is that old pattern of thought which must come out, and you must allow that to happen, so that the outcome may be totally clean personality.[8]

Yogi Bhajan's tantric yoga, then, has a consciously psychotherapeutic purpose: what he has called "burning the subconscious mind," that is, eliminating the restrictions on life in the present resulting from negative memories and patterns (karma) from the past. Beyond this individual goal the tantric yoga of 3HO has a corporate aim: to move people from habitual "individual consciousness" or mere self-reliance to a habit of "group consciousness" and then to "universal consciousness." The group consciousness is symbolized in the collective nature of the endeavor; and the state sought through the exercises is an analog of the "cosmic body" awareness of kundalini yoga: a way of experiencing fundamental ontological unity with a harmonious universe, a new source of motivation for action.

The lecture ends abruptly—"All right, set yourselves"—and the exercises begin. Tantric yoga exercises in 3HO generally have four characteristics in common in addition to requiring men and women to exercise together. First, they are usually of quite long duration, often thirty-one to sixty-one minutes. Second, they are difficult, either physically or emotionally; they may involve strong physical effort to the point of great pain, of holding one difficult position motionlessly for the whole time; or they may evoke strong emotions (such as fear, anger, or love). Third, they provide strong aids to concentration; since one has to maintain a precise position or motion and repeat a complicated mantra in an exact rhythm and in conjunction with a partner, the mind cannot easily wander. Fourth, there are strong subjective aftereffects: you may feel "stoned" or physically exhausted or emotionally drained or elated; sometimes

8. Ibid.

parts of your body tingle with energy or are temporarily paralyzed. Tantric yoga is strong business indeed.

Today's session is typical.[9] The first exercise involves holding a precise position in which the eyes of the partners are only a few inches apart. Yogi Bhajan directs the people to concentrate on their own reflection in their partner's eyes while everyone rhythmically clicks his tongue for a few minutes and then joins in a continuous chant of *Ong* ("Creator"; the sound itself is supposed to have a beneficial "vibratory effect" on the pituitary and pineal glands). This lasts for thirty-one minutes. After a rest period a more physically demanding exercise begins, and the couples kneel, facing each other. Maintaining their hands in a particular "mudra" (position), they rise up on their knees (so that their faces almost touch) and then kneel back down again, maintaining eye contact, in time with a complicated eight-part mantra chanted alternately by the men and the women. Although this lasts for sixty-one minutes without pause, in the concentration required to perform it properly all sense of time disappears. With every rising, great pain builds in the thighs and challenges one's will to continue. Locked in the tantric lines, though, the continuing effort of all the others is an encouragement to "keep up," to participate in the "group consciousness" of the exercise and not drop out because of individual discomfort. The concentration and the pain—communicated through "the antennae of the eyes"—and the hypnotic force of the mantra create a specific altered state of consciousness, in which individual ego is dissolved into this shared activity and disappears for the duration. Many said that by the end of this exercise they were conscious only of "being the activity," or identifying with the process itself.

In the last tantric exercise of the day, the partners sit cross-legged, facing one another, with their hands in another precise position. For thirty-one minutes the men chant *Ha* followed by the women chanting *Ri*; together (in the *combination* of male and female) the mantra is *Hari*, a name for God. Again some say that they experience not two partners chanting but only the exercise, the mantra whole and full beyond the polarity of man and woman, doer and act, individual and group. A brief prayer ends the tantric session for the day.

9. This is a composite account drawn from several tantric sessions. Because of the powerful nature of the exercises and the need for close supervision, they are not described in sufficient detail to be done by the reader, who is hereby cautioned.

Yogi Bhajan has said that the purpose of the exercises is to replace negative habits of mind with positive ones, and that the beneficial effects may not be felt until much later, even after Solstice. But under the discipline of silence there is no opportunity to share what has happened over the past four hours, or even to make sense of it in any terms but your own.

In the afternoon there are voluntary assorted classes: T'ai chi and Aikido and Kung Fu (everyone in 3HO is admonished to learn self-defense); pressure-point massage for aiding physical ailments; music and the techniques of chanting texts from the *Siri Guru Granth Sahib;* homeopathic medicine; a session on ashram publicity and public relations. About a dozen merchants set up their wares: yoga clothes and turbans, meditative beads, posters, Sikh jewelry, and other adjuncts to a particular way of life. Other booths offer new services within the 3HO family: a prepaid group legal plan for Californians, a computerized astrological data service, a place to subscribe to the 3HO publications. The mood is that of a country fair, albeit a strangely silent one.

The classes end with the call to dinner, a substantial meal: garbanzo beans and rice (for protein), cooked beets and raw celery (for vitamins, minerals, and to "purify the blood"), and curried cauliflower (to include garlic, onion, ginger, and beneficial spices in the diet). Even though at Solstice 3HO food is the same every day, it is so well prepared and seasoned that it is eagerly awaited.

After dinner there is the evening kirtan (session of spiritual singing). The medium is guitar (both acoustic and electric), the idiom is folk and rock. 3HO's musicians have developed dozens of ways to sing the main mantras in a modern American style, and they have written their own songs as well. Suddenly the group seems like any other group of young Americans grooving to the music that is uniquely theirs. It is part rock festival, part summer camp, part joyful worship. But always the spiritual content goes along with the musical form, so that even when the music is hottest people may be singing *Ek Ong Kar Sat Nam Siri Wha Guru.* The music goes on into the night but people gradually drift away; by nine-thirty the session has broken up.

The long demanding day has been a good one for most. At home in an ashram, so much would never be packed into one day. There would be the morning sadhana certainly, with a similar pattern of exercise, chanting, and meditation; that is the center and source of 3HO's life wherever it may be. Most of the other events would occur over the run of days and weeks of life together. But Solstice is a time to work intensively and full time at which the participants are and wish to be. They have enjoyed the days and the work of building themselves, each other, and their new society toward a nation they hope will stand the test of the times and emerge finally as a healthy, happy, and holy brotherhood.

FROM THE PERSONAL TO THE INSTITUTIONAL

Most of the dynamic of Solstice works at the level of the individual, to strengthen each person's commitment to the 3HO life-style and thereby to build a company of strong individuals on the way to spiritual liberation. Solstice is also the major occasion for developing the group consciousness of the members of 3HO—generally through shared participation in the disciplines and specifically through three major public events: induction into the Sikh community, Sikh ordination, and a mass wedding. These events work to build 3HO as an institution in the same sense that the daily disciplines build individuals.

Yogi Bhajan continually asserts that he has come to America not to create disciples but to train teachers—that is, not to establish a population of dependent followers but to develop independent, spiritually liberated people who can spread the teachings and be an example to others of God consciousness. So there are no rituals for becoming a personal disciple of Yogi Bhajan, or even for becoming a member of 3HO. But there are opportunities to make personal commitments to the 3HO dharma; foremost is the ceremony of becoming formally a Sikh.

On the ninth of the ten days of Solstice, those who wish may join the Sikh Dharma Brotherhood. The ceremony is simple: a brief address by one of the regional teachers, several appropriate readings from the *Granth* in English; and then each person who wishes to comes forward in turn and bows to the ground before the holy book as a symbol of his loyalty. By this action a person symbolizes his willingness to make the following specific formal commitments, which are the Sikh Dharma:

1. To accept that there is but one Creator God, and to accept the *Siri Guru Granth Sahib* as his only Guru until death.
2. To arise each day before the sunrise and to meditate on God (through doing morning sadhana) in the "primal hours of the day."
3. To keep his physical form "as God made him," which means to keep the hair uncut and not to shave. The man also promises to wear his hair in a knot on top of his head and covered with a turban, the woman to wear her hair up and covered also.

4. To follow a vegetarian diet, abstaining from meat, eggs, alcohol, tobacco, and all mind-altering drugs.
5. To earn his living righteously "through the sweat of his brow," without deviousness or exploitation; to share with the 3HO brotherhood, help the poor and needy, defend the weak, and be of service to the community.
6. To live the life of a householder with one wife or husband for life, being neither celibate nor promiscuous.
7. To be available for military service in case of national attack—or for alternate service if one objects to the military.

This ceremony does not change one's life; rather it is a formal announcement of a way of life already taken up and internalized. Those who remain in contact with 3HO come to live a disciplined life in some degree; when the disciplined activities become a normal part of one's life, there is no reason not to formalize it. Yet the step is symbolically significant, for one thereby becomes a Sikh and accepts a whole culture and a foster nationality as well as a new way of life. Many people have begun to live some aspects of the Sikh life-style even before they come into contact with the 3HO; they tend to find in 3HO a way to integrate the piecemeal elements of a life-style they had picked up elsewhere. Most people had come through a "hippie" period and were ready for some sort of discipline. But it is a longer step from hippie to Sikh—and in one sense that is what 3HO is all about.

On the last day of the Solstice, everyone not previously ordained who was then heading a 3HO ashram—and his or her spouse as well—was made a Sikh minister through a simple series of promises made in the presence of the Guru (Granth). But those who were ordained—about eighty—were not made 3HO ministers; under the law 3HO is a nonprofit educational corporation, not a religious organization. So the men and women are ordained as "ministers of the Sikh Dharma," ministers without a church even though they head the 3HO ashrams. They are responsible to Yogi Bhajan directly, who as "Minister of the Sikh Dharma for the Western hemisphere" (appointed by the Sikh hierarchy in India) is in effect their bishop. These ministers are responsible for 3HO's religious center without having any formal institutional connection with it. Again there is a tightly structured Sikh core to what at first seems to be a more generally oriented collection of 3HO ashrams.

The Sikh wedding ceremony on the last day of Solstice consisted of four readings from the Granth about the spiritual goals of marriage (in Punjabi and then in English), after each of which the twenty couples being married bowed down to the ground before

the Guru as a sign of their commitment first to God and then to each
other. From this spiritual center, however, comes a strong and more
general commitment that relates to 3HO as a broader social movement than merely Sikhism. There is a strong commitment to life in
the world, symbolized by the requirement that 3HO members live
as householders with families. 3HO marriages also represent a social
critique of American culture in general. Yogi Bhajan teaches that
only emotional and spiritual stability in the home can create stable
children, and only through stable positive children will a stable
society arise. He sees the insecurity of the home and family as the
major source of America's social neuroses; hence, he expects 3HO
marriages to be strong, spiritual, and permanent. Great stress is
placed on the heavy commitment of marriage within 3HO; the day
before the ceremony Shakti Parwha, the middle-aged general
secretary of 3HO, said to the group:

Let it be understood: Unless you're getting married because of spiritual
urge, to build a family, to build a nation, to participate in what 3HO stands
for, go somewhere else to get married; you don't need Yogi Bhajan. . . .
Unless your intention is to start out a life which will be a shining radiant
example of two bodies living as one soul in the seeking of God consciousness, forget it. We don't need you.[10]

Out of this commitment to traditional monogamous marriage
comes a revaluation of the place of women in American society.
3HO would agree with the women's liberation movements that
American women have been exploited and treated as sexual objects;
but the two movements differ strongly in their prescribed alternatives. Rather than striving to make women the exact equal of
men, 3HO would restore women to a place reflecting their "proper
differences" from men. Women are "the grace of God," the first
guru of their children, and the source of social stability in a society.
It is their place to be reflective of the more directly active male
energy in a spiritual partnership, to be one pole of a relationship
that tries to move beyond polarity, as in the tantric exercises. This
does not mean that "a woman's place is in the home," it means only
that her special and proper responsibility is for the stability of the
home, in a life that may include any amount of activity in the wider
world. The fact that women in 3HO are ordained as ministers—for
the first time in the history of the Sikh religion—is a strong indication of their fundamental equality.

The public ceremonies, then, indicate the institutional direction

10. From Shakti Parwha's address, 26 June 1973.

and goals of 3HO. Though its forms are broad and the ethos broader still, 3HO's central core is Sikhism. Just as the Sikh mantras pervade the otherwise "practical" yoga traditions, so do the Sikh symbols and rituals pervade a life-style that on its surface is not so different from the life of many contemporary secular sectarian movements. Recruitment to the committed Sikh core is through helping people realize that the way they have come to live through 3HO is really Sikh, so that there is no reason to avoid taking the formal step and confirming that choice of life-style. It is all quite benevolent and also very conscious, an effective way of building a *Sikh* Aquarian nation out of a sympathetic post-hip generation.

PEOPLE

Who are the people 3HO attracts? who see themselves as the foundation of the Aquarian nation abuilding? Where have they come from, what are they like now, and what has their experience in 3HO been like? To find some answers I administered a questionnaire to about half the people attending the 1973 Solstice Sadhana.[11] There follows a selection of findings from that questionnaire, along with my own observations from more than two years of contact with 3HO. I have also compared 3HO responses with responses to the same questions (included in a spring 1973 survey[12]) by a representative population of people from sixteen to thirty years of age living in the San Francisco Bay Area, although the two populations are not rigorously comparable.

Background

Briefly, 3HO people have been more affluent, more educated, more experienced with drugs and demonstrations, and more politically liberal than the Bay Area youth sample, as table 1–1 shows. This indicates that 3HO people overall fit a picture of the background of the youths who made up the counterculture of the late 1960s and early 1970s (when most were of college age). Almost everyone now in 3HO can talk about an earlier period of active involvement in several aspects of a life opposed to the values of the dominant culture.

11. Of the 450 questionnaires distributed on the ninth day of Solstice, 250 were returned, nearly equally divided between men (126) and women (122) and between residents (128) and nonresidents (122) of 3HO ashrams.

12. This survey is the one reported on by Robert Wuthnow in Chapter 13, below.

Table 1 – 1

	Bay Area Sample, 16-30 years old	3HO
	%	%
Median reported family income when respondent was in high school	($10,285)*	($15,000 approx.)
Education		
At least some college	58	84
Finished college	18	31
Attended graduate or professional school	7	13
Drug use: Had ever used mind-affecting drugs	53	95
Political activism: Had ever taken part in a march or demonstration	30	59
Political stance: Self-description by one of nine categories		
In one of the three most liberal	40	60
In one of the three most conservative	12	1
	(N = 328)	(N = 250)

*This figure is the national median family income in 1971, (source: U.S. Census Bureau).

Socioeconomic Patterns

All but a handful (fewer than fifteen) of the thousand or so people at Solstice were white and fairly young: the median age for both men and women was twenty-two. Two-thirds of the people were between twenty and twenty-five, inclusively, and only 5 percent were over thirty. About half the respondents were then residents of 3HO ashrams; almost all the rest had attended a previous Solstice gathering or an intensive yoga course. Table 1−2 summarizes some socioeconomic comparisons.

The data suggest that most 3HO people have not fully made the transition from the fluid life-style of the counterculture to the more rooted style that is the 3HO norm. Despite the strong encourage-

Table 1—2

| | Bay Area Sample | |
	16-30 years old	3HO
	%	%
Presently married	33	27
Working		
Full time	39	33
Part time	17	24
Going to school (not working)	21	11
Time at present job		
Less than 6 months	25	51
More than 24 months	45	11
Moved more than three times in the last two years	10	45
Annual Family income		
Less than $4,000		61
Less than $5,000	46	
More than $15,000	14	5
	(N = 328)	(N = 250)

ment of marriage within 3HO, for example, only a minority of 3HO people are married. Although about as many 3HO people as Bay Area young people are working or going to school, a far greater proportion of 3HO people have held their current jobs only briefly and almost half had moved more than three times in the previous two years. As would be expected for a young and growing movement, 3HO apparently involves a great number of people still in the process of changing the basic pattern of their lives.

Although about as many 3HO people are working as are Bay Area young people, the average income of a 3HO family is far lower. This reflects the decreased economic requirements of ashram life (room and board for a couple in one Bay Area ashram in the summer of 1973 was $162 per month). It also indicates the type of employment most 3HO people are engaged in—maintenance or gardening work, restaurant or bakery work (sometimes in 3HOfounded businesses), housecleaning or babysitting, and the like. The occasional 3HO lawyer or doctor or teacher is an isolated exception.

The 3HO Process

On the questionnaire I asked for open-ended responses to three questions: what the respondent's *original reasons* had been for becoming involved with 3HO, what his *present reasons* were for continuing in 3HO, and how his *life had changed* as a result of his contact with 3HO. Answers to these three questions provide a sketch of how a person came into 3HO and has been affected by it. The responses of several committed individuals give a personal sense of the 3HO process when it works for someone.

Many have stayed with 3HO because of the everyday beneficial changes they have noticed. Typical is a twenty-two-year-old man from California who got into 3HO eighteen months ago because the yoga "helped chronic backache." Now, as an ashram resident, he says that 3HO "has become my way of life, a way to obtain peace within and become a better person . . . less tense, more serene, more stable in my job life."

Many others in 3HO were specifically searching for God, truth, or a way of life even at the beginning. A twenty-one-year-old man who had been involved in conservative Christianity in his college days said that when he encountered 3HO in October 1971 he had been "searching for a pure life-style, a flowing relationship in harmony with myself and the Creator." Now, he says simply, "Freedom found!" Because of 3HO, he says, "My God consciousness has risen and my entire life has undergone a drastic change. From a drinking, smoking, flipping-out hippie I have become a child of God."

Most typical is the person who has found his or her motivation changed from physical to spiritual. One twenty-three-year-old woman became involved with 3HO because "the yoga made me feel healthier"; she was still in it six months later "to be one with our Lord; to share, love, live gracefully and righteously." She has come to know that "all and everything is God. We are all one, and materialist things don't go with us. Love is all we need." In discussions with 3HO people I often encountered this change of motive, where people who originally had no particularly salient spiritual awareness have become oriented by a new-found spirituality. The source of the change is in the yoga itself, which they claim to be a direct and objective means of stimulating this new spiritual consciousness.

Others have found in 3HO a means to end negative habits that they found limiting. Often that negativity had to do with drugs; a twenty-one-year-old man who had been in 3HO for only six months said that for several months before his first contact he had been wanting something else for his life than to be a drugger; though he does not yet live in an ashram, he has "become much more aware of myself and of the oneness of all [and] I'm no longer taking drugs." (Overall, 90 percent of current ashram residents said their former drug use had stopped entirely, and another 7 percent said it had decreased.) Others have found 3HO to be a means of changing their sexual image of themselves. An eighteen-year-old woman who had been in 3HO for seventeen months said, "I have changed my way of thinking pretty much—not a radical feminist any more but a grace of God lady."

Finally, some people have come into 3HO primarily because they see in it a means for creating a new society. One person with two years' experience in 3HO says, "I originally just got high from the yoga, and that's still true, and now I feel strongly about creating a New Age Society." Others expressed their feelings in more specifically Sikh terms: "I now hope to live according to the Sikh Dharma and help [Yogi Bhajan] to build a strong and spiritual nation under God."

Although more people have come through the process I call "physical to spiritual" than any other, none of these paths is considered the normative one for a member of 3HO. Individual motives are diverse and multiplex, and this is accepted as natural. It does not matter whether a person considers himself a physical culturist or a yogi or a Sikh; each person is expected to find the most comfortable path. The social unity arises from morning sadhana, shared by all; given participation in that, any reasonable path can lead to the goal of liberation.

Nor is the 3HO path itself considered normative for all. There is certainly not "One Way"; almost any sincere spiritual path is compatible with 3HO's goals.[13] Although most people end their involvement with 3HO before becoming fully committed to it (one yoga teacher estimated that of every one hundred people who take yoga classes only four or five wind up living in a 3HO ashram), this does not produce any crisis of explanation or self-identity for 3HO

13. In San Francisco, for example, members of 3HO (with Yogi Bhajan's encouragement) were instrumental in the founding of the "Meeting of the Ways," a confederation of diverse spiritual groups which fosters interaction among their leaders and members.

members. They recognize that their way is good for those who remain in it, though not suitable for everyone. They acknowledge
that the Aquarian nation will be a family of groups with compatible
spiritual purposes, not a Sikh aristocracy.

THE PROLEPTIC ETHIC

The Healthy-Happy-Holy Organization is filled with seeming
paradoxes, component elements that rarely go together anywhere
else. In India the Sikh religion and the many traditions of yoga have
nothing to do with each other; in this country some native Indian
Sikhs denounce Yogi Bhajan for attempting to join them. Nor are
personal spirituality and social concern or patriotism and leftist
political views usually combined in one organization. But it is
precisely this blend of polar elements that distinguishes 3HO as a
movement attempting to get beyond normal polarities and social
constraints into a more fundamental experience of the unity of all
things. It is just this process, with unity as a goal, that 3HO sees as
the underlying dynamic of the transition to the coming age of
Aquarius. Its attempt to go through the process *now*, therefore, is at
the core of its self-image as a pioneering social movement.

One of the most unusual apparent contradictions in 3HO is that it
represents an "Eastern worldliness"—neither the socially escapist
path that many Eastern religions have offered to Americans nor a
secular reform movement. The source of this characteristic is deep
within 3HO's theology. The central name for God is Sat Nam—
both transcendent, unchanging truth (Sat) and that truth as it is
manifested in the shifting forms of the creation (Nam). God himself
is beyond the polarities of transcendence and immanence, a pervasive unity more fundamental than the apparent contradiction. On
a more practical level, 3HO people do not chant *Om*, the familiar
mystical syllable, because they say it represents the vibration of the
divine *apart from* the world. Instead they chant *Ek Ong Kar*—
Creator and creation are *one*—a paradoxical unity with which they
seek to attune themselves. And their personal goal is to become
jivan mukt'—spiritually liberated while still alive in the physical
world. These theological images imply that the search within 3HO
for the most fundamental unity of mind and life must be pressed in
both polar-opposite directions: inner personal experience of the unchanging divine and life in the transitory world. This is the core insight which Sikhism contributes to 3HO.

It is not surprising, then, that 3HO is seeking a course other than the polarities of exclusively inner religious concern and exclusively outer social involvement. 3HO's chosen alternative—a familiar one in American history—is that of exemplary prophecy. Exemplary prophecy is precisely the establishment of a comprehensive lifestyle that embodies one's goals for society; by manifesting and enjoying proleptically (before the time of widespread fruition) what one expects the future to bring, one hopes to influence society and bring nearer the time of fulfillment or ease the transition.

For 3HO, then, social reform is advanced by living, now, the lifestyle of the coming age of Aquarius. In a society that it perceives and experiences as sexist and sex obsessed, for example, 3HO does not directly challenge sexist institutions and attitudes but instead creates strong egalitarian marriages and establishes a "Grace of God Movement for the Women of America"[14] through which women can learn their proper way in the world. Or in a society it feels to be preoccupied with money and possessions and riddled with economic inequities, 3HO does not abet Marxist-style class conflict but rather demonstrates a better way: living simply and communally, sharing with others.

What this approach precludes, of course, is direct confrontation with the institutions of society being criticized. There is in 3HO a tendency toward political (as distinct from worldly) aloofness, toward avoidance of direct involvement in the day-to-day contentions for ordinary social power. 3HO's concern with ends and not means is a manifestation of its thorough idealism and represents an unwillingness to consider how social institutions will be changed.

Perhaps this implied criticism of 3HO makes the issue too simple, for 3HO's sense of the sufficiency of moral example derives not only from its immediate experience but also from its long-term historical vision. As in many reform movements in American history, 3HO's perceived dynamic is eschatological—history is unfolding according to a fixed plan, and "in the fullness of time" the correctness of the chosen path will be revealed to all and established everywhere. Previously in America the course of that eschatological dynamic has been the dualistic Christian tradition, with its transcendent Lord of History developing his plan; 3HO's eschatology derives from an immanent or monistic vision. God is the universe and is above or beyond only the categories (polarities) men use to describe him. There is no "infinite qualitative distinction between God and man," but rather a continuity; "God is the infinite of me; I am the finite of

14. Founded in San Francisco at the Autumn Equinox 1971, the GGMWA provides special exercises and reading materials for 3HO women.

God." The dynamic history is a dynamic of organic growth, influenced by internal "genetic" controls, not by an external agent; and the outcome of the historical process now under way will be a gradual fruition rather than a sudden divine intervention. Therefore, it is more important for members of 3HO to be in harmony with the new order than to be in conflict with an order that will pass away. The new age *will* come; the very existence of 3HO as a strong example shows that the transition has already begun. Since politics by definition deals with embodiment of the present order, any preoccupation with institutions or politics is for 3HO a misdirection of energy, a frivolous activity.

The role of proleptic language is unique, and those who assume it often see themselves as a chosen people with special opportunities. Since the overall outcome of history is set, one must only "keep up"—live attuned to the life-style set by the eschatological vision—and life will unfold as it should. With the global future fixed, all of one's efforts can go toward making of one's life a manifestation of the future. But one must keep up the life-style, for this is the only way to demonstrate that one is truly a member of the chosen vanguard.[15]

This proleptic ethic is a powerful motivation for activity in the world, for every act is a potential vehicle for establishing the truth of one's belief. One's own inner life, one's family, one's living situation, one's economic arrangements, and one's community all become charged with a strong proleptic imperative: all must become new, the future must be manifested now in every area of life. In 3HO all must become fully healthy, happy, and holy.

It should be easy to understand why the Summer Solstice Sadhana is for 3HO the cornerstone of its corporate life. For the individual, it is a time to strengthen one's exemplary life-style and to grow in the anticipation of one's liberation. Corporately, Solstice is an "errand into the wilderness"; like the Pilgrims of an earlier America, 3HO's goal is to be a "city set upon a hill," a saving moral example for the larger society.[16] Since this example can be manifested most purely in apartness, the very isolation of Solstice

15. It is just this sort of dual impetus—a combination of special opportunity and the inner need to demonstrate one's coming salvation—which Max Weber saw at the core of the "Protestant ethic" he described. Although it comes from monistic rather than dualistic spiritual sources, the same general dynamic seems to be at work in 3HO.

16. The "errand" image is drawn from Perry Miller's famous essay *Errand into the Wilderness* (Cambridge: Harvard University Press, 1956).

makes it the strongest source from which more normal ashram life can draw.

3HO's proleptic ethic explains the attraction of the stringent disciplines at the core of the 3HO life-style. For the disciplines do not merely prepare one to live the life, they *are* the life. They are not just physical and spiritual calisthenics, they are means and end in one package: dharma. The early morning sadhana is not a temporary burden; it is a joyful opportunity to participate in God's future now by experiencing a proper physical, mental, and spiritual harmony with the universe. And all the strenuous physical and emotional effort of tantric yoga is a marvelous opportunity, now, to get past the male-female polarities and the limitations of the individual ego that the whole world will have to struggle with for years to come.

3HO's members have chosen to emigrate from an American culture they have found either lacking or destructive. They are the new pilgrims, to a new space within America, marked off by boundaries of appearance and activity and experience rather than physical distance. To be a Sikh—dressed in white, crowned in a turban, living a visibly disciplined life—is a way of manifesting that space, that moral apartness. Sikhism is in this sense an acquired ethnicity, a consciously chosen distinctiveness of a sort that most of 3HO's population had chosen earlier by becoming "hippies" and "freaks."

The members of 3HO are, by and large, patriotic despite their liberal-to-radical political persuasions. In 3HO it is no contradiction with leftist views to raise the American flag and sing "God Bless America," for this is a way to claim a new space within American culture, a space delimited by the founding myths taken as literal exemplars. 3HO's radical political critique derives from a sort of fundamentalist patriotism and not from any foreign ideology. Thus 3HO's plan for the future represents a populist rather than Marxist kind of socialism—communitarian, but not Communist, motivated by proper consciousness, not by economic forces at large.

3HO's multifaceted idealism explains to some extent the nature of its population. 3HO, like many movements that have arisen from the recent counterculture, is largely composed of the cream of America's youth, the white upper-middle class, those who have been given material and educational advantages and yet have turned their backs on "the best" that America had to offer. It is, in part, *because* these young men and women have been trained to be idealistic, to be interested in the possible more than the actual, that a strong vision like that of 3HO appeals. Anyone who does not believe in the possibility of positive change, and who is not willing to try to manifest that change proleptically in his or her own life, will not remain long in 3HO.

PROSPECTS

It is too early to guess what 3HO will become. A movement less than five years old at this writing, 3HO has not yet needed to face the long-term problems that an exemplary movement must overcome if it is to survive and prosper. 3HO is only beginning to move away from its economic dependence on the dominant society; its children are too young to present an internal challenge to the group's way of life; Yogi Bhajan is still an active leader, able to head off any factionalism or differing interpretations of the teachings; and any tension between mass appeal and purity of life-style is not yet salient in a still rapidly growing movement.

Yet 3HO's resources for doing what it says it is going to do are considerable: the yoga disciplines for health and for strength of body, mind, and emotions; the group life for reinforcement of individual gains in a testing social setting; and the Sikh center for its explicity spiritual sources. Perhaps—for the members of 3HO at least—the age of Aquarius is truly not far away.

2

The Hare Krishna in San Francisco

GREGORY JOHNSON

On a street bordering Golden Gate Park in the Haight-Ashbury section of San Francisco stood the Krishna Consciousness temple. A large athletic stadium loomed over the street's three-story-high wooden buildings. One side of the street was zoned for businesses, which included a small bicycle store, an auto-repair shop, a dry-cleaning establishment, and the Krishna Consciousness temple. Above the entrance to the temple were the two-foot-high wooden letters "Hare Kirshna." The large storefront windows were covered with red and orange patterned blankets.

The sounds of chanting and music filled the street. Inside there were dozens of brightly colored paintings on the wall, thick red rugs on the floor, and a smoky haze in the air. This smoke was incense, an element of the ceremony in progress. The people in the room were softly chanting barely audible Sanskrit words. The room was nearly full, with about fifty people who all appeared to be young sitting on the floor. Assembled in front were about twenty persons wearing long, loose-fitting orange and saffron robes, with white paint on their noses. Many of the men had shaved their heads except for a ponytail. The women with them also had white paint on their noses and small red marks on their foreheads. The other young persons in the room appeared no different from other denizens of the Haight-Ashbury, costumed in headbands, long hair, beards, and an assortment of rings, bells, and beads, and they were also enthusiastically participating in the ceremony. The ten or so persons sitting in the rear appeared to be first-time visitors.

The chanting ceremony (mantra) increased in tempo and in volume. Two girls in long saffron robes were now dancing to the chant. The leader of the chant began to cry the words: *Hare Kirshna, Hare Krishna, Krishna, Krishna, Hare, Hare; Hare Rama, Hare Rama, Rama, Rama, Hare, Hare.* The entire group repeated the words, and attempted to maintain the leader's intonation and rhythm. Many of the participants played musical instruments. The leader was beating a hand drum in time with his chanting. The two swaying, dancing girls were playing finger cymbals. One young man was blowing a seashell; another was beating on a tambourine. Two others were playing harmoniums (droning, reed instruments), and a young girl was playing a Panpura (a small flute-like instrument) and staring at a picture on the wall of an Indian girl playing a similar instrument. On the walls of the temple were over a dozen paintings of scenes from the *Bhagavad-Gita.*

The music and the chanting grew very loud and fast. The drum was ceaselessly pounding. Many of the devotees started personal shouts, hands upstretched, amidst the general chant. The leader knelt in front of a picture of the group's "spiritual master" on a small shrine near the front of the room. The chanting culminated in a loud crescendo and the room became silent. The celebrants knelt with their heads to the floor as the leader said a short prayer in Sanskrit. Then he shouted five times, "All glories to the assembled devotees," which the others repeated before they sat up.

After the chanting concluded, three female initiates went to a room behind the altar and returned with large containers of food and paper plates. They proceeded to serve the meal. Each plate was passed back hand-to-hand to the people in the rear of the room until everybody had been served. The food was rich, spicy, and strictly vegetarian, without meat, fish, or eggs. After the meal one of the devotees began to explain the objectives of the temple. He outlined the development of the movement and the reasons it had come to San Francisco.

THE ORIGINS OF THE MOVEMENT

The Krishna Consciousness movement was founded in New York in 1966 by a seventy-year-old Indian expatriate, A.C. Bhaktivedanta. The spiritual locus of the movement, Bhaktivedanta was believed to be the direct link to the deity Krishna. He had been a successful businessman in India, and he relinquished his job and family to move into the East Village section of New York City in 1965 to establish an American version of an Indian religious discipline that has existed since the fifth century. He gathered around him a coterie of followers, including the poet Allen Ginsberg.[1] Initiation into the movement involved adherence to certain ritual practices and beliefs stipulated in his interpretation of the *Gita*. Besides conformity to strict standards of dress and behavior, membership required residential insulation from the outside world. Full membership was granted only after a trial period of about six months during which one demonstrated sufficient spirituality and knowledge of the sacred texts.

Early in 1967, Bhaktivedanta relocated himself and about half of the thirty members of the New York temple to San Francisco, for two significant reasons: to continue as a city organization rather than retreat to the country in order to become contemplative and nature-oriented, like many similar groups; and to make a conscious effort to recruit young persons, whom the swami was convinced were open to the particular message of Krishna. The group moved into a reconverted laundromat near the center of the Haight-Ashbury area in early 1967. Coinciding with a large migration of young people to the area, this move proved to be a windfall for the movement. The migrants acted as a vast reservoir of potential recruits; Jainanda, one of the temple's leaders, estimated that over the years of 1967 and 1968 from 150 to 200 persons became full converts at the temple. Many became the mobilizing force behind the movement's later expansion to the rest of the United States and Western Europe. By July 1974 the movement had grown to fifty-four temples throughout the world.

As the youthful denizens of the Haight-Ashbury diffused outward to other cities throughout America, the International Society of Krishna Consciousness (ISKCON) followed them like a shadow. During the early 1970s temples were opened near centers of college-age student enclaves in Los Angeles and Berkeley; Boston; Seattle; Boulder, Colorado; Santa Fe; Columbus, Ohio; and Buffalo. Foreign temples had been opened in Vancouver and Montreal, in London and in Hamburg. Jainanda attributed the movement's growth to the original dissemination of devotees from the San Francisco temple: "The temple here is like a seed bed for Krishna. We plant the seeds and the devotees come up like flowers for Krishna all over the world. We have boys going to Hawaii and Europe and the East Coast, to serve Krishna and tell people of his glories."

1. For an account of the initial activities of the movement in New York City, see the *New Yorker* magazine, August 17, 1968, p. 63, in "Paterfamilias-I," by Jane Kramer.

I became personally interested in this movement in 1968 when a close college friend converted to its ranks. The sudden manner in which he relinquished his prior friendships, political ideals, and material possessions bewildered me. It became possible to pursue this initial interest when I was employed as a research assistant in a project designed to interview residents of the Haight-Ashbury area. For about three years I examined this movement in San Francisco, utilizing observations, interviews, and analyses of its documents.

The student of any social movement faces an inevitable analytic dilemma: how to balance his own sentiments with those of the movement. Being personally compelled by many aspects of Eastern thought, this dilemma would have been most acute if I had chosen a movement whose philosophy was similar to my own. The Hare Krishna movement, however, expressed principles so distant from my own that I was not conscious of this problem.

THE WORLD VIEW OF THE MOVEMENT

The stated beliefs of the movement were based on the *Bhagavad-Gita* as translated by its founder, A.C. Bhaktivedanta. At all times, the devotees attempted to reduce the sacred text to simple yet comprehensive directives that would apply to the lives of persons in the Haight-Ashbury. For the residents, the ideology became especially sensible once one granted a crucial assumption, which seemingly corresponded to experiences within the Haight-Ashbury: the present age was undergoing a decisive transformation, characterized by unprecedented confusion and turmoil. Events had shown that previous beliefs did not work; people were searching for a spiritual absolute that would lead them beyond war, strife, and chaos. In articulating these positions, the devotees claimed that the world was near the end of the materialistic age of Kali-Yuga, the last cycle of a four-cycle millennium. If the populace could be aroused, this age of Kali-Yuga would be concluded; and a new age of peace, love, and unity would be discovered.

Furthermore, this new age would arrive through the transformed consciousness of millions of people. Most important, this transformation would be a psychological one, within the minds of individuals, rather than through changed institutions. This position held that, if each person practiced the bhakti yoga discipline, he would be eternally blissful as well as protected by Krishna. "Someday there will be only one political party," one member predicted. "People will not vote, they will chant." Within this scheme, what were called "social problems" would automatically disappear, because people would be unified by Krishna Consciousness.

The material world (*maya* in Hindu scriptures) was portrayed as superficial and unreal. Advertising, supermarkets, movies, and newspapers were all senseless diversions. Every person had a potential for both tranquility and ecstasy, which would be achieved only through renunciation of superficial distractions. This renunciation would lead man to his natural state of being; he would be able to breathe better, work better, sleep better, eat better, love better, and be a happier person. A flyer handed out on the streets in the summer of 1968 described the discipline:

It is the essential track above the suffocating pleasure trips advertised by billboards. Such a linear odyssey through plastic form is a diversionary movement offered to superficial and coarse creatures for captivating their whims, while the Ultimate Express (Krishna Consciousness) is running unnoticed into the kingdom of God.

The devotee's rejection of the world is applied to the entire physical environment; when I asked why the temple does not move to a mountain retreat in the country, away from the materialism of the city, one devotee replied:

The city is better, because it is so ugly. One can appreciate the ugliness of the temporal world much easier in the city, so it is easier to escape it and find Krishna. The country deceives you, because its beauty and serenity make one think that he achieved liberation when he really hasn't. His head is still the same. They are all the same; country and city are material worlds.

Many of the devotees were convinced the movement had provided them with truths that were timeless and absolute. "Why should I go back to college when I have already learned everything there is to know through Krishna?" said a twenty-year-old woman, a former student at San Francisco City College. This position was also stated by Tamal, the leader of the temple, when he spoke after group chanting (*kirtan*). "Vedic knowledge is transcendental and cannot be understood by educational procedures. It is something that one can study, but simply studying it will only take you so far. In order to understand it, one must practice it."

Thus, the absolute insight experienced by a devotee could not be interpreted by words or logic. It was something that each person "knows" when he "feels" it. The devotees stressed that all logical, rational arguments about truth are worthless; logic will lead only to disagreement, never to one path as the answer, but to many paths.

This perspective rejected formal education, in which knowledge is specialized in terms of disciplines. The devotees accepted as valid some of the forms of traditional schooling: the teacher, the student, the book (the *Gita*), as well as certain "tests" of knowledge. But the substantive content was profoundly different from traditional education. This knowledge was completely unified and grounded in personal experience. The end of learning was not questioning and communicating with others, but self-realization.

The movement's espousal of personal enlightenment was given a specific emphasis, directed to the interests of the denizens of the Haight-Ashbury; a most important interest at that time was the use of hallucinogenic drugs—mescaline, lysergic acid (LSD), and psilocybin. The temple's appeal to persons who had experimented with these drugs was indicated by a four-foot-high multicolored poster on the wall of the temple:

Stay high forever. No more coming down. Practice Krishna Consciousness. Expand your consciousness by practicing the Transcendental Sound Vibration. Hare Krishna, Hare Krishna, Krishna Krishna, Hare Hare, Hare Rama, Hare Rama, Rama Rama, Hare Hare. The chanting will cleanse the dust from the mirror of the mind and free you from all material contamination. It is practical, self-evident, and requires no artificial aid. Try it and be blissful all the time. *Turn on* through music, dance, philosophy, science, religion and prasadam (spiritual food). *Tune in.* Awaken your Transcendental Nature! Rejoice in the Ocean of Bliss! The process of Sandirtan brings about transcendental ecstasy. *Drop out* of movements employing artificially induced states of self-realization and expanded consciousness. Such methods only lead to spiritual laziness and chaos. *End all bring-downs,* flip out and stay for eternity. Bhakti yoga has been practiced for many centuries and is authorized by India's great acharyas. Swami Bhaktivedanta is in the bonafide line of Krishna's discipline succession. He has especially come to this country to spiritually guide young Americans.

The above statement indicates how the movement made a sophisticated effort to translate its appeals into contemporary form. A centuries-old belief system was revised to appeal to the alleged concerns of the youthful residents of the Haight-Ashbury.

That the movement was fairly accurate in anticipating the concerns of its potential recruits (including a belief in the sudden transformation of the world, the importance of personal revelation, and an expressed relinquishment of material goods) is shown in values expressed in the journalism, writing, and personal statements of members of the Bay Area youth culture.[2] Although such values

2. See John Weakland, "Hippies: What the Scene Means," in *Society and Drugs,* ed. Richard Blum (San Francisco: Jossey-Bass, 1970); and David Whittaker

were sincerely held by many young persons in the area, they were not generally articulated in a public context. The philosophy of ISKCON represented an organized, detailed delineation of sentiments that had been formless and unshared.

It would be a mistake, however, to emphasize the values and doctrines of the movement as the sole reason for its growth. In attracting adherents, its chanting ceremonies seemed to be much more significant than its doctrines. On many occasions I observed visitors who had been fully absorbed in chanting and dancing leave the temple quietly when the post-mantra doctrinal discussions began. It seemed apparent that the chanting ceremonies were the movement's distinctive contribution to the residents of the Haight-Ashbury. Three times daily the mantras provided a freely accessible opportunity for collective emotional release. Moreover, it was an activity that demanded complete involvement, in contrast to the passive, audience-like participation in most events in the area, such as rock music concerts.

Thus, any interpretation of ISKCON must incorporate its doctrines and its rituals—the music, the chanting, the smell of incense, the oil paintings on the wall, the artifacts, and the musical instruments—into a composite cultural picture. What were the successes of these appeals? How did this movement, in its attempt to embody many of the values and practices of the counterculture, originally emerge and later expand from the Haight-Ashbury? Who joined the movement? Why would a young person raised to maturity in postwar America voluntarily relinquish his home, his possessions, and his prior conduct and enter an Eastern monastic order?

SOURCES OF COMMITMENT TO KRISHNA

The large-scale dislocation accompanying the migration of young people to the Haight-Ashbury created a large, continually walking gathering of unattached persons. Several members noted that they had first discovered the Krishna Consciousness movement by accident—in walking by the temple or hearing the mantra performed in the park. Others had heard about the movement from friends or accidental acquaintances. Oftentimes the individual was alone when first attending the temple.

and W.A. Watts, "Personality Characteristics of a Non-Conformist Youth Subculture," *Journal of Social Issues* 25 (1969): 65–89.

Physical Inducements of the Temple

The immediate area around the temple was characterized by extensive foot traffic. Below the large "Hare Krishna" sign on the outside of the temple was a smaller placard: "Stay High All The Time, Discover Eternal Bliss." Inside, the incense, paintings of ancient scenes, and pictures of the swami seemed calculated to convey a distinctly alien impression to the visitor. The strange musical instruments, the cherished ritual embellishments (such as a pillow that holds the *Gita*), and the prayers in Sanskrit (a language understood by none of the devotees) fortified the exotic symbolism.

Interpersonal Strategies of Recruitment

Any person who walked into the temple was a potential recruit. Many were drawn in by the sounds of the chanting ceremony and the music or by the smell of incense and food. A devotee who acted as doorman asked the visitor to take off his shoes. This was a convention within the temple, but it also served to make the outsider immediately aware of his presence in a special place. When the chant was taking place, the visitor was invited to be seated on the carpet and participate.

The proselytizing devotees seldom gave the visitor something to read, but relied on face-to-face contact instead. Primarily, the devotee talked about the sublime experience of Krishna Consciousness and pictured it as an experience surpassing all worldly pleasures. The strategy was one of empathy—the devotee identified his preenlightened self with that of the potential convert. If drugs were mentioned, the devotee would voice the dictum that Krishna Consciousness is a way to stay high all the time, that drug use does not compare even slightly with the overwhelming joy of the bhakti yoga discipline. The devotee usually mentioned the spiritual guidance in the timeless wisdom of the *Bhagavad-Gita*.

Exposure to the Ritual

Agreement about doctrine was insignificant compared with the potential convert's feeling about the kirtan ceremony. Logical discourse was not nearly so important to the devotee as the surges of joy and ecstasy generated by the mantra. When asked what they liked most about Krishna Consciousness, the members almost always mentioned the chanting. "Kirtan is the most exciting and sublime experience I have ever had. Every day I feel it again," said one. Clearly, if a person is immediately seduced by the mantra, he was a likely convert; if he was not, the likelihood of his joining was much less.

SELF-SURRENDER AND THE QUEST FOR ORDEAL

On entering Hare Krishna, all aspects of the convert's prior identity were surrendered. The hair of a male was shaved. Clothes, money, and personal effects were given to the temple. The initiate relinquished his previous name and was assigned a Sanskrit name from the scriptures of the temple. Personal finances were superfluous since all the members' needs—food, clothes, and travel—were supplied by the movement. The initiate was given a set of Hindu robes (usually orange, sometimes yellow), which were worn at all times. This alteration of appearance was fortified by a rigorous set of prohibitions on conduct: strictly forbidden was the eating of meat, illicit sex (outside marriage), gambling, all intoxicants, cigarettes, and drugs. These proscriptions were based on A.C. Bhaktivedanta's interpretation of the Vedic texts and were crucial to the bhakti yoga discipline.

This life of self-imposed poverty and ascetic denial seemed especially dramatic in contrast with the origins of most devotees. The best available indications are that most devotees came from prosperous homes: a questionnaire study of the life histories of thirty-one devotees conducted in 1971 disclosed that the annual incomes of the fathers of the respondents averaged over $20,000.[3] This finding was confirmed by inferential impressions gained from interviews I conducted: of fourteen persons who discussed their preconversion lives, seven indicated home communities that were suburbs of San Francisco or Los Angeles. All the devotees were white. All indicated that they had attended college, although only two had finished.

In this light, conversion to Krishna seemed to be an emphatic rejection of conventional affluent America. In contrast with the solely ideological rejection characteristic of youthful political radicals, many of whom retained the trappings of middle-class life such as televisions, automobiles, and stereo equipment, the convert to Hare Krishna made a complete revision of the course of his life. This was a rejection expressed through actions rather than words. The roots of this decisive transformation of identity were expressed by a re-

3. This study was conducted by Dr. Stillson Judah and is summarized in his book *Hare Krishna and the Counterculture*, (New York: John Wiley and Sons, 1974).

cent convert when he explained why he believed that so many young persons were discovering spiritual enlightenment: "Like most everybody else, we were given everything when growing up. Our parents thought that material possessions meant spiritual satisfaction. But we knew it was false. Even then, we knew that true spiritual happiness was in an energy of a higher form. Many other young people have come to understand this principle. Material gain is illusory. It brings nothing but unhappiness."

This suggests that the rejection of the material benefits of American affluence was only a surface indication of a more deeply rooted, less tangible form of rebellion. The comfortable affluence of the life of the American dream seemed, for many youths, to lack a sense of ordeal, of challenge or hardship. Designated life plans (such as college, graduate schools, and professional employment) were merely carefully prescribed expressions of parental ideals. The alternative life is based on one's free choice, its constraints the result of personal decision, as opposed to the external forces of school, family, or employment. Robert Bellah has discussed this phenomenon in terms of a general historical trend toward personal choice of values and style of life in opposition to the imposition of cultural tradition: "Culture from being conceived as an exo-skeleton, is becoming an endo-skeleton, *something self-consciously chosen and internalized, not immutably given from without.*"[4]

In this context, many young persons seemed to pursue vigorously the hardships and obstacles denied by affluence. In the process, they hoped to attain precisely the rewards that had escaped their fathers: community, self-insight, and a rich and varied experience. The ordeals of politically oriented youths over the 1960s are well documented: this decade saw several variations on this theme, from the migration of northern white youth to rural southern poverty regions in the early 1960s to the jailings, police-riot beatings, and chemical warfare subsequently suffered by student dissidents. A different version of the same theme is offered by the segment of youths oriented toward drug use; these person explored hazardous psychological territory while living in cold-water poverty in San Francisco's Haight-Ashbury or New York's Lower East Side.

The strict adherence to a religious discipline can be comprehended as another decisive example of a selected ordeal. The preparatory preentrance stage of such religious disciplines required

4. Robert Bellah, *Beyond Belief: Essays on Religion in a Post-Traditional World*, p. 219. Emphasis added. (For publishing data on the titles in the footnotes, see the references at the end of the chapter.)

a constancy of motive, a dedication to purpose, and an endurance of self-sacrifice that were perhaps equal to the most rigorous medical or professional school in the land. This seems especially true of the Hare Krishna movement, whose regulations were the strictest of the many groups appealing to the counterculture. Perhaps the most striking element of devotional service was its selflessness. This quality was characterized by Nukunda, a veteran devotee whom I asked if the devotees ever missed the old pleasures of the material world. "One must serve Krishna constantly without ever thinking of yourself. We are filled up with pleasure by our service to Krishna. All the old pleasures are meaningless because they are selfish. You can serve yourself and Krishna too." This divestment of past pleasures seemed to be a result of a radical transformation of the ego: rather than oneself, the group (as the representation of the deity Krishna) became the reference point for all desires and aspirations. How did this transformation of the ego occur? The accounts of the devotees suggest that the answers to this question lay in their experiences with hallucinogenic drugs prior to conversion.

THE APPEAL OF NONCHEMICAL TRANSCENDENCE

When I asked Tamal how many of the other devotees had used hallucinogenic drugs prior to conversion, he replied:

Almost all of us, I suppose. . . . maybe 95 percent or more. . . . Such experiences affected me and I was much different afterwards. This is true of others too. But these experiences were unsatisfying because they were temporary. . . . Drugs provided temporary knowledge, perhaps, but not wisdom. . . . Nothing like the wisdom from Krishna.

Although drugs were strictly forbidden in devotional service, many devotees freely discussed their past drug experiences. Several described drugs as a necessary but insufficient precondition to achieving a psychological state permanently sustained by the bhakti yoga discipline (its chanting and food especially). "It opened the door, but Krishna let me step through," said one devotee. "It freed my mind, it washed out the old structures," claimed another. Rather than the pleasurable or sensual aspects of drug use, the devotees stressed the use of psychedelics as a means to internal discovery. The sense of ordeal so prevalent in the discipline of devotion to Krishna seemed also essential to drug-induced enlightenment. In criticizing the extensive proliferation of the use of LSD and mescaline in the Haight-Ashbury, Tamal said,

Most of the people in the Haight are destroying their minds on drugs

because they don't realize the powers they are dealing with. They have to
be dedicated. It is like becoming a devotee of Krishna almost—you must
be dedicated to the correct ways to spiritual knowledge. Also you must
listen to those who have gone before. Like the spiritual master is to us. . . .
When I first took acid I was guided by a friend who had taken it many
times before. Many people now do not do this. They don't realize that acid
is not just for sense gratification. It is a serious matter. They find this out
too late and many of them end up crazy.

In pioneering with hallucinogens, the devotees seemed to conclude that they were special caretakers of the pathway to revelation.
There existed only specified ways of travel along this path, and
deviation would lead to an unrewarding and confusing experience.
This perspective assumed limited accessibility to the active devices
(LSD, mescaline, or psilocybin) that initiated the journey. After
1967, however, these substances proliferated widely. Accessibility
was no longer exclusive; self-medicated enlightenment was directly
available to many people. Very little was asked of these drug users
in terms of commitment, sacrifice, or suffering. Jainanda described
the process: "Somewhere it all changed; acid was distorted into a
pleasure trip. It became just sense gratification. People were feeding their heads like they were feeding their mouths. It was used to
bring out the human's animal nature rather than his spiritual
nature."

The Krishna temple afforded the controls and regulations in the
journey to enlightenment that were absent in haphazard self-
medication. Most important, to be worthwhile, enlightenment must
be an ordeal. The attainment of spiritual wisdom was not easy. It involved a rigorous discipline of self-denial and sacrifice. The
movement's strict prohibitions against personal pleasure were
necessary for spiritual dedication. This adherence to predesignated
pattern was reflected in the execution of the mantras. If enlightenment were to be attained, the mantras had to be performed in
specified ways. Particular words, intonations, and ways of holding
oneself were especially significant. These requisites were reminiscent of a set of procedures surrounding drug ingestion. However,
the sect's procedures were not personally devised or idiosyncratic;
its pathways to spiritual wisdom were perceived as comprehensive
and timeless in their wisdom.

Preconversion experiences within the Haight-Ashbury seemed to
disconfirm any vestiges of "psychedelic utopianism" in the devotees:[5] the belief that the ingestion of psychedelic chemicals would

5. Psychedelic utopianism is a quasi-magical belief in drug use as a means to
effect widespread world transformation.

inevitably produce persons who were peace loving, communally oriented, and antimaterialistic was decisively deflated by events in the Haight-Ashbury.

As drug use proliferated, it became merely one of many consumed commodities, including waterbeds, records, stereos, and motorcycles. Most important, the proliferation of drug use was simultaneous with both the increase in police pressure and the involvement of organized crime in drug marketing. Dealing and buying drugs became precarious as risks of thievery, beatings, and contact with police informers were greatly increased. Furthermore, the widespread misrepresentation of the contents of drugs meant that the consumer could no longer be certain of the substances he was ingesting. One devotee of three months summarized his feelings about this period in the Haight-Ashbury:

Most of us thought we had the answer in drugs. It took me a long time to figure out that drugs were just another object of ego gratification and selfishness. They are illusory objects that are placed in front of you to make you want them and feel important. It makes no difference whether it is a new car, a pretty girl, a meal in a fine restaurant or the best acid that you can find—they are all the same. They create anxiety because as soon as you have one you want more. The only way out is to give it all up. Not just one or two, but all of them. Then you will realize that you don't need objects to feel important.

A central theme underlying commitment to the movement was the rejection of the pursuit of personal pleasure, of which drugs were an integral part. This placed the movement in fundamental opposition to the larger counterculture. If the counterculture was unified, it was unified in its obsession with personal experience; within it, an individual was not subordinate to a social role, an ideology, or a group; existing legal and normative controls were largely rejected; each individual was urged to pursue freely a personal state of ecstasy. The discipline of Krishna Consciousness represented a conservative reaction to this passionate assertion of self.

Max Weber has pointed out how the successful attainment of the mystical search requires separation from the concerns of the material world; the mystic must reject the life of persons who are "forever involved in the burdens of created things."[6] The interviews suggest that it became impossible to pursue chemically induced transcendence in the context of a materialistic drug culture. The acquisition and ingestion of the drugs necessitated contact with

6. *The Sociology of Religion*, p. 171.

the material world, which was unreconcilable with a spiritual search. Drugs became merely another item in the realm of "created things."

COLLECTIVE VALIDATION AND FELLOWSHIP

For many devotees, the hypnotic quality of the mantra seemed to be an experience equivalent to hallucinogenic drug use. Not only did the mantra generate feelings of ecstasy or transcendence, it also involved a community—something lacking in the drug experience. The hallucinogenic drug experience is not generally amenable to collective validation; by its very nature, the experience is a solitary one; the user confronts his innermost feelings of fear, awe, and fantasy.

In contrast, the individual's experience of transcendence within the temple became regularized and predictable. The group's daily chanting rituals (mantras) became the expression of feelings previously reserved for the drug experience. The drug culture was one of resignation and passivity, whereas the Krishna movement stressed participation and affirmation. Each devotee had a part in the preparation and execution of the mantra. The purpose of the mantras, like that of drugs, was to separate the experiencer from the controls of "objective" reality; but unlike drug use, which was individualistic and isolating, the purpose of the mantras was to merge with a collective meaning.

Private feelings of enlightenment can be difficult to sustain unless the individual is fortified by a group of other persons who the individual is convinced are realizing the same internal feelings. This principle was expressed by Tamotsu Shibutani: "The founder of a new religion goes forth to report on his conversations with God; were it not for the acceptance of his associates, anyone claiming such experiences would be incarcerated as insane."[7]

The absence of collective validation for drug-induced revelations was perhaps a reflection of the transient quality of relationships in the Haight-Ashbury. Many devotees described preconversion life as a series of chance fragmentary experiences. One convert described his prior experience in the community: "Everybody was just walking past each other up and down the streets. It was like being in a parade except that nobody was in step with anybody else. . . . Everyone thought they had the answer and no one could stop and

7. *Society and Personality* (Englewood Cliffs, N.J.: Prentice-Hall, 1961), p. 528.

talk to anyone else. When they did, they were talking *past* each other, not *to* each other. Nobody is doing anything together except the devotees of Krishna." In contrast, the sect afforded the members an intense and lasting group. The practices, symbols, and doctrines of the movement were centuries old, conveying an impression of timeless wisdom. Furthermore, one's mobility was not restricted: a full devotee could travel to other movement temples in cities throughout the country. This provided the member with an ongoing series of communities to which he had "guaranteed" acceptability.

A devotee of eighteen months said that the best aspect of life in the temple was "the other devotees. Without them I would not stay here. They are so great. . . . We see Krishna together every day." Analysts of contemporary communal endeavors among young people have commonly offered explanations that emphasize the family-like characteristics of these ventures. Communal living can be thus interpreted as either a continuation of the "personalistic" intimacy of the nuclear family into postadolescence[8] or as a belated correction of its prior absence.[9] A close examination of the ongoing nature of this communal fellowship in the Hare Krishna movement revealed a paradox: although the devotees were in close day-to-day proximity, the quality of the relationships lacked a specific personal intensity. Smiles, warm personal greetings, physical touching and hugging were virtually absent. (Also absent were corresponding expressions of anger or hostility.)

While painting the cart for the movement's annual Juggernaut parade, Jadurani, a female devotee, described the nature of personal feelings in the temple. "We show our love by our engagements for Krishna. Painting the cart is a good engagement. Making *prasadam* (the temple's daily meal) is a good engagement too." The expression of fellowship through collective tasks ("engagements") meant that personal feelings of intensity were diffused to the entire temple rather than directed toward specific individuals. Without question, the most significant of such engagements were the continually chanted mantras. It was in the mantras that feelings and

8. See Richard Flacks, "The Liberated Generation: An Exploration of the Roots of Student Protest," *Journal of Social Issues* 23 (1967): 52−75; and his "Social and Cultural Meanings of Student Revolt: Some Informal and Comparative Observations," *Social Problems* (winter 1970): 340−57. See also Thomas Robbins and Dick Anthony, "Getting Straight with Meher Baba," *Journal for the Scientific Study of Religion* 11 (June 1972): 122−40.

9. See Philip Slater, *The Pursuit of Loneliness* (Boston: Beacon Press, 1970).

sentiments, constrained from interpersonal expression, seemed to be given free reign. The object of these feelings, however, was not individual devotees but an abstraction, a deity as embodied in the earthly form of the movement's founder, A.C. Bhaktivedanta.

THE REGULATION OF EMOTIONAL ATTACHMENTS

The survival and growth of the Krishna movement within the encompassing counterculture presented a paradox; in a community allegedly based on the forces of universal love (rather than force or coercion), one of the few intentional communities to survive severely restricted the expression of love as it is commonly defined: exclusive two-person attachments. The entire rule structure of the temple served to deindividualize personal relationships. The shaving of the hair was an important initial event in deindividualizing (and symbolically desexualizing) the recruits. Sex between men and women was regulated.

The redirection of intense personal feelings has always been an important aspect of religious commitment. In many cases, the most devoted forms of spiritualization can be interpreted as the sublimation of eros. "Sex is easily forgotten when you give all your love to Krishna. He gives you infinite pleasure in return." One way in which the temple regulated emotional expression was through trial celibacy. Rather than permanent renunciation, vows of celibacy were required only during the devotee's brahmachari period, for a new convert a period of sacrifice, withdrawal, and contemplation, during which he was not allowed to permit attachment to any mortal to interfere with his devotion to Krishna. Another way was through devotional marriage, between a male and female devotee, in a match approved by the spiritual master, who often performed the marriage ceremony according to ritual procedures. One important regulative condition: procreation rather than enjoyment was the sole purpose of sexual relations between the couple. Hence, married couples tended to continue living within the confines of the temple rather than seeking a separate private residence. (One ISKCON temple in Los Angeles comprises about thirty married couples and their children. In most regular temples men outnumber the women by about two to one.) Such controls on exclusive two-person relationships seem to be a critical precondition to the survival of intentional communities.[10]

10. Rosabeth Kanter has emphasized this point in her study of the organizational characteristics of ninety-one such communities. Despite wide religious and

In imposing such controls, the temple seemed to avoid many of the potentially divisive influences of interpersonal love (such as jealousy, envy, and personal possessiveness). Such sentiments were elevated to a supernatural domain and directed to an impersonal deity—"objectified" love. Thus, the Krishna temple successfully generated what the larger counterculture had failed to accomplish: the establishment of a unified community based on the noncoercive authority of love.

The appropriate expression of intense personal feelings is perhaps the most important task of any intentional community. The potential divisiveness of intense emotional expression was intensified by the confined living quarters within the Hare Krishna temple. A "solution" to this potential problem was facilitated by the movement's resocialization process: in the requirement for complete divestment of the recruit's prior identity, his grounds for dissension and disagreement were significantly diminished. The strict prohibitions on emotional expression solidified his decision to relinquish everything.

Furthermore, the movement's continual chanting rituals were critically significant in providing a structured expression of the emotions constrained by its prohibitions. Each devotee participated in collective chanting at least three times daily—a public expression of feelings normally reserved for intimate relationships. Such personal relationships were categorized as frivolous "entanglements" causing introspection and self-analysis, which sapped one's dedication to Krishna. Affection for other human beings was completely forgotten in the ecstasy of spiritual devotion. Thus, it was in the mantra that private emotions became regularized, predictable, and collectively affirmed.

Its restrictions on the pursuit of personal pleasure most radically demarked the movement from its neighbors. Numerous persons in the area became regular participants in its ceremonies without formally entering the movement. Resistance to the group's prohibitions on conduct were most often noted as the reasons for unwillingness to join. One potential convert said, "I like the chanting, but they are too dogmatic for me. I could never say that I was going to give up something like sex. I am still part of the material

---

ideological differences, the most "successful" communities ("success" being defined as existence for over twenty-five years) were characterized by the regulation of exclusive two-person relationships between their members. "Commitment and Social Organization: A Study of Commitment Mechanism in Utopian Communities," *American Sociological Review* 33 (August 1968): 499–517.

world." Thus, it is likely that by modifying or relaxing its prohibitions the movement would have expanded its formal membership. This alteration, however, would also have undermined the
movement's distinctive identity as well as its primary source of unity—the sense of shared zeal derived from collective sacrifice.

CONCLUSIONS

The evolution of the Haight-Ashbury exemplified the failure of the
counterculture. Rather than having a coherent, sustained vision of
an alternative community, its participants remained motivated by
vague and unarticulated aspirations. Theirs was a reaction rather
than an affirmation. At the level of a community-wide aggregation,
a clearly defined counterculture was never actually established.
Only when scaled down to the microcosmic form of a small community could a genuine culture be sustained. Only at this level
could a system of meanings, symbols, and conduct in opposition to
the larger society be established.

The Hare Krishna movement initially emerged because it effectively translated its ancient rituals and doctrines to meet contemporary needs. Two specific features seemed especially significant:
(1) an apocalyptic ideology. The world was portrayed as being in
danger of imminent collapse—which would render meaningless
any previous desires for personal achievement or material acquisition. The movement's selective emphasis of these elements of its
doctrine represented a deliberate effort to resonate with the an-
ticipated attitudes of its neighbors in the Haight-Ashbury. (2) Participatory rituals. The movement's chanting ceremonies were
perhaps more significant than its ideology in generating involvement; unlike the audience-like behavior at episodic musical events,
the mantra allowed full personal participation within a collective.

For its recruits, the movement seemed to embody many of the
aspirations for an alternative community not fulfilled by the
Haight-Ashbury. Conversion to Krishna served to sustain the
promise of "psychedelic utopianism" within narrowly defined (and
legally immune) limits. Perhaps the most significant aspect of
hallucinogenic drug use was its redefinition of the possible
pathways to knowledge. In a similar fashion, the ceremonies of the
Krishna temple offered direct unmediated communion with supernatural transcendent forces. The experience became regularized,
controllable, and predictable within the bhakti yoga discipline.
Transcendence became a routine state of being.

Personal commitment to the movement was sustained because the temple offered something generally lacking in the drug experience: a unified and supportive community that validated the transcendent experience by sharing its expression. This community, in order to survive, required a binding sense of mutual sacrifice by each of its members. By relinquishing all aspects of their prior identity, the devotees were instilled with a powerful motive to sustain the faith. Moreover, each devotee, through his sacrifice and the rigor of his devotional training, was offered the very rewards denied to him by his affluent origins: the sense of accomplishment derived from the completion of a genuine ordeal involving risks of both material and psychological hardship.

In imposing such controls, the movement seemed to realign its members with the moral imperatives of the larger society. The behavior of the initiates was drastically changed: they forsook many of their previous activities (some viewed by society as illegal or questionable) and lived an ascetic life. In some ways, theirs was a model life. They abstained from drugs, alcohol, cigarettes, and sex. They cut their previously long hair and kept it short when it grew back. The conservative, world-acceptance teachings of the *Gita* led to a resolution of personal disputes with society. Employment, for instance, was no longer a sellout. The previously deviant life-style was channeled into different directions, which were no longer illegal but merely strange, amusing, or perplexing. They could not easily be placed in a category (such as "hippie") by the public at large. Interviews revealed that this was an important facet of the movement. "Krishna Consciousness is all our own; it was begun by one master amidst the people, totally independent of the news media." The devotees were immune from formal societal sanction because illegal drugs had been renounced. In this sense, they could be compared to a drug-rehabilitation organization, such as Synanon, in which the members also cut their hair, became isolated from the outside world, and practiced rigid adherence to certain rules. But the comparison was not complete, because only the members' outwardly deviant behavior was changed: practicing Krishna Consciousness, the members frequently explained, was a way to stay "high" all the time. Everlasting euphoria was achieved, which was superior to a more transitory, drug-induced state. Theoretically, this posed an interesting problem of deviance. Did the movement reaffirm the individual's preexisting deviant life-style? Or did it reconcile the individual with society?

On the surface, the latter alternative seemed feasible. Some

members secured employment, ceased to be concerned with changing the social order, and renounced illegal drugs. From the standpoint of the larger society, these people were no longer factors of in-
stability and were contributing more productively. At the level of
the individual, however, it would seem that personal alienation had
not decreased. In Weber's terms, the person was "in the world" but
not "of the world." Disaffection from the larger society was merely
reaffirmed and revitalized in a different symbolic package. The individual continued to exist within the Haight-Ashbury, but in a
situation that was unified by a different set of expectations. The
members had already rejected traditional life patterns and values
when they entered Krishna Consciousness. The movement ideal-
ized, organized, and dogmatized many of the members' previous
hippie attitudes. This represents a threshold in an alienating
process. The individual was no longer merely personally disaffected
by existing society—he refused to believe it worthy of his attention.

POSTSCRIPT

The Krishna movement has dramatically expanded beyond its
isolated cadre of dedicated followers in San Francisco. In July 1974
ISKCON consisted of approximately five thousand members in over
fifty temples throughout the world. The movement's annual Juggernaut Festival in Golden Gate Park in San Francisco was the
largest in its history. The movement employed an advertising agency to publicize the event, which attracted nearly ten thousand persons. The four-hour festival featured dancing, music, and chanting
amplified by an elaborate and expensive sound system. The celebration was interspersed with short speeches, culminating in a brief
talk by A.C. Bhaktivedanta, who entered the park in a chauffered
Mercedes sedan, with a police escort.

    Although the movement is at its largest and most extensive in its
history, several factors suggest that ISKCON may have reached the
peak of its growth. Most important is the diminishing significance
of the college-age drug subculture, the movement's primary
recruitment base. Further developments within the movement
seem to have isolated it from the larger society, sapping its
proselytizing energies. Beginning in 1971, many of its members
were relocated to rural settings, the most important of which was
New Vrindiban in West Virginia. Since that time, approximately
seven hundred recruits have been sent to India to the original Vrindiban, the movement's sacred place, the supposed birthplace of Sri

Krishna. Most are sent to India with the intention of permanent devotional service, never to return to America in this lifetime.

Although these factors point to the possible fragmentation of the movement, perhaps the most important test of its survival will be the reaction to an eventual crisis of leadership succession. Such a crisis is likely because of the absolute centrality to the movement of its seventy-eight-year-old spiritual master, A.C. Bhaktivedanta. On his eventual "passing from the life cycle," Krishna Consciousness seems unlikely to survive in its present form.

REFERENCES

Bellah, Robert. *Beyond Belief: Essays on Religion in a Post-Traditional World*. New York: Harper and Row, 1970.

Bourque, Linda B. "Social Correlates of the Transcendent Experience." *Sociological Analysis* 30 (1969): 151–63.

Bourque, Linda B., and Kurt Back. "Society and Transcendent Experience." *Sociometry*, March 1971, pp. 1–21.

Cox, Harvey. *Feast of Fools*. Cambridge: Harvard University Press, 1969.

Davis, Fred. *On Youth Subcultures: The Hippie Variant*. New York: General Learning Press, 1971.

Davis, Fred, and Laura Munoz. "Heads and Freaks: Patterns and Meanings of Drug Use among Hippies." *Journal of Health and Social Behavior* 9 (1967): 156–64.

Goleman, Daniel. "The Buddha on Meditation and States of Consciousness, Part II: Typology of Meditation Techniques." *Journal of Transpersonal Psychology* 4 (1972): 151–210.

Howard, John R. "The Flowering of the Hippie Movement." *Annals of the American Academy of Political and Social Science* 382 (1969): 55–62.

Lewis, I.M. *The Sociology of Ecstasy*. London: Penguin Books, 1971.

Pahnke, Walter, and William Richards. "Implications of LSD and Experimental Mysticisms." In *Altered States of Consciousness*, edited by Charles Tart, pp. 399–428. New York: John Wiley & Sons, 1969.

Roszak, Theodore. *The Making of a Counter Culture*. New York: Doubleday, 1969.

Shepherd, William G. "Religion and the Counter-Culture—A New Religiosity." *Sociological Inquiry* 42 (1972): 3–9.

Weber, Max. *The Religion of India*. Glencoe, Ill.: Free Press, 1958.

———. *The Sociology of Religion*. Boston: Beacon Press, 1964.

———. *Max Weber: On Charisma and Institution Building*. Edited by S.N. Eisenstadt. Chicago: University of Chicago Press, 1968.

Yablonski, Lewis. *The Hippie Trip*. New York: Pegasus, 1968.

Yinger, J. Milton. *The Scientific Study of Religion*. London: Collier-Macmillan, 1970.

Zablocki, Benjamin. *The Joyful Community*. Baltimore: Penguin Books 1971.

3

Guru Maharaj Ji and the Divine Light Mission

JEANNE MESSER

Who Is Guru Maharaj Ji? is the title of a book and a popular topic of conversation for thousands of Americans, most of whom either have or intend to have a firm opinion. Guru Maharaj Ji is most easily described as a boy guru, successor to his father's disciples, who was persuaded to bring his movement to the West by a handful of Western devotees who had discovered him in India. Since August 9, 1971, more than eighty thousand Americans have become his devotees. East and West, the movement itself is called the Divine Light Mission.

Maharaj Ji's masterhood at the age of eight (when his father died) seems no less presumptuous to the average Indian than it does to the average Westerner. We have at least the example of Christ preaching in the synagogues at the age of twelve to inhibit spontaneous dismissal of his claims. But we share the habit of expecting holy men to have renounced material pleasures—witness what we pay our preachers—and to be aged and erudite. This leader of some five million devotees is really a child and a lover of machine-age toys: cars, airplanes, stereos, rock band equipment, even computers, which fascinate him.

What he teaches, however, is not new. I first saw him when he was thirteen, sitting in a white satin-covered chair, surrounded by roses and prostrating devotees, in a Unitarian church in San Francisco. On the walls of the sanctuary were inscribed the verses "The Kingdom of Heaven is within you" and "What doth the Lord require of thee but to do justly, and to love mercy, and to walk humbly with thy God?" And Maharaj Ji's short speech was a succinct version of the Gospels. "The Kingdom of Heaven is within you. And I can reveal it to you." That was sum and substance,

followed by an invitation to see him the following day if one was interested—a possibility to which I did not admit for months
afterward. He only said of other religions that he had come not to
start a new church but to make perfect Christians, Buddhists, or
Moslems. He denied that he himself was perfect, asserting only that
he could show one perfection. "If you want to learn about
mathematics, you go to a mathematics master. If you want to learn
about perfection, you go to a Perfect Master." And he urged anyone
who felt he had a way to know God to pursue that way and to keep
him in reserve. "If you cannot find God any other way, then come
to me." A substantial percentage of his devotees are, in fact, people
who have seriously sought God or God realization on other paths,
whether as devout Christians or Jews or as followers of other
Eastern teachers.

KNOWLEDGE VERSUS BELIEF

Suppose that modern "rational" man's greatest presumption—and
greatest error—has been to treat the scriptures of the world's major
religions as records of primitive mythologies. In rejecting the
premise that we live in a teleological universe, many have given
themselves no "rational" alternative but to reject the underpin-
nings of history's great religions.

What Guru Maharj Ji's devotees claim to have is a direct experience of that teleological center, the force that operates the
cosmos. Rennie Davis, one of the Chicago Seven defendants and
now a devotee of Maharaj Ji, told his fellow radicals in Berkeley that
"God is that energy which physicists tell us cannot be created and
cannot be destroyed. What the physicists don't tell us is that that
energy is *conscious*."

Guru Maharaj Ji's claim is that God is that entity which unifies
the cosmos, and that one can *know* God directly—a superb promise
to make to a rationalist who cannot meet the requirements of faith
or conviction. His teaching consists simply of what he calls "giving
knowledge," not of any extensive set of moral precepts. Unlike most
Eastern religious teachers, he generally refuses to give concrete in-
structions regarding what one should eat, how one should make a
living, or what one's disciplehood should involve. All of truth is in
"the knowledge."

"The knowledge" is really two different experiences, neither of
which can be empirically demonstrated to involve Guru Maharaj Ji.
Those who agree to become his devotees are permitted to "receive
knowledge." This first experience of the knowledge consists of four

events which take place in a "knowledge session" conducted by a *mahatma* (at this writing, all but one of Guru Maharaj Ji's some two thousand mahatmas are from India or Tibet) with a group of fifteen to twenty-five initiates.

1. "If thine eye be single, thy whole body will be filled with light" (Jesus of Nazareth, Matt. 6:22). Indians of many sects believe this to be a literal truth, that one can see inward with what is called the "third eye" and perceive God in the form of light within the self. Guru Maharaj Ji's devotees are shown individually an intense light within themselves, and then are shown how to meditate on that light independently. This light is described in all scriptures and in many accounts of ecstatic drug experiences, but few people see it with any frequency or predictability. After a knowledge session, devotees report seeing that light regularly in meditation, and with increasing intensity over time. At its most intense, it is brilliant white light; it can also be a many-hued light show. Many devotees also report seeing images or pictures in the light.

2. The "music of the spheres" or "sound of sounds" appears in all scriptures. Maharaj Ji's devotees are made aware of its presence and are shown how to listen for it in their private meditations. The sounds devotees report hearing range from water sounds—similar to, but richer and more varied than, those heard in a seashell or conch—to crickets in the grass on a summer night to stringed instruments and choirs.

3. Devotees are told of a nectar flowing in the body which they can taste, and they are instructed to meditate by tasting that nectar at all possible times. The nectar has been described as tasting like a combination of butter and honey.

4. Devotees are made aware of an internal vibration and are told to meditate on it at all times, waking or sleeping. This is said to be the Word or Name of God, as in the verse "In the beginning was the Word, and the Word was with God, and the Word was God" (John 1:1).

What occurs in a knowledge session beyond these four events is not clear even to an initiate. The existence of light, music, nectar, and the vibration is no secret to either Eastern teachers or scriptural scholars. In the East, however, disciples are usually taught that these experiences will occur, with the grace of God, after many years of patient meditation, devotion, and service to God. In the West, they are generally treated as metaphor. Yet they occur unmistakably in the knowledge session and thereafter (but with less intensity) for Maharaj Ji's devotees. What creates the intensity in that session is unclear, but there is no obvious autosuggestion or other accompanying ritual or activity to account for it. A few weeks after such a session, most new devotees report the discovery from their own meditation that the experience is addictive, that is, one thirsts for more of it, and that they cannot create that experience with the same intensity for themselves. The few who have tried have apparently failed to reveal anything to nondevotees beyond the form of the meditation technique.

Devotees are also asked to attend Sat Sang regularly—informal and leaderless discussions among devotees of their experiences—and to do "service" for Guru Maharaj Ji. The nature of such service is unspecified. It is clear that it includes letting others know that the knowledge is available; but one would do that, if satisfied, without instruction. Otherwise it appears at first to be a matter of choice. One might arrange speaking tours for mahatmas—disciples who are authorized to conduct knowledge sessions—or chat in coffee shops with strangers or simply tell one's friends.

"This knowledge," says Guru Maharaj Ji, "is not the Knowledge. The Knowledge is in the meditation." That tells new initiates very little and the uninitiated less. But devotees report a remarkable transformation of consciousness in a very short period of time. I have tried below to describe that transformation fairly and to avoid any generalization that does not apply to all practicing devotees, but the sequence of events should not be taken as fixed. I was a thoroughgoing atheist at the time of initiation and was looking for a tranquilizer, not God. But for the many who require no convincing, that stage in the transformation is experienced simply as *confirmation*, not as transformation. There may be other similar variations from devotee to devotee.

The first obvious change is the discovery that meditation is a source of energy—a discovery common among those engaged in many forms of meditation. Devotees are simply less fatigued, less easily disoriented when they meditate regularly, and they become rapidly dependent on the meditation as a source of rest, energy, and personal integration. Fifteen minutes of meditation—even with poor concentration—is a healthy substitute for an afternoon nap and is often more restful psychologically than sleep.

The second change is an increasing awareness of what Rennie Davis calls "that remarkable series of coincidences on which Divine Light Mission runs." It is the beginning of an awareness of cause and effect as different from what they once seemed to be. One begins to feel that events in one's life are being arranged for the sole purpose of *getting one's attention*—as if the external and internal worlds were working together without one's conscious cooperation. One devotee reports feeling "directed" to pick up hitchhikers, who turn out to be devotees. Another devotee's car window exploded inside the car door and rained glass all over her, with no injuries and no apparent cause, and she experienced the event as a demand that she meditate. Most devotees are not consciously looking for signs; they feel *confronted* by signs requesting their cooperation. For some, these experiences begin shortly before they actually receive the knowledge, though after they began to consider it.

What follows, ranging in time from six weeks to a year, is an increasing awareness that reality is not quite the way it looks and that it is arranged to look the way it does for the one who sees it. With this is a growing and unshakable conviction that one is accompanied, tended, loved, and taught by God, and that the God within is remarkably like the child guru: happy, playful, insistent, unpredictable, loving, and perfectly benevolent.

Guru Maharaj Ji tells his devotees that "everything this Knowledge touches becomes perfect," and devotees report that things do. Their marriages, their work, their finances, their relations with family and peers—all improve in a manner conspicuous to everyone around them. Devotees become lighthearted and lose much of their tendency to depression or despondency. Many report a change in their relation to right and wrong. A fixed moral code becomes a desire to respond to the internal cues without reference to any existing standard. With that change, devotees indicate that guilt disappears; that is, there is no pool of guilt that is evoked by wrongdoing. One regrets a lack of "responsibility" in its generic sense, but the self-hatred associated with shame is lacking. One begins to feel and act toward one's self and others as one experiences God acting within the self: playful, loving, and benevolent.

What comes out of this whole area of changing consciousness is an extraordinary dialogue among devotees. Miracle stories—from pure trivia to the really remarkable—are exchanged by the hundreds and with delight and laughter. Everyone is overcome by the irony that seems to fill their lives: nothing they ever *thought* was true. This leads inevitably to much talk about the nature of thought and of the mind.

THE MIND, IN THE EAST AND IN THE KNOWLEDGE

Westerners approaching Eastern teachers from any school are confronted with constant reiteration that the mind is the barrier to enlightenment, whether enlightenment is described as complete nothingness or as perfect bliss or as knowledge of God. Needless to say, that truth could not be accessible to the mind. Westerners are generally accustomed to identifying themselves with the boundaries of their bodies, the thoughts in their minds, and with their emotions, such as depression or ecstasy; to be told that their identity is *essentially* different is to be informed of nothing. Maharaj Ji's devotees claim, however, that it is possible to experience that fact, whether or not the mind is willing to acquiesce. There is no way—functionally at least—to bypass the premises of rationalism except to introduce experience where the mind says experience is not possible—that is, to provide incontrovertible evidence to which the mind has no alternative but to acquiesce. To assert that the mind cannot comprehend God is not to assert that the man cannot, if one is accustomed to that distinction; but many of us are not so accustomed, and have long asserted that God is an entity in whom one *believes*, an entity, that is, beyond experience.

I raise this here as a purely pragmatic question, not as one involving philosophical distinctions. If it is true that one can know God, can engage in dialogue with God, then the assumptions on which Westerners commonly lead their lives are called into question. In describing the experiences of Guru Maharj Ji's devotees below, I am necessarily limited to description, from the same root as the word *scripture*, and can transmit none of the experience itself. But the question of what impact this movement might have on Western social order rests entirely on the nature of the experience and the consequences of the experience, and not on the nature of any beliefs.

There are, of course, other religious sects in the West that stress experience as well as belief, and that are probably seeking and perhaps finding the same experience that Maharaj Ji's devotees report. Nevertheless, the larger Christian denominations stress belief, not experience, and morality, not obedience to God in the direct sense of responding to commands. Prayer, for instance, is a one-way conversation, which God is assumed to hear and to answer; but it is not common for Westerners to report *hearing* God's response. Most Westerners point to the beauty of nature or of infants to demonstrate God's love; it is rarer for them to report *feeling* loved, feeling fathered with all that that implies, feeling guided or directed in the moment rather than in the abstract. And most base what we call "conscientious" behavior on fixed moral precepts—the Ten Commandments, perhaps, or the Golden Rule, or local cultural norms. There exists a set of rules about right behavior to which one can refer.

For Maharaj Ji's devotees, fixed referents begin to dissolve as they practice meditation. New initiates are caught up in the same dogmatic and philosophical questions that most of us are. "Who is Guru Maharaj Ji?" is answered in terms of new cosmologies designed to fit this young man into the universe, into history, and into the major religions as well as one's own experience and philosophy. Common answers from new initiates, for example, are that Guru Maharaj Ji is Christ, that Christ has been on the earth many times, as Jesus, as Buddha, as Mohammed, as Krishna, or that Christ has always been on the earth (this inferred from Guru Maharaj Ji's assertion that there is always a Perfect Master on the earth). Others assert that he is God himself, but still others that he is simply a guru, of whom there are many, with remarkable power. All devotees try to deal with the fact that Maharaj Ji comes from India, and they absorb great quantities of what they understand to be Hindu dogma, though Maharaj Ji gives little suggestion of being Hindu in religion.

New devotees spend hours trying to "figure out" the knowledge. It is obvious that the four objects of meditation block the sensory apparatus of the body. That is, the internal light is experienced as light seen with the eyes, even though the eyes are designed to pick up external images only, and the blind perceive only the internal light. Sound, which seems to be perceived with the ears, is heard also by the deaf. The nectar occupies taste and smell; the vibration, touch or feeling. Devotees amuse themselves by discussing this novel approach to undermining "illusion" as recorded by external senses, and by otherwise making up conceptual frameworks or reality structures into which they can fit this new activity.

All theories begin to dissolve in short order, however, as they are replaced by an awareness that simply bypasses language and the mind. It is not that one cannot think any more; it is just that one cannot think of any way to articulate the experience accurately or to explain it. God is not experienced as "energy"; one mahatma suggests that "energy" is simply a twentieth-century handle for the subject-that-cannot-be-discussed, and that is how it begins to seem. None of the experience gives one a sense that Maharaj Ji is a series of manifestations of Christ. One's notions of right and wrong are neither confirmed nor undermined by the experience; they are simply replaced by a sense that one is being instructed constantly, and the notion of an unchanging code of behavior fades into the

background. The only fixed referent becomes the meditation itself.
If one is not sure what to do next, one is probably not meditating on
the Holy Name, the vibration; and uncertainty becomes a reminder
to meditate, not a reality of any duration. The devotee resumes
meditating, and his next move becomes "obvious," that is, he feels
inclined to do thus and so with no admixture from any other inclination.

Although what devotees feel compelled to do looks increasingly
like what the New Testament suggests is right behavior, the
behavior feels spontaneous or responsive, not righteous. Maharaj
Ji's devotees report, for instance, feeling as if they were overflowing
with love, as if there were not enough love objects available when
they are meditating. Brotherly love then becomes an experience,
not a righteous idea. Devotees also report that giving Sat Sang (that
is, talking to others about one's experience) and listening to Sat
Sang (listening to others talk about their experience) become
irresistibly delightful, a way to "get high," in contemporary par-
lance. Acts of service become extraordinarily rewarding, but the
reward is not to the ego or a sense of right action; it is simply the
reward of happiness. When practicing devotees leave off meditating
or service for whatever reasons, happiness is displaced by despair or
depression accompanied by a strong desire to "get happy" again.

The happiness devotees report bears no resemblance to the
amiability of the oblivious. Devotees, though decreasingly inclined
to be anxious about the future and less able to remember an unhap-
py past clearly, are prey to all the difficulties of a day-to-day
existence, and days go up and down as emotions do. It is the foundation of one's self-experience that is altered; where there was
chaos or an abyss there is a good feeling toward the self and toward
the world, which is unaffected by day-to-day ups and downs, a kind
of indestructible happiness that is not easily contaminated by
difficulty or sorrow.

A tale passed along by devotees seems to epitomize their experience of their minds after some months of meditation. The story
is a once-upon-a-time tale, in which a man travels through most of
his life with a lizard on his shoulder, whose opinion he respects
above all else. For years he goes where the lizard suggests and shifts
course with the lizard's whims. If they go to the city, the lizard ac-
quires a quick dislike of cities and demands that they go to the
country; if they go to the country, the lizard becomes bored.

One day the lizard tells the man that he's heard of a great train
ride one can take to a place called Heaven, a perfect place. "Let's

catch that train," says the lizard, "I'm tired of this place." The man agrees, as is his habit. As they begin to board the train, the conductor stops them. "No lizards allowed on this train," he says; "you'll have to leave that lizard behind if you want to come." The man steps off the train unhappily and the lizard protests. "Hide me in your breast pocket," hisses the lizard; "I want to take this train." So the man hides the lizard and boards the train. When the train is well under way, and the man is thoroughly and happily engrossed by the scenery, the lizard slips out of his pocket and onto his shoulder. "This isn't so great," complains the lizard. "Is this all you've seen so far?" "I like it," says the man firmly. "Well, I don't," frets the lizard. "Let's get off at the next stop." They are still arguing when the conductor pops up and spots the lizard on the man's shoulder. "We don't allow lizards on this train," he reminds the man. "Either get rid of that thing or get off the train." The lizard suggests they get off, happy that the confrontation suits his purpose; but the man hesitates, then looks defeated and unable to reject the companion to which he is so habituated. He looks despairingly at the conductor, who tears the lizard from his shoulder and flings it from the train. The lizard's back breaks and he turns into a beautiful white stallion. The conductor places the man on the stallion and gives it a hit on the rear, and the man rides off to Heaven on its back.

Not too subtly, the lizard is the mind, the train is Maharaj Ji's knowledge, and the conductor is Maharaj Ji. Devotees love this tale, particularly the part where the man tries to hide the lizard and take it with him on the ride. The joke is on themselves, since they have certainly not broken any lizard backs yet; and they love it, presumably because they can at least dimly comprehend the distinction between the mind and the man, a liberating comprehension once one begins to enjoy it. The suggestion that the mind should serve the man, like a stallion, and not the reverse, has also become comprehensible to practicing devotees, most of whom have begun to understand their goal in similar terms. All are convinced, because they experience it intermittently, that it is possible to become a perfect instrument of God, a perfect servant, if one can only shut the lizard up long enough to hear the Father calling. Response to the Father, they insist, is natural and spontaneous, if one hears his voice over the static in the mind. Meditation, then, becomes at minimum a technique for quieting the mind so that one can hear the truth from its Creator and then obey. In hearing and obeying is the "bliss" of which the scriptures speak, but which they cannot transmit, because words transmit information about experience, not the experience itself.

"MANIFESTING" THE KNOWLEDGE

What happens to any one individual consciousness is, of course, of concern only to the immediate beneficiary or to someone who observes the outward manifestations and is attracted to them or interested in their origins. If this particular guru and his meditation techniques make a lot of people privately content, yet affect their behavior not at all, it is of little interest to anyone else and of no interest to social scientists.

It is what is manifest, therefore, that is of concern here. I choose that word deliberately because it is also part of the argot of devotees. Devotees maintain that just as one can know God, rather than simply believe in him, one can also manifest his activity in one's self and one's relationship to him in one's behavior. That is, it is the activities of Maharaj Ji and his devotees that will bring others to the movement, not a set of convincing precepts or conceptual schema. That does not mean that enthusiastic devotees do not go around trying to present convincing arguments for conversion, for they do. It does mean that they consider those arguments a poor substitute for the reality of manifest God realization.

What is first visible to others about a devotee is undoubtedly his increasing happiness, manifested as amiability, greater flexibility in interaction, evenness of temper, and an ability to hear the truth about himself and to tell the truth about what he himself sees. (Many devotees, especially those who are deeply involved in organizational activity from the beginning, become aggressively dogmatic during the first months of meditation, which certainly covers and slows these changes.) That is, happiness is linked closely to a sense of security which permits devotees to be open where they were previously vulnerable and therefore closed. Most agree that in their first few months of meditation they feel progressively better, but only half consciously, until they begin to experience what they describe as an overflowing of good feeling and joy, a sense that the source of this good feeling is limitless. The more convinced they become that there is no limit to this feeling, the less vulnerable they feel, and the more open to further personal changes they become.

There follows an increasing willingness to rejoin the mainstream of society, in whatever area they felt alienated or separated. Many keep their distance from both Guru Maharaj Ji and Divine Light Mission for months, until they feel secure enough to approach more closely the question of where their new experiences originate and to deal with social pressures from fellow devotees which are concentrated in the person of the Mission itself. At this point it becomes difficult to distinguish changes stemming from the knowledge in its pure sense from changes linked to an increasing group consciousness. Devotees are told from the beginning that Sat Sang and service are as necessary as the meditation to the realization of the knowledge. At this juncture all three activities begin to overlap, and in this context one is able to observe the activities of this burgeoning religious movement as a social movement with potential implications for the rest of the social order. This, then, is where one begins to look at "manifestations of the knowledge" on the group level.

I once watched a reporter interview a mahatma and devotees at the San Francisco Divine Light Mission ashram; the reporter set out to identify significant characteristics of the group of about two hundred persons. Using only a show of hands, he concluded that every age group was represented, as well as every occupational and education group. This writer's impression was that the group was predominantly young (twenty to thirty years) and middle class in origin, though a surprising number of older adults were present.

Most devotees, whatever their background, are employed full time, have short hair and own suits if they are male, and generally present a conventional face to the world. They do this deliberately and self-consciously to avoid alienating the world at large from Guru Maharaj Ji for the sake of some earlier social identity of their own. There are young devotees whose parents became interested in the knowledge because "Anybody who can get that kid to cut his hair can't be all bad." But having made their physical appearance uninteresting, they make more significant the substance of their organizational activity, and that is precisely their aim.

DIVINE LIGHT MISSION

Divine Light Mission is a worldwide organization dedicated to the propagation of Guru Maharaj Ji's knowledge. It operates as a cluster of organizations engaged in innumerable activities; these are tied together financially (sometimes) and by their general aim of "service to Maharaj Ji" (always). There is nothing tidy or systematic about the operations of the Mission as a whole, and at present (1974) it is difficult to divide it into meaningful sectors even for discussion purposes.

Divine Light Mission (DLM) maintains all ashrams (coeducational households of devotees who have devoted all their time and possessions to service) and their activities: promotion of public programs; hosting mahatmas, members of Maharaj Ji's family, or

Maharaj Ji; maintenance of a center devoted to the giving of knowledge, meditation, and Sat Sang. The Mission also coordinates the itineraries of mahatmas and Maharaj Ji and his family and the periodic national or international gatherings of devotees.

International Activity

Since all countries share Maharaj Ji, those few mahatmas he has permitted to leave India, and Maharaj Ji's family, there is continuous cooperation with respect to itineraries (though this is one area dominated by Maharaj Ji's personal decisions), travel and housing arrangements, and presentation of programs. Since 1971, there has been a festival each year to which all devotees were invited, which required months of cooperation in the organization of charter flights, housing, and finances. In 1972, for instance, American devotees chartered six 747s to fly to India, and the price per seat was set so that South American devotees could fly from New York to India free of charge. Other countries made similar arrangements to accommodate the poor. Millenium '73, to which devotees throughout the world were invited, was held in November 1973 at the Houston Astrodome. Seven international flights flew devotees to Houston. Divine Light Mission International paid for many of the flights.

Otherwise, Divine Light Mission is separately incorporated and operates independently from country to country. All ties between countries are cooperative rather than formal.

National Activity

The Divine Light Mission's national headquarters in the United States are in Denver, Colorado—the fiscal center for the country and the bureaucratic hub of all Mission activity. All ashram residents are assigned to their residences by Denver. Anyone needing funds applies to Denver; most of those contributing send funds to Denver (though some local activities are locally supported).

About 4 percent of the practicing American devotees are engaged in full-time service for the Mission. Perhaps half of these are in local ashrams or other devotee centers. The balance, perhaps five hundred, work with or through the national headquarters in Denver and are recruited from all over the United States. These people are involved in organizational activity, which has been centralized, partly because this is more efficient and partly because the activity is so young (it began in mid-1972) that there are too few in any one city to support it adequately.

Denver itself houses most of the centralized activities. Shri Hans Educational is an organization of devotees with teaching interests and credentials working to establish boarding schools and child-care centers across the country. In cities with interested devotees who do not want to join the effort in Denver, there are collaborative groups working locally. Denver also houses Shri Hans Publications, Inc., which published and promoted the Mission's monthly magazine, *And It Is Divine*, and the international semimonthly newspaper, *Divine Times*, until publication was suspended after Millennium '73. Also in Denver is Divine Travel Services, which handles all travel arrangements for Maharaj Ji, his family, mahat-mas, and devotees on Mission business, as well as the charters for national and international gatherings. There is a Women's Spiritual Right Organization dedicated to reaching out to persons in prisons, mental institutions, and hospitals. Groups of devotees in Denver operate such businesses as gas stations, restaurants, and stores. Other cities also have centralized operations. Los Angeles, for in-stance, is the home of the Shri Hans Productions, Inc., the film and recording studios operated by the Mission.

Since the number of American devotees continually increases, the manpower pool for full-time service has grown from six people in 1971 to over one thousand in early 1974. Because both manpower and income are (in theory) increasing geometrically (through propagation), every project has its sights set far beyond its im-mediate capabilities; for DLM hopes to include all humanity in its membership.

Local Activity

All local activity is supportive or propagational. In the San Fran-cisco Bay Area there is one ashram (in two households) which has about thirty residents. Ashram residents are celibate; eat no meat, fish, or eggs; drink no alcohol; and smoke no cigarettes. They are expected to obey their general secretary (assigned from Denver), to be ready to transfer to another area at any time, and to do whatever work is assigned. Most hold full-time jobs outside the ashram and put in two hours of service in the evening; all adhere to a rigid schedule of Sat Sang, service, and meditation from 5:30 to 10:30.

Despite the apparent severity of ashram regulations, the house-hold operates as a brotherhood (housing both men and women), though the general secretary has the final word. A good general secretary is a good brother and a good administrator in the business sense.

Most ashram residents are either employed outside full time or self-employed. Residents operate a small business called Divine Services Company, which provides such miscellaneous services to households as hauling, painting, plumbing, and electrical repair. The ashram also coordinates maintenance activities for Divine Sales, a used-goods store in a poor district in San Francisco. Maintenance includes manning the store and "jumbling," or going from door to door soliciting donations for the store's inventory.

The ashram is responsible for coordinating the service of all devotees in the Bay Area, for keeping all devotees informed of financial needs or scheduled programs, for housing mahatmas and other distinguished visitors and Maharaj Ji, for preparing all public programs, for coordinating child care for devotees engaged in service or attending Sat Sang in the ashram, and for any other task that might be assigned from Denver.

There are ashrams operating similarly in almost every state in the United States and in over fifty countries. Almost all the United States ashrams operate a Divine Sales outlet and a Divine Services Company. There are two ashrams in California, in San Francisco and in Los Angeles.

"Premie Centers" are communal households of devotees which are subject to moderate regulation by Denver, primarily through the local ashram. These may have married, noncelibate couples, and children residing in them. They turn over at least 30 percent of the household income to national headquarters, must keep a "presentable" household, and must not eat meat, eggs, or fish, or smoke or drink on the premises. Although they are not otherwise subject to orders from the Mission, they have obviously made a serious commitment to service to the Mission and to cooperation with its activity.

A "premie house" is simply a household of devotees. It may have only a husband and wife or as many as thirty individuals living together. Such households are not subject to external regulation and are held together by a common commitment and cooperation. Devotees seem inclined to combine households as their devotion increases, and these households are natural clusters of devotees, often with strong personal attachments to one another.

The Bay Area has two formal Premie Centers, another five premie houses with seven or more residents each, and over one thousand practicing devotees, many of them in smaller premie houses. Devotees who are not in one of the more formal households are hard to keep track of, and estimates of their number vary. The best estimates are based on attendance at unadvertised programs when Guru Maharaj Ji or one of his mahatmas is in town. Since many new devotees will appear only for programs, it is some time before the ashram can actually identify those who practice the knowledge after receiving it.

Activities and numbers have developed more slowly in San Francisco than in many other American cities. Other cities operate numerous small businesses and have specialized households of painters or musicians or others of similar interest organizing to earn funds for the Mission cooperatively.

Finances

In spite of the superficial order of DLM bureaucracy and organization, the Mission runs on the energy generated by devotion and what devotees call "grace." Since the first order of business is to spread the knowledge, only a small percentage of the Mission's operations are profitable because the scope of activity is always larger than resources can technically afford. *And It Is Divine*, for instance, sold for a dollar a copy; but many thousands more copies were given away than were sold, because it was a primary vehicle of propagation. It was a full-color, slick, seventy-page magazine with international news; features on subjects of humanitarian interest like old age, ecology, or the history of Arab-Israeli conflict; and Sat Sang. The October 1973 issue had full-page color advertisements for Natural Resources Defense Council, Humane Society of America, and *Organic Gardening* magazine—all donated by the Mission. Advertising was not sold.

Divine Light Mission operates almost entirely without capital, and this is the source of great numbers of "grace" stories. In 1972, for example, the Mission wanted to buy a small plane to transport Guru Maharaj Ji and his family around the United States. They had negotiated a price and secured a loan from the bank. The down payment was nearly $18,000, with no serious chance of generating it even in donations. The owner of the plane eventually put up the money himself, to satisfy the bank, because he "liked Guru Maharaj Ji." That is not a common reason for such unbusinesslike behavior. The owner of DLM's national headquarters building has repeatedly paid for extensive alterations to the building as activities burgeoned, though he ostensibly has no relation to the Mission other than landlord. To devotees these are miracle stories, and there are hundreds of them.

Grace operates at all levels. Devotees are agreed that anyone who decides to go to India, for instance, will come up with the money to go; and devotees report finding hundreds of dollars in kitchen drawers, being approached by strangers and offered unsolicited money, and other bizarre tales of money being generated by devotion. This alters the premise on which most of us operate, that financially we are on our own; neither devotees nor the Mission itself are bound by that notion. The Mission decided to hold Millenium '73 in the Houston Astrodome, to house all devotees in hotels and motels, to feed all attenders, and to fly people from poorer nations like India free of charge and made arrangements for all activities on the assumption that the necessary funds would be forthcoming. At this writing, DLM is still heavily in debt from that function, is restricting some operations, like *And It Is Divine*, but is no less optimistic.

In theory, all funds on which the Mission runs are donations, which come from a number of sources:

1. All income of ashrams and businesses belong to the Mission, which in turn provides each ashram with a household budget. Presumably, the income of an ashram or household operating a business in the Mission's name is greater than the funds needed to support the local unit. This does not account for the costs of supporting new businesses and new ashrams that do not yet operate in the black; and since DLM is above all a growing concern, it is hard to estimate how these balance out.

2. All devotees are encouraged and nagged to donate funds of their own. They are also encouraged, on rare occasion, to solicit funds from nonmembers. Some devotees have signed pledges to donate a dollar a day to provide the Mission with some reliable income.

3. Premie Centers turn over 30 percent of their household income to the Mission. This provides the Mission with a regular income, though centers are not yet numerous.

4. Periodic crises require fund raising across the country. To pay the debts remaining from the Houston event, devotees all over the country turned over their own possessions to Divine Sales, which had crash garage sales, attended flea markets, and invented numerous activities to dispose of the goods.

Efforts to get more concrete information on funds is futile, since all emergencies are covered somehow and the pending emergencies are expected to be resolved by devotion and grace. Since that is the usual outcome, there is no empirical reason for devotees to question their faith. The simplest economic explanation of how the Mission manages to stay solvent is that, because the number of supporting members increases so rapidly, it is always possible to pay yesterday's debts, even though it seems impossible that tomorrow's will be paid. Like an inflating economy, the Mission is protected only so long as it expands.

All Mission activities depend entirely on volunteered labor and funds. The knowledge itself, the primary source of satisfaction to devotees, is independent of the Mission proper, and DLM has no power to discipline or enforce agreements. Devotees move in and out of service roles or financial commitments, and DLM has little chance to predict or control income or staffing.

Nevertheless, most ashrams are crowded, as are most premie houses, which cannot find suitable housing as quickly as needed. Volunteers for full-time service arrive in Denver every day, and those who will go anywhere or do anything can be assigned to areas where manpower is needed. These numbers depend entirely on the success of the propagation effort. Their willingness to be assigned anywhere is generally a consequence of their relation to the knowledge and to Guru Maharaj Ji.

Devotees find Divine Light Mission to be unreliable and un-predictable, and usually unreasonable. No devotee goes to work for DLM because the Mission makes a good employer. One loses con-trol over where one lives, what one eats, whether one gets medical care or a new shirt when needed, and whether one gets the kind of work one prefers. The Mission encourages devotees to feel that they should not need such control and that the apparent chaos is really God's order working through them; their role is to surrender and flow with the reality. To many, DLM is a discouragingly unrespon-sive employer. But they donate their services anyway, whether from extra time or full time, and do whatever work is assigned, rarely with any grumbling once they have begun. When I returned from a month in India in 1972, I asserted that the most important lesson learned there was "to never let Divine Light Mission have control over my life again." That feeling quickly faded, as it did for most of the four thousand who had made that trip, and was replaced by a strong sense that the entire trip was grace. Why?

It was stated earlier that the impact of this movement on Western social order rests entirely on the nature of the religious *experience* and on the consequences of that experience, not on the nature of any beliefs. Devotees consistently claim that it is the experience that moves them, not Divine Light Mission and not conviction, which is sometimes quite unstable. Guru Maharaj Ji's devotees have met God in the flesh, as many understand their experience, and their gratitude and enthusiasm dominate their lives and activity.

The first and most concrete consequence of the meditation is an increase in energy and in personal integration, which permits devotees to invest tremendous time and effort in Mission activity and in propagation without fatigue or disorientation. For a rapidly growing, multipurpose organization with executive power concentrated in the hands of youth, these are invaluable attributes to the labor force. It does not explain why devotees engage in service, but it does explain how they have managed to do as much as they have in less than two years and with no real letup in pace.

The growing sense of devotees that reality is not quite what it has always seemed produces an extraordinary tolerance of irrational behavior and contributes to their ability to live in chaotic, constantly re-forming communities and activities with peers who are themselves in the midst of great personal change. Devotees claim that what seems absurd is simply the Creator's trying to call one's attention to something, that conflict is a vehicle for expanding one's awareness.

It is in the experience of Christ as the intercessor—the real medium of communication between man and God, and man and man—that devotees become oriented toward the call of the Creator rather than the irritations of the immediate context. All experiences, then, become lessons with cosmic significance, and the devotee's role is to surrender to the lesson. To become wrapped up in anger or intolerance is to refuse to listen to the lesson, to become so occupied with one's own definition of the situation that one cannot learn the Lord's.

The rest of the power of the movement is the power of happiness itself: where it is indestructible the individual becomes a less demanding person, and it is contagious. A great amount of unskilled labor is required of devotees, though devotees are often quite well educated and middle class enough to prefer more demanding work. The Mission could not function if it used only the best-sharpened skills of each devotee, if only because it is not efficient enough to arrange that. All activities depend on a large group willing to do whatever needs doing, and ego satisfaction must come from some source other than work, or place of residence, or physical comfort. Devotees explain that they will do anything they can to express their love for Guru Maharaj Ji, and nothing they can do will ever express it fully. Perhaps their general sense of well-being alleviates any need for the more conventional rewards of American life, and meditation is in fact a substitute for these.

One possible explanation of unconditional devotion is that Maharaj Ji's devotees are so rewarded by God himself that other potential rewards pale in significance. Another involves the nature of "worship" among devotees, most of whom had a normal young-adult reluctance to be dependent on anyone or to prostrate themselves before another human being or to let anybody tell them what to do, and all of whom rapidly lose that reluctance when they practice meditation. One devotee, a near-Ph.D. in sociology and very skeptical of the knowledge for some time after receiving it, said, "I once thought I could never prostrate myself before any man, that it was obscene. Now I find it difficult to pass his picture without falling on my face with gratitude." The gratitude is the primary key, perhaps, together with the sense that devotees share that the God within and the guru without are not distinguishable, and that he runs this universe with no other object than to love and reward them. That is a powerful experience, whatever its foundation, and unconditional service is a small return.

Since the primary business of Divine Light Mission is propagation, and since its activities seem to rely on constant increase in numbers, the giving of Sat Sang is the primary service of every devotee. There are devotees who heard about Maharaj Ji from strangers in bars and coffee shops, who came through friends or relatives, who read the magazine or the newspaper, who stumbled on a campus or other public program and were fascinated. But most simply become acquainted with some happy person who convinced them that the happiness was available for the asking from that boy guru, whoever he is.

If one believes he has met God in a house across town, he is going to drag every friend he can find to share the experience. This is the prime mover of the propagation effort, and it is a bit different from more traditional propagation movements. It is very common for a group of converts—whether to Communism or Christianity—to seek company and increase of their numbers, but such groups usually are held together by their belief that they *will see* perfection. Maharaj Ji's devotees are moved by the sense that they *have seen* it, that the kingdom is "at hand." While they do not claim to be instant buddhas themselves, they do claim to be living in perfect happiness, and they have a strong desire to share it.

It is that overflow of good feeling that makes this movement so contagious around the world. Particularly for a generation exhausted by conflict, the idea that one can fall in love with the world and know it to be perfect is a compelling one. Guru Maharaj Ji sets out little dogma to attract followers. For those who find asceticism attractive, there are mahatmas telling them that all activities are right in moderation; for those who think everyone should live in an ashram, there is Maharaj Ji's mother telling them that the householder performs the highest service, that of providing shelter and training for the children of God; and for those who are attracted to Eastern mysticism and alienated from Christianity, there is Maharaj Ji himself asserting that Jesus was the Word made Flesh, and therefore God, and therefore always here in the human heart, in the Spirit. The promise is a simple one, and all efforts of devotees and nondevotees alike to complicate it backfire rapidly.

Maharaj Ji says, "Give me your love and I will give you peace. Give me the reins of your life, and I will give you salvation. I am the source of peace in this world." He says only that, and devotees propagate by swearing that he can prove it to any who receive his knowledge and meditate on it for a few months at most.

THE KNOWLEDGE IN THE FUTURE

Where this movement fits into companion movements throughout the West, and whether it will endure and expand to affect the social order, are big questions. People are unlikely to abandon experiences where they feel the potential of their actions is being fully met, which differentiates this movement from unsuccessful political movements, for instance, and which may also differentiate it from contemporary millennial movements that require external miracles to come to fruition. Though many of Maharaj Ji's devotees are convinced that Maharaj Ji himself is the promise of Revelation, and the very Christ that many await, their conviction is simply the icing on the cake. If Maharaj Ji told them that Jesus was coming soon, they would be delighted at the new revelation and would modify theology to fit their experience.

Although Maharaj Ji is himself from India, is a guru, and offers a meditation technique, he is not clearly Eastern and is a subject of great controversy in India, where he is also a major heretic. Any man who says that all scriptures are true, that Buddha, Mohammed, Moses, Jesus, Krishna, and a host of others were all Christ, is a heretic everywhere. To many Western devotees he is plainly a Christian, but there is no clear definition there either. As a consequence, it is difficult to place Divine Light Mission among the religious movements in the West, and it operates as a bit of an outcast, refusing to join associations of different groups and simultaneously refusing to admit that they are not also "premies, though they don't know it." Devotees will listen to Sat Sang from anyone and will give it to anyone, treating none who are not also devotees as if they had the whole truth and none as if they had missed the boat entirely. It is disconcerting to a Jehovah's Witness, for instance, to hear a devotee agree with every word he says and then respond with, "Except that He's already here; I know what you say is true because I've *seen* it."

That is always the sticker: if Maharaj Ji's devotees are experiencing what they say they are, then this movement is nowhere near its end; if they are not, it may reach its limits at any time. Devotees agree to that and recommend to the skeptic that he "try it." Always the issue is reduced to the question of proof, since this particular movement asserts that evidence is available for the asking and that to demand it is legitimate. That often puts critics on the defensive, which may partly explain the hostile media treatment of this movement.

I doubt that the entire world population will be caught up in this movement, but the intensity of feeling many seem to have about it—whether for or against—suggests that it poses some issues important to this culture. The most basic issue is tied up with the worship by seemingly sane, educated, and articulate youth of a fellow human being rather than some less tangible deity. I have heard horror expressed by Christians who were unmoved by the suggestion that Christ had worshippers in his lifetime. Complete humility before a fellow mortal seems difficult to swallow.

On whether this movement will visibly and independently affect the social order, I can offer no opinion. It is distinguishable from popular American movements like *est* or Transcendental Meditation or Scientology by the emphasis on worship. But other Eastern movements, like 3HO, carry the same component, though not the suggestion that the master is indistinguishable from the deity. The outcome of any one movement seems clearly tied up with the futures of the other contemporary movements, both because there is obviously some competition for membership and because we do not yet know whether people will progress into more deeply religious movements and experiences if they begin with the more secular ones. Perhaps most will simply return to old business from their present involvement and pursue no further the questions raised by the wave of self-realization efforts.

PART II
New Quasi-religious Movements

The chapters in this section describe movements that cannot be fitted easily into either the Asian or the Western religious traditions. They derive primarily from developments in modern "secular" culture, and some of them would reject the term religious *altogether. For several of them the word* science *is an important symbol. We use the term* quasi-religious *to indicate that these movements do in one way or another put their adherents in touch with ultimate meaning, relate their followers to the sacred in the sense of that which is most central and important in human existence.*

This question arises perhaps most acutely in connection with the chapter on political radicalism. Many political radicals not only do not use the word religious *to describe themselves but denounce religion as a form of "mystification." Fortunately, we do not have the obligation to give any final answer to the recurrent problem of whether the sociological analyst is justified in describing as "religious" or even "quasi-religious" groups that reject the term. Chapter 4 is concerned very much with the self-consciously religious Left and its vicissitudes with respect to the larger movement. Certainly no one can deny the contribution of religious people to left-wing political movements in the last twenty years. But neither can the sociologist avoid observing that a group like the Symbionese Liberation Army, which was spawned in Berkeley and which we did not study, though one of its prominent members was briefly on our secretarial staff, seemed far more oriented to ritual and symbol than to anything approaching practical politics.*

The Human Potential movement is less consciously concerned with rejecting the appellation "religious," and indeed there are many borrowings from religious traditions, particularly those of Asian origin. But the main sources of this movement have been modern social science, particularly psychology and sociology.

When the search for "community" becomes an end in itself and
when the provision of "therapy" begins to give answers to the
basic questions of human existence, it is perhaps not too much to
speak of the groups in question as at least quasi-religious. Just as
some political radicals may be concerned only with certain discrete
political issues and may avoid turning radicalism into a totalistic
world view (even though the pressure to do that is very great), so
some followers of one or another human-potential movement may
seek only a technique to combat insomnia or attain orgasm. But
when particular training systems purport to help their trainees to
discover "it," and when the "it" in question is expressed in stories
and riddles derived from Sufis and Zen Buddhists, then clearly
something more than attention to segmental symptoms is going
on. Donald Stone's chapter nicely describes how the therapeutic
modulates into the religious and back again.

Synanon is something of a marginal case with respect to the
larger Human Potential movement. Although it shares much of its
ideology with the larger movement, it has a kind of organization
that is quite atypical. The authoritarian leadership and totalistic
group structure that Ofshe describes so well is more reminiscent of
the groups described in Part I than of most other human-potential
groups. In the latter too, as in most of the groups we have studied,
charismatic leadership is central. But in most of the human-
potential groups the leader claims less authority over the lives of
his followers and does not seek to set up a separate residential
community.

Our research did not lead us to conclude that there was a
widespread rejection of science among any of the groups that we
studied. The groups described in this section all have an explicitly
positive attitude toward it. Those political groups which have
adopted some form of Marxism see it as a "scientific" theory.
Rather than rejecting reason, they feel that they are truly rational
and that it is their opponents who are irrational and mystifiers.
Among the human-potential groups too there is a positive attitude
toward science, at least "humanistic" science. The use of biofeedback devices to improve meditational technique is not seen as
threatening. Even belief in auras and other "magical" phenomena
is often justified in terms of purely natural properties of the
cosmos that science itself is beginning to discover.

Whether science as the working scientist knows it is an effective
concept for either political radicals or the Human Potential movement may be doubted. "Science" has itself become in the modern

world a magical term redolent of the sacred. This had already occurred in the nineteenth century when Mary Baker Eddy started her Christian Science church (a movement whose followers frequently designate simply as "science"). That "science," at least in America, is by no means necessarily the opposite of "religion" only adds a further problem to the many difficult ones that the sociologist of religion must deal with.

If religion and science are not really polar opposites, neither are tradition and modernity. Modernity itself has become a tradition. That aspects of modern culture—politics, psychology, sociology —can provide the scaffolding for the construction of new religions or quasi-religions is, after all, what the sociologist of religion would have expected. The need to make sense out of reality as a whole, sense that empirical science can never provide, remains a generic human need no matter how "secular" culture has become.

4

The New Consciousness and the Berkeley New Left

ROBERT N. BELLAH

From FSM (Free Speech Movement) to SLA (Symbionese Liberation Army) Berkeley has been a stage upon which left-wing
movements have entered the world. Indeed in the late 1960s the
word *Berkeley* was more likely to conjure up a vision of radical
politics than of new religion. From the middle sixties to the middle
seventies, the political side of the new consciousness has been just
as prominent in the Bay Area as the religious side, if not more so.
We could have spent our time researching political attitudes and
groups as profitably as religious ones. Even though our limited
resources and our primary interest in the sociology of religion
prevented our giving equal treatment to politics, we did decide
early on in our study to pay at least some attention to the political
dimension because it was so important intrinsically and so in-
tertwined with religious change and innovation. As Emile Durkheim pointed out for the nineteenth century, socialism and religious
revivals were two aspects of the reaction to the crisis brought on by
industrial society. That crisis continues to deepen in the late twentieth century, and radical or socialist politics and new religious
movements continue to emerge in response to it.

If the effervescent phase of the counterculture—its radical psychedelic outpouring—had passed by about 1971, when our study
was getting under way, so had the effervescent stage of the political
movement. The upheaval brought on by the invasion of Cambodia
in the spring of 1970 was the last major political outburst. Just as we
had to study the "successor movements" of the counterculture to
get at new religious consciousness during the period of our study, so
we would have had to study successor movements to the political

wave of the late 1960s. Since our resources did not permit such a study, what follows in this chapter is a general summary of the political background and atmosphere in which our religious groups operated, along with a few impressions about what political successor groups we would have found had we been able to study them.

If we can take the Civil Rights Movement under Martin Luther King as the preparatory phase of the cultural revolution of the 1960s, we can say that religion and politics were indissolubly joined in that initial phase. King and many of his followers and supporters were motivated primarily by religious and ethical concerns, but the issues raised were intensely political and when pushed far enough led to fundamental questions about the American political system. Only gradually during the sixties did the religious and the political dimensions of protest begin to come apart and they never did so completely. The psychedelic revolution of the middle sixties in drugs, music, and life-styles might seem to be and often was apolitical. But the sense that there was something drastically wrong with the American system, that the whole middle-class career pattern was some kind of pointless game playing, had obvious political implications. And the political critique of bureaucracy, exploitation, and manipulation tended to pave the way for religious utopianism as one possible response. Timothy Leary's "liberation" by the Weathermen to join Eldridge Cleaver in Algiers and Rennie Davis' conversion to the boy Guru Maharaj Ji were two examples of how the tendencies could cross over. Nonetheless, we should not underestimate the tensions between them. Often the choice of one precluded the choice of the other, at least for a time. If politicos considered the religion freaks to be "copping out," the latter considered the former to be wedded to the "world of illusion."

THE FREE SPEECH MOVEMENT

The San Francisco Bay Area has a long tradition of liberal politics and continues to this day to vote well to the Left of the country at large. San Francisco has been a union town since early in the twentieth century, and Berkeley had a Socialist mayor in 1911. More recently, the university was the scene of a major confrontation over loyalty oaths in the 1950s, and Berkeley students mounted a bitter demonstration against the House Un-American Activities Committee in 1960. Still, it was the Free Speech Movement in the fall of 1964 that put Berkeley on the political map and set off a chain of explosions that would affect virtually every major American university by the end of the decade.

The Free Speech Movement was an offspring of the Civil Rights Movement, which had involved students from all over America for several years previously. Hundreds of Berkeley students had participated in civil rights work in the South and in California, where there was a concerted effort to get business and industry to hire more members of minority groups. Just before the beginning of the fall semester, there occurred the most reactionary Republican presidential nominating convention in decades, a convention that ended up nominating Barry Goldwater, a man committed to positions that would have reversed all the civil rights gains of the preceding years. It was the recruiting of students to picket the San Francisco Cow Palace, where the convention was being held, that precipitated the attempt of the Berkeley administration to ban political recruiting tables on Sproul Plaza.

There is no need to detail here the events that followed—the attempted arrest, the surrounded police car, the thousands of students, the eventual victory. It is enough to note the essential continuity with civil rights tactics. The students were clean cut, short haired, often with ties and jackets. Their resistance was nonviolent. The tone was set by Joan Baez when she said before the sit-in of December 2, 1964, "When you go in, go with love in your hearts." That was the message of Martin Luther King.

There is no need to romanticize the FSM. All the stupidity and bad faith were not on the side of the university. Doctrinaire devotees of Old Left splinter groups tried to use the situation for their own ends almost from the beginning. By the spring of 1965 the Free Speech Movement had degenerated into the "filthy speech movement," a development that is worth some consideration in its own right. But justice was surely on the side of the students. Elementary political rights were being denied to students under pressure from conservative political elements. The victory on the immediate issues at stake proved one of the more solid and irreversible victories of the sixties. But the events of 1964 would set in motion a political momentum that would lead in directions quite unforeseen at the time.

How a clean-cut and idealistic movement for free speech could end up a few months later in a public shouting match of four letter words is a question that created consternation at the time. Without overemphasizing the filthy speech movement we can nonetheless see it as a sign of a much deeper cultural alienation than was at first apparent in the Free Speech Movement. Cultural alienation is also old in the San Francisco Bay Area. Outcasts and misfits from other parts of the country have long drifted to California. Wholly differ-

ent visions, oriental or utopian, have frequently had an appeal to
northern Californians. In the late 1950s San Francisco was the chief
center for the "Beat" culture that broke through the conservatism
and conformity of those years with a sharp and often nasty sting.
Beatniks were not "nice" and they didn't talk nice. They didn't
have much good to say about middle-class America. Perhaps the
filthy speech movement was a harbinger of the transition from
"beatnik" to "hippie" that was just beginning to occur, and that
would carry anarchistic and bohemian life-styles to a far larger
proportion of young Americans than ever before in our history.

That there was something "religious" about the FSM and about
the frenzied waves of political activism that followed is not simply
the opinion of the observing sociologist. Michael Rossman, a
leading figure in the events of 1964, looking back ten years later,
wrote,

During the months of struggle there was born among us a new vision of
community, and of culture, to make whole the vision of social justice that
had moved us to action in the New Left. . . . Emboldened to risk and dare
only by each other's presence, we were out there on the existential edge,
where what we knew dropped off into the unknown, toward a vision of a
different reality. Everything was torn loose for a time. Our careers cast off,
our lives at times in jeopardy, our very conceptions of who we were and
how to be a person among persons were shaken and revised as profoundly,
though differently, as in any current transcendental conversion. In this
chaos and mystery, alone together and equal, facing the unknown, no one
led or followed. We were cast into a desperate spontaneous democracy,
which was our ultimate and only magic.[1]

Even if we must discount some of this language as a nostalgic
reinterpretation, the juxtaposition of politics and magic was already
occurring in the middle 1960s. The great Be-in in Golden Gate Park
in January of 1966 attracted activists as well as hippies. A style of
dress and personal adornment was beginning to appear that made a
large part of the youth generation look like homeless vagabonds.
Long hair became almost an insignia. By looks alone one could not
tell whether an apparent hippie was a Buddhist or a Marxist. Attraction to rock music, psychedelic drugs, and group living arrangements united both political and religious radicals, even if an interest
in Zen meditation, also pioneered by the beatniks, did not have
quite so catholic an appeal. Clearly, by 1967, with the Vietnam War
replacing, though not obliterating, racism as the chief crime of the
United States government, the disaffection reached an intensity

1. "A Tale of Ten Years: A Son and A Father," *Rolling Stone*, May 9, 1974.

that was more than political, more even than cultural, and that for many could only be called religious in its breadth and intensity.

PEOPLE'S PARK

As the counterculture grew in the Haight-Ashbury district of San Francisco and in Berkeley, political confrontations increased in frequency and intensity, though the two trends were more parallel than identical. In the fall of 1966, there was a sit-in and student strike against navy recruiters on the Berkeley campus. In the fall of 1967 there were violent demonstrations against army recruiting in Oakland, with many injuries to students and police. In the fall of 1968 there were major demonstrations and sit-ins when credit was denied for a student-originated course taught by Eldridge Cleaver at Berkeley. All during this period bombings and arson attacks were increasing. Frequent targets of attack were the ROTC building and the Institute for International Studies, but the worst incident was a major fire in a reading room of the main university library. Increasing militancy was taking its toll among students in the form of bitter factional quarrels over strategy and tactics. For some it became a contest to see who could outdo whom in daring and bravado, or as someone said, who could be "more Mao than thou." The impulses that would lead to the Weather Underground and the SLA were already visible in these years.

Berkeley was only one part of a far-flung upheaval that involved hundreds of thousands of young people and approached the proportions of a national insurrection. To objective observers it was never a serious military threat to the United States government, but its political consequences were indeed major. It undermined the legitimacy of Lyndon Johnson and probably contributed to his decision not to run for reelection in 1968. Even more serious, the student upheaval convinced certain political advisers of the new Nixon administration that took office in January 1969 that it was indeed a serious revolutionary menace, thus setting off a series of decisions that led to the first resignation of a president in the history of the United States.

It was in this atmosphere that the height of political insurgency in Berkeley was reached in the People's Park incident in the spring of 1969. Like all of the political events of the late 1960s, People's Park was neither as innocent as some of its supporters believed nor as Machiavellian as some of its opponents imagined. The basic grievance was real enough. Nearly a square block of land in the area

south of the Berkeley campus had been cleared of houses preparatory to university construction. The lot, however, had been
neglected for months, allowing cars to park among the rubble
amidst the winter mud. It was an unsightly and abandoned scene.
Thus, there was a spontaneous response to the call issued in the underground *Berkeley Barb* on April 18, 1969, to build a "people's
park." The scale of the work that began on April 20 certainly
suggests that there was more than pure spontaneity at work. Certainly anyone who had eyes to see in the spring of 1969 knew that
the attempt to "liberate" a piece of property for which the Regents
of the University of California had paid upward of one million
dollars would not go unchallenged. Certainly there were many
political activists in Berkeley who were not blind.

Nonetheless, for many students, street people, hippies, and
Berkeley children, People's Park was a fiesta while it lasted. Much
ingenuity went into the design of the park and many of its features
were creative and aesthetically pleasing. The park became a
hangout for singing, storytelling, and smoking dope. Campfires and
cookouts proliferated, and some began to take up residence in temporary structures. Naturally, neighborhood complaints about noise,
pilfering, and occasionally ugly incidents late at night also began to
appear.

Under pressure both from the regents and from local elements
alarmed at the expropriation, the university opened negotiations.
Whether the university was deliberately obtuse in failing to find a
"responsible group" with which to negotiate or whether there were
those in the leadership of the park who wanted negotiations to
break down, or what is more likely, both, is hard to determine at
this remove. At any rate, events moved to their inexorable conclusion when, at 4:30 A.M. on May 15, 250 California Highway Patrolmen arrived in the vicinity of People's Park and the Berkeley
Police dispersed those encamped with a minimum of disturbance.
Shortly thereafter a construction crew began putting up an eight-
foot-high cyclone fence around the park.

Some 6,000 students gathered for a noon rally in Sproul Plaza.
There were several speakers, but during the talk by Student Body
President Dan Siegel something happened that terminated the
rally. Siegal was, according to his later interpretation, in the process
of weighing alternatives for action when he suggested the possibility that "we go take the park." At that, elements in the crowd took
up the chant "take the park" and began moving toward Telegraph
Avenue in the direction of the park. From that point on, the colli-

sion between the crowd and several hundred Berkeley Police, Alameda County Sheriff's Deputies, and California Highway Patrolmen was perhaps inevitable. In the disturbances that followed one young man was killed, another blinded, and dozens were injured. A large part of South Berkeley was teargassed, including a neighboring junior high school. During the next few days Berkeley was occupied by 10,000 national guardsmen, subjected to further teargassing, and first amendment rights were suspended. The then governor, Ronald Reagan, defended what many believed to be an excessively violent response as perfectly appropriate.

THE HERITAGE OF THE SIXTIES

What had begun in the early sixties with civil rights marches, and matured in 1964 as the Free Speech Movement, ended in 1969 with tear gas, shotguns, firebombs, and molotov cocktails in Berkeley and all over America. The fate of the New Left was in part determined by the behavior of the American state. The administration persisted in a war it could not win unless it employed means that were unacceptable to world opinion, the American people, and finally even to itself. Each step of "escalation" only revealed all the more plainly the pointless and fruitless brutality of the war. When opposition at home became bitter, extreme, and violent, first Johnson and then Nixon moved to repress it, but again with methods that goaded further opposition rather than suppressing it. In the end, as we now know, it was a draw. Both sides collapsed from inner fatigue more than outer defeat. Given the inequality of the forces involved in this David and Goliath encounter, we would have to declare the New Left the undisputed winner, were it not for its near total disarray well before the collapse of its bitterest opponent.

This is not the place to attempt to explain the collapse of the New Left, but certain observations are necessary if we are to understand the political atmosphere at the time of our study in the early 1970s. Perhaps the deepest reason for the collapse of the New Left was the weakness verging on nonexistence of an old Left for it to be the new Left of. By 1960 the old Socialist and Communist parties were mere shells, tiny cabals of enfeebled and discredited leaders. The assorted Trotskyite and other esoteric leftist parties were even more hollow and impotent. There was, then, no context of organization and leadership with which the New Left could interact as it rose to prominence and influence in the middle sixties. Nor was there any specifically American heritage of radicalism and socialism that might have provided some guideposts to a new strategy and tactics, or if there was such an American heritage it was far too buried to be readily available. The early leaders of the Students for a Democratic Society (SDS) provided the beginnings of ideological innovation when they spoke of "participant democracy" so that the individual would "share in those social decisions determining the quality and direction of his life."[2] By the middle 1960s, under pressure to develop a more complex social and economic analysis, Greg Calvert and other SDSers came up with the idea of a "new working class" which included technicians and the lower echelons of the bureaucracy that runs this country. Like the old working class of blue-collar workers, these too have been deprived of ownership of the means of production and have only their labor to sell. The universities as the training ground for the new working class could be, they argued, a major organizing center for the disaffected. But as the pressure mounted after 1967 and "resistance" turned into "revolution," at least in the minds of the most active leaders, there was no time to develop these promising beginnings; the tendency was to fall back on the lowest common denominator of revolutionary theory: vulgar, predigested Marxism, whether of Stalinist or Maoist origin. As the ideological battles became more convoluted, the activists became more isolated from the mass of their sympathizers, more inclined to encapsulation in revolutionary communes or affinity groups. What happened to the Berkeley SDS in the fall of 1968 presaged what would happen to the entire movement in the summer of 1969. A split occurred between an adventurist group that wanted direct confrontation and a doctrinaire Maoist group, known as Progressive Labor, that wanted to push a mythical worker-student alliance with no appeal to either workers or students. At the height of student interest, the SDS committed suicide.

One aspect of the increasing loss of contact with reality among the youthful leftists of the late sixties that is of particular interest to us is the active hostility to religion that appeared at the time. From 1967 on as confrontations became more violent, there was a conscious repudiation of pacifism, now denounced as liberal and counterrevolutionary. The increasing glorification of violence, though usually, except in the most extreme groups, violence against property rather than violence against persons, went hand in hand with an old Left dogmatism committed to materialism and determinism

2. From the Port Huron Statement, quoted in Kirkpatrick Sale, SDS, N.Y.: Vintage, 1974, p. 52.

that considered religion to be nothing but mystification. That what was happening was itself the emergence of a mystique of violence and class warfare among an elite group of activists cut off from the main currents of American history would become apparent only in retrospect. A group like the Berkeley Free Church, which began in 1967 as a ministry to hippies and street people and became more and more political in the years that followed, tried to maintain a religious presence in the midst of the most militant Left but was itself pulled down in the ultimate collapse. Translating religion finally into nothing but politics, it lost its raison d'etre and, incidentally, its community support and funding.

In evaluating the political experience of the sixties we should not, however, concentrate solely on the most mobilized of the activists. The far larger numbers of young people that the activists gradually left behind were changed in ways that had important implications for the future. The many who found confrontation and violence an increasingly bum trip and who could not see the world exclusively through Marxist-Leninist glasses gained no new illusions about the American state. While not identifying with third-world guerrillas to the extent of trying to emulate their violent tactics, as some of the extreme activists did, the average student remained nonetheless profoundly disaffected with American society and convinced that it stood in need of radical change. This disaffection expressed itself throughout the period of our study in a number of ways, which can be summed up perhaps by saying that even after militance had passed, the Left—meaning a position distinctly more radical than traditional American liberalism—continued to hold a cultural and ideological hegemony among students and many others in Berkeley and to some extent in the Bay Area generally. This hegemony can be traced in student, city, and congressional elections. The district that includes Berkeley has sent throughout this period one of the most radical of all congressmen, Ronald Dellums, to the House of Representatives, a man who also happens to be black, though the district is predominantly white. Since 1973 four of the nine Berkeley City Council members have been radicals and the rest have been liberals, indicating how the whole political spectrum has been skewed to the Left. Left-wing political parties have consistently dominated the student government at the university during this period. Voting is only a general indication of a pervasive atmosphere in which leftist assumptions are taken for granted, or at least set the terms for most political and many cultural discussions. In our area the pervasive disaffection and the leftist ideological hegemony—expressed more in negative terms than in any clear positive program—have been largely shared by those attracted to new religious groups, though they, even more than the average young person, have given up active political participation. But the heritage of the sixties has not been simply pervasive and negative. It also lies behind a number of more specific tendencies and movements.

THE POLITICAL SUCCESSOR MOVEMENTS

While most of the developments of the early 1970s have involved a turn away from direct political action, we must first chronicle briefly those groups that continued and even intensified the militance of the late 1960s into this period. Part of the background for this development was the Black Panther Party, with its headquarters for a time in Berkeley, that emerged in the late sixties. It was then in its most militant phase, and its slogan and practice of "armed defense" became a stimulus to that wing of the SDS that would become the Weather Underground. Locally the most militant group to emerge from the wreckage of the SDS was a group called Venceremos, in which Bruce Franklin, a Stanford English professor, was active. Beginning out of confrontations on the Stanford campus, it grew increasingly interested in prisons and prisoners, where the Black Panthers had previously been active. Venceremos, as the name implies, adopted a Che Guevara style of armed militance. Identifying, as did the Weather Underground, with third-world and American black revolutionaries, its own membership was largely middle-class white. The Venceremos involvement in the escape of a black prisoner (during which a guard was killed) effectively ended it as an open organization. But in 1972 it included among its members Emily and Bill Harris as well as Joseph Remiro. Others of the group, which first made itself known in the fall of 1973 as the Symbionese Liberation Army in connection with the assassination of Oakland School Superintendant Marcus Foster, were earlier participants in the prison visitation program of Venceremos. The escape in March 1973 of Donald DeFreeze from Soledad Prison, where he had been visited by members of the Venceremos group, was perhaps the impetus for the formation of the even more militant SLA that summer. This is not the place to recount the events of the assassination of Dr. Foster or the kidnapping of Patricia Hearst from a south Berkeley apartment in February 1974. Perhaps what is most important for our purposes is not the group itself, which probably never numbered much more than a dozen, but the fact that it survived for weeks on end in the Bay Area, moving easily between San Francisco and the East Bay, in spite of one of the most massive manhunts in modern history. That fact indicates that if there was not a sea, there was at least a considerable pond in which the fish could swim. The uncooperativeness of many potential witnesses indicates that in our area sympathy for even the most extreme and violent groups lingers on. Many, even those violently opposed to the SLA and its philosophy, would hesitate to turn them in to the American state.

For most of those in the Bay Area Left, however, the events connected with Venceremos and the SLA have been only a staccato drumbeat in the background, communicated through the mass media rather than direct experience. Far more of those involved in the cataclysmic events of 1968 to 1970 have turned to quiet politics or withdrawn from politics altogether than have become hypermilitant. Indeed, the burned-out activist was almost as common in the early 1970s as the burned-out drug user. For many of them "getting my head together" became the first priority. Every one of the new religious groups, from the Zen Center to the Christian World Liberation Front, has had its share of former activists for whom the group has helped to provide a new and more coherent personal identity. Many who did not opt for a tightly organized religious group found a niche in the "alternative community" that survived in Berkeley and San Francisco or in nearby rural areas. Arts and crafts and other marginal economic activities provided a subsistence in a culture that was at the same time "spiritual" and "political." Others chose to return to the main structures of society—to finish their education, often including graduate school, find a job, and start a family. Even for many of these, and for the large numbers of young people who had never been activists at all but found themselves coming to adulthood in the Bay Area with its pervasive left-wing atmosphere, political causes and political movements were not entirely a thing of the past.

The one major movement to survive the sixties with not only undiminished but actually increased vigor has been the Women's Liberation Movement, perhaps the center and fulcrum of political thought and action on the Left in the early 1970s. The Women's Movement itself was a product of the sixties, though it emerged relatively late in that decade. Clearly visible by 1967, it remained overshadowed by the Vietnam War and the increasingly serious confrontations of the late sixties. Since 1970 the movement has generalized beyond the narrowly political sphere. Consciousness-

raising groups among women have been endemic in the Bay Area
and have embraced a broad spectrum of usually, but not always,
young and middle-class women. The movement has been in part
explicitly political, with its demand for full equality in all avenues
of American life. Efforts for the implementation of equal opportunity for women in hiring have gone ahead even in the face of a
worsening economic situation. Women have moved into prominence in left-wing politics in such diverse contexts as the SLA and
the Berkeley City Council, which after the April 1975 elections had
a majority of women members for the first time.

But equally, if not more, important has been the rethinking of a
whole range of political and cultural issues in connection with a new
evaluation of the meaning and value of the feminine. The Women's
Movement is not itself entirely agreed on some of the basic issues,
but at least a significant wing of the movement asks not only equality with men but a new orientation toward sex roles. In attacking the
macho syndrome of dominance, competitiveness, and violence,
many women are not so much asking for the same privileges
(though they do defend the right of women to be active in the world
without being criticized as "pushy" or "castrating") as questioning
whether such macho attitudes and behavior patterns are healthy for
any human being. Male dominance over women has been related to
the exploitation of the poor by the rich and "conquest" of nature by
"man." Rejection of one kind of oppression leads to rejection of the
others. Further, though some women see men as basically "the
enemy," others see men too as in need of liberation. The macho
pattern demands that the man repress his own tender emotional
side and refuses to allow him to express his fears and anxieties. A
freer and more accepting attitude toward women, in this perspective, means a freer and more accepting attitude toward deeper
levels of the male self. Another by-product of a less anxious
masculinity would be that homosexuality would be less threatening
than it has traditionally been to the American male. Gay Liberation,
not incongruously, has grown in the shadow of the Women's
Liberation Movement. Likewise, the militant lesbianism of some in
the Women's Movement was not only the ultimate claim to independence from men, but also a rejection of the dominance/sub-
mission hierarchy of traditional heterosexual roles.

At an even deeper level Women's Liberation has raised rather
fundamental questions about the relation of human beings to the
universe. Perhaps, some have said, the suppression of goddess
worship since the Iron Age has been deeply pathological. A new in-

terest in the femininity, the "motherhood," of God has been expressed in some Christian circles. A return of the long-repressed
feminine side of consciousness could lead, some have argued, to a
new, simpler, more celebrative, more natural way of life, a way of
life more in accord with the long-run survival of life on this planet.
In this regard the Women's Movement has converged with the new
emphasis on ecology.

In these ways at least a part of the Women's Movement has come
closer to the new religious orientations than might have seemed
likely in the late 1960s. It is ironic that many of the religious groups
themselves remain committed to older patterns of male/female
relationship in which equality and mutual acceptance are far from
the norm. But in many of the groups we studied, even ones where
change in this area comes hard, like the Christian World Liberation
Front, the effect of the Women's Movement has been significant
and new possibilities for women have opened up.

Another tendency that survived the collapse of political militancy
in the 1960s is the organization of self-consciously radical groups in
the professions. "Radical caucuses" in some academic associations
have become more institutionalized and have even begun to
publish their own journals. A vigorous chapter of the Union of
Marxist Social Scientists is active in Berkeley. In nonacademic professions, such as law, medicine, and social work, similar organizations can be found in the Bay Area.

RELIGION AND POLITICS TODAY

The most overt link between religion and politics is probably to be
found among liberal Christians. During the 1960s many campus
ministers became radicalized and their offices became centers of
political activity. Partly for this reason and because of economic
problems in the denominations, denominational support for campus ministries has greatly declined and the number of denominational groups still active has decreased. Though some groups have
turned toward more liturgical or inner experiential emphasis, others
have continued to be politically activist, though not necessarily at
the expense of worship. The university YMCA in Berkeley, long a
center of social concern, seems of late mostly involved with yoga,
meditation, and jewelry making, though student volunteer programs for tutoring the culturally deprived and helping emotionally
disturbed children continue. The University Lutheran Chapel
houses the Berkeley Emergency Food Project, which daily feeds

about 200 needy street people. Unitas, the headquarters of an ecumenical Protestant ministry, is more directly involved in politics and indeed provides something of a center for the nonsectarian Berkeley Left. The Catholic Newman Center is also the focus of considerable left-wing activity. It was there, for instance, that the major Berkeley meeting was held to protest the murder of Chilean President Allende and the destruction of his regime, though the Newman Center also hosts a charismatic prayer group. The New-man Center has been especially active in support of Ceasar Chavez' United Farm Workers, a cause with wide appeal to liberal Chris-tians. Berkeley is also the home of a Christian collective that began publication in 1974 of a journal called *Radical Religion* which is ex-ploring the relation between American religion and radical politics.

Theologically more conservative Christian groups are distinctly less radical politically, though the Christian World Liberation Front, loosely linked to the Jesus movement, is critical of the American status quo. Its newspaper *Right On* has something of the flavor of the underground press and carries some sharp cultural and social criticism. Groups like Campus Crusade for Christ and Inter-Varsity Alliance, which still survive at Berkeley, are relatively con-servative or nonpolitical.

Most of the new religious groups that we studied are close to the theologically conservative Christian groups in being largely non-political. Our survey shows that the political attitudes of those at-tracted to oriental religions, however, are distinctly more radical than the attitudes of those attracted to the neo-Christian move-ments, as will be seen in chapter 13. Further reflections on the political significance of the new religious movements will be found in chapters 13 and 15.

Just as many of those involved with religion are nonpolitical though generally sympathetic to left-wing political beliefs, so many of those involved in politics are nonreligious though vaguely sym-pathetic to "the spiritual trip." Hard-line antireligious beliefs are not uncommon on the Left but less evident today than in 1970. Even the Black Panthers discovered in the early seventies that when they opposed religion they cut themselves off from their own com-munity.

It cannot be said, however, that after twenty years of close in-terweaving of religion and radical politics in Berkeley (or in Amer-ica generally) a clear understanding of the appropriate relation between them has emerged. The major theoretical resources of left-wing thought do not allow it to take religion seriously, even when there is some recognition of religious communities as sources of potential allies in the political struggle. This deficiency is one of the major theoretical weaknesses of the Left, which has never understood why religion has been important in all American social movements from the abolitionists to civil rights. Indeed, the weakness and lack of continuity of a radical Left in America is closely related to the inability to link up with the indigenous American ethical and religious tradition of social concern. Militant secularism has made sense in some societies but has never been politically practical in the United States. The early sixties, when the New Left was at its most flexible, was a period when this weakness might have begun to be overcome; but the opportunity was missed and has not yet returned.

By and large the religious groups have not been much better at thinking through the relation of religion and politics than have the political groups. Conservative Christians and many of the new oriental groups assume that only through changing individuals can we change society. This insight is not to be neglected. Mass changes in consciousness do have important structural consequences. But taken alone this personalist approach is hardly adequate. Only among theologically liberal Christians is there a serious effort to relate the religious and political dimensions of the contemporary world. In the last decade or so there has emerged internationally among both Catholics and Protestants a position that has been variously called "liberation theology" or "theology of hope." Latin America and Europe have provided important contributions as have some black American theologians. Liberation theology, which is attracting much attention at the Graduate Theological Union in Berkeley and its constituent seminaries as well as among students influenced by Unitas and the Newman Center, is basically an effort to link Biblical thinking to contemporary social issues. Its major resources beyond the Bible itself tend to be Marxism and neo-Marxism. Oriented heavily to third-world problems, it cannot be said that liberation theology has as yet developed a clear understanding of the American situation. Not for the first time the American Christian community has imported a theology largely formulated abroad without really assimilating it to the American scene. It is of course premature to conclude that the as yet only nascent liberation theology will not eventually develop a productive understanding of American religious and political realities. If it is to do so, however, it seems likely that it will have to expand the range of its theoretical resources and in particular to come to terms with specifically American experience.

THE FUTURE OF THE LEFT

In a period when American society is beset with increasingly severe problems and the American "free enterprise" (capitalist) system has ever fewer ardent defenders, the time would seem to be ripe for a serious left-wing political movement to raise questions about fundamental alternatives to our present social and economic system. Much that has happened in our area would seem to provide the cultural preparation for such a movement. Though Berkeley is well to the Left of the country, there are many areas with comparable if less-developed trends. Yet a responsible, organized Left with wide appeal in the society seems as far from reality as ever. There is some tendency on the part of those on the Left to explain this fact as a result of "repression." But the causes seem more internal than external. The factionalism, extremism, and immaturity that tore apart the SDS at the end of the 1960s are still visible in muted form in the microcosm of Berkeley. A sense of historic continuity, so essential to a movement for sustaining itself through many setbacks, is largely missing. Movement "alumni" are discarded and abandoned, though they must by now number in the hundreds of thousands. No coherent center keeps them involved in the political process.

Nobody predicted in early 1964 that the American campus, beginning at Berkeley, was about to explode. Nor can anyone say that there are no circumstances that might set off another series of explosions. But the foundations of a serious and responsible Left political movement that could sustain itself through explosive periods and quiescent periods alike is not yet visible in Berkeley or perhaps anywhere else in the United States. The religious and political movements of the sixties have changed consciousness. The successor movements of the early seventies have kept the new consciousness alive. But the political organization of that consciousness to effect significant change in American society is a matter for the future.[3]

3. Harlan Stelmach is the member of our research group who worked most closely on the New Left. Data and insights provided by him were essential in the writing of this chapter.

5

The Human Potential Movement

DONALD STONE

The one who knows his self knows God.
SAYING OF MUHAMMAD[1]

As American culture continues in the pursuit of loneliness, the consumption of plastic experience, and the erosion of meaning from everyday life, the psychologically minded of the middle class have sought more direct experiences of living through growth groups, body-awareness techniques, Eastern spiritual disciplines, and Western-style mind training. The most active participants in these groups and disciplines consider themselves part of a general consciousness-raising movement that has come to be called the Human Potential movement. Rather than taking direct action to change the political structures or setting up an exemplary countersociety, members of these groups seek to transcend the oppressiveness of culture by transforming themselves as individuals. They see that, if society is to realize its potential, they must first realize theirs. This potential includes greater insight, body awareness, and communication with others. It refers increasingly to heightened spiritual awareness and the possibility of feeling at home in and at one with the universe.

There are scores of disciplines, groups, and trainings whose more committed participants would consider themselves part of this broad movement. These include encounter groups, Gestalt Awareness Training, Transactional Analysis, sensory awareness, Primal Therapy, Bioenergetics, massage, Psychosynthesis, humanistic psychology, *est*, Arica Training, Transcendental Meditation, psychic healing, biofeedback, mind-control training, and yoga (especially when used as a supplementary technique outside its Indian cultural

1. Sufi saying attributed to Muhammad, quoted in Claudio Naranjo, *The One Quest* (New York: Ballantine Books, 1973), p. 124.

context). Encounter groups are the best known of these. There are estimates that six million Americans have participated in and considerably more have read about them.[2]

A hallmark of the movement is the extent of multiple participation and eclectic borrowing among these organizations and disciplines. Groups that exert strong pressure for organizational loyalty or orthodoxy of belief and ritual can be considered on the fringes of the movement. Thus, Synanon and Primal Therapy are on the periphery, and growth centers such as Esalen are at the center. Of all the disciplines, gestalt therapy is probably considered the greatest common denominator.

Participants in human-potential groups typically join a weekend training or weekly evening sessions in an extended program for personal growth and development of latent abilities. They learn practical methods that enable them to enter into an experience of "present centeredness." They give their full attention to mental processes and bodily feelings in the here and now. They adopt a less judgmental, less evaluative frame of mind, which allows a more fully conscious experiencing and a more complete picture of the object of attention.

This state of consciousness is termed *gestalt consciousness* in this essay. Gestalt consciousness is the common experiential basis for all groups in the Human Potential movement. Gestalt consciousness not only is the viewpoint for new personal insight and body awareness, but it is the foundation in some disciplines for further training in transcendental awareness. Participants in these "transpersonal" disciplines report experiences of tapping into cosmic energy, of being at one with the universe, or of realizing the true Self.

Transpersonal, a recently coined human-potential term, refers to a variety of transcendent experiences and encompasses a wide range of phenomena, including mystical experience and parapsychologi-

2. "The ground rules of encounter are that participants be open and honest in a group setting, that they avoid mere theorizing and instead talk about their feelings and perceptions. There is often an emphasis on eliciting emotions which lead to positive or negative confrontations rather than away from them. The focus of encounter is to explore interpersonal relations. Over the past years encounter has evolved into a broad approach incorporating several related disciplines to achieve its aims."* (In these brief descriptions of human-potential disciplines, passages in quotation marks are in the words of a teacher of the discipline; those marked with an asterisk [*] are taken from the Esalen Institute Catalogue.) The estimate is, as of 1969, by psychologist Warren Bennis, according to Bruce L. Maliver, *The Encounter Game* (New York: Stein and Day, 1973). Three million and six million are rough estimates printed in *Psychology Today*, February 1970, p. 54.

cal events. In an advertisement for the *Journal of Transpersonal Psychology, transpersonal* is defined as "metaneeds, ultimate values, unitive consciousness, peak experience, being, essence, bliss, awe, wonder, self-actualization, ultimate states, transcendence, spirit, sacralization of everyday life, oneness, cosmic awareness, cosmic play, individual and species-wide synergy, the theories and practices of meditation, spiritual paths, compassion."

To the extent that this movement increasingly provides experiences of transcendence, cosmic consciousness, the Self beyond the self, or of nothingness, it may be considered religious. Although this is the direction of the movement as it moves beyond its encounter-group phase, even disciplines that train for transpersonal experiences are reluctant to describe themselves as religious. The term *spiritual* has fewer establishment connotations and is more frequently used. Generally, the religious motif can be overexaggerated. For many, particularly in the body-oriented or sensitivity trainings, participation is more narrowly therapeutic or recreational. Whether participants seek cosmic bliss or the pleasure of the moment, they all have in common the quest for direct experience through an expanded consciousness or awareness. These pilgrims respond to the vacuum of legitimate authority in society by filling it with the charismatic authority of direct personal experience.

VARIETIES OF HUMAN-POTENTIAL GROUPS

Disciplines in the Human Potential movement correspond to the evolution of the movement. Its origins may be traced to sensitivity training in the late 1940s and the National Training Labs at Bethel, Maine.[3] The study of group dynamics and interpersonal problem solving became a nationwide movement in the 1960s. Schools, church boards, corporations—even the army—tried sensitivity training as a means to efficiency through improved communication. As it became clear that groups released forces that had a strong impact beyond the group sessions, they began to take on a more explicitly therapeutic air. Many psychotherapists adapted encounter techniques to their group work. Reports of changed lives and provocative techniques such as nude encounter marathons attracted journalists. Encounter became a household word.[4]

3. Kurt Back, *Beyond Words: The Story of Sensitivity Training and the Encounter Movement* (Russell Sage Foundation, 1972, and Penguin Books, 1973). See especially chapters 2 and 9.

4. Most of what has been written about this movement has been by psychologists and journalists, who focus on techniques or on the more sensational

During this period, bodily integration methods such as massage, sensory awareness, and Rolfing grew in popularity and were often incorporated into encounter-group experience.[5] By the 1970s the name *Human Potential movement* came into use, and there was a growing emphasis on transpersonal and spiritual experience, partly through the adaptation of Eastern disciplines into Western settings, for example, Psychosynthesis, *est*, and Arica Training.[6]

This evolution during the last twenty years represents a change in emphasis from the self-transcendence of going beyond the routines of everyday life to the self-transcendence of merging with infinite cosmic energy or ground of all being. Within the movement there has been a long-standing interest in Eastern religions and in research on transpersonal phenomena such as creativity and self-actualization, but trainings have been a later development. One encounter-group center has diversified into offering yoga, T'ai Chi,

---

aspects of encounter groups and on the booming interest in parapsychological phenomena such as extrasensory perception. There are only two sociological accounts of encounter groups, and none that treats the movement as a whole. *Beyond Words* and *The Encounter Game*, cited above, do not take the religious aspects of the movement seriously.

5. "Massage is seen and taught as a caring relationship between two people. Consideration is given first to the feelings and the sensory experience of both partners, and after that to technique. Workshops may be attended by both couples and singles."* "Sensory awareness is Charlotte Selver's name for the work she studied with Elsa Gindler in Berlin and brought to the United States in 1938. Workshops in sensory awareness aim at a state of intellectual quiet in which each activity can be fully felt and allowed to find its natural way, free of inhibitions, techniques and images. . . . Sensory awareness brings the essential character of meditation to every aspect of daily living."* Rolfing and structural integration: "By realigning the body structure, the [Ida] Rolf method of structural integration attempts to release excessive tensions so that the person may experience greater physical freedom and balance. Structural integration is a process of direct physical manipulation and deep massage. Working with a trained practitioner, the process is usually completed within ten sessions."*

6. Psychosynthesis: "Starting with each person's existential situation as he perceives it, personal growth is organized into a process aiming at the integration of personality and the emergence of an effective unifying center of being and awareness, the Self. The practical work of psychosynthesis chooses in each situation the *appropriate* progressive activities among many techniques and methods available."* *est* (Erhard Seminars Training): Werner Erhard, the founder, states, "The purpose of the *est* training is to transform your ability to experience living so that the situations you have been trying to change or have been putting up with clear up just in the process of life itself. . . . It produces results that traditionally have taken years, in only days. The combination of data, processes and group sharing enables people to get in touch with a part of themselves that has always been there and in most cases has been unexperienced. It's the part of them that is truly

Bioenergetics,[7] meditation and Value Clarification workshops, a trend of many growth centers that began with encounter and are now accommodating a more explicit search for transcendence.

The term *transcendence* refers to spiritual states and is used in many ways. Abraham Maslow listed thirty-five various meanings, including loss of self-awareness, mystical fusion, integrating dichotomies, becoming godlike, attaining Taoist objectivity, overcoming limitations.[8] John Lilly, a noted brain researcher and audacious explorer of inner spaces, describes an experience during the first Arica Training:

This is the way I felt . . . just completely pure; like a baby in the womb. Totally without deviation or sin; no responsibilities and yet responsibility for everybody. . . . No contradictions; in total tune with the universe. I had never known what that meant before, being right in tune with matter —with the cosmos and nature with other people absolutely all on the same wave length—everything.[9]

Many people participating in human-potential disciplines testify to having experiences like these, and often these were not the experiences they initially sought.

Transpersonal trainings such as Psychosynthesis, *est*, and Arica represent one direction in which the movement is heading. These groups present a more elaborated world view or comprehensive "theology" than is found in encounter or bodily disciplines. The

---

able, and perfect. This experience of their own nature transforms people's ability to experience life." "A training process is a method by which a person experiences and looks at, in an expanded state of consciousness, without judgment—what is actually so with regard to specific areas in his life. The result is a release to spontaneity." Arica Training began under the direction of Oscar Ichazo near Arica, Chile. "We use a system of techniques drawn from many different disciplines. Practiced intensively, Arica exercises lead to the complete realization of a human being. Practiced moderately, they dramatically improve the quality of personal life. A small commitment of time and effort brings the individual a more elastic energized body, a clearer mind, and more expressive emotions." "Arica meditation techniques tune us to our own energy source and the energy sources around us. Meditation and breathing, meditation in sound and movement, and visual meditation are taught."

7. Bioenergetics is based in part on the work of Wilhelm Reich and Alexander Lowen. "The body is viewed as an energetic process that participates *as* the world *in* the world of instinctual, social, imaginative and creative realms. Bioenergetics seeks to develop an individual's range of expression by working through this energetic process."*

8. Abraham H. Maslow, *The Farther Reaches of Human Nature* (New York: Viking Press, 1971), pp. 269–79.

9. John C. Lilly, M.D., *The Center of the Cyclone: An Autobiography of Inner Space* (New York: Julian Press, 1972, and Bantam Books, 1973), p. 198.

training for charismatic experience is being institutionalized to provide opportunities for long-term involvement, attraction of a more diverse following, and increased numbers of training groups. As the training of children of participants is provided for, these groups are turning from cult to churchlike social structures.

PARTICIPATION IN THE HUMAN POTENTIAL MOVEMENT

The movement is concentrated on the East and West coasts, and the Bay Area is its acknowledged center. Within commuting distance of San Francisco there are at least twenty-five growth centers, a dozen institutes or universities engaged in research, and hundreds of therapists, teachers, and clergy who use the techniques and have the view of human nature espoused by people within the movement.

The Association for Humanistic Psychology (5,000 members) has its main office in San Francisco and is the professional and research arm of the movement.[10] Founded in 1962, it grew out of a *Journal of Humanistic Psychology* begun by Maslow and Anthony Sutich several years earlier. Other founders were Eric Fromm, Carl Rogers, Viktor Frankl, Rollo May, James Bugenthal, and Charlotte Buhler, who brought a neo-Freudian and existential psychoanalytic perspective to the movement. The association was one of the first organizational manifestations of what came to be called the Human Potential movement.

Esalen Institute (Big Sur and San Francisco), the best known of the growth centers, has over twenty thousand persons in its programs each year. Esalen symbolizes the confluence of humanistic psychology and Eastern spiritual disciplines, bringing together such offerings as encounter, massage, gestalt, T'ai Chi, meditation, Psychosynthesis, and Sufi teachings. Esalen Big Sur is characteristic of many centers; tucked away in the mountains or countryside, they offer fresh air, natural food, and communion with others, self, and nature. The atmosphere resembles a church retreat except that people say "om" instead of grace, and less effort is made to keep the men's and women's sleeping quarters separate. Another difference is the cost: from $50 to $150 for a weekend.

10. Humanistic psychology is the scientific study and applied research of "those capacities and potentialities that have no systematic place either in positivistic or behavioristic theory or in classical psychoanalytic theory, e.g., creativity, love, self, growth, self-actualization, etc., etc." Severin Peterson, *A Catalogue of the Way People Grow* (New York: Ballantine Books, 1971), p. 205.

Several years ago Esalen enlarged its San Francisco program to make the sessions more accessible to an urban and college population and to reduce weekend costs. Evening lectures are offered at a nominal cost. This arrangement is almost identical to several Bay Area university extension programs that offer many of the kinds of experiences first presented by growth centers. Like Esalen, they are staffed mainly by itinerant leaders who are paid a percentage of the enrollment fee.

Participation in human-potential groups is not mutually exclusive. While the disciplines are distinct, they are usually complementary, and many people enroll in several groups in the same period. For instance, one leader of encounter groups who has been Rolfed and who participated in the Arica Training is receiving gestalt therapy in exchange for Swedish massage and Polarity therapy.[11] The ease with which people join and leave groups is characteristic of this movement, in contrast to most religious movements that claim to provide intense experience.

Persons who identify most strongly with the movement are those whose vocation keeps them in contact with these disciplines as trainers, therapists, or members of the helping professions. A high proportion of group leaders are trained psychologists or therapists. Some psychiatrists are adopting human-potential techniques and perspectives—enough to lend a modicum of professional legitimacy to many leaders who have little formal training or credentials.

Some of the more prominent leaders who have offered sessions at growth centers as well as under their own sponsorship are Fritz Perls (Gestalt Awareness Training)[12], Alan Watts (Zen meditation), Stanley Keleman (Bioenergetics and neo-Reichian therapy), and William Schutz (encounter).

NEW DIRECTIONS: TRANSPERSONAL TRAININGS

Veterans of encounter generally face up to two facts. First, the interest in encounter in the Bay Area is not growing as rapidly as in the late sixties. Second, the amount of psychic energy required for intense interpersonal encountering tends to leave group facilitators

11. "Polarity therapy is an intensive pressure point massage system similar in both theory and practice to Chinese acupuncture. . . . Its purpose is to realign posture and to release blocked energy throughout the body."*

12. "Gestalt is a theory and approach to personality integration first developed by Fritz and Laura Perls. . . . The goal of the training is to assist the participants to utilize *excitement* and *awareness* and to develop *responsibility*. . . . Everyone in

"burnt out." They frequently take up a private therapy practice, often in affiliation with a growth center. An increasing number have become leaders in disciplines that have developed into large-scale organizations, which present an assortment of techniques in discrete packages, under an incorporated name. Thus, Silva Mind Control, T.M., *est*, Arica, and Psychosynthesis offer a comprehensive program, with distribution through local branches. These groups and their offshoots have nearly doubled in size each year since 1970.

This growth is the result of using Western organizational techniques to offer Asian-inspired disciplines at less cost to more people with more uniformity and with a minimum of delay. For instance, in San Francisco, *est* offers a two-weekend training at least once a month to over two hundred trainees at a cost of $250. The training entails a synthesis of many techniques and is based on what resembles Zen and Taoist assumptions about reality which somehow are successfully translated into plain English and personally experienced during the sixty-hour training.

Economies of scale, uniform quality, and minimizing risk are organizational advantages of such a package. Seasoned pilgrims who found the way on their own are more critical of these chartered trips, the standardization of fees, and the overzealousness of the travelers. In the face of protests that neither the experiences nor the gurus are authentic, many persons claim to experience states of awareness that have been previously enjoyed only by an esoteric elite. From 1970 to 1974, twenty thousand have been involved in Arica, thirty thousand with *est*, nearly a thousand with Psychosynthesis.[13] Transcendental Meditation and Silva Mind Control together have involved over a million persons.[14] (These two groups are on the fringes of the movement in their organizational ex-

the workshop may work simultaneously with some awareness exercise, or in interaction with each other. More traditionally . . . participants [will work] individually with the leader. The starting point for such individual work is whatever is here and now of most involving concern for the organism: a fantasy or dream, an interaction with another person, a memory, or a physical posture."*

13. The Arica figures are from "Facts about Arica Institute, Inc." (mimeo 1974). Two thousand "graduates" have completed the forty-day training. The Psychosynthesis figure is an estimate by an instructor at the Palo Alto headquarters. The *est* figure is for 1974.

14. The TM figure was 500,000 as of January 1975 and 100,000 as of 1971. The Silva Mind Control figure is 350,000 since 1966, with 100,000 in 1974. "Transcendental Meditation as taught by Maharishi Mahesh Yogi . . . is practiced for a few minutes an evening as one sits comfortably with eyes closed [It] improves clarity of perception, . . . develops creative intelligence, . . . expands awareness,

clusiveness.) This rapid and continuous growth has provided funds sufficient for increased services, such as research, follow-up activities for recent initiates, and wide dissemination and promotion of the techniques for clergy, teachers, and medical professionals at less than cost.

TRANSPERSONAL AWARENESS

Transpersonal techniques are used to achieve the sense of realization of Self beyond the everyday self. Put another way, they facilitate an encounter with one's being. While not many human-potential disciplines have transpersonal experience as their primary purpose, Psychosynthesis is an approach that explicitly trains for these realizations. Roberto Assagioli, the Italian psychiatrist who designed the discipline, describes the euphoric state of spiritual awakening through the exercises:

A harmonious inner awakening is characterized by the sense of joy and mental illumination that brings with it insight into the meaning and purpose of life; it dispels many doubts, offers the solution to many problems, and gives a sense of security. At the same time there wells up a realization that life is one, and an outpouring of love flows through the awakening individual towards his fellow beings and the whole of creation.[15]

Such experiences arise when the self is experienced as neither mind nor body nor emotional forces. These partial definitions of self are replaced by a realization of being an aspect of that which creates all. The true Self has no point of view other than it creates and is part of. A relevant Psychosynthesis exercise takes the direct form of repeating in a relaxed state: "I *have* a body, but I *am not* my body. I have an emotional life, but I am not my emotions or my feelings. I have an intellect, but I am not my intellect. I am I, a centre of pure consciousness . . . of awareness, will and power."[16] In *est*, different

---

... insures full development of the individual in a natural way." "After meditating, an individual naturally engages in activity more effectively without accumulating stress and strain" (from a pamphlet by Student's International Meditation Society). The brochure for Silva Mind Control states it is "the science of tomorrow . . . today" for greater "productivity, problem-solving, habit control, memory, health, controlled esp, increased vitality. . . . Students . . . learn in just hours of classroom instruction to function at lower brain frequencies without the use of bio-feedback equipment." "Silva Mind Control: Alpha-Theta Brainwave Function," Institute of Psychorientology, Laredo, Texas, 1972.

15. *Psychosynthesis: A Manual of Principles and Techniques* (New York: Viking Press, 1971), p. 46.

16. Ibid., p. 117.

processes are used to attain similar realizations of dis-identification with the body and mind, and re-identification with oneself as chooser, being, and source.

In the transpersonal disciplines, gestalt consciousness serves as a platform from which it is possible to explore this "higher" self. In gestalt consciousness, with the usual stimuli from the body or the feelings or the mind put gently at rest, the participants can explore physical sensations, emotions, or mental images as outward layers of a being or true Self situated beyond or above the everyday self. In gestalt consciousness training, the participants are told to act "as if" they are the chooser. In transpersonal awareness the participant *experiences* self as source.

After a peak experience of Self-realization or a glimpse of the being, there is usually a euphoria that may last for weeks. The phenomenological description is much the same as that of Guru Maharaj Ji devotees after they have received the knowledge. Attractive as this euphoria may seem, the trainers do not value it as an end in itself. At its best it serves as an experience on which to draw the inspiration and enthusiasm to serve others. However, the ideal of service is not stressed in transpersonal disciplines, because it is assumed that people can serve the needs of others only after they have clarified their own.

TRANSPERSONAL EXPERIENCE AND BELIEF IN GOD

Many participants in transpersonal disciplines say that the word *God* is not meaningful to them. Those who do relate to the term rarely have an anthropomorphic image in mind. Rather than Father, Lord, or Friend, the image is more likely to be "my ground of being, my true nature, the ultimate energy." The most common image of God is the notion of cosmic energy as a life force in which all partake. Rather than something Wholly Other, it is open and accessible. This is the *chi* of T'ai Chi Ch'uan and the *ki* of Aikido.[17] God is process rather than reification. "Everything is a manifestation of the playfulness of a single divine substance. . . . God is immanent, homogenized into the single stuff that makes the universe."[18]

17. "Aikido is a Japanese art of self-defense with the emphasis placed on centering, harmony and blending. It is presented as physical manifestation of energy and spiritual laws of the Universe."* "T'ai chi is an ancient Chinese exercise discipline practiced for health, meditation, energy flow and self-defense."*

18. Sam Keen, "Transpersonal Psychology: The Cosmic *versus* the Rational," *Psychology Today*, July 1974, pp. 58–59.

Others do not experience God as the fullness of things, but have an experience of nothing. Sometimes there is a feeling of loss or initial terror as the participant comes to sense that "there is nothing out there." This nothingness is not necessarily a negative experience. It can be a holy void: there may be a sense that only out of nothingness is there anything. Thus, nothingness and the inevitable cycle of creation and destruction is affirmed and less feared. Whatever the image of God, the evidence for this image must be drawn from personal experience.

Subsequent to experience in groups many expand their interest in religious questions and become involved in the Jewish or Christian traditions of their upbringing and in Eastern disciplines. Some ministers will affirm how their faith and trust was strengthened by the self-discovery that came with group experience. It is common for liberal ministers to lose their resistance to people who take biblical miracles literally and to be open to the appropriateness of life after death.

The Hindu concept of karma—uncompleted experience accumulated in this lifetime (and in previous ones)—is widely used. This "unfinished business" has to be dealt with before man's evolution toward being at one with the cosmos continues. Evil is seen as man's refusal to take responsibility for what he has created. Thus, mankind is the author of evil, and to the extent responsibility is not assumed, evil abounds.

Transpersonal experience may also decrease interest in organized religion and diminish the use of God language. A psychiatric social worker said she formerly used terms like *God* to explain suffering and the source of happiness and love. Subsequent to the *est* training, she did not use these terms so often, sensing that she is god in her universe and the creator of what she experiences.

GESTALT CONSCIOUSNESS

Training for transpersonal experiences involves a level of awareness and a philosophy of life that seems to be common to all human-potential groups. I have termed this common state of mind and set of assumptions *gestalt consciousness*. It is both behavioral and ideological. It underlies transpersonal experience as well as body work and encounter. As a state of awareness it is similar to the results of Eastern meditation in the way perceptions are organized and in the techniques used to attain it. Gestalt awareness is an altered way of looking at experience with the aim of witnessing it in a more direct, nonevaluative, noncognitive way. The techniques are

designed to focus attention on an immediate situation in order to
stay in present time in the present continuum of awareness. This is
frequently called staying in the "here and now" or "present
centeredness" or "going with the flow." A cat watching a ladybug
climb a twig shows a gestalt awareness.

Gestalt consciousness is *ideological* in that those who seek it have
an underlying rationale or explanatory framework. These assumptions include a belief in an unexplored potential to control inner
physiological and emotional states. It is assumed that mind and
body can be harnessed in the service of developing a feeling of integration, wholeness, and increasing range of expression and com-
petence for achieving whatever people truly want. The implication
is that what humans want is to be at one with themselves, with each
other, and with the cosmos.

In this ideology, mind and body are seen as positive assets, or at
least as tabula rasa, in potential service of man's being or true self,
which is often conceived of in beneficent terms as well. The body is
said to harbor chaotic forces so long as they are repressed, and the
mind is the source of hubris and self-justification only so long as it is
unbalanced in favor of its rational rather than its intuitive mode.
Humans, therefore, are not victims of their bodies, their emotions,
or the physical universe. Rather they have the potential to work in
harmony with these. A heuristic device is to assume that man has *no*
limits. Even gravity or the necessity of death may be questioned.
Choice, awareness, and truth are the building blocks of human-
potential ideology. There is no choice without awareness. And there
is no awareness without telling the truth.

Underlying human-potential disciplines is a paradoxical theory of
change: "Change occurs when one becomes what he is, not when
he tries to become what he is not."[19] This orientation toward "what
is, is" differentiates this ideology from mere "positive thinking." In
summary, these disciplines emphasize values of present centeredness and responsibility for this behavior.[20]

Behaviorally, gestalt consciousness is associated with relaxation,
with unblocking emotions, with feeling, intuition, and nonlinear
thinking. The descriptions of this state of awareness are similar to
accounts of psychedelic drug experiences, and indeed most of the

19. Arnold Beisser, "The Paradoxical Theory of Change," in *Gestalt Therapy
Now: Theory, Techniques, Applications*, ed. Joen Fagan and Irma Lee Shepherd
(New York: Science and Behavior Books, 1971), pp. 77–80.

20. John Enright, "An Introduction to Gestalt Techniques," in *Gestalt Therapy
Now*, p. 113.

early participants in this movement used drugs and also conducted the early research on them.

The disciplines that train for gestalt consciousness take place in a safe supportive setting, to attain a relatively nonevaluative, non-judgmental "experiencing of experience." Sometimes this is described as emptying the mind, or deautomatizing the selectivity of perceptions of everyday consciousness.[21] There are many techniques for narrowing concentration or distracting the mind from its usual patterns of thought, such as gazing at a mandala, hypnotic induction, reciting a mantra (Hari Krishna), *asanas* (physical postures and breathing exercises—3HO), visualization (*est*), guided imagery (Psychosynthesis), concentrative meditation, or even pressing nerve endings in the cranium (Divine Light). Any combination of these techniques may be used. Approaches that are physically rigorous or painful (tantric yoga as used in 3HO) serve similar purposes, but require a more controlled and structured setting as well as more commitment and preparation than most persons in the human-potential groups are willing to undergo.[22]

The subjective experience of gestalt consciousness varies enormously from technique to technique, but all have the common goal of cultivating an alternative point of view as a means to circumvent usual investments in old patterns and habitual self-images. This consciousness breaks down habitual distinctions between what is important and unimportant, between self and other, between right and wrong. The self is momentarily freed to take a different position or attitude toward experiences, particularly bothersome ones, and to transform the meaning of this experience and its reflection on the self.

Usually there is an accompanying release, or a sense of completing or making whole an experience that was formerly experienced incompletely or unconsciously. I call this consciousness "gestalt consciousness," rather than "cosmic consciousness" or "mystical experience" or "peak experience," because it does not necessarily involve such strong feelings of being at one with the world or of the fittingness of all things that other terms imply. It is often more a gentle "hmm" than an ecstatic "aha!" It is a process where aspects of experience that have been disowned, discounted, or evaluated negatively have the opportunity to surface. In the case

21. Arthur Deikman, "Deautomatization and the Mystic Experience," *Psychiatry* 29 (1966).

22. See Robert Ornstein, *The Psychology of Consciousness* (San Francisco: W.H. Freeman, 1972), chap. 6, for an excellent survey of meditation methods.

of a memory, the surfacing allows a complete picture to emerge, a whole picture, a gestalt. This is considered to be integration beyond mere insight or cognitive knowledge of hidden events. Gestalt consciousness is not so much opening up the closet door to see what skeletons are there as it is mentally entering the closet to find out that skeletons are familiar friends that were once denied.

As one example of how gestalt consciousness facilitates a more holistic sense of self, here is an account of a restless, domineering, manipulative woman, who has a dream of walking down a crooked path in a forest of tall trees. She is asked by her therapist to become one of the trees. As she loses her self-consciousness and "becomes" a tree she describes a feeling of being more serene and deeply rooted. Taking these feelings into her current life, she experienced both the lack of them and the possibility of achieving them. Imagining herself to be the crooked path, her eyes filled with tears as she experienced more intensely the devious crookedness of her life and again the possibility of straightening out a little if she chose.[23]

Gestalt consciousness shows the experiencer that reality is not as "hard" as it seems to be. What was once a fixation or a historical fact becomes very malleable. Following on this is the realization that reality is personally constructed and reconstructed all the time.

EXTENT OF PARTICIPATION IN BAY AREA GROUPS

The Bay Area New Religious Consciousness survey for 1973 (see chapter 13) indicates that 17 percent of the Bay Area population had participated in an encounter group or similar kind of training, such as sensory awareness, sensitivity training, a T-group, or growth group. The survey shows that group work with a therapist and sensitivity training in college and high school account for the most frequent exposure to growth groups. Other settings in the order of frequency include on-the-job vocational training, church groups, centers such as Synanon and Esalen, and women's consciousness-raising groups.

The survey reports that persons under thirty had more than double the rate of participation of older persons (29 percent *versus* 12 percent). In both age groups more than 75 percent had participated in more than one group; more than 30 percent had gone back for a third group. Ninety-five percent said they found the group(s) "very" or "slightly" helpful; 3 percent found them "slightly harm-

23. John Enright, "Gestalt Techniques," p. 121.

ful" and 2 percent, or 3 persons of the 173, found them "very harm-ful." The survey shows that the average age is about thirty-five, that there are an equal number of men and women, and that they are better educated than Bay Area residents with the same incomes. Politically they are liberal to radical; religiously they are slightly less likely than the Bay Area population to go to church, or to have a Christian denominational affiliation or a traditional belief in God.

Some of the life-style characteristics that appear to go along with participation in human-potential groups are never having married, a recent change of address, and a tendency to join groups and try out new experiences. Fifty-two percent said they had "experienced being 'high' on drugs," and nearly half of these said it had "a lasting influence on my life." Psychotropic drugs are an important introduction to the alternative realities conjured up by these groups and to the vision of alternative ways of living.

VARIETIES OF ATTRACTION

A wide variety of appeals motivate participation in human-potential groups: from therapy to thrill seeking, from intensive group ex-periences to being centered within oneself, from meeting new friends to diffusing into cosmic bliss—all with an underlying quest for direct experience. The movement attracts persons who would rather quiet the chatter in their heads naturally than take tran-quilizers, or who would rather know God than believe in him.

The range of attractions may be seen as social, sensual, thera-peutic, as well as transpersonal. Often several of these spark an ini-tial interest in a group or discipline, and these interests shift with greater acquaintance with the movement and its offerings. For ex-ample, Stuart Miller, now a director of Esalen, describes in his autobiography how he spent a sabbatical year at Esalen to increase his effectiveness in academic group situations and to add to his sex-ual prowess.[24] By the end of the year, he had abandoned his career and was contentedly waiting on tables, thereby providing Zen-like service to humanity.

SOCIAL ATTRACTIONS

Many persons initially join a group, particularly an encounter group, looking for acquaintances or friends. The desire for human

24. Stuart Miller, *Hot Springs: The True Adventures of the First New York Jewish Literary Intellectual in the Human Potential Movement* (New York: Viking Press, 1971).

fellowship and community increases in contemporary society with the decline of primary groups located in the extended family, at the place of work, and in the local church. Persons who find themselves unwelcome at social gatherings or on the fringes of many groups may be attracted by the encounter group's moral commitment to take all its members seriously.

Persons are also attracted by the opportunity to meet others in a direct, honest way, unencumbered by the usual social norms. Groups generally reverse many of the normal conventions of society, so that race, age, and social status lose their stratifying and distancing powers. It is testimony to the poverty of everyday life that many persons claim that a human-potential group provided their first frank exchanges with someone of the opposite sex, of another ethnic background, or on the other side of the generation gap. Sometimes the feelings of love and acceptance engendered in groups are powerful enough that participants talk of their group or seminar as their "family." The ethos that persons are to be taken seriously, as persons, is aided by the knowledge that the group will last only a little while and will not interact with society at large, where the discrepant social worth of the members would be accentuated.

INTENSIVE GROUP EXPERIENCE

Human-potential groups seem to satisfy the basic human thirst for intensive group experience that is exemplified in religious gatherings and fraternity initiations. Thomas Oden has pointed out the similarity of encounter groups with the house meetings of the early Methodists and with the festivities of Hassidism.[25] As an intensive group experience, weekends at growth centers show many similarities with the Cursillo, with the Summer Solstice of the Aquarian nation, or the traditional church retreat, where renewal and rebirth are emphasized. These retreat experiences create a temporary society where the members can try out new ways of relating and new

25. Thomas C. Oden, *The Intensive Group Experience: The New Pietism* (Philadelphia: Westminster Press, 1972). A book that argues for the use of encounter techniques as part of religious training is Gerald J. Jud and Elisabeth Jud, *Training in the Art of Loving: The Church and the Human Potential Movement* (Philadelphia: Pilgrim Press, 1972). Marilyn Wilmot has analyzed a psychotherapy group as analogous to a religious community and its therapist as a modern day shaman in her Ph.D. dissertation, "Ideology, Leadership, and Following: A Study of Group Therapy," York University, 1973.

behaviors. Persons are encouraged by the specialness of the occasion, by the group support, and by the prompting of the leaders to
explore new patterns of behavior. Groups provide opportunities for
owning up to negative feelings of self and for releasing guilt. This
process of self-revelation resembles the "opening of the heart"
sessions in early Methodism, the "house parties" of Moral Rearmament in the 1930s, and the "game" in Synanon today.

In most religious settings the admission of wrongdoing is tied to
contrition and the expected promise to mend erroneous ways.
Human-potential groups use confession less as a means for social
control. Some leaders even admonish the contrite not to make
promises regarding future conduct, for these might simply set them
up to break their word. Wrongdoings that might be confessed in a
short-lived encounter group rarely affect the survival of the group to
the extent they would a live-in community. Human-potential
groups can therefore afford not to set up ethical proscriptions to
regulate the selfishness, jealousies, and power seeking that can
break up more long-lived communities.

SENSUAL ATTRACTIONS

Human-potential groups, especially the body-oriented disciplines,
provide a dignified setting for the exploration of sexual and sensual
feeling. In automated America there is an enormous appeal for simple physical touching, particularly in an undemanding, sexually
nonthreatening atmosphere. For example, the atmosphere created
by a leader of a massage workshop permits people of the same or
opposite sex to touch without the usual ambivalences toward what
it will lead to. The common associations of massage with sleazy sex
seem to vanish with the simple expression of warmth, affection, and
sensuality. While the initial attraction of a nude encounter may for
some people be fantasies of sex orgies, many others are attracted to
groups because of the possibility of physical expression that is *not*
limited to genital sexuality. Many body disciplines, such as Rolfing
or Structural Patterning,[26] are less oriented toward interpersonal
physicality. Their purpose is to facilitate reacquaintance with one's
own body, making friends with it, learning how to listen to it so that
it may be more available as a servant and channel for energy flow.

26. "This system, developed by Judith Aston, is based on the premises of Structural Integration [Rolfing]. Structural Patterning is the use of specific movement
patterns at each hinge to bring the body toward better balance and alignment in
relation to gravity."*

THERAPEUTIC ATTRACTIONS

Some persons join a growth group or undertake a discipline in a search for assistance in problem solving. They may be encouraged by their own therapists to join a group. Problems may concern a spouse or lover, parents, sexual identity, decisions about work, or simply general malaise. Human-potential groups may also serve as way stations where persons may discover whether they are interested in a more explicitly therapeutic setting.

The range of problems that group participants seek to solve can be described on a continuum according to *social* definitions of severity. At one end of the continuum are chronic problems and life crises such as marriage dissolution, sexual identity, severe health condition, drug addiction, and intense loneliness. Toward the middle of the continuum are normal, "healthy" neurotics who have similar problems on a smaller scale. They may have marriages that are "OK, but not great." Although they may not have a drug or an alcohol problem, they may chain smoke or depend on coffee for alertness or on marijuana for relaxation. Some may feel trapped in traditional roles; others may feel they are in a rut of unconventional behavior.

In this middle range are a number of younger enrollees from a countercultural background who are seeking more discipline and order in their lives. They want to clarify their values and intentions and to accomplish something lasting and tangible. They do not want to rejoin society at the point where they dropped out; they seek new gurus and models who are successful in terms of some of their parents' values: clarity of purpose, power in the marketplace, organizational continuity, financial security. Many of the leaders mentioned in this volume are sought out for being successful *in* this world without being *of* this world.

Toward the other end of the continuum are the successful, those who have the symbols of success without fully experiencing success. At an *est* guest seminar, Werner Erhard told the audience that they were tremendously successful in having the first eleven and three-quarters inches of life. He went on to say that what was often missing was the last quarter-inch, the satisfaction of fully experiencing the success already achieved. People still think there is something more, something around the bend, some enlightenment that will fit the pieces of the puzzle together.

Carl Jung nicely characterizes the two ends of this continuum, this yardstick of living:

To be normal is a splendid ideal for the unsuccessful, for all those who have not yet found an adaptation. But for the people who have far more ability than the average, for whom it was never hard to gain successes and to ac-·complish their share of the world's work—for them restriction to the normal signifies the bed of Procrustes, unbearable to boredom, internal sterility and hopelessness. As a consequence, there are many people who become neurotic because they are normal.[27]

Group participants talk in terms of seeking "fresh experience," "wanting to taste the fruits of my life," or wanting "a feeling of catharsis and a new vision." At this end of the continuum, concerns are as much with the meaning of life as with specific problems. Some may wonder "Who am I?" or "How did it all begin?" or "Why is there war and suffering?" This search for the last quarter-inch may be characterized as a quest for transpersonal experience. People in this movement say that it comes when experiences no longer "happen" to them, when they know they are the ex-periencer.

TRANSPERSONAL EXPERIENCE AS SHORTCUTS TO POWER

The quest for transpersonal experience may also be the search for power with ego transcendence. Some want to acquire special powers external to the self that can be utilized without the loss of ego or surrender of control that accompanies the transpersonal or body trainings previously mentioned. For instance, preoccupation with astral projection or out-of-the-body experiences may over-shadow an interest in gaining awareness of being *in* the body. There is a growing preoccupation with controlling inner states as a way to feel better and to gain influence over objects and other people. The movement serves as a respectable entree into the occult. This response to the lure of psychic power as a means to get a head start on life is an indicator of the feeling of powerlessness in society generally. It can also be attributed to the growing interest in the efficacy of biofeedback, psychic healing, and extrasensory percep-tion.[28]

There appears to be little concern in the movement that paranor-mal powers and spiritual abilities might be used as tools of domina-

27. *Modern Man in Search of a Soul* (New York: Harcourt, Brace, 1933), p. 55.
28. Biofeedback is the electrical amplification of changes in the body (such as occur in heartbeat or brain-wave frequency) and conversion into a light or sound so that a person can identify the cues of internal changes as the first step in learn-ing to control them. It assumes that the mind is the manager of the body's func-tions, and gains voluntary control over normally unconscious physiological

tion. The general current of optimism about human nature and human potential results in the belief that, if there is magic, it must be white magic. There may be some basis to this belief. Several participants have said that the initial attraction of a movement discipline was as a shortcut to the domination of life and the manipulation of others, and that they realized from their subsequent involvement that what they wanted was to be more open to life and to serve others.

THE ATTRACTION OF STRUCTURAL FEATURES
OF THE HUMAN-POTENTIAL GROUPS

All of the various attractions of the movement—making friends, sensuality, therapy, occult practices, and spiritual trainings—are more directly met by groups and settings outside the movement. There are, for example, Sierra Club outings or bars for meeting people, rock climbing and casinos for thrill seeking, modern dance classes for body expression, psychotherapists for problem solving, and a variety of new religious groups for spiritual encounters. The following features show some of the special appeal of the movement.

One feature is the low level of commitment required. Growth group sessions are less expensive than psychoanalysis and faster than *zazen*. In comparison with the opera or tithing for a church, some human-potential group fees are modest. Most fall in the range of $3 (for an evening of Aikido) to $600 (for forty days of Arica Training). The more explicitly therapeutic and "complete cure" disciplines are costlier. Primal therapy, for example, may cost $8,000.[29] Participation does not require altering one's life-style or joining a special community, as in Synanon or 3HO. The movement is not ascetic or prudish as are many Eastern religions. There are usually no total prohibitions against the use of drugs outside the

processes. Psychic healing is the healing of bodily impediments (and sometimes emotional problems) by the force of will or the concern of another person, who assists in the seemingly miraculous and spontaneous healing in a way that cannot be accounted for by medical science.

29. "Primal Therapy . . . forces the patient to relive core (Primal) experiences, i.e., those moments in infancy and childhood when the patient found reality too painful to endure and took refuge in the comfortable half-world of neurosis. One of the indications that the re-experiencing of childhood denials has been reached—and thus recovery is in sight—is the release by the patient of the blood-chilling, terrifying Primal Scream." From the bookjacket of Arthur Janov, *The Primal Scream: Primal Therapy, the Cure for Neurosis* (New York: Dell Publishing Co. 1970).

group meetings. Discreet and honest sex is usually permissible and may even be an important attraction for some people. At present the hedonistic quality of the movement gains some moral sanction for being based on an ethic of openness and honesty rather than puritanical hypocrisy.

The assumption that authority is based on personal experience rather than on a holy text or divinely appointed avatar is attractive to independence-loving Americans. Formal belief and ritual are played down. There *are* assumptions that persons are expected to try out *as if* they were useful or true, but which they are not required to accept.

Perhaps the most important appeal is that human-potential groups are not as stigmatizing as are many special-interest groups. While it may serve many of the same functions, participation in a growth group does not entail the same onus as going to a head shrinker, or a lonely hearts club, or even a Pentecostal church service. Because of the many motivations for joining growth groups, it is more difficult to stereotype and stigmatize the participants.

IS THIS NEW RELIGIOUS CONSCIOUSNESS?

The search for a direct experience of the holy has been a common theme for cults and revivals throughout history. Participants in the Human Potential movement often lack the historical perspective to see that their movement has some precedents. Some of the accounts of St. John of the Cross are indistinguishable from the writings of contemporary pilgrims and mystics in this movement. The techniques used in the movement are often as old as India. The notion of God outside law has much in common with the underground stream of antinomianism that periodically wells up.[30] The excitement about the immanence of a divine force has much in common with the revivalism of the Great Awakenings.

Although there may be historical precedents to experiences provided by human-potential groups, there are several distinctive aspects of gestalt consciousness. What is probably new is the authoritative basis of direct experience without necessary reference to God or revelation. Many of the participants claim to have a greater sense of a cosmic presence or of a higher force after they stopped "believing in" or "beginning with" God. Coming from a

30. See the provocative account by Nathan Adler, *The Underground Stream: New Life Styles and the Antinomian Personality* (New York: Harper Torchbooks, 1972).

secular culture where there is little energy left for debating whether God is dead, the feeling of the transcendent is different. Although there is no longer a sense of covenant, there is a sense of immanence and that the universe is not capricious.

There is also a different basis of authority for the relationship between trainers and seekers. As children of the age of relativity, a significant number refuse to give up their minds totally or permanently to any system, guru, or symbol. While surrender and submission are always involved in the search for direct experience, the submission is less to an unchanging authority and more to the authority of the moment. Reality is taken as a personal construct, and as such is manipulable. Reality and authority develop as the constructor develops. As John Lilly puts it, "Every belief is a limit to be examined and transcended."

This movement appears to differ from other revitalization movements in that its participants seem to suffer more from existential uneasiness and the oppression of Weber's iron cage than from the social and economic deprivations that, sociologists have claimed, typically motivate persons to join new religious movements.

Throughout history, new religious movements have sprung up during periods of rapid social change as people grasped for a new authority that would make their dislocated world intelligible and indicate how they should act. When the authority that guaranteed their social status crumbled, a common maneuver has been to assume a special status in a religious movement. By joining a church one might become a member of the elect. This creation of a compensatory status, or the attempt to create moral capital out of scarce economic and social resources, is a way for those on the fringes of society to confer dignity on their lives.

There seems to be a different nuance of status deprivation with many seekers of the movement who are squarely and securely located in the modern world and are still not satisfied. They report a feeling of being "off balance," not centered within themselves. Somehow the quest of people who are functioning well, but still have a feeling that life could be better, seems less like compensation and more like growth. In addition to problems, they have "unexplored potential."

Significant numbers of participants in the movement have backgrounds of affluence and advanced education. Having satisfied their basic needs for economic security, sociability, and public recognition, they find themselves trapped in a highly rationalized and technological society where asceticism has lost its sacred underpinning. The Human Potential movement is one of the arenas where they seek a way out.

6

Synanon: The People Business

RICHARD OFSHE

Synanon is the name of a string of communities located primarily in California. These house approximately eighteen hundred individuals who lead an alternative life-style in environments virtually free of crime, violence, and the use of drugs and alcohol. Synanon is also two analytically distinct social entities that occupy the same physical space. It is first a corporate entity that has no owner or stockholders in the usual sense and has grown from a capital worth of little more than the cost of the incorporation to an institution that controls assets in excess of 15 million dollars, has yearly cash receipts of more than 3.5 million dollars, and receives yearly donations of goods estimated to be worth between three and four times the amount of its cash receipts.[1] The second entity is the community—the aggregate of people who reside at Synanon, together with the unusual pattern of social organization that has evolved during the transition from a self-help therapeutic community for the rehabilitation of narcotic and alcohol addicts, from which rehabilitated addicts "graduated" (returned to the larger society), into a social movement that is intended to provide an alternative way of life for former drug abusers or anyone else who wishes to live the style of life developing within Synanon.

The analytic distinction between the corporate entity and the community is important, because the two entities, although certain-

1. Data on Synanon's economics came from a lecture by Ron Cook (a regent of Synanon and financial director) entitled "Synanon Economics" in a Synanon Research University lecture series, 1972. Estimates of the value of goods donated to Synanon are based on figures given to me independently by several Synanon residents.

ly affecting each other, have a good deal of independence. The corporate entity has a continuity through time that the population of the community lacks because of the exceedingly high rate of population turnover. The founder, Charles Dederich, is probably the only remaining member of the original community; he was a member of the Alcoholics Anonymous offshoot group from which Synanon evolved and of the club that preceded the incorporation of the Synanon Foundation. It is estimated that from the time of incorporation to the present over fifteen thousand persons have resided in Synanon.[2] In one study it was found that even now, with an organized program leading to permanent residence in Synanon, 50 percent of a group admitted during a four-month period departed within the first month of residence and only a third were still present after six months. Even for those who survive the early period of high attrition, Synanon's history has always been one of rapid population change. Of the population in 1972, 61 percent had been in residence for longer than one year, 44 percent had survived two years, and only 11 percent had been Synanon residents for longer than five years.[3]

A second reason for making this distinction is that all wealth generated by the population of the community accrues to the corporate entity rather than to the members, and the members do not own Synanon, the corporate entity. Synanon Foundation, Incorporated, is a nonprofit corporation which, if it were dissolved, would be required to donate its assets to some other nonprofit corporation rather than divide them among Synanon residents. With two qualifications,[4] all profit (here defined as the difference between the value of labor and the cost of maintaining a worker) from the labor of residents of the Synanon community accrues to the corporate entity. Everyone, except for children and the infirm, works at a full-time job either within Synanon or in the larger society. All Synanon residents receive from the corporation their food, clothing, shelter, medical care, education, occupational training, and access to recreational activities. Residents who work for the Synanon corporate entity also receive cash for "walking-around money," which begins at

2. From *An Instant Guide to Synanon*, Synanon News Bureau, Oakland, California.

3. See Edward L. Maillet, *Report on Research Visit to Synanon Foundation.* (For publishing data on titles in the footnotes, see the references at the end of the chapter.)

4. The qualifications are the salaries paid to residents who work for Synanon (maximum $50 per month) and monies earned by those who work outside that are not contributed to Synanon.

$1.50 per week and increases in small amounts as their period in residence lengthens. Residents of five years or more may be designated employees and receive a salary of $50 per month. Residents of the community who are not former drug abusers and who work on the outside are known as life-stylers. For the goods and services enumerated above, they pay a monthly fee to the corporation—for a single person a minimum of $300 per month, the estimated amount required to meet the costs of maintaining a person in Synanon. Fees for families are adjusted according to family size. Life-stylers are encouraged to donate to the corporation the remainder of their incomes so that they leave themselves the equivalent of the $50 monthly employee salary plus special expenses such as those connected with travel to and from work. Life-stylers who are hired by the corporation (doctors, lawyers, teachers, draftsmen, accountants) assume employee status, work within Synanon, and receive the $50 monthly salary.

Finally, all power exercised in the various Synanon facilities rests with the corporate entity; privilege is unequally distributed within the community. The degree of inequality is determined by the corporation, and the personal prestige of community members is determined by position in the corporate structure. Corporate affairs are managed by the appointed officials and executives of the corporation. The general membership of the community has no formal power over the appointments to corporation positions. Naturally, the corporate management is sensitive to community reaction to new policy decisions, and decisions or programs that meet with widespread disapproval can be reversed. But if the corporation management decides that a policy or a new rule is significant and beneficial for both corporation and community, a great deal of dissatisfaction from the community can be withstood.

In 1968 Synanon formally ceased to be a stopping and rebuilding point in an addict's life and became the point of entry into a new life-style for both addicts and "squares" (nonaddicts). Corporate management had decided that Synanon was to become an alternative society and the formerly transient community was to be conceived and planned for as a permanent population. Certain programs would be abandoned, planning for expansion of those functions necessary to handle support of a cradle-to-grave population (schooling, occupational training, child care and rearing) would be undertaken or expanded, and the understanding of the legitimate relationship between the corporation and the community would be changed. Planning for one's life outside of Synanon became no longer acceptable.

When Synanon was a therapeutic community, most new arrivals left before completion of the program (it took from two-and-a-half to four years) and most Synanon residents left within a few years. The corporation has decided however, to move in a certain direction, presumably with the expectation that individual attitudes toward the corporate decision will be brought into line through the mechanisms of social pressure for conformity to community standards, selective loss of individuals with discrepant attitudes, and selective recruitment of individuals willing to accept at least the idea of a lifetime commitment. At present, however, Synanon is characterized by the high turnover rate noted above.

The range of privilege distribution within the Synanon community is narrow in comparison with the outside community. At the lower end of the scale a person receives a dormitory room, basic clothing necessities, adequate food, walking-around money, and limited recreational activities. The upper end of the scale provides an individual with an apartment or small house, a vehicle for personal transportation, higher quality clothing, better food, higher salary, and expanded recreational activities. The material differences between the most and the least advantaged within the Synanon communities are not great, however. The power to determine how great the differences will be, as well as to determine the absolute level of affluence, rests with the corporate power structure.

In Synanon, as in all societies, personal prestige is determined by occupational position. Because of unusual characteristics of Synanon society, the specifics of the system are different from the system in the larger society. Most Synanon residents work for the Synanon Foundation, and prestige in the community is therefore primarily a function of position in the corporate power structure rather than of evaluation of an individual's particular occupation.

To obtain a significant position in the corporate structure, an individual must demonstrate sufficient commitment to the corporate enterprise to suggest that he will remain with Synanon. Length of residence in Synanon is therefore an important qualification if for no other reason than that it demonstrates willingness to accept the values of the society, to live under the highly authoritarian social system that prevails, and to accept the demands for conformity to corporate rules that define life in the community. An individual might demonstrate commitment by donating his capital to the foundation, by transferring all of his occupational activities to Synanon, or by bringing to Synanon skills that permit the corporation to undertake new activities that are expected to be profitable.

Residents who begin their careers in Synanon as drug addicts or abusers, alcoholics, juvenile delinquents, or criminals are distributed across the entire range of power positions in Synanon society. Unless they possessed occupational skills when they enter and can therefore direct some special activity (for example, construction, accounting, auto repair), the opportunity for upward mobility within the Synanon corporate structure and therefore within the Synanon community is through a management position (for example, director of food service or transportation, director of a facility, or regent of the corporation).

Life-stylers as a group are well treated in Synanon with respect to privilege, since they are substantial contributors to the Synanon economy. They are somewhat compromised with respect to prestige within the system, since they work on the outside and therefore are not totally involved with Synanon society. Life-stylers who become employees of the foundation are usually professionals or offer some skill to the corporation and therefore typically occupy positions that are respected within the community. By being "employees," they solve the problem of outward orientation that tends to compromise the status of life-stylers who work on the outside.

Upward mobility within the corporate structure results in increased formal privilege within the society as well as increased personal prestige within the community. Since formal position within the corporation is given by appointment, the corporation power structure effectively controls an individual's social position within the community. In a very real sense, Synanon is a company town without even the rudiments of a government independent of the company.

I have made this distinction between the entity Synanon Foundation, Incorporated, and the aggregate of individuals and social patterns that comprise the Synanon community because it permits analysis of Synanon's history, which is the history of the development of the corporation, and analysis of Synanon's function, which can be understood in terms of the reasons for and consequences of involvement with the Synanon community by those individuals who cycle through the various Synanon facilities.

THE CORPORATION

Synanon sometimes describes itself as "the people business." This is, I believe, a quite appropriate, if somewhat cryptic, description of the activities of Synanon Foundation, which was chartered in 1958 for the purpose of doing good things for people. Although this is not the language of the organization's formal charter as a nonprofit corporation, a charter that defines an organization's legitimate purpose as rehabilitating drug- and alcohol-dependent individuals, helping character-disordered individuals, and educating people would allow all sorts of good works and activities necessary for the performance of these good works. Synanon emerged initially as a business that was going to rebuild the character of heroin addicts, or at least forcefully assist heroin addicts in their own rehabilitation.

Considered strictly as a business enterprise, Synanon's history might be described as follows: Synanon Foundation, Incorporated, began operating in 1958. It entered the marketplace by providing a service, a program that was advertised as leading to a "cure" for heroin addiction. At the time Synanon began operation, there existed a variety of federal, state, and private programs for the treatment of drug addicts. These programs all had extremely low success rates, and they were too much alike to permit any judgment concerning which type of approach appeared to have potential success.

Synanon's program had characteristics that were different from its competitors in a number of ways. Since the program was completely voluntary, it was possible to define and treat an addict as desiring and willing to work for his own rehabilitation. Addicts were made to work for their rehabilitation in two ways: they were put to work around the Synanon house to keep it running, and each participated in everyone else's therapy.

The arena for therapy is the Synanon game, an aggressive encounter group in which people are told in no uncertain terms what is wrong with their behavior and how to correct it. The game itself focuses on concrete behavior rather than on hypothetical constructs and internal dynamics. More than anything, Synanon demanded from individuals the continual efforts to live up to the rules under which they had freely agreed to live. The experience itself of living in Synanon, under its military-like authority system and in its family-like atmosphere of concern, must be recognized as part of Synanon's therapeutic program. The demand for personal discipline was made in settings other than just the game. For example, individuals who violated Synanon rules were given "haircuts," verbal beatings delivered by administrators and those further along in the process of their own rehabilitation. Finally, Synanon had no paid or professional staff. Everyone present shared an important status characteristic: they were all "outsiders." If participation in Synanon did not do an individual any good, whether by providing a place to go when there was nowhere else or by actually helping to end drug dependence, then there was no reason for anyone to be there and no reason for Synanon to exist.

Rehabilitation was a full-time job for everyone residing in the Synanon community. Although an addict was put to work as soon as he was detoxified, work was primarily maintenance activity around the Synanon house. Since Synanon was not a government- or foundation-supported enterprise and the addicts had no significant personal resources or jobs to generate income, the corporation had serious financial problems from the beginning. Because Synanon was performing a public service, it sought support from the public—in its early days through donations of food from storekeepers, used furniture from individuals, and so forth. Essentially, Synanon began selling its services to the general public in a manner similar to that used by most nonprofit organizations. It was attempting to perform a service that was recognized as valuable by a significant segment of the general public and it solicited philanthropic support for that activity.

In the late 1950s and early 1960s Synanon began receiving a great deal of publicity because it was *appearing* to have some success at producing drug-independent former addicts and was also provoking a hostile reaction from some segments of the public. This was newsworthy, and Synanon received attention from Los Angeles television, newspapers, *Life* and *Time* magazines, state and federal government committees concerned with drug addiction, and professionals concerned with drug rehabilitation. The image of Synanon that reached the public was of a poverty-stricken, courageous group of individuals who were freeing themselves from the horror of drug addiction through new therapeutic techniques and self-help.

In 1959 Synanon moved its socially disreputable and racially integrated population from a slum in Ocean Park, California, to a three-story former National Guard Armory in Santa Monica. This set off a furor in this middle-class, conservative city; and the fight that ensued involved hysterical attacks on Synanon by ultraconservative elements, the use of minor violations of the building code in an attempt to drive Synanon from Santa Monica, and an attempt to define Synanon as a hospital and therefore in violation of zoning law. Dederich was sent to jail for twenty-five days for a zoning violation, and Synanon's visibility increased. To the neutral or positively inclined elements of the general public, these attacks cast Synanon into the position of a target of the forces of unreasoning prejudice. Synanon was a group of outcasts in the process of re-forming themselves, who were being attacked by rich and powerful opponents capable of bending local government to their wills.

In its early days, Synanon established a public image that allowed it to solicit support successfully from the general public. It developed a practice called "hustling," which was the solicitation of donations from private individuals and corporations. Since Synanon was a nonprofit corporation, donations of cash were tax deductible at full dollar value; and until the tax laws were changed in 1969 companies that donated goods to Synanon could deduct the selling price of an item rather than the cost. In Synanon, hustling has become a well-developed speciality. From the practice of getting day-old sandwiches, bread, aging fruit and vegetables, and other discards from local merchants and the general public, it has developed into a full-time operation for a segment of Synanon's population. Hustlers are usually former addicts with long histories of heavy drug use, living proof of Synanon's good works. Goods from hustling have been estimated to have a value of about three to four times the corporation's cash income. Given a cash income of 3.5 million dollars in 1972, hustling would have produced goods having a value of between 10.5 and 13.5 million dollars. Hustling means more now than making the rounds of local merchants. Hustlers produce nearly all of the goods that are consumed by the community in its day-to-day operation and seek to supply whatever is needed for special projects (for example, construction materials, computers, heavy equipment of different sorts, and cattle for Synanon's ranching operations). Hustlers routinely travel around the country in search of special commodities as well as to increase their territory.

Synanon Industries was inaugurated in 1965. This is the division of corporate Synanon that conducts its various business ventures. Synanon Industries has operated gasoline stations in California and developed the second largest distributing business in the country of volume-advertising gift items (imprinted pens, key rings, and so forth). Since at present Synanon Industries operates only one gasoline station, nearly all of its revenue is generated through the advertising specialty business. In 1972 Synanon Industries had gross sales of approximately 4 million dollars, and net income from its operations amounted to approximately 1.3 million dollars.

The products and services of Synanon Industries are sold to the general public in the normal fashion and are clearly identified as being a part of Synanon, the drug-addict, self-help, rehabilitation program. Industry salesmen, like those in the hustling operations, are usually former addicts, who can point out to a potential customer the benefits they have received from Synanon and how doing business with Synanon supports these sorts of activities.

Synanon's primary "people business" was and still is the rebuilding of drug addicts and abusers. In its earliest days Synanon's addict population was made up almost entirely of adults with long histories of heroin addiction. Over the years, the population has changed in composition to the point where its "dope fiend" (Synanon's classification for *anyone* who enters for a drug-related reason) population is on the average young and has a relatively short (compared with the early days) history of drug use with a variety of drugs, including heroin. The average age of a Synanon resident is between twenty-two and twenty-three; the average age of entering dope fiends may be somewhat lower.

Synanon, as a corporate entity, derives little income directly from its work with dope fiends. In 1972 it received from newcomers a total of $30,000 and took in over a thousand new residents. Synanon also receives payments from county and state funds (largely from the state of Michigan) in the amount of $13 per day for juvenile residents of Synanon. This amounted to $71,000 in 1972. The total cash coming to Synanon as a direct consequence of its rehabilitation work with drug abusers was $101,000, or about 3 percent of its cash income in 1972.

Synanon, as a corporate entity, is able to generate a great deal of income in the form of cash and goods received as an indirect consequence of its dope fiend business. This fact together with its historical starting point accounts for Synanon's choice of a public image. Like every corporate entity, Synanon manages its public image. Since Synanon depends so heavily on its image for survival (maintaining its tax-exempt status, solicitation of donations, and appeals to concerns about social welfare as an element in its sales activities), it is especially concerned about its public self. The public self that corporate Synanon most frequently presents of the Synanon community is based on those activities that present it as a rehabilitation business.

The dope fiend business serves as the foundation on which Synanon has built and from which it has expanded. Synanon's expansion in its fifteen years of existence has taken it from a single storefront operation in southern California to a complex of five substantial facilities in California, including ranches, apartment buildings, a former beachfront club in Santa Monica, an eleven-story former athletic club in Oakland, and a large former paint factory in San Francisco. Synanon also operates a facility in Detroit and one in New York City. Using standard notions of corporate growth, Synanon has demonstrated steady development in terms of its net worth, assets controlled, and volume of business in its basic support activities of hustling and specialty-item sales. This corporate expansion is matched by an expansion of the activity that originally justified Synanon's existence. There is a steady stream of drug abusers initiating contact with Synanon and experiencing its variety of therapy for differing lengths of time.

In the middle 1960s Synanon diversified the services it offered to the public and created what are called game clubs in each of Synanon's urban facilities. By joining one of Synanon's game clubs a nonresident could play Synanon games and participate in many of the other activities that define life in a Synanon house. In these game clubs Synanon offered its services to that segment of the general public that was not drug dependent. The service was similar in intent to services offered by individuals or organizations that conducted encounter or sensitivity training groups. Synanon's first basic diversification engaged it in what has come to be known as the human-growth or human-potential movement.

Synanon was able to use its visibility (based on its involvement with drug abusers) as the basis for starting its new business. In addition to seeking donations from the general public Synanon has always attempted to involve members of the public in its activities, in the form of open houses every Saturday evening, where those who were curious about Synanon's activities could see for themselves something of life in a Synanon house and meet its residents. The open houses served as a point of contact between "dope fiends" and "squares" and between corporate Synanon and the public that supported it. During its early years Synanon received considerable publicity, the Synanon game was known to be a form of encounter group to a substantial segment of the public, and Synanon had a large number of residents with considerable experience at playing the Synanon game. To enter the human-potential-movement business, Synanon had only to advertise the fact that the general public could play Synanon games by joining a Synanon game club. During the mid-sixties when Synanon entered the encounter business, California was a hothouse for new varieties of encounter groups. Unlike orthodox psychotherapy, which was still fashionable but which carried the stigma of illness or of an inability to cope, encounter-group ideology focused on the idea of movement toward perfection. Encounter groups provided growth experiences rather than treatment for problems.

Prior to launching its human-potential business, Synanon had served a clientele that was outside the mainstream of acceptable middle-class existence in America, since the most significant social characteristic of those who arrived at Synanon's door was their drug addiction. The human-potential movement appealed to a basically middle-class market.

Synanon's version of an encounter-group business was markedly different from its competition. Synanon's therapeutic ideology focuses on behavior rather than underlying cognitive structure and demands change in behavior from the very beginning. Therefore, participation in Synanon's game club meant participation in Synanon life. I would characterize Synanon's therapeutic or growth ideology as one which postulates that an individual is highly responsive to his social environment and that in a controlled (that is, designed) environment the habits that define a life pattern can be changed by careful reinforcement and structured experiences. In this sense, Synanon's techniques are highly behavioristic in that attention is paid to overt behavior, and it is overt behavior that is modified. Synanon therapeutic ideology also includes the postulate that cognitive structures consistent with the facts of behavior eventually develop.[5] Therefore, it is possible to change self-image and value preferences if an individual can be induced to behave in a manner consistent with the desired values. Individuals who joined Synanon game clubs, therefore, found themselves participating in a therapeutic experience significantly different from that offered by other human-growth businesses, since they were encouraged to identify with and become involved in the Synanon life-style. From Synanon's perspective this identification and involvement was essential in order to benefit from contact with Synanon.

Synanon's human-potential business was organized in a fashion different from its dope fiend business, where treatment costs were paid by the general public largely through donation and patronage of Synanon's commercial operations. Here, the clients themselves paid the corporation for its services. The exchange relation, like the

5. A more complete discussion of Synanon ideology may be found later in this chapter. For a discussion of the techniques used to produce change, see Ofshe et al., "Social Structure and Commitment to Synanon." For a somewhat different perspective on Synanon's therapeutic ideology, see Steven Simon, "The Synanon Game."

therapy itself, was different from the typical fee-for-service arrangement in other human-potential businesses. For example, dues for membership in a Synanon game club have varied over the years from a high of ten to twenty dollars a month to a low of a penny a month. Synanon's game clubs have always been a bargain in the human-growth market.

The encounter-group business benefits the corporation in at least four ways: cash, services, public relations, and recruitment of game players into life-styler status. Since Synanon's therapeutic experience necessitates involvement with Synanon's good works mission and its problems, game players are induced to make cash donations to Synanon commensurate with their ability to pay. Because the token formal fee for membership in a game club is low and the majority of middle-class game players can afford to make larger donations, and because Synanon is always in need of additional funds to expand in order to serve more people, the game players frequently find themselves vulnerable to suggestions that they increase their donations. In 1972 Synanon received approximately 7 percent of its cash income from game players. This amounted to approximately $237,000.

Corporate Synanon benefits from its involvement with game players through the donation of the game players' services. The middle-class game-player population provides a talent pool that includes doctors, lawyers, dentists, and architects, for example, all of whom are able to donate valuable necessary services. Synanon's physical-plant expansion program frequently involves the donation or purchase of a run-down property that can be dramatically improved with a substantial investment of skilled labor, a demand that can be partially satisfied through labor donations by game players.

The admission of nonresidents into closer involvement with Synanon's life-style has resulted in a large number of people with first-hand experience with the organization, hence a more realistic picture of its goals and activities than they are likely to obtain through media exposure to Synanon's activities. Anyone who had had contact with Synanon for even a few months could not fail to recognize the humanitarian content of Synanon's value system and the manifest good works performed by the organization, even if they did not find it beneficial for themselves or were repelled by other aspects of the organization.

Finally, the game clubs serve as a filter through which potential life-stylers pass before they decide to move into Synanon's alternative society. In 1968 the program leading to the graduation of former drug addicts from Synanon was abandoned, and Synanon embarked on the task of establishing an alternative society that was to be capable of housing a person from the cradle to the grave. The alternative society was to be open to anyone who wished to adopt the Synanon life-style. The corporation undertook to create a model society that was to experiment with new forms of social and interpersonal organization as an extension of the therapeutic activities it had engaged in throughout its history. For those who chose residence, the benefits were participation in this social experiment and complete involvement in Synanon's therapeutic human-growth-oriented social structure.

"Squares" who are personally attracted to Synanon and its experiment in communal living constitute an important segment of Synanon's population. As relatively successful members of the larger society who see Synanon's life-style as preferable to those in the outside society, they confirm the validity of insiders' commitments. They also provide a talent pool that enables Synanon to develop those services that a socially independent society must be able to provide for its members. Any community that seeks to provide for its population a relatively complete range of essential social services must be able to operate schools, provide health care, conduct its internal economic operations, and oversee economic and legal relations with the outside world. Life-stylers bring to Synanon training and experience which Synanon as a separate society is not presently able to provide. For example, of approximately eighteen hundred residents in the various Synanon communities, eight are physicians, who can easily provide basic medical care for Synanon's population; and since those who are "employees" of Synanon are paid only the $50 per month maximum salary, it is economically feasible to attempt innovations in the organization of medical care.

Life-stylers who do not bring to the organization scarce talents or training continue to work in the larger society and pay Synanon a fee judged equal to the amount necessary to maintain an individual in the community. In this way Synanon's nonprofit corporate status is not endangered. Most life-stylers contribute to Synanon a substantial proportion of their incomes in addition to the fee they pay for residence. In 1972 it was estimated that approximately 17 percent of Synanon's population consisted of adult squares. In 1972 Synanon derived approximately 37 percent of its cash income from residents who worked on the outside. This amounted to about $1,300,000.

THE COMMUNITY

The residents of the various Synanon facilities at any point in time, together with the patterns of social organization that structure their lives, constitute the Synanon community. The style of life in Synanon is noticeably different from the pattern of life lived by Americans of any social class. The most obvious formal differences between the Synanon life-style and that of the society from which it emerged involve rules regulating the use of stimulants and norms governing interpersonal hostility and cooperation. Alcohol and all recreational drugs are prohibited, as is all physical violence and threats of violence—hostile exchanges between residents are banned with special exceptions. Although traditional forms of politeness are carefully observed, traditional norms of privacy do not hold, and inquiry is permitted into any aspect of one's life. Social life is organized around the collective use of facilities: meals are served in dining halls; social intercourse is conducted in public rooms; many residents live in dormitories or share apartments, though married couples usually have private sleeping quarters and unmarried couples seeking privacy are given temporary use of guest rooms; even children live in dormitories, rather than with their parents.

Life in a Synanon house is characterized by a pleasant feeling of comfort and ease, with a variety of activities in the public rooms, with people moving from one group to another and appearing to know and to have something to say to members of virtually any group that has formed for the moment. The norms of life in a Synanon house are structured to produce an atmosphere in which anyone is welcome to join almost any group. Outside visitors and visitors from another Synanon house are made to feel welcome, and efforts are made to include them in the activities. "Family-like atmosphere" fairly describes the feeling one gets from observing and participating in life in a Synanon house.

The social structure that produces this atmosphere is consciously designed, and considerable effort is made to maintain this exceedingly pleasant ambience of Synanon facilities. For example, Synanon facilities are small (the largest houses about five hundred), most people both live and work within the facility, and individuals periodically rotate from one facility to another. Most, therefore, have friends spread throughout the various facilities. The unique factor in Synanon is that all participants interact with one another in Synanon games and therefore come to know about one another's lives in an intimate way.

In general, life is oriented inward. There is a recognized norm (the rule of containment) that energy is to be invested within the community rather than directed outward. The tendency is to invite outsiders to come to visit a resident in Synanon rather than for the resident to visit on the outside; friendships with persons who are not in some way involved with Synanon are discouraged, as are activities that cannot be conducted within Synanon and with other Synanon residents. The policy is to invest one's energy in Synanon activities and in Synanon people.

Synanon facilities support a variety of internal community activities and forms of entertainment for residents: a public library system, television, collections of phonograph and tape recordings of music available in public rooms, and periodic new film releases shown at the various facilities. Most of the facilities host Saturday night parties and other activities open to the public. As one might expect in a small socially isolated community, interest groups form to pursue various crafts, and study groups form around issues of common interest. There is always some building project under way or some special project for which there is insufficient labor available from the occupational labor pool of the community; hence, there are calls for volunteer labor to help transform some part of the environment and make some aspect of life more pleasant. This gives a Synanon house something of a pioneer feeling.

The major behavioral dividing line in Synanon is between what is called "in the game" and "out of the game." Outside of the game, "on the floor" in Synanon argot, one is expected to be the model of a relaxed, friendly, pleasant, helpful person who is happy in his work, on the best of terms with everyone, and satisfied with the way others are conducting themselves. One is to act as if life is exactly as pleasant as it appears to the casual visitor. This is the ideal to which members of the community aspire. In the game, however, one can reveal whatever feelings and attitudes are being suppressed "on the floor." In the game it is not only acceptable to criticize the mistakes and stupidities of others or to reveal one's negative reactions to someone else's behavior, it is the purpose of the game. The game is the arena in which strong emotions are displayed, individuals learn how others react to their behavior, and demands are made to correct errors.

The subject matter that can be brought up in a game is in no way restricted, and games are used to address any interpersonal or organizational problems within the community. This includes such diverse matters as conflicts among members of departments and work groups within the organization, marital problems, developing a consensus about the norms of Synanon society, and leading individuals to reject undesirable aspects of their past behavior and to accept the values consistent with their new behavior patterns.

The basic Synanon game is an encounter group with from ten to fifteen participants. Games have an aggressive tone, since they usually proceed on the basis of indictments in which one participant points out the defect, transgression, or error of another. The norms of the game call for the group to support the indictment, and unless the indicted individual can quickly fend off the attack, he finds himself opposed by the entire group with various members adding their observations in support of the original charge. One class of indictment involves some problem between two or more individuals in which difficulties in their interaction are surfaced and solutions are sought. Since the subject matter of an indictment is overt behavior, the two contending parties talk about those aspects of each other's behavior that are causing problems, and the group acts as judge, with various members offering evidence in support of charges and offering possible solutions. Solutions usually involve argument by one or both of the parties to modify the problematic behaviors.

The second class of indictment involves violation of Synanon norms. This sort of indictment has the status of offense against the community and produces strong emotional reactions. Violations of Synanon norms are especially significant for two reasons. First, Synanon is attempting to construct a social system different from the one residents left and from which they bring habits that are in discrepancy with the habits Synanon seeks to establish within its boundaries. The differences between life within Synanon and life on the outside are not regarded as arbitrary differences in Synanon's value system. The differences are strongly preferred to the norms of behavior on the outside. Second, from Synanon's point of view, changing a character-disordered or drug-addicted or neurotic individual's behavior means changing his basic pattern of life. Synanon seeks to rebuild persons, and acceptance of the normative system under which Synanon residents live is essential in producing the changes that are sought.[6]

The Synanon game, together with its variants,[7] and the way in

6. For extensive discussions of the Synanon game and its relation to behavior change, see Simon, "The Synanon Game"; Ofshe et al., "Social Structure and Commitment to Synanon."

7. Variants on Synanon games include stews, dissipations, hi-frequency games, and various games that take more than three hours. Each variant has some distinguishing characteristic, such as the setting (with or without a gallery) or a

which the game is integrated into the routine of Synanon life make
up the distinguishing characteristic of Synanon social organization.
Game interaction consumes a considerable number of hours of each
resident's time per month. Steven Simon estimates that a typical
Synanon resident participates in three or four three-hour games per
week to fulfill a mandatory game requirement. Synanon residents
will also play in a variety of noncompulsory games, which serve as a
common form of entertainment and social activity in Synanon.[8]
Social games differ from compulsory games only with respect to the
duration of the game and the composition of the group of players.
Games may be organized within friendship groups, for married
couples, for parents and children, and so forth. Insofar as the
Synanon game is considered a therapeutic experience, it is clear
that Synanon residents participate in a social system in which one of
the major sanctioned activities is the promotion of therapy and
growth. According to Simon, the residents of the various Synanon
communities fall into three classes with respect to expected consequences of involvement with Synanon and reasons for being in
residence. He distinguishes among these three types of residents as
follows: "(1) the character disordered or anomic personality; (2) the
antinomian or hippie-character type; and (3) the square or normally
deficiency-motivated personality" (p. 290).

Simon's three categories correspond to (1) adults with long
histories of drug addiction and criminal activities; (2) young adults,
dropouts with a history of drug use including psychedelics, speed,
and heroin; and (3) "squares" who have no serious histories of drug
use but can be termed "the 'average person,' the 'basic neurotic,' or
the 'adjusted American'" (p. 294).

Given the typology of character disorders and personality deficiencies into which Simon categorizes Synanon's population, it is
reasonable to infer that the main motivation for coming to Synanon
for all segments of the community's population is egocentric in that
they seek personal change which they view as desirable. However,
many current Synanon residents were initially motivated partly by
pressure from parents, or by a choice between Synanon and commitment to some other drug-treatment program or a jail sentence,
by a desire to live in an environment that offers the family atmosphere found in Synanon houses, by a desire to become involved
in an alternative life-style intended to be a prototype for finding

device to bring together from distant Synanon communities people who coor-
dinate the activities of the corporation. The basic interactive techniques are
similar, however, to the standard Synanon game.
    8. Simon, "The Synanon Game," pp. 73, 74.

solutions to major social problems, or by a desire to raise children in the sort of environment Synanon offers.

One of the reasons for distinguishing between corporate Synanon and community Synanon is that the corporation has had a continuous existence, while the community is characterized by a high rate of population turnover. Despite the fact that in 1968 Synanon ended its formal program of ex-addict graduation and presently operates no programs that lead directly to reintegration with the larger society, data collected in 1972 reveals that only 44 percent of Synanon's population had been in residence for longer than two years and only 11 percent had residence histories of five years or longer. However, these figures are only for residents and do not report mean length of involvement for "square" game players. The undisputable point about Synanon's demography is that nearly all the individuals who initiate contact with the organization spend relatively short (as measured against an expectation of a lifetime commitment) periods of time involved with it, and a small number of individuals appear to become psychologically committed enough to the organizations and its good-works program to integrate their occupational and social lives with it and become committed to the corporate enterprise. The division between the apparently permanent and transient populations of Synanon corresponds to the division between that segment of the community which manages the corporation and directs Synanon's activities and that segment of the population which is simultaneously the staff of the corporation and the clientele for its good-works activities.

To understand further the nature of the relationship between corporate Synanon and the community, it is useful to focus on the difference between those Synanon residents who can be conceptualized as having a relatively short-term, instrumental relation with the organization and those residents who identify strongly with its mission and fill the executive and decision-making positions within the corporate structure. The vast majority of those who have had contact with Synanon would fall into the former category. Of those who have ever had contact with Synanon, relatively few have chosen to remain in residence on a semipermanent basis. Of the community's eighteen hundred residents in 1972, less than two hundred had residence histories of longer than five years. The picture is of a proportionally small core of persons who have careers tied to the conduct of Synanon's people business and good works, and a proportionally large segment of the population that eventually chooses to terminate its relationship with the Synanon corporation and the community.

There is no available scientific evidence about the consequences of temporary participation in Synanon's social and therapeutic environment. There are no data available, so far as I know, concerning the proportion of former Synanon residents who return to drug use or return to their former patterns of "neurotic, deficiency motivated" behavior. It is clear that individuals do undergo substantial change in their behavior while in residence in Synanon or while a game-club member with substantial involvement with the Synanon community. Drug users stop using drugs, and difficult people are likely to become more pleasant to get along with. If someone stays in residence or in contact with Synanon, he has no choice but to make changes of these sorts. To what extent these modifications in behavior are sustained outside of the Synanon environment cannot be answered without objective evidence.

During the year that I was a participant-observer at Synanon, I met numerous individuals in the Bay Area who are either former Synanon residents or former game-club players. I found that those who had lengthy involvement with the organization felt that their relationship with Synanon was valuable to them. The reason for leaving usually revolved around a conflict between the demands of the organization for strict conformity to its rules and the desires of the individuals to conduct any aspects of their lives differently. Conflicts were usually not about major issues, but rather over norms which considered separately would have to be classified as minor, or matters such as the degree to which a game player had integrated his life into Synanon's structure. It seems to me that I was being told, "I came to Synanon to accomplish something and needed help. I was therefore willing to do as I was told. As I gained confidence in my ability to do what I had previously doubted I could accomplish, I saw less and less reason to continue to accept all aspects of Synanon's social system."

What I was hearing made sense given what I see to be the nature of Synanon's system for producing behavior change and resocialization. The philosophical principles on which Synanon's value system is based rest on traditional American notions of individual responsibility for action, the idea of finding within oneself the strength to control one's life, and the faith that one can, in some mystical way, look within oneself and know what is right. The two writers who express these ideas and are used as references for Synanon's ideology are Ralph Waldo Emerson and Abraham Maslow. Emerson formulates these ideas in a semimystical fashion, with reference to God-given knowledge and the need for individuals to find truth within themselves and to act on the basis of that truth. Maslow writes of the self-actualized individual, who happens to possess the same general characteristics as the person Emerson sees. Although Maslow uses the vocabulary of modern psychology and Emerson the vocabulary and conceptual system of early American Puritanism, they both represent American traditions of individualism. To become more like the sort of inner-directed individual written about by Emerson and Maslow is the philosophical goal toward which Synanon residents are to direct themselves.

Synanon's operating system for producing this sort of individual is demanding and forces an individual into a position in which his actions are known to the public, and he must either successfully defend himself or change his behavior. Throughout Synanon's history the organization has been attacked for being authoritarian and demanding nearly absolute conformity from its residents. It seems to me that the core of Synanon's therapeutic system is precisely the fact that absolute demands are made on the individual. In considering Synanon's authoritarianism we must not lose sight of the substance of what is demanded. The demands are, in the main, for adherence to the highest principles of honesty, rejection of behavior regarded as undesirable by those undergoing change and by the society in general, and pursuit of perfection. Synanon offers a life-organization system intended to produce certain sorts of changes in individuals. Like most systems of resocialization, it demands conformity to the rules of the system. Unlike most therapeutic systems, Synanon offers a totally structured environment intended to support the change it demands. Resident-clients of Synanon are subject to demands for strict behavioral conformity to the rules of Synanon communities and for assent to philosophical arguments that strength comes from within them. Insofar as the system is successful, it results in persons who modify their observable behavior in socially acceptable ways and come to believe that they are in control of their actions and able to govern themselves.

That there is some essential contradiction between an authoritarian system of social control and a philosophical belief system that stresses individual responsibility is what I seem to hear from those who were at one point involved in Synanon. One might interpret their mixed feelings and decision to leave Synanon as the result of a growing belief in their abilities to control themselves, coupled with involvement in a system that does not readily provide opportunities to exercise that control. The only way to exercise control within Synanon is to become part of the core population that manages the community. If one has status in the community, one is able to participate in the decisions that organize life at Synanon. The only way

to attain status in the community is to demonstrate that one is committed to the good-works mission of the organization and is not part
of the population with a short-term, instrumental relation with
Synanon.

POSTSCRIPT

Although what I have written to this point may contain errors of
fact and of interpretation, it represents a conscious effort to carry
out the craft of sociological analysis. I was initially attracted to the
idea of what a social experiment on the scale of Synanon might
produce and to the fact that it was engaged in activities that
benefited people in desperate need of help, and I met many people
there that I liked very much. As I became more knowledgeable
about the community and the corporation I came to see an endless
conflict between the desires of individuals and the desires of the
corporation, with the corporation being vastly more powerful.

While Synanon's authoritarian power structure might be functional for an organization dedicated to helping people gain control
over some particular aspect of their lives, as the basic power structure around which to build a society in which people are to spend
their entire lives it seems to me to leave much to be desired. I came
to see Synanon as a prescriptive society in which peoples'
possibilities for action were being steadily reduced in number, and
where only those of their desires that could be shaped into
something beneficial to the corporation would be permitted. I
believe that the fundamental cause of this is that Synanon is mod-
eled along business lines and therefore at its core measures its
success in terms of growth, expansion, and organizational survival.
A business cannot readily judge either the social value of what it is
doing or the absolute quality of its product. It is too easy to use standards such as sales figures and capital worth as an index of
meaningful success.

Synanon's purpose is supposed to be the curing of drug addicts,
the creating of self-actualized people, and the creation of a model
society, any one of which is a substantial task. In seventeen years
Synanon came to define these as its aims. How well it has succeeded
in any of these tasks is a matter for debate, since the organization
seems little concerned with self-evaluation.

I came away from Synanon with the belief that it probably does some good for the people who have a transient contact with it, and that it is a business that has created a core of "company" men and women who manage it and who therefore have a considerable personal stake in its continuation—a business, not a revolution.[9]

9. This paper was prepared during the author's tenure as a Guggenheim Foundation Fellow, 1973–74.

REFERENCES

Cook, Ron. "Synanon Economics." Lecture delivered in Synanon Research University lecture series, San Francisco, 1972.

Maillet, Edward L. *Report on Research Visit to Synanon Foundation*. Fort Sam Houston, Texas: Health Care Research Division, U.S. Army Medical Field Service School, Brooke Army Medical Center, 1972.

Maslow, Abraham H. *Towards a Psychology of Being*. New York: Van Nostrand, 1962.

Ofshe, Richard; Nancy Berg; Richard Coughlin; Gregory Dolinajec; Kathleen Gerson; Avery Johnson. "Social Structure and Social Control in Synanon." *Journal of Voluntary Action Research* 3, no. 3–4 (1974).

Simon, Steven I. "The Synanon Game." Ph.D. dissertation, Harvard University, 1973.

Yablonski, Lewis. *Synanon: The Tunnel Back*. Baltimore: Penguin Books, 1967.

PART III

New Religious Movements in the Western Tradition

Among the myriad forms of new religious consciousness are some whose inspirations come from Western religious traditions. This should come as no surprise. Judaism and Christianity were themselves once new forms of religious consciousness and they, especially Christianity, have been spawning offspring in amazing variety and number ever since.

Many of these offspring have lasted only as long as the conditions that brought them into being. In American alone, it has been the experience of hundreds to flower briefly, only to die—the Oneida Perfectionists, the Shakers, the Dunkers, the House of David, the Llano Colonies, the Pillar of Fire, to mention only a few. At the same time, a remarkable number of the offshoots of traditional religion have survived and remain permanent and sometimes very vigorous fixtures on the religious landscape. Movements such as Christian Science, the Jehovah's Witnesses, the Church of Jesus Christ of the Latter-day Saints, and the Seventh-Day Adventists thrive virtually as well today as during any other time in their history.

Before now, the last groundswell of new religious consciousness in America occurred during the depression years of the 1930s. Then, as now, there was some input from Eastern religions and from sources other than traditional Western religious thought. Comparatively, however, movements grounded in Western religious traditions were considerably more prominent than in the present resurgence. Only remnants of the major depression-born movements survive, though at their height some groups—such as Father Divine's Peace Mission, the International Church of the Foursquare Gospel, I Am, and Psychiana—attracted followers in the tens of thousands.

In the religious resurgence that accompanied and survived the

*counterculture, Western religious traditions have provided once
again the seeds for the birth and growth of new religious
movements. Among the better known of the new offspring are the
Jesus People, Jews for Jesus, and Catholic Charismatic Renewal.
Compared with their depression-born counterparts whose appeal
was primarily to middle-aged and older people, these new
movements are considerably more oriented to youth. They are also
more modern in style and spirit. The new movements differ less
from past ones in the religious message they seek to convey. Once
again, the call is for a return to forgotten fundamentals rather than
for rallying to new revelations.*

*The new movements in the Western tradition studied as part of
the new religious consciousness project were the Christian World
Liberation Front, Catholic Charismatic Renewal, and the Church
of Satan. The Christian World Liberation Front is a Berkeley-
based offshoot of the Jesus movement, sharing the same theology
as that movement, but less conservative in its political outlook.
Catholic Charismatic Renewal is seen by some as a Catholic version of Pentecostalism, although the connection is disputed by
others who trace its roots to Roman Catholic sources. The movement, only a few years old, has become a force to be reckoned
with in the Roman Catholic church. San Francisco is among the
areas in which the movement has taken a substantial hold. San
Francisco's Church of Satan has generated nationwide attention as
a result of the bizarreness of its religious message and the flam-
boyance of its self-proclaimed high priest, Anton LaVey. While
the Church of Satan has not attracted a substantial number of
followers, its emergence reflects the abiding presence of the occult
in the Western religious tradition.*

*The chapters on these movements, as earlier chapters in the
volume, are not informed by a single perspective. Rather, once
again, the chapters illustrate the rich variation in outlook from
which the phenomenon of religion can be observed and interpreted. In his report on the Christian World Liberation Front
Donald Heinz affords a demonstration of the insights to be gained
from focusing attention on a movement's processes of symbolization. His chapter brings out the very different meanings that
attach in the CWLF to the figure of Jesus and the significance of
these meanings in the movement's birth, growth, and sustenance.*

*Ralph Lane adopts a more traditionally ethnographic approach
in his study of Catholic Charismatic Renewal. He seeks to afford
descriptive insight into the character of CCR through examination*

*of the unfolding of one of its principal rituals—the prayer
meeting. He also treats the movement more analytically to assess
its present course and future directions.*

*Randy Alfred's chapter on the Church of Satan is perhaps the
most unusual in the book, for the practice of witchcraft has been
studied only rarely by social scientists. Alfred is the member of our
research team who switched from covert to overt observation
midstream in his study. The reader will want to watch for the
response he obtained when he revealed his true identity.*

7

The Christian World Liberation Front

DONALD HEINZ

Ecstatic shouts of "One Way!" and index fingers pointed heaven-
ward became a part of the American consciousness with the
emergence of the Jesus movement between 1967 and 1969. Photo-
journalism, television, and Jesus buttons pinned under happy faces
in a hundred places proclaimed that something new was happening
in evangelical Christianity. By 1971 the Jesus movement was voted
the Religious News Story of the Year: *Time* and *Newsweek* rewarded it with cover stories, the *Christian Century* editorialized, and
regular fan notices appeared in *Christianity Today.* Paperback
reports began to appear, and even a few sociologists paid attention.

In Berkeley, too, the Jesus movement took hold. In April 1969
three men and their families came from Los Angeles to "make
Christ an issue" on campus, to confront political radicals with an
alternative, and to preach the gospel to the street people. They
succeeded in planting what was to become the Christian World
Liberation Front (CWLF) in the area south of the University of
California.

There was a celebrative, searching religious atmosphere, not
without its darker sides, in Berkeley at that time—perhaps not unlike that period in the Roman Empire when the civil religion was in
decay and numerous mystery religions and cults rose up to flourish.
The missionaries who founded CWLF wanted to be in the center of
a mecca that attracted so many pilgrims.

At the beginning, the small group of Christians infiltrated the
campus, especially radical student organizations, talked to students,
and befriended street people on Telegraph Avenue. Eventually,
they began to provide space where an emerging family could come

143

home to, the beginning of the ministry of the "Christian houses." When it became necessary to call themselves something for the sake of registering themselves on campus, they frankly altered the name of a popular radical group, the Third World Liberation Front.

Their presence became known through baptisms in Ludwig's Fountain in Sproul Plaza on campus, confrontations with radical student leaders, political rallies, and ever-present leaflets, posters, and announcements. With such fanfare they were able to attract a steady stream of recruits, first from the street people, then a few from campus, and eventually small numbers of talented people from around the country who wanted to be part of the work in Berkeley.

Within three months CWLF was producing a monthly newspaper, *Right On*, which has remained the cornerstone of its ministries. The best of the newspapers to come out of the Jesus movement, it has evolved in the direction of the thinking Christian and non-Christian, away from the street culture to which it originally spoke. Early on, several Christian houses were also started, a cross between Christian dormitory and commune. Subsequently, at various times in CWLF's evolution, these have been crash houses, communal homes, convenient living arrangements for those on CWLF's staff, family homes for married couples with children, who were also interested in having a few of the brothers and sisters stay with them. A ranch in northern California flourished and then passed out of usefulness; it served as a haven where new children in the Lord could get away from the hassles and temptations of Berkeley long enought to experience and grow into a Christian family.

By 1972 a street-theater group had come into being, addressing the issues of life in a low-key approach. More recently, a kind of free university has been struggling to find an audience, a style, and a structure. In addition, there have been tutoring ministries, a coffee house for Berkeley high school students, a ministry to people with problems of sexual identity, programs every summer for interns. At any one time, about thirty-five people are on CWLF "staff," functioning at subsistence-level support solicited through prayer letters to the Christian community and friends. The average longevity for staff members seems to be about two years. The number of people within the larger CWLF family at any one time varies from one hundred to two hundred.

Compared with the rest of the Jesus movement, CWLF almost from the beginning has been without flamboyant leadership, charismatic emphases, "total community" structures, and authoritarian social control. In its six-year history, the women's issue has been fought through and won (by the women), a kind of participatory democracy has replaced a more hierarchical system of elders, and a theological style has emerged that is somehow true to evangelicalism and true to Berkeley. The Bible is clearly considered the inspired Word of God, but it seems less wooden in CWLF's hands. Culture and world are dying, but there remains room for engagement and occasional affirmation. There is a loose style and few taboos. There has emerged an instinctive sympathy, almost solidarity, with most leftists causes, though not with Marxism.

CWLF has moved from a mission to the streets and campus, to a coalition of ministries, to, in 1975, a kind of church—which nevertheless retains something of all the previous stages. Now in its seventh year, CWLF seems confident about its future and secure in the form it has reached. Though vastly different from the ministry that began in April 1969, it is intact and strong and still able to recruit people to its work and family.

In describing and interpreting a particular movement there are many approaches available, as this book makes clear. The approach of this chapter is to attempt an understanding of CWLF by studying the Jesus of the movement. Who is One Way? How is Jesus symbolized within the group and to the outside? It is assumed that symbolization will be related to the social-psychological shape of the group, that the imagery of Jesus will answer the needs and experiences of those who come to adopt it. It will be demonstrated in what follows that there are several Jesuses in the group and that they mean something, individually and together, to the group and about the group.

"THE QUEST FOR THE HISTORICAL JESUS"

From the days of the New Testament people have pressed and been pressed for an answer to the question, "What do you think of Christ?" Every age, it seems, tries to get back to Jesus himself. Albert Schweitzer has chronicled the eighteenth- and nineteenth-century quest for the historical Jesus in his classic book. He describes how "each epoch found its reflection in Jesus; each individual created Him in accordance with his own character."[1] Schweitzer passionately lamented the efforts to strip Jesus, the imperious eschatological figure (Schweitzer's Jesus!), down to size:

1. Albert Schweitzer, *The Quest for the Historical Jesus* (London: A & C Black, 1911), p. 4.

Notice what they have made of the great imperious sayings of the Lord, how they have weakened down His imperative world-condemning demands upon individuals, that He might not come into conflict with our ethical ideals, and might tune His denial of the world to our acceptance of it. Many of the greatest sayings are found lying in a corner like explosive shells from which the charges have been removed. No small portion of elemental religious power needed to be drawn off from His sayings to prevent them from conflicting with our system of religious world-acceptance.[2]

Although Schweitzer's work seemed to prove a contemporary location for every "historical Jesus," his work did not settle the matter. Since its appearance, new quests for the historical Jesus have been a part of every generation. The death of God movement of the middle 1960s seemed for the moment to make the issue irrelevant, but no sooner had it appeared than some proclaimed: God is dead, long live Jesus.

By the end of the sixties a new historical location for Jesus had taken shape. The youth culture out of which the symbolizations of Jesus discussed in this paper arose looked like the following at the end of the sixties: hippies with wilted flower power, active and passive drug experimenters, burned-out radicals, children of permissive parents looking for benevolent authority, dropouts from banal Protestant churches, questers for experience and meaning, some still optimistic easy riders and eternal trippers, some in deep ambiguity or despair. The scene has been described by Marxists as the American mother country in the last throes of a decadent capitalism and collapsing empire, by Alvin Toffler as a generation suffering future shock, by Theodore Roszak as a counterculture in the making, by Philip Slater as American culture at the breaking point, by Charles Reich as the beginning of the greening of America, by Robert Jay Lifton as protean, and by Robert Bellah as one offering no direction home.[3]

The young were bewildered and challenged by confusing alternatives in matters of religion, morals, vocation, life-style, and future. They were products of affluence and sensory overload and were controlled by their influence in American life. Few could es-

2. Ibid., p 398.

3. See Alvin Toffler, *Future Shock* (New York: Random House, 1970); Theodore Roszak, *The Making of a Counter Culture* (Garden City: Doubleday, 1969); Philip Slater, *The Pursuit of Loneliness* (Boston: Beacon Press, 1970); Charles Reich, *The Greening of America* (New York: Random House, 1970); Robert Jay Lifton, "Self," in *Psychological Man in Revolution* (New York: Random House, 1969); Robert N. Bellah, "No Direction Home: Religious Aspects of the American Crisis," in *Search for the Sacred: The New Spiritual Quest*, ed. Myron Bloy, Jr. (New York: Seabury Press, 1972).

cape the conveyor belt of technology, and the whirr of the machine was in everyone's consciousness. Insufficient defenses did not permit them to settle down successfully with a schizoid world. Instead, estrangement, indifference, and depersonalization met them at home, in the culture, and at college. Some of those who looked inward after the failure of one revolution confronted equal disaster. There were no rose gardens except in regressive fantasy, or the East, or drugs.

In the East, in the human-potential movement, in astrology and the occult, in quiet alternative life-styles, in nature and diet, many thought they saw a new way. The culture did not lack hope and possibility and visions of a new commonwealth—or at least a subterranean network of alternatives. One of the answers people found was Jesus.

Perhaps inevitably, hippies on the West Coast rediscovered Jesus as a funky character to groove on. It was obvious to them, as it had been to David Friedrich Strauss when he wrote his epochal *Life of Jesus* in 1835, that the accretions of church history and doctrine would have to be stripped away. Since they were people committed to experiencing everything, they began experiencing Jesus too. The mystery of his person, as Schweitzer had written, was always at hand in the culture, and beckoning anyone interested to thoughtful meditation. Jesus was becoming fascinating again, also in the counterculture.

By the late 1960s Jesus was "in." Christian publications and religious hucksters, the latter before the former, soon caught on. There appeared Jesus posters, sweatshirts, bumper stickers, watches, jockey shorts, and bikinis. There was "gold at the top of Jacob's ladder."[4] Eventually there were Surfers for Jesus, Skiers for Jesus, Karate for Jesus, and Ham Radio for Jesus.

The emergence of the figure of Jesus, then, became a central fact in one kind of religious experience in the late sixties. It was a fact so clear that the movement which grew up around that experience was quickly dubbed the Jesus movement. The people who came to Berkeley as missionaries and founded CWLF were ready to take that interest in Jesus and redirect it to the Jesus in whom they believed.

The brothers and sisters of CWLF tend to assume that a direct return to the Jesus of the New Testament is possible and necessary. New converts discover that the Bible is thought to be God's re-

4. Ronald M. Enroth, Edward E. Erickson, Jr., C. Breckinridge Peters, *The Jesus People* (Grand Rapids: Eerdmans, 1972), p. 154.

vealed Word, uniquely and verbally inspired. Jesus is the divine
Son reliably revealed in the New Testament. The Bible tells all one
needs to know, and the Jesus who the twentieth-century believer
knows in his heart is believed to be this very Jesus of the Bible.

The return to the New Testament has often been linked with a
move away from something else—priests, the church, the vagaries
of current theology, factionalism. The cry "Back to the sources!"
may arise in any age or circle of people who are distressed, deprived, unchallenged, or unhelped by whatever has gone immediately before. To go back far enough is to rediscover life, certainty,
joy, purity, the fountain of youth. Such a cry connects to the
nostalgia currently engulfing America or to the good old days every
age tries desperately to remember.

In the CWLF, this Jesus of the Bible legitimates a divorce from
the past. One long-time member reflects bitterly on her Lutheran
upbringing: "If they knew all this that I have come to know, why
didn't they tell me? If they didn't know it, what is their excuse?"
The Jesus of the Holy Dependable Book is also counted on as a
dependable Deliverer, one who with power and authority rescues
from bondage, drug addiction, meaningless sexual quests, acute
personal dilemmas, anomie. He promises and delivers new life,
meaning, purpose, joy, and ultimately eternal life in heaven. To
read the pages of the New Testament with the glasses of one's own
recent experience and now suddenly answered questions is to see
that my Jesus and the Jesus of the Bible are one.

But the Jesus of the Bible is complex, and in the CWLF the
oneness just referred to is achieved in more than one way. Different
symbolizations of Jesus are held simultaneously by the group's
members; but in the ebb and flow of the movement's evolution,
particular symbols have been ascendent or descendent at different
points in time. The changes are a reflection of structural changes in
the life of the movement as well as of variation in the composition
of members and of the needs that they bring to and get resolved by
their membership.

In what follows, there is an attempt to understand CWLF
through an encounter with its symbolizations of Jesus. The symbolizations that are focused on emerged from nearly two years
which I spent with CWLF as a participant-observer. I have tried to
describe the nature of each symbolization and its origin and evolution in the group. I have also sought to convey what is being rejected and what affirmed through particular symbolizations and to
afford a sense of how the different symbols function in the life of the
group and in the lives of the members.

JESUS THE ALTERNATIVE

The provision of alternatives was a sine qua non of many of the innovations spawned by the counterculture: radical politics, free schools, communes, food conspiracies, encounter groups, humanistic psychology, Esalen, body awareness, primal screams, to name only a few. Paralleling these developments, there emerged in evangelical Christian circles a kind of utilitarian evangelism, which touted the Biblical Jesus as being a far more effective alternative than anything else. In the early church Jesus was often described as the radical Alternative—the difference between light and darkness. Such symbolization, newly discovered, became of central importance to the Jesus movement in general and to the CWLF in particular.

CWLF especially attracts people solid in their Christian faith but perplexed about their Christian identity. The non-middle-class Jesus of the CWLF looked like considerably better news than the carefully controlled gospel they had heard all their lives. Here was an alternative they were hungry for—authenticity in commitment and life-style. To Jack, a new seminary graduate, it looked like a new frontier for real theological work. To Frank, it was a chance to offer his creative gifts in an accepting atmosphere, unencumbered by all the rules of an evangelical youth organization. To David, it was a chance to write, create, and lead in ways his Brethren church would not tolerate. To Elizabeth, it was a chance to let living in Berkeley be the test of her Christianity.

Jesus the Alternative was also a symbol for those who arrived at CWLF through other than Christian channels. A burned-out radical named Susan, a convert to CWLF, saw Jesus as a love alternative to hate tripping. For a woman heroin dealer in her thirty's, Jesus was an alternative to pushing, living out of wedlock, and occasionally losing her two small children. For a macho agnostic brother named Pedro, Jesus meant the end of pointless wanderings.

The symbolization of Jesus the Alternative was at once a source of recruitment to CWLF and a symbol capable of taking members of the group in a variety of directions. For some, simply finding the way produced utter relief and immediate closure. Social-psychological complexity is wiped away. The devil is the answer to the problem of evil. Social critique and social understanding are unnecessary. Such a Jesus is the answer to loneliness, insecurity, and self-doubt. The good news of salvation is elevated and solidified as a total and complete faith. This first rush of salvation prematurely creates a Jesus who is a totem of absolute, unwavering certainty, a

Jesus symbolizing more a rejection of the past than an affirmation of the future.

For others, the symbolization of Jesus the Alternative is an affirmation of a new future, but of the simplest kind. The new believer takes the role of wide-eyed perceiver, receiver, and sharer of Truth. "If you're saved and you know it, clap your hands." This direction might have as its motto, "First and last Jesus." If the apostle Paul had said, "I am determined to know nothing but Christ the Crucified," these joyful believers seem to be saying, "I am determined to know nothing."

But most in CWLF come to say, "First Jesus and then— whatever." A new way of confronting and responding to the world and to themselves grows out of their new evangelical faith and the context in which it has been nourished. Bryan begins to discover the Lord "handing me my problems back to deal with them." Susan goes back to radical politics. Joyce, once a schoolmarmish evangelical, becomes involved in prison ministry and reform. Carolyn, a gentle southern belle exuding Jesus songs when she first came to CWLF, is now engaged in feminist political action and may leave CWLF to devote herself wholly to such a ministry. A famous slogan in the Jesus movement goes: "After Jesus everything else is just toothpaste." These CWLFers might say instead, "Before Jesus everything was just toothpaste." They are now capable of an excitement about life and a vigorous engagement of reality which sees all creation waking up for the first time to rebirth. Theirs is not a defensive alternative but a free and affirming one.

The toothpaste slogan is scarcely ever mentioned today in CWLF, though occasionally it may be blurted out as a fond recollection of an earlier naivete the group may be in danger of losing. What factors could account for this change? For one, the group's straining toward greater theological maturity (read inclusiveness) and an enriching of the symbolization of Jesus; for another, the group's growth in maturity and sophistication sparked by the existence among its members of persons with strong backgrounds in higher education for whom a Jesus narrowly sectarian or legalistic is not tolerable. The shape of the Berkeley situation within which CWLF is not only committed to minister but to which it is greatly attracted is also a source of change. People who tune a message to their listeners may begin to hear the message differently themselves. The words that St. Luke reports the Apostle Paul as saying to the men of Athens sound similarly tuned to the situation of the preacher's listeners.

Nevertheless, a kind of detour in the evolution of this symbolization from a narrow one way to an inclusive Christology is the
apparent resolution of many to want to "stop the world" at the location of the "hour I first believed." For them Jesus the Alternative
remains a way to absolutize a countercultural life-style, with its
celebration of spontaneity and cultivation of improvisation as a permanent way of living. When a small group of CWLF leaders
returned in 1973 from a three-week tour sharing with Christians
around the country what God was doing in Berkeley, one could hear
a near smugness in the joy with which they returned to the true
authenticity of Berkeley. Their mission seemed to have been a
greening of the churches, which meant in part: Become more like
us. The suspicion that the counterculture (and not Jesus) might
have become the real alternative led one CWLF couple to return to
the South, seeking there to raise a family in the kind of tradition
they still loved and to use their talents within the straight church.

The symbolization of Jesus the Alternative has been carried
farthest by only a few. They are talking and writing about an
authentic "third way" for dealing with reality, the world, and the
self. Sharon has taken *Right On* from the immediate reality of
CWLF in her attempt to make it a newspaper of such a third way.
David left CWLF to become a teacher in a Brethren seminary and
dreams of founding a journal that will represent such a way to
would-be radical Christians. The One Way that these voices express
is open and engaging; it is the One Way of people who have been
around and who have felt themselves pulled by Jesus the Alternative to a fresh, satisfying answer, one they argue with vigor.

JESUS THE EXPERIENCE

The counterculture's revolt against the academic establishment has
been spurred, in part, by the call for experience. Professors without
the credentials of experience have been belittled. In the drug
culture, in experimental life-styles, in the evolution and development of alternative institutions, and in their interpersonal relationships, the young sought and insisted on experience. The vacuity of
so much liberal Protestant piety could not possibly have made a
connection with such a mentality, but the warm religiosity of many
of the evangelical missionaries was instantly understood by many of
the young.

Billy Graham has called the demand for an experience with Jesus
Christ a primary characteristic of the Jesus movement. A *Christian*

Century editorial called the movement's Jesus "a fresh green growth in a sere landscape, a lift from the boredom in a bland conservative-and-liberal church, a voice of authority and a beckoning hint of love in a world where the young seek simplicity and innocence."[5] The Christian evangelists who came together in settings out of which the Jesus movement arose were devotees of "heart religion." The direct experience of Jesus in one's heart and life is also an omnipresent element in the Christianity of the CWLF.

"God, I'm offering you my life, such as it is. If you want it, if you are out there, show yourself to me. Let me feel you moving in my life now." Such a prayer has been learned and prayed by most of the brothers and sisters who have come into CWLF. Feeling one's heart warmed by the "God who is there," sensing that the Person on the other end of the line has not hung up, experiencing a personal relationship with the Father—all come with breathtaking power in the discovery that they are coming true for oneself.

Experiencing Jesus in the CWLF means many things. For some it is a conversion. For some it is a startling disconfirmation of all their previous experiences with churches. For some who have adopted a countercultural world view and for those whose desperation has emptied them emotionally, the experience of Jesus offers authenticity and trustworthiness. The potential member of the Forever Family is taught to expect the experience, particularly the experience of God's being your friend, of your being important to him, of your coming into his plan and design, of starting anew with someone you can depend on.

For those in the CWLF, Jesus the experience is the preeminent reality in their new life and faith. Jesus is someone to relate to, to feel in one's heart, to talk to, and to expect a response from. This experience of Jesus is a fact of CWLF's religious life that warms and unites the whole group. The kind of ecstatic cheekiness and wide-eyed wonder at what the Lord is doing, observable at many Monday night family meetings, signals that Jesus the experience is being worshipped and praised and passed around the community. The blissful smiles belong to those returning again to their own conversion experience or staying high on the testimony of others. The emotional highs, the rapturous joy, the ecstatic assurance does not, in CWLF, move to the unique experience of a bodily healing. No one in the community has been taught to expect that kind of experience, though anyone can discover it at one of CWLF's competitors, Resurrection City's Night of Miracles, just down the street.

5. *Christian Century*, editorial, June 23, 1971.

In CWLF, Jesus the Experience is shaped in communal worship, in individual witness to those still searching, and in the response to times of doubt, uncertainty, and lack of direction.

It has been no small task to keep this Jesus alive as CWLF has become more and more involved in nonevangelistic ministries and has been evangelizing less on the streets than in the early years. Complaints are often heard these days that the old excitement and spontaneity and life and enthusiastic sharing that characterized the movement's beginnings are no longer as much in evidence as they used to be. Still, Jesus the Experience is always the baseline to which one returns, the wellspring to which one goes back for nourishment, the common denominator that binds the group together.

The move into a newspaper, into street theater, into engagement with competing religions, into political involvement has required more than Jesus the Experience, however. When a new ministry is being launched, when Transcendental Meditation is being exposed as a false religion, when the community is struggling with the women's question, when CWLF is trying to find an identity as church, then other symbolizations are required.

JESUS IS ONE OF US

Many early observers of the Jesus movement labeled it "hippies with religion." The new Jesus was revolutionary, mellow, and antiestablishment. He practiced wine making and food distribution without a license and encouraged communal living. He was rejected by the religious professionals, a deviant discovered and embraced by deviants.

The Jesus who is one of us is a symbol adopted by CWLF followers early in the group's history, as is reflected in the following full page notice which appeared in the second issue of the CWLF newspaper, *Right On.*

REWARD

Jesus. Alias: the Messiah, Son of God, King of Kings, Lord of Lords, Prince of Peace, etc.

Notorious Leader of a world-wide liberation movement.

Wanted for the following charges:

Practicing medicine and distributing food without a license.

Interfering with businessmen in the Temple.

Associating with known criminals, radicals, subversives, prostitutes, and street people.

Claiming to have authority to make people God's children.

Appearance: Unknown. Rumored to have no regard for conventional dress standards.

Hangs around slum areas, few rich friends, often sneaks out into the desert.
Has a group of devoted followers, formerly known as apostles, now called
    freemen (from his saying, You will know the truth and the truth shall set
    you free.)
Beware—This man is extremely dangerous. His insidiously inflammatory
    message is particularly effective with young people who haven't been
    taught to ignore him yet. He changes men and sets them free.

WARNING: HE IS STILL AT LARGE!

This text, in a slightly different version, has appeared before in
America's religious history. In this form, it excited attention once
again, and it was reprinted over and over again in evangelical and
other religious periodicals throughout the world.

The symbolization of Jesus as one of us, like the other symbols
discussed here, was a magnet that attracted followers to CWLF.
"Here," reports Jerry, a former Haight-Ashbury resident who came
to Berkeley a year after CWLF had begun, "God showed me a
group of hip Christians. Here was a little group in Berkeley—excited, overflowing, full of joy and love. It was thrilling, people of my
own type, long hairs, so exciting to see that God is not abandoning
the hip world. I had such a burden for the hip scene."

The Jesus who is one of us resonated with every attempt to justify
one's deviant path, to feel worthwhile, to celebrate what others reject, and somehow, at the same time, to pay whatever debts to majority goodness and truth are still nagging. It was also unimaginably
good news for those whose guilts or pasts seemed too much to bear.
This Jesus was deliverance and salvation, theological legitimation
and approval. Outside evangelical control, such a Jesus could also
be a Weatherman, black, bisexual, Zen, honest to God, secular, a
clown, a devotee of the Old Gnosis against the scientific establishment.

This imagery of Jesus was enough to put CWLF at odds with the
straight churches. Not long after Jack Sparks began what was to
become CWLF, one of his supporters warned him that he was "losing touch with the good people of America." But it was of immense
importance, especially in the early years of CWLF, for its followers
to know that Jesus was not middle class. To have freshly stolen him
back from the churches, where he had been kept for years, was a
major cause of group cohesion and strength. To celebrate this Jesus
was to celebrate oneself. He takes us as his own. We take him as our
own. He is a song of ourselves—a trophy captured in the contest
over which is the real "sacred canopy," a rival altar set up in the
face of the religious establishment.

This symbolization of Jesus has not been abandoned as CWLF has matured, but now the concentration is more on our being one of Christ's than on his being one of us. The shift is a sign that CWLF is becoming more sure of itself, that its community's boundaries are becoming more certain, and that the group is responding to a larger Jesus.

JESUS IS COMING SOON

The expectation of Jesus' return has always been strong among the religious groups of the West who reject the world. For them the new community is an ark to get them through the raging waters engulfing a condemned world. Apocalyptic literature and preachers have always arisen in times of distress and hopelessness. The apocalyptist calls down not only judgment on an evil world, but God himself. The lively hope of an imminent return provides the comfort and strength to get through the present.

As in movements before it, prophecy and apocalypse have been integral to the Jesus movement. Prophecy has come to mean the prediction of the future, especially the future just prior to the return of Christ. Apocalyptic refers to that genre of literature and expectation devoted to mysterious allusions to and signs of the last days of world history. It is filled with an often frenzied and impatient expectation that God will act soon to deliver his people from terrible circumstances.

Jesus songs, Jesus rallies, and Jesus preaching are filled with the Jesus who is coming soon. "Maranatha," an Aramaic expression the early church used, meaning "Our Lord come," has been used in songs and slogans and has even become the name of a publishing, recording, and promoting outlet for the Jesus movement. A popular Jesus ballad sung by Maranatha's "Love Song" singing group goes like this:

Chorus: Maranatha! Maranatha! The Master's coming home.
We must prepare our hearts so we can meet him.
Maranatha! Maranatha! The Lord is coming back.
We must be filled with love to truly greet him.

The Master went away from us two thousand years ago.
He left us with his promise to return—
How my heart does long for him, I miss the Master so,
I must keep the faith and let the fire burn.

He left this world a tragedy, He let them take his life.
He sacrificed his blood on his own choice.

When he returns in glory he'll come to claim his flock.
The Master loves the ones who know his voice.

The rapturous assurance that Jesus is coming soon is a substitute for the future. The only future is the return of Jesus. "It won't make a bit of difference if Jesus is coming back tomorrow, will it?" If Jesus is a substitute for the future, he can also be a deliverer from the present. Sometimes it is a deliverance one calmly waits for, sometimes a deliverance preached with frenzy. The excitement of apocalyptic certainty may be not unlike that of some radicals who thought a new America was aborning in Chicago, 1968, and that they were the midwives: "As radicals saw matters, America in June was shuddering at the epicenter of the imperialist world. America's trouble excited them. It whipped their resolve and tickled their imagination with the persistent fantasy of revolution. When the radicals went to Chicago, they really thought that they might soon be contesting for control of the United States government."[6] That excitement alternated with despair, "a despair that suggested we were the first generation that could imagine declining its bid to inherit the earth."[7]

The alternative to that kind of revolution is that ultimate emigration, apocalypse. Such an emigration was already practiced in the drug culture by those who dropped out of the prevailing definitions of reality and quietly or boisterously rejoiced in the truth of their own deviance. To some Jesus people it looked as if the revolution of the radicals had failed and the Lord himself was on the way.

In the CWLF, the expectation of a literal second coming of Christ is a part of the Biblical message which is proclaimed and from which comfort, hope, and assurance are drawn. But, unlike some parts of the Jesus movement, the symbolization of Jesus as coming soon has never made engagement with this world irrelevant. Though a returning Christ is never absent from proclamation and piety, the symbolization is there as a source of strength, not as a rationale for copping out. A Jesus who makes tomorrow irrelevant interferes with the printer's deadline for *Right On*. The Jesus who may open up God's largesse by the end of the month distracts from the personal responsibility the elders are trying to inculcate in the new babes in the Lord. Of course, that need not be so. Some rural Jesus communes that think of little else other than the imminent

6. Roger Kahn, "The Collapse of SDS," in *Smiling Through the Apocalypse*, an *Esquire* anthology, compiled by Harold Hayes (New York: McCall Publishing Company, 1969), p. 624.

7. Jacob Brackman, "My Generation," ibid., p. 637.

return of Jesus vest enormous amounts of energy and hard work getting ready for him. In the CWLF, however, a literal return of Christ is only one important part of the Christian apologetic and philosophy of life which is proposed as an alternative to those that presently prevail. At the same time, the expectation of the return never has become a substitute for apologetics or discipleship or attempts to live out a Christian life-style in ways that catch the world's attention.

OTHER SYMBOLS

Not all of the symbols of the Jesus movement or of the CWLF are lodged in the person of Jesus. The movement itself and one's being a part of it assume additional symbolizations, most notably that one has "come home" again. Homecoming is a powerful image. George McGovern in 1972 wanted to utilize its evocative power in his campaign slogan, "Come Home America."

What is this homecoming? After long and tortuous wanderings, after crushed hopes and burnt-out lives, suddenly there is the discovery of peace, comfort, healing, security, rest, salvation. You ease tiredly down on the bed and take off the heavy shoes with the dust of the road, a brother runs for a cold glass of water, you sleep soundly, and the family table is set when you awake. Many a brother or sister has experienced exactly this when led up to CWLF's Dwight House, three blocks and a million miles from Telegraph Avenue in Berkeley.

Whence the image of homecoming? It is in the unconscious of humankind, in old revival hymns, in countless testimonies. Sometimes it is a regressive if not escapist longing for fusion. Sometimes it may symbolize a return to values and ideals long since rejected but now reaffirmed as a way out of present dilemmas. It is the hope that beginnings may rejuvenate us as we struggle toward ends.

For most in CWLF, this home is a base of operations, a safe house from which to sally forth against the world, a place of meaning and rearmament from which one goes to engage the culture, a source of identity. "Now that I know who I am I can do what needs to be done." When Charlie found the time and space to be who he was, he began using his time in street theater. When Clancy came home and stayed awhile, he ventured out as filmmaker, all-purpose handyman, political radical, and general hard worker. David and Sharon developed an understanding of themselves in terms of radical Christianity and launched effective lives writing and teaching.

Depending on when you arrive in CWLF's history or the shape of your needs, home was where you were comforted or challenged. Sometimes CWLF was a little flock in a chaotic city. If you left home briefly, it was only to pull back home a few others still left in the streets. Sometimes CWLF was a center for creative ministries. Home was where you returned at night, where you did the necessary homework in preparation for your real work in the world. For some in CWLF, especially those most sure of their Christian identity, home was not a primary locating reference at all. You visited home while in the service of your ministry, responding to the call of a somewhat different Jesus—to teach, to lead prayer, to put out a paper, to provide some artwork, to supervise a Christian house.

CWLF was also, especially early in its history, a symbol of being part of something larger than oneself. Being part of a powerful movement is important if not essential for any true believer. The sense of a large "Movement" (always capitalized and referred to without adjective by leftists) had already been significant for recruiting young radicals. And evangelicals traced their entire history to revival movements and movements of the Spirit. The new believer would like to believe he is not alone.

People leaving behind a losing movement (hippies and drugs) found in CWLF a successful and powerful means of rejecting the past. In their new life CWLF functioned to keep them thinking big, to hold discouragement and frustration at bay, to fire their enthusiasm. God looked to be doing something big in Berkeley; how fortunate they were to be part of it. When the day for movements passed in Berkeley, this symbolization lost some of its power. Yet even now the news of what God is doing all over the country is often an exciting and faith-strengthening ingredient in family worship, as brothers and sisters traveling through Berkeley come to share the news. Probably the early church, too, was excited to be a part of the movement of the Spirit described in the Book of Acts.

CONCLUSIONS

While much of the Jesus movement seems to have fixed on symbols that lead to closure, blissed-out rapture, and introversion, CWLF and some other offshoots of the Jesus movement have seen those symbols decline. In their place is a Jesus who calls to creative, culture-engaging ministries, to deeper theological studies, and to the attempt, still halting, to fashion a Christian philosophy and life-style that will be a vigorous third way, even if only a remnant is committed to it. The latter is an attempt audacious, promising, and easily derailed.

It is one thing to fix on a Jesus whose dimensions and underpin-nings are not likely to lead the group into disintegration; CWLF seems to have accomplished that. It is another to fix on a Jesus who does not carry the movement so rapidly or thoughtlessly into in-stitutionalization that all the original charisma is lost and there simply occurs another splinter in the sectarian establishment. CWLF seems to be winning that battle, though it remains to be seen whether its original charisma will have been tied to the streets and to the atmosphere of the late sixties in which the Jesus move-ment first arose. If it was, then all its presently creative ministries and bold attempts may flounder—either because insufficient new recruits are found or because many will leave to find a better theology or to reject, perhaps unconsciously, one that is no longer nourishing.

But it would be no small accomplishment were the group, and others like it, to fix on a Jesus who could lead to a creative "third way," who could produce a remnant whose attractive introversion would be a beacon to the larger society. May we expect a creative breakthrough, inducements to or proleptic anticipations of societal change, *new* religious consciousness? Probably not. There are two reasons, one in the nature of the group, the other in the symbols chosen.

CWLF has drawn too few of the elite of the youth culture, too few of those potential leaders who have experienced the present situation most deeply, given themselves to visions, and who possess the creativity, intellect, sensitivity, charismatic authority, and effec-tive articulation to lead others, inspire change, and require or produce the kind of symbolization likely to evoke change and new consciousness. (It is likely that those few in the Jesus movement who fit the above description have moved on in their Christian con-sciousness; and if so, the movement will not have been without its effect.)

Within CWLF some have not been able to transcend the narrowness of vision that too often has characterized evangelicals and certainly fundamentalists. Some have allowed an early closure to keep their vision of Jesus from expanding, a closure born of the ecstasy of sudden deliverance. They came too soon; the world's climax is no responsibility of theirs. That relationship is severed.

One may say that theological conservatives are not likely to take responsibility for the world in the way liberals have done. That has saved them from the kinds of rationalizations liberals use to excuse their acculturation. But it has also excused them from the heavy weight of concern for constructing a theology that will never let the world out of its sight. (Of course, the intense desire to convert the whole world may be the evangelical answer to this charge.) In Ernst Troeltsch's terms, they have never committed themselves to the new "completion" in the world of that radical Gospel which has transformed them personally.

Yet this may overstate the case. To underestimate the value of remnants erecting small tents outside the sacred canopy, to refuse to grant visionary sectarian communities (there are some) the powerful role that secular utopianism has often played, is to join the liberal bias against introversionist communities. (Recently Protestant mainline theologians have been talking about how minority communities and actions can anticipate the Kingdom, foreshadow the visionary commonwealth when God will rule.) Some in CWLF want to develop such remnant communities. As yet the peaks are too low to signal the way to others, to afford significant new landmarks on the road to change and new consciousness—or the Kingdom of God.

What about the symbolization itself? There has been little attention to Jesus the Logos, the one the second-century church fathers with courage and flair saw infusing all culture and ideas. Jesus the Alternative still lacks Exodus or sociological dimensions, although CWLF itself is instinctively leftist and politically active. The corporate consciousness of the prophets and of Pauline theology is absent. There is, in addition, that literalism inherited from fundamentalism and much of evangelicalism which reduces the power of symbols. Until recently, there was little ecclesiology, and some of those most committed to an Anabaptist remnant community have been least ready to commit themselves to the emerging shape of CWLF as a church. There is, on a personal scale, some of the "presocialism" in the CWLF community which Henri Desrosche thought he saw in the American Shakers.[8]

If CWLF should succeed in recalling and embodying the strengths of the intentional community, in living visibly and undefensively outside the system, in discovering and symbolizing a Christ ready to lead in such endeavors, great things could yet

8. Henri Desroche, *The American Shakers: From Neo-Christianity to Presocialism* (Amherst: University of Massachusetts Press, 1971).

happen. There are seeds in the old root cellars of the church waiting to be replanted and mutations yet to occur. If the group feels called to look, to work, to think and dream hard enough, to strain after the largesse of the God behind its symbolizations . . . alas, that does not seem too likely.

8

Catholic Charismatic Renewal

RALPH LANE, JR.

THE BEGINNINGS

The Catholic Charismatic Renewal (CCR)—or Catholic Pentecostal movement, as it was originally known—traces its origin in the United States to events in the early part of 1967 at Duquesne University in Pittsburgh, Pennsylvania. It was reported that two young lay members of the theology faculty at that institution were filled with the Holy Spirit after having prayed with and for each other and after having made contact with and attending a prayer meeting of a Protestant neo-Pentecostal group in Pittsburgh. Edward O'Connor, noting that Duquesne is conducted, "appropriately enough, by the Holy Ghost Fathers," relates that the two faculty members had made a pact with each other in the spring of 1966 to pray for each other "that they might be filled with the gifts of the Holy Spirit, and they agreed to recite daily the hymn . . . [which begins] Come, thou Holy Spirit, come!" Until then they had been engaged in a variety of religious endeavors that left them disappointed, since "it struck them that they did not seem to have the ability to proclaim the gospel with power as the early Christians had done."[1]

They were faithful to the pact from spring 1966 until the singular experience in January 1967, when they were filled with the Holy Spirit and received the gift of tongues and other charisms. One cannot explain why these particular individuals at that time and place should have had the kind of experience reported—a sociologist has

1. *The Pentecostal Movement*, p. 14. (For publishing data on the titles in the footnotes, see the references at the end of the chapter.)

neither the appropriate psychological data nor insights into the workings of the Holy Spirit even for conjecture. Nevertheless, the rapidity and extent of the spread of the charismatic movement would seem to provide a link to more general and widely repeated events that are amenable to sociological analysis.

By February 1967 twenty faculty and students at Duquesne had formed a prayer group and were involved in charismatic activities, following the lead of the two original members. Within a month the activities had spread to Notre Dame, Indiana, where many of the faculty participants from Duquesne had done graduate work and where they maintained links through networks of friendship. Similarly, it spread also in those early weeks and months to Michigan State in East Lansing and later to the University of Michigan in Ann Arbor by way of this same network of mutual background and interests. By mid-April stories of what was taking place were appearing in local papers and in the *National Catholic Reporter*. *Time, Newsweek,* and *Life* sent correspondents to investigate, although, in O'Connor's rueful phrase, they apparently did not find the story "important enough to carry."[2]

The movement has grown spectacularly since the spring of 1967. From all accounts, the way in which it spreads seems everywhere the same as that observed in the San Francisco Bay Area, where the research for this study was undertaken. Lay persons who had been at Notre Dame as students and had been in prayer groups there moved to the Bay Area in 1969. They maintained contact with each other, continuing to pray together and introducing new friends to weekly prayer sessions. By the summer of 1970 they were able to establish a central weekly prayer meeting on the campus of the University of San Francisco, a Jesuit institution. Word spread rapidly of the activities, attracting more and more recruits. As at the earlier locations, first the religious and later the secular local press provided relatively "sympathetic" coverage. This, in turn, brought more recruits, and eventually the number of groups increased. Since "membership" is variously defined and there is no rigid organizational structure to which an accounting of members must be made, claims concerning size vary. Nevertheless, by 1973 it seemed likely that the movement had attracted well over a hundred thousand recruits in the United States and had spread to more than two dozen foreign countries. A firmer indicator of the accelerated growth rate is given by attendance figures for the annual conventions at the University of Notre Dame in South Bend, Indiana. At

2. Ibid., p. 71.

the first such weekend meeting in 1967 there were ninety persons and at the fourth conference in 1970 there were about fourteen hundred; by 1972 the number had reached ten thousand and in 1973 more than twenty thousand.

Before attempting to account for this spread in sociological terms, it might be well to describe the way in which the Catholic Charismatic Renewal actually functions. We shall look first at the prayer meeting and related activities and then at the organization of the movement as a whole. We can then return to the task of understanding the social context in which it has taken place.

THE PRAYER MEETING

Prayer meetings invoking the Holy Spirit were held three or four times weekly on the Notre Dame campus until the end of the academic year in May 1967, with as many as two hundred persons attending, according to O'Connor's account. The atmosphere of those meetings, the types of activities, and the themes that predominated appear to be prototypes for the prayer meetings held weekly by the hundreds of local branches of the CCR. The spiritual experience and expressions of prayer meetings are distinct from modes traditional among Catholics before Vatican II and to a large extent after. The prayer meeting has become the meaningful badge of identification for CCR participants.[3] For the recruit it is usually the first point of contact with Catholic Pentecostalism in action. The prayer meeting is where the recruit learns how to and the full-fledged participant is able to give expression to the special modes characteristic of the Catholic Pentecostals—generally the charisms or gifts of the Holy Spirit, but other inspired activities as well.

In the traditional setting for collective prayer, whether at Mass or at any of the special devotions such as recitation of the Rosary, ritual expression is emphasized more or less as an end in itself. Whatever efficacy such prayer might have for the individual in the long run, there is never the expectation of supernatural presence here and now. The Pentecostal prayer group, in sharp contrast, puts a premium on the feeling or experiential dimension. This feeling may be very generalized, especially for the neophyte, expressing itself in such phrases as these: "Something very different is happening here that I can't explain," or, "You just know that God [or the

3. The description of the prayer meeting and related activities is based on personal observation of a relatively large prayer group (200 to 300 participants) which meets every Saturday night as what has become the San Francisco Bay Area regional center of the CCR.

Lord, or the Spirit] is here," or, "I can feel him." As the experience is repeated, however, feelings become increasingly specific both in interior disposition and form of manifestation. Thus, some participants begin to report a new sense of tranquility or of joy, or a release from tensions, a relaxation because they have given themselves over to the Lord. They relate having the experience of knowing and of being guided by the Spirit. The ultimate goal in the development of the interior disposition is Baptism in the Holy Spirit. This is not expected to happen to the solitary individual as it happened to some mystics or contemplatives of the past. Rather, it is generated from or induced by the prayer-meeting dynamics and is, in turn, recognized as legitimate or authentic by fellow participants in the group.

There is no specific empirical test of when one has received the Baptism in the Holy Spirit. Among the participants there is an ambiguity (akin to what we are told being "in love" is like) concerning the peace and joy one is expected to experience. One is assured that it will be thoroughly recognizable when it comes along. Nevertheless, the individual is not simply set adrift to arrive at the Baptism in the Spirit by himself without any indicators. The initiated will pray with or over the recruit who has indicated a willingness to seek the Baptism, and will sometimes lay on hands. The recruit's progressive receptivity to these reassuring prayers and gestures is a tangible sign to him and to the group that he is moving toward the Baptism. Virginia Hine lays stress, correctly it seems, on the transformation of personal orientation, the "before" and "after" feeling, which is reported by those who have received the Baptism.[4] From the perspective of the movement, it is functional insofar as it signifies commitment both ideologically and in terms of interaction with others within the group. The inner joy and peace one feels eventuates in greater love and trust of one's fellow Pentecostals. An important feature of the prayer meetings is this mutual rapport and support. Participants often smile at one another in a relaxed camaraderie, giving evidence of the peace they feel in each other's presence.

On the reception of the Spirit one or another of the charisms or gifts of the Holy Spirit is generally manifested by the individual, leaving no doubt in anyone's mind that the person has received the Spirit. These are not viewed as absolutely necessary accompaniments, but presumably they would not normally occur unless the Baptism had been received at or near the same time. Apparently, it

4. "Pentecostal Glossolalia: Toward a Functional Interpretation."

would be highly unusual if at least one gift was not received, for it is the exercise of these gifts at prayer meetings that sets the Pentecostal off from other modes of religious expression.

The most usual or frequent gift is that of tongues, or glossolalia. The vocalizations themselves are linguistically unintelligible or un-communicative. They take on a pattern unique to the individual, although groups apparently have fixed ranges of expression. Furthermore, all glossolalia has recognizable phonetic features that cross cultural lines. Altered mental or emotional states, before, dur-ing, or after the vocalizations, are commonplace. Here again the in-tensity or visibility of such behaviors is apparently patterned by the group. They may range from extremes of involuntary motor activity to trance to a relatively calm state in which the speaker lapses into glossolalia more or less at will. The CCR, however, tends to dis-courage emotional displays, which it associates with more fun-damentalist Protestant groups. Virginia Hine points out that glossolalia can be a "bridge-burning" act, which symbolizes one's commitment to the movement in a way that all can see and which accompanies the personal reorientation along the lines of the Pentecostal movement rather than those of non-Pentecostal reli-gious commitment.[5] Hine and Felicitas Goodman agree that these are learned behaviors.[6] The interactive context in which they are learned is the prayer meeting itself, which we shall now examine.

When persons come to a prayer meeting for the first time, they are given an orientation lecture beforehand in a room set aside for that purpose. In keeping with the relatively low-key atmosphere of the CCR, in contrast to the more enthusiastic and earlier Protestant Pentecostals, the leaders of the orientation meeting do not try to sell the movement. They stress the normality of what will take place in the prayer meeting that is to follow; and most important in terms of recruiting pitches, they stress the normality of the skepticism that newcomers feel, a skepticism that they, the leaders, had themselves felt. The idea is implanted that the curiosity that flows from the skepticism may, itself, be a sign that God wants the newcomer there.

The normality the leaders try to establish is not only psy-chological. Frequent references to biblical passages that recount the first Pentecost and to those that refer to the works of the Holy Spirit help to establish the legitimacy of the CCR within the Roman Catholic church. The citations are all more or less familiar, so that

5. Ibid., p. 224
6. See their articles on the subject of glossolalia in the *Journal for the Scientific Study of Religion*, fall 1969.

the newcomer is not made to feel that he is trespassing in a foreign country. Mention of Pope John XXIII and his aspiration for a new Pentecost makes the CCR appear to be not just a return to the past, to the early days of the church, but a genuine renewal. There is a preference for referring to the movement as Charismatic Renewal rather than Pentecostal. The former label gives it a currency much more appealing to middle-class adherents than the reactionary fundamentalism historically associated in the United States with Pentecostalism.

The leaders of the orientation meeting effectively balance the themes of familiarity and innovation. The priest, who in this case is chief spokesman, wears a clerical collar along with a well-worn argyle sweater. He identifies himself as "father," followed by a contraction of his first name and his family name. He relates that he has been baptized in the Spirit and has the gift of tongues. He had been a skeptic, but he marvels at what he has witnessed in the lives of his fellows.

Next, a young man introduces himself and tells about his own conversion. His narrative includes allusions to his own acquaintance with the drug scene and a fruitless search for meaning in many spiritual directions throughout the world. Finally, while visiting a local scene of Marian devotion he felt impelled to seek out the CCR, which he had heard about from friends. The Marian theme appears time and again, almost in opposition to the post-Vatican II tendency in Catholicism to play down Mary as an object of veneration. It suggests to the recruit that the well-worn paths are not being abandoned. The young man's message is not received with much enthusiasm by members of this night's recruit audience, even though he admits to speaking in tongues and to a new inner contentment. As it turns out, previous drug usage is not common among recruits to the CCR. On this night the recruits come from an age group a bit too old to appreciate the kind of spiritual struggle the youth has described.

A woman in her mid-fifties then arises and tells at length of her personal misfortunes. Her husband has left her after gambling away all their money. Her children have grown up and have gone off in search of a stability that she was unable to give them. Her chronic state of ill health and general malaise have prevented her from keeping the responsible job she had held in a brokerage office. She continually failed to recognize what the Lord was trying to tell her, and she had assumed through it all that she, herself, could straighten out her own life. Filled with skepticism and despair, she came to a prayer meeting at the invitation of a friend. On that very night she knew herself to be healed. The sense of healing may be in both body and spirit, though she makes no attempt to divorce these. She has the gift of tongues and of prophecy. At the end of her recital there are murmurs of approval from the twenty or more persons who are attending the orientation. There are several utterances from among the recruits of "Praise the Lord," in which the priest and the young man join as through hearing her for the first time. On the way down the hall to the large room in which the prayer meeting will be held, some of the newcomers remark on the obvious sincerity of the woman who has been healed.

Before the orientation meeting is over the newcomers are informed that they may attend the half-dozen or so Life in Spirit seminars which, like this meeting, are held just before the prayer meeting each week and which will make them more familiar with the CCR. In presenting potential recruits with individuals with whom they can identify, the leaders establish the essential legitimacy of the movement and of charismatic gifts before the experience of the prayer meeting itself.

The prayer meeting is held in a large room that is carpeted from wall to wall. It does not have the intimacy associated with the living-room gatherings of the early days or of the small groups that are currently more characteristic of the CCR. However, the seating is arranged so that everyone looks toward the center of the room and can see the faces of many other persons, as one would in a home gathering. This is quite unlike the traditional church arrangement, where all eyes are directed toward the celebrant in the sanctuary. Seeing each other's face facilitates gestural exchanges of affirmation and support, a sense of sharing religious experiences within the community.

The physical arrangement also makes it possible for the neophyte to learn the appropriate prayer postures without instruction. Although chairs are provided in the outer part of the circle, most participants sit cross-legged on the floor. During prayers, hands are placed on the knees, with palms upward, a posture believed by participants to indicate an open or receptive interior attitude to the workings of the Spirit.

The private prayers and tongue speaking occur only periodically throughout the evening. The meeting begins at the direction of a young man who sits on a low chair at one end—farthest from the entrance of the room—of an oval space in the center of the room in which no one is seated. In the division of labor necessary to the orderly conduct of the weekly meeting, he has emerged as a leader in what the participants feel is a perfectly natural or spontaneous way. That he plays his part so effortlessly and graciously, and that he is accepted so readily by the community in this role is, for the participants, further indication of the love and trust that the Holy Spirit has sown among them.

The leader of the meeting suggests a warm-up song. Some of the participants have guitars and there is a tambourine. All seem to be singing, and the hymn is the familiar "Amazing Grace." It does not end so much as trail off into the glossolalia, private prayers, and aspirations, all of which blend in a curious way, sounding as though they are being recited in unison, and the tone seems more important than the content. From this point on, throughout the entire meeting, which lasts somewhat longer than an hour, there are periods of song—which may be suggested by someone other than the leader—of individual prayers, of called-for silences, of individual petitions, of psalms recited aloud, of biblical texts that the participant indicates he has *received,* of biblical-sounding aphorisms later acknowledged as prophecies.

These latter texts and prophecies are important elements in creating the sense of unity in the meeting, since they are later woven into a theme for the evening, in an interpretative narrative delivered by, in this case, a priest whose *gift of discernment* is acknowledged. He discerns the message that the whole evening is meant to convey. But, as with all the charisms, they are believed to be the property of the community even though they reside in the individual as a vehicle of the Spirit. This communal as opposed to individual gift is an important development in the CCR. This collective exercise of discernment may be seen throughout the evening as the participants nod approvingly or smile pleasantly, as though to indicate that the right chord has been struck by what has been said or sung.

What has been reported about the meeting thus far suggests a highly routinized ritual. To some extent this is the impression given, and it is certainly intended as an antidote to freakiness. At the same time, however, there must be room for virtuoso charismatic performances and for considerable lay participation. Otherwise the prayer meeting would be indistinguishable from traditional devotional exercises. The virtuoso outlet is partly provided in glossolalia and in discernment, but there are those who say prophetic words and those who *receive* a proper biblical text. A person with the gift of prophecy simply breaks into phrases that sound as though they come from the Bible but which the person recites with eyes closed, when the inspiration comes. They do not have a time-bound quality, just as biblical prophecies do not. That they are prophecies may be acknowledged by the initiated in their prayers or by the priest who discerns.

Many of the initiated bring well-worn paperback Bibles with them. If one of the initiated has a text, he will—in the appropriate pauses, usually at the end of a prayer—rise to his feet and announce that he has a text. (Texts and prophecies are given as frequently by women as by men.) There may be some explanation of the circumstances under which the text was received. For example:

As we were preparing to come here tonight, right after supper, I said to my wife that I had been thinking of a problem that was disturbing to me and I opened my Bible to a text that seems to me to speak to the problem. My wife wanted to know how I could be sure it would fit into the meeting and how I could be sure it was from the Lord. I told her we would just have to trust that, if it were from the Lord, we would know. He wouldn't send me something that didn't fit.

Although the ethos of the prayer meeting allows for individual inspiration, the form that it may take is regulated by strong, if tacit, group norms. An incident involving the "Twenty-third Psalm lady" illustrates the way in which group control is exercised. At the only meeting at which I noted her presence, the "Twenty-third Psalm lady" placed herself on the floor immediately in back of the inner oval of participants. She arranged her skirt decorously and thrust her legs out to the side. She propped her torso first on one arm and then on the other, in decided contrast to the way in which the initiated ordinarily position themselves.

In the early stages of the meeting she shifted her legs occasionally, but did not appear especially flustered or discomfited. Following one of the early silences she appealed, sotto voce, to persons around her for a recitation of the Twenty-third Psalm. It is difficult to say why her neighbors failed to oblige her. After much agitated movement in the direction of one or another of her neighbors on the floor, sometimes moving on her knees, crouched down to avoid being conspicuous, she managed to borrow a small volume containing the words of the Psalm. She got to her feet and read it aloud. The recital was not greeted with particular enthusiasm in the form of aspirations from the participants, but it certainly was not disruptive. From this point on, she seemed unable to find a comfortable sitting position, frequently shifting her legs or her supporting arm, and yanking at her skirt.

A crisis of embarrassment was reached for her when, fifteen or twenty minutes after her reading, she started to her feet and began to say something that sounded like "I'd like to . . ."; but she did not continue, for the young man who had discussed his text with his wife rose slightly ahead of her and indicated, in a louder voice than hers, that he had a text. They were about ten feet apart, he standing erect, she on her knees but with her back straight and head up. When he heard her voice breaking into his announcement, he turned in her direction and appeared to smile at her. She mumbled softly, "I'm sorry," and slowly sank to her sitting position on the floor. When he finished reading she got up, walked to the nearest wall, sat down, and propped her back against the wall for the remainder of the evening.

To describe the way in which she was eased out does not suggest that the actors in this little drama were conscious of the control mechanisms at work. Yet time after time these became operative to establish the limits of acceptable behavior. This is not to say that the leaders will not engage in direct and conscious control of the meeting. Sometimes persons who say or do something that could disturb the smooth operation of the meeting are told that their behavior is disturbing. This is done, however, with sensitivity to the person creating the disturbance. Sometimes the gift of healing is employed to restore the disturbed person to an appropriate emotional state. Deviant testimonials are enough of a problem to merit discussion at a conference of regional leaders. A member of the national leadership posed the question of how to deal with a prophecy that the world will end next week.

Near the end of the prayer meeting the priest who will interpret the texts and prophecies speaks. His remarks make very explicit the continuity of the community of this particular prayer meeting and over time. The young man who has begun the service makes last-minute announcements: "Father Wilson will hear confessions in Room 209; if people would like to be prayed with, go to Room 206. Who needs a ride? This lady. Where to? Here's someone going that way." More rides are solicited. The community cares. Some persons stay on for coffee and talk, especially those who have been initiated. Since the hour is late, others leave in friendly little groups. Although the ethnographic account ends here, the community reassembles the next Saturday for still another ritual exercise. In the words of one young informant, "The first part of the week is one big let down. Along about Wednesday I begin to think about how great it will be Saturday night and I can hardly wait."

THE ORGANIZATION

The prayer meeting is the chief arena for proselytization and for enactment of the cultic rituals. From the outset, however, the CCR has concerned itself with more than providing what one informant refers to as "a spiritual service station." O'Connor insists that, "while members of the community are thus active in a multitude of ways, there is no apostolate or work proper to the whole community except the weekly prayer meeting."[7] This may represent a point of view more than it does empirical reality. The accommodation of the movement to the institutional Catholic church demands a strategic approach,[8] which suggests to the observer that organizational goals of the CCR are viewed from within as entirely ancillary. Yet O'Connor's description of the first few weeks at Notre Dame includes an account of a meeting that addressed itself to settling disputes over the form the activities of the group should take and over relationships to the institutional church. As O'Connor recognizes, the local operation of the movement on a week-to-week basis demands ministerial performance, which in turn poses the problem of continuing leadership.

With the elaborate regional and national bureaucracies and international ties that have proliferated in the space of a few years, there has emerged a vertical organization, with headquarters at Notre Dame but which has relied heavily on key figures in the Ann Arbor community. The monthly newsletter, *The New Covenant*, is published at Ann Arbor, and comment is made in it on a wide variety of the organization's concerns. The Communication Center at Notre Dame dispenses books, manuals, and cassette tapes by recognized leaders of the CCR. The books may be inspirational for participants everywhere; some, along with the manuals, provide guidance to leaders at the local level for the conduct of a host of activities. In the manual on the Life in the Spirit seminars there is a program for leading persons to the Baptism in the Holy Spirit. John Thompson shows that local chapters that do not follow the models provided by the national Communication Center—which have been developed after considerable experience and discussion—tend to flounder and ultimately dissolve.[9] This suggests that the need for organizational support is not only felt at the top but is also part of the indigenous dynamics of the movement. At Notre Dame a directory of chapters

7. *Pentecostal Movement*, p. 106.

8. See Michael Harrison, "The Adjustment of a Social Movement to Its Organizational Environment: Pentecostalism within the Catholic Church."

9. "Catholic Participation in the Charismatic Renewal Movement."

is maintained, and the effort to keep it up to date requires staff time. The annual conventions are held at Notre Dame also, and massive planning efforts are required because of the scale they have attained.

THE SOCIAL LOCATION OF AN EMERGING CCR

To understand fully these organizational developments it is necessary to consider the social situation in which Catholic Charismatic Renewal emerged as a movement. To begin with, the movement clearly owes much to the stimulus of Vatican II. The changes the council legitimized in 1962 touched on every conceivable dimension of religious expression within Roman Catholicism. It de-emphasized or discarded altogether some modes of belief, ritual, and experience, as well as intellectual underpinnings and ethical posture, that had enjoyed almost a century of preeminence, at least in the United States and probably throughout most of Roman Catholicism. At the same time, it ushered in an atmosphere of innovation with respect to all these dimensions, the long-range effects of which are still being worked out.

The net effect of the Second Vatican Council was to create a vacuum in which routines of the past were suspended and new forms could rush in to fill it. During the 1960s a host of new (or renewed) practices emerged, accompanied by a theological renaissance chiefly at academic centers throughout the world.

There is no evidence that in Catholic institutions of higher learning departments of theology themselves fostered the development of the CCR. In fact, there is continuing friction between the intellectuality of departments of theology and the more spiritual emphasis of the CCR. Much more influential in sparking the movement were Newman centers and other forms of Roman Catholic campus ministry at secular and Roman Catholic universities. Stimulated by Vatican Council II, persons associated with them came to be highly critical of the spiritual stagnation of the past and equally impatient with the majestic pace at which efforts toward change seemed to be proceeding within the church.

While it is evident that Vatican II made possible the emergence of CCR, the movement has considerably older roots in the church. Over its long history, the church has been confronted with frequent attempts to break with its institutional mold. New religious orders, new sects, new esoteric cults emerging within the church are not uniquely contemporary phenomena. They have appeared periodically throughout the history of the church, and most, if not all, of them have included a desire to return to an enthusiastic form of religious expression.

In the past, however, control of religious expression rested in the hands of the religious hierarchy, a control enhanced by the recitation of the Mass in Latin. Some highly expressive practices did develop, of course, at the shrines of Lourdes and Guadalupe, for example. These were more tolerated than encouraged and were, in any event, kept under the watchful scrutiny of the hierarchy. The same was true for devotions growing up around particular saints in preference to attendance at the obligatory Sunday Mass. Such devotional adjuncts functioned as outlets for pent-up zeal.

Those attracted to these ancillary practices, to judge from rather widely scattered data, were disproportionately from folk societies or from ethnic pockets in industrialized societies. The elderly were also overrepresented, although most evidence indicates this to be true of adherents to any ritual expressions. In any case, these deviant activities, while tolerated, were effectively contained by the church hierarchy from becoming movements that would threaten the smooth functioning of the mundane operations of the church. Vatican Council II effectively changed all that, so that what had previously been latent in the church could become manifest.

Among the more immediate precursors of CCR were groups such as the Catholic Worker and Friendship House, which addressed themselves to the needs of the poor and oppressed. They established neighborhood or settlement houses, staffed in large measure by lay persons who had assumed a communal life-style very much akin to that of religious orders but with considerably more flexibility and only a nodding acquiescence to episcopal authority. Such groups attracted attention both through their own publications and through the wider Catholic press, particularly that which concerned itself with a social conscience. To some extent these movements had about them a ring of what would later be dubbed the counterculture. These seem to have been especially appealing to those who maintained their Catholic identity in academic settings.

Other predecessor movements to CCR were the Christian Family Movement (CFM), Young Christian Students (YCS), and Young Christian Workers (YCW). These had started in Europe as Catholic responses to Communist-cell organization. They combined collective action with collective prayer and discussion, and afforded a working model of organization for the efforts that would follow.

Perhaps most salient of all the forerunner movements is known as the Cursillo (literally, short course), an intense weekend-retreat movement which began in Spain in the late 1950s. It called for immediate sharing among the retreatants of whatever feelings of enthusiasm and renewal of faith they experienced. In earlier retreats the typical pattern was protracted periods of silence so that the individual could meditate on his own spiritual state and discuss it only with the retreat master, who was a priest. The reported camaraderie generated at a Cursillo created a climate in which participants were encouraged to plumb deeply into the experiential dimension of their religiosity and to give it open expression.

Cursillo is important to the genesis of CCR because, as a largely middle-class movement, it legitimized for middle-class laity modes of religious expression that had been long repressed. The rapidity with which the Cursillo movement spread from its beginnings in Spain to the rest of the world, especially via Mexico to the United States, in a very few years is indicative of the responsive chord it was able to strike among a laity longing for ways to experience their religiosity. The preparatory role of the Cursillo is important only in historical context, however. The subsequent growth of CCR membership is not chiefly from the ranks of the cursillistas.

Turning now to the features of the beginning of the CCR that are linked to the American scene, it is necessary to consider the general ambience in which new modes of religious consciousness have taken root in this society and also the appeal of Pentecostalism. With respect to the former, this essay can do no more than suggest that the whole volume of which it is a part is an attempt to explain what is perceived as a new situation, what Robert Bellah describes as a "post-traditional world."[10] One supposes that the counterculture is indeed symptomatic. It should be emphasized, however, that the phenomena in question, whether new religious or secular modes of consciousness, are part of developments that flowered in the late 1960s and that have been primarily middle-class in appeal, finding the most willing audiences in university communities. In view of all that has been written on the subject, it may be unfair to offer a shorthand characterization; nevertheless, a central element of the counterculture has been dissatisfaction both with the society as it has operated and with the attempts to reshape it from within. It is clear that this double theme of discontent contributed to the rise of new modes of religious expression within Roman Catholicism.

The direct catalyst for the emergence of CCR came from the visits of the two Holy Ghost Fathers with a Protestant neo-Pentecostal group in Pittsburgh. Beyond that exposure and since

10. See *Beyond Belief*.

the early days of the movement at Notre Dame, the CCR has been little influenced by Protestant counterparts.

There are many parallels with the neo-Pentecostal groups, indicating that the CCR arose out of a more general American ambience. Neo-Pentecostals had as their purpose the awakening of members of established denominations to the Pentecostal experience. This is to be distinguished from the Pentecostal movement of fifty years earlier, which attempted to convert people to a new sect. In the late 1950s, through the efforts of a neo-Pentecostal movement, practice of the charismatic gifts was reported among Episcopalians, followed in the early 1960s by American Lutherans and Presbyterians.

Neither CCR nor neo-Pentecostals appear to come from low-status backgrounds. The Full Gospel Business Men's Fellowship, founded in 1953, exemplifies the air of respectability that sets neo-Pentecostals off from fundamentalists and earlier Pentecostals. CCR recruits also come from the educated middle class. Michael Harrison demonstrates that at the University of Michigan there are no significant socioeconomic differences between Pentecostal and non-Pentecostal Catholics.[11]

Like its Protestant counterpart, and despite its emergence from college campuses, the CCR exhibits a thread of anti-intellectualism and a literal belief in the devil. O'Connor illustrates this element of the world view.

It is characteristic of the Pentecostal movement that, along with renewed faith in the Holy Spirit, there comes a greater awareness of the evil spirit. Perhaps this is because a keener spiritual sensitivity makes a person more perceptive of evil influences as well as good ones. Perhaps it is because, when the Holy Spirit begins to act in a more manifest way, Satan retaliates by doing likewise. (May it not be that the widespread modern disbelief in the reality of the devil is simply a counterpart of the modern neglect of the Holy Spirit?)

In any case, experience has taught people in the Pentecostal movement to take very seriously that aspect of the Christian life that has to do with warring against the evil one. One very intellectual leader of the Pittsburgh community, of decidedly liberal tendencies, used to maintain that Satan was only a mythical expression for the dark forces latent in human nature. Not long after the events of February and March, 1967, someone asked him whether he believed in Satan now. "You better believe I do," he replied—laughing, but dead serious.[12]

11. "Sources of Recruitment to Catholic Pentecostalism."
12. *Pentecostal Movement*, p. 79.

FUTURE DIRECTIONS

Although prediction is a hazardous undertaking, it seems unlikely that CCR will be arrested at the expressive stage of development we have discussed. The theme of sharing the spiritual exercises and of the charisms within an expressive group has already been transformed into much more pervasive interpersonal relationships and networks. The sense of a community of participants who come together weekly from their diverse roles in the workaday world changed very early for some into a community in which participants shared all except their occupational roles. Even work roles in these new communities may overlap so that participants do not lose substantial contact with one another for any protracted period.

In San Francisco, those who have received the Baptism in the Spirit, perhaps seventy-five to a hundred of the two to three hundred who attend the weekly prayer meetings, find themselves meeting at least one other night each week to pray and to discuss what they are doing. The discussions range from liturgical arrangements for the Saturday night prayer meetings and other housekeeping details associated with it to ways in which the members of this initiated group can help each other. Since the number of baptized has risen rapidly, this larger cadre of initiates has subdivided into eight or ten more manageable groups, whose representatives meet together.

Flexibility also exists with regard to the variety of community ties from which one can choose. For example, small groups of single men or of single women or of couples with small children may choose to live under one roof, sharing not only in the necessary secular routines but in prayer regimes and other spiritual exercises as well. Sometimes adjacent housing units are available to one or more such groups, so that a neighboring community of participants is readily established. Although no fixed pattern seems to have emerged, these various units articulate with each other in an interlocking network that is geographically near the locus of the prayer meeting.

Early in the history of the movement only university campuses and their surroundings were conducive to this type of communal development. An alternative model has come into prominence more recently. Urban territorial parishes have been turned over to the members of the CCR. This does not mean that the bishop has relinquished ultimate control over a unit within his diocese. It means that parishes which have been losing members through migration or through diminished lay participation can be renewed through the efforts of the CCR. The pastor and the curates themselves would be participants in the movement, so that all the liturgy could be integrated around common charismatic themes. If the parish has a school, the religious order that staffs it (usually women) are also participants. The lay persons who are participants in CCR have considerable influence in shaping both liturgical and educational directions, and assume active ministries in both enterprises.

The belief that the Holy Spirit is working in and through the community has become increasingly stronger, and the solution of secular exigencies is testimony of this efficacy of the Spirit. For example, one young man described efforts he and others had made to find housing for a young widow and her several small children. They had located a suitable apartment which she could afford on her modest salary; however, neither she nor they had the money to furnish it. They prayed for help and guidance. That very day a leader of the community had received a telephone call from a prosperous businessman visiting from a city where he is active in the CCR. He wanted to know if the leader knew of anyone who could use several hundred dollars. The sum, as the young man related, was just what the widow needed and the need was met.

This little story, which is told often in one form or another by Pentecostals, Catholic or not, captures the elements of the world view that dominates as the movement develops along communal lines. There is the idea that one can expect to turn to one's fellow participants for ministrations and that one ought to reciprocate when called on. Of course, this is a simple expression of love of neighbor, but the definition of neighbor is more literal or personal. It is this element that has been at the root of the controversy between the CCR and the social activists within the church. The debate is not really over whether to be active but over the proper arena for action. It finds its parallel in the nonreligious sphere between, for example, the views of what is called the liberal establishment and those of what is labeled the counterculture. The former have in common with the social activists a commitment to *causes* that tend to treat neighbors and their needs in a class sense. The CCR and the counterculture share the view that this established approach to social problems depersonalizes or dehumanizes both giver and receiver and, in the long run, fails to solve the problems it addresses, since it only creates bureacratic structures whose chief goal is self-perpetuation. The social activists point out that in a highly differentiated society the person-to-person approach advocated by the CCR is exclusive and tantamount to a kind of isolationism, and that failure to recognize the existence of classes may mean that the needs of many will be ignored. The intention here is not to mediate the dispute in any way, but merely to suggest that these two world views should have profoundly different structural consequences for both the church and the surrounding society in terms of how resources are allocated for solving social problems.

REFERENCES

Bellah, Robert. *Beyond Belief: Essays on Religion in a Post-Traditional World*. New York: Harper and Row, 1970.

Gerlach, Luther, and Virginia Hine. "Five Factors Crucial to the Growth and Spread of a Modern Religious Movement." *Journal for the Scientific Study of Religion* 7 (1968): 23–40.

Goffman, Erving. *Interaction Ritual*. Garden City, N.Y.: Doubleday, Anchor Books, 1967.

Goodman, Felicitas. "Phonetic Analysis of Glossolalia in Four Cultural Settings." *Journal for the Scientific Study of Religion* 8 (1969): 227–39.

Harper, Charles L. "Some Speculative Notes towards a Theory of Catholic Pentecostalism." Paper presented at the annual meeting of the Society for the Scientific Study of Religion, Chicago, Illinois, 1971.

Harrison, Michael I. "The Adjustment of a Social Movement to Its Organizational Environment: Pentecostalism within the Catholic Church." Paper presented at the annual meeting of the American Sociological Association, Denver, Colorado, 1971.

———. "Sources of Recruitment to Catholic Pentecostalism." Paper presented at the annual meeting of the Society for the Scientific Study of Religion, Boston, Massachusetts, 1972.

Hine, Virginia H. "Pentecostal Glossolalia: Toward a Functional Interpretation." *Journal for the Scientific Study of Religion* 8 (1969): 211–26.

O'Connor, Edward D., C.S.C. *The Pentecostal Movement*. Notre Dame: Ave Maria Press, 1971.

Ranaghan, Kevin, and Dorothy Ranaghan. *Catholic Pentecostals*. New York: Paulist Press, 1969.

Stephan, Karen H., and G. Edward Stephan. "Religion and the Survival of Utopian Communities." *Journal for the Scientific Study of Religion* 12 (1973): 89–100.

Thompson, John R. "Catholic Participation in the Charismatic Renewal Movement." Paper presented at a symposium at the Institute of Religious Studies, University of California, Santa Barbara, 1974.

9

The Church of Satan

RANDALL H. ALFRED

Although the major focus of this chapter will be on a specific form of Western witchcraft, the phenomenon is neither localized in this culture alone nor isolated from other trends within it. Witchcraft, magic, and sorcery are found widely distributed around the globe. In our society, the recent growth of interest in witchcraft and magic is part of a more general "occult revival" that includes astrology, Ouija boards, and interest in such prophets as Edgar Cayce. The popularity of such novels and films as *Rosemary's Baby* and *The Exorcist* indicates a widespread interest in matters magical and Satanic and has brought these themes to at least the peripheral attention of most Americans. What are the realities behind these popular images?

WITCHCRAFT IN THE UNITED STATES TODAY

The contemporary practice of witchcraft in the United States is arrayed along two orthogonal dimensions. First there is a continuum between the practice of black magic and the practice of white magic. Although witches of either stripe generally make more of this distinction than is warranted, there are some genuine differences. Practitioners of black magic are more willing to employ their arts for ends regarded as evil by the surrounding society, consider themselves more in league with demons and dark spirits, and call more upon satanic tradition for both ancient technique and the legitimation of modern innovation. White witches and warlocks (the technical term for male witches) are careful to dissociate themselves from magic employed for any but supposedly beneficial ends, ritually protect themselves from the influence of evil demons (even when these are invoked for the performance of certain functions), and call more upon the European witchcraft tradition, which seems to be an underground survival of pre-Christian paganism and nature worship.

At right angles to this dimension is a continuum involving degree of organization. At one end, we find individuals (with perhaps a small, local, and informal following) practicing magic as a folk craft. At the other, we find organized groups practicing canonical witchcraft according to specified tradition.

Among white witches who practice individually are those who have earned or learned their witchcraft status through kinship with or apprenticeship to another solitary witch, those who have picked up the art from reading or more tenuous media contact, and those who have "invented" their practices, usually inspired by highly visible cultural archetypes and often with the aid of psychedelic drugs. Combinations of these types are, of course, possible. The vast majority of those in the United States who consider themselves witches are probably practitioners of these sorts. Typically, one finds them casting spells for the health and success of family and friends and celebrating nature festivals, such as plantings and harvests, and astronomical and astrological events, such as new and full moons, new years, solstices, equinoxes, eclipses, and the appearance of comets.

It has been found that members of the drug-using community who become interested in witchcraft continue the use of hallucinogenic drugs in their use of witchcraft. The wide popularity among young people of anthropologist Carlos Castaneda's three books on the mystical practices and philosophy of a drug-using Yaqui shaman undoubtedly encouraged this trend but is by no means solely responsible for it.[1] In its minimal and probably most widespread form, this psychedelic new-Druidism is drug-assisted nature worship; it consists of retiring to a mountaintop or other natural setting with friends, perhaps to watch a sunrise or an eclipse, under the influence of a psychedelic drug. (LSD is most commonly used because of its availability, but the biologicals peyote cactus and psylocibin mushrooms are preferred as being more "natural.") Here is an instance of unclear boundaries between playful and profound involvement in the occult, for regardless of the admixture of recre-

1. *The Teachings of Don Juan; A Separate Reality;* and *Journey to Ixtlan.* (For publishing data on titles in the footnotes and for other selected source material, see the references at the end of the chapter.)

ational and spiritual motivations, profound ("heavy") worshipful and celebratory emotions and attitudes regarding nature and one's place in it often result, and they may be more than transitory.

An indeterminate number of magical "circles" practice nude ceremonies as either pretext for or introduction to sexual orgies. These have their counterparts in black magic, differing from the former primarily in the use of a Black Mass rather than spell casting as a prelude to the sexual activity. The witchcraft activity itself is not especially central to these groups or the experience of their members and is thus usually neither very "black" nor very "white."

Organized or canonical white witchcraft groups are usually called covens and consist theoretically of precisely thirteen members, although they usually range from ten to fifteen. Estimates of the number of these groups in the United States today range from fifty to three hundred. There is much competition among these groups regarding claims of traditional legitimacy. Scholars cannot agree on whether this tradition is entirely a survival of pre-Christian practices in Europe or whether much of it arose in response to the publicity of the Inquisition. It is more likely, I believe, that this kind of inversionary sect is more important in the satanic tradition than in white witchcraft groups. Before the middle of the fifteenth century, the Roman Catholic church denied the existence of witchcraft and punished people for believing in witches; after that time it accepted the fact that such practices occurred and punished people for them.[2] The famous European witchcraft trials of the sixteenth and seventeenth centuries are regarded by some as trials for the heresy of unbelief rather than for the working of magic against the community or its members. At any rate, the claims for traditional legitimacy made by any contemporary witchcraft group are weakened in light of the virtual eradication of witchcraft during those centuries.

Witches in these covens today are unlikely to use drugs in their rituals and are frequently antagonistic to the use in any context whatever. This may constitute a major break with pre-Inquisition European witchcraft. Michael Harner believes that plant-based, hallucinatory ointments (notably Datura, henbane, mandrake, and atropine) were rubbed between the thighs and on other areas of sensitive skin by medieval witches. The trance state thus induced frequently included, among other hallucinations, the experience of flying on the branch or broomstick used to rub the ointment be-

2. Jones, *On the Nightmare*, pp. 213–31.

tween the thighs. Castaneda experienced the sensation of flight after rubbing a Datura paste on his genitals and other sensitive areas. Despite the general success of the Inquisition, the utilization of these drugs may have survived in a few isolated places in Europe and possibly even in the United States.[3]

Those involved in black magic include solitary Satanists who believe they have made pacts with the Devil. Relatively unorganized black-magic groups include not only sexually oriented groups but also the highly publicized, though rare, Acid Satanists of the Charles Manson variety. Such groups are almost completely untraditional and revolve around the hypnotic or charismatic nature of the cult leadership. As the name "Acid Satanism" implies, the use of drugs, especially LSD, is central to these cults. The authoritarian nature of these groups has led to the use of the term "acid fascism" as well.[4] Satanic flagellation societies, which are sadomasochistic versions of the black-magic-and-sex groups, may also be seen as non-drug-using versions of such cults.

Organized black-magic groups include the Church of Satan, headquartered in San Francisco, and schismatic groups such as the Church of the Fountainhead. The schismatic groups are generally short lived and less organized, and practice ritual magic not quite as "black" as that of the Church of Satan. As it is worldwide and there is no central (white) witchcraft organization or hierarchy, the Church of Satan must be considered the most highly institutionalized of the various forms of witchcraft. The rest of this chapter will focus on this particular group.

THE RESEARCH

The primary method of study was covert participant observation. I approached the group in April 1968 as an outsider and indicated an immediate interest in joining. My feigned conversion to Satanism was accepted as genuine and I made rapid progress in the group, as measured by my advancement in ritual rank, my being given administrative as well as magical responsibilities, and my appointment to the "ruling" body of the church.

From April 1968 to August 1969 I attended fifty-two of the group's weekly rituals, participating in all but eight of these early

3. See Harner, "Shamanism, Witchcraft, and Hallucinogens"; "The Role of Hallucinogenic Plants in European Witchcraft"; and Siggins, Harner, and Alfred, "Witches, Demons, and Other Fly-by-Nights."
4. Felton, *Mindfuckers.*

on. I was also present at twelve meetings of the ruling council, at twelve classes on various aspects of Satanism, and at six parties. All these occasions included much discussion and conversation, and most were followed by early-morning visits to local restaurants with the group's leadership corps. I slept overnight at the church headquarters as the guest of the high priest on six occasions. There were several times when I visited socially with, attended movies with, or met on the streets and talked with members of the church. Between August 1969 and November 1973 I was in contact with members or leaders of the group on another twenty or so occasions, under a variety of such circumstances.

Altogether, I was with the group or its members on about a hundred separate occasions, totaling about six hundred hours and recorded in about that many pages of research notes, which were written as soon as was practical after leaving the group on each occasion. In addition to these notes, this report is based on over fifty pieces of media coverage; the three books published by the high priest, Anton Szandor LaVey; all forty-four copies of the *Cloven Hoof*, the group's newsletter, from July 1968 to August 1973; and about two dozen pieces of correspondence which I exchanged with the church headquarters.[5]

Throughout the research, I tried to minimize reactivity, that is, my own effect on the group I was studying. I was generally nondirective in my comments and conversation, demurred in first requests for suggestions or ideas, answered subsequent requests with suggestions made previously in similar situations by others, and even selected at random pages from books out of which I was asked to read something of my choice. Even in the group's ruling council I was able to avoid undue influence, since it was an advisory rather than a legislative body. (LaVey could and frequently did override the council by means of appeals to his own charismatic authority or to satanic tradition.) Such efforts and devices, however, did not completely solve the problem of reactivity; I often had to choose what ideas to second, since I was generally perceived as a high-status member and since my behavior was interpreted by others as flowing from genuine satanic conviction and devotion to the church rather than as random acts or simple yesmanship.[6]

Since my ideas about the ethics of covert participant observation

5. See the references at the end of the chapter for these book titles and other LaVey sources.

6. For a novelistic and satirical approach to reactivity in the sociological study of religious cults, see Allison Lurie, *Imaginary Friends* (New York: Coward-McCann, 1967).

changed, I resolved to tell LaVey what I had been doing and to ask permission to publish the results of such research. As I had suspected from a few comments that he had made half-jocularly in the past, he had surmised all along that I was doing research. His impression had been, however, that my interest was genuine and primarily personal, with research as a sort of back-of-the-mind possibility. From a purely sociological point of view, this was not the case; I had joined the group to do research and later got personally involved. But from a satanic perspective, my deception and covert aims, my playacting and feigning, and my use of other people for my own ends were all components of lesser magic, that is "wile and guile obtained through various devices and contrived situations, which when utilized, can create 'change, in accordance with one's will.'"[7] Thus my feint was typically satanic, so I was not feigning; and the last diabolical laugh is not mine after all.[8]

SATANISM IN THE OCCULT REVIVAL

According to *The Satanic Bible,* written by LaVey between the foundation of the Church of Satan in 1966 and 1968, there is really no difference between white and black magic, except for the hypocrisy of white magicians who believe their altruism and benevolent spells do not offer them any gratification or personal power. And the Satanist hardly regards the attainment of power or self-aggrandizement as evil or "black," since these are viewed as the fitting and proper pursuits of all intelligent humans. A 1972 issue (July-August) of the *Cloven Hoof* further denigrates white witchcraft as a reversion to submissive nature worship, whereas Satanists worship none but themselves. The Satanist is expected not to worship diabolical deities but rather to manipulate them as symbols for the purpose of one's own glorification and gratification. But despite LaVey's statement of "no real difference," the fact is that ceremonial magic as practiced by the Church of Satan relies largely on diabolical symbolism and the positive valuation of many activities conventionally considered "evil," and is thus properly categorized as black magic.

7. LaVey, *The Satanic Bible,* p. 111. Lesser magic as taught by LaVey includes a great deal of micro-manipulation of behavior, based on the micro-observations of social scientists generally, sociologists specifically, and Erving Goffman in particular.

8. Or as Kurt Vonnegut wrote in *Mother-Night,* "We are what we pretend to be, so we must be careful about what we pretend to be."

"The stars may affect no one," says LaVey, "but astrology affects everyone."[9] A Church of Satan tract on this subject, subtitled "The Stars: A Vitamin Supplement for Weak Egos," states;

A wise sorcerer "believes" in astrology, because he knows that the majority of the peoples of the civilized world believe in astrology (at least part of the time); and if enough people are motivated by a hoax, then the hoax becomes as reality. Therefore, in the manipulation of humans who are affected by astrology, it is necessary to know how, where, and when the stars will supposedly guide their human followers, so the manipulator will be waiting first in line to deal with his star-led subjects.

Despite this attitude, there was always much talk of astrology among church members, even in the presence of LaVey.

The official attitude toward astrology is also the attitude toward other areas of the occult. LaVey was not only a lion trainer and a calliope player when he was with the circus, he was also a palmist and fortune-teller. He spent many years studying various occult subjects in what he now regards as a wandering in the wilderness before stumbling on the true path, the "Left-Hand Path," of Satanism. He has amassed a library of several thousand volumes on occult matters, and he gave many public lectures on occult subjects. These lectures served both to enrich the Church of Satan and to introduce it to those interested in other areas of the occult.

The Church of Satan strongly condemns the use of illegal drugs. The rationale for this is twofold. First, it is believed that drugs, especially the hallucinogens and LSD particularly, act to reduce one's active control over the environment and are a means of withdrawal.[10] Magic, on the other hand, is conceived of as an extension of such control. The use of the legal drug alcohol is viewed as acceptable and even desirable in moderate amounts to reduce inhibitions and increase imagination. A heavily spiked punch called Satonic or Globin Juice was served (from a commode) at the quarterly parties marking the church's official holidays; a shot of bourbon was used by LaVey or other lecturers to "loosen the tongue" before public appearances; and a beverage of personal choice—almost always alcoholic—is prescribed for satanic rituals. It is deemed both foolish and unmagical, on the other hand, to become wholly intoxicated while attempting an act of magical control.

9. Truzzi, "The Occult Revival as Popular Culture," p. 20.

10. Hippie-acid culture developed in San Francisco almost simultaneously with the Church of Satan, and the corner of Haight and Ashbury is a scant two miles, as the demon flies, from the church headquarters. It may be that LaVey's intense animosity stems from the rivalry of two would-be global social movements fighting for the same local turf.

Second, such drugs are illegal. A satanic magical formula is "nine parts respectability to one part outrageousness." (This combination of the acceptable and unacceptable is found in more equal proportions in the very name "Church of Satan.") The following neo-Edwardian rule of etiquette was expressed by LaVey in the church newsletter of July 1968 (then an encyclical letter from the high priest to active members): "We Satanists pride ourselves on being ladies and gentlemen—sinful, perhaps—but nonetheless, ladies and gentlemen." LaVey is in many ways a law-and-order man, and once served as a police crime-laboratory technician. He has a chaplain's badge for the San Francisco Police Department and has many friends on the force, a few of whom are church members. His attitude toward drugs was shared by most members, and several younger members who openly referred to their use of marijuana and amyl nitrite ("poppers") eventually found their way out of the church, more or less voluntarily.

THE ATTRACTIONS OF SATANISM AND ITS PHILOSOPHY

The philosophy of contemporary Satanism is expounded at length in *The Satanic Bible*. The most succinct summary is found in these "Nine Satanic Statements," a diabolical equivalent of the Ten Commandments.

1. Satan represents indulgence, instead of abstinence!
2. Satan represents vital existence, instead of spiritual pipe dreams!
3. Satan represents undefiled wisdom, instead of hypocritical self-deceit!
4. Satan represents kindness to those who deserve it, instead of love wasted on ingrates!
5. Satan represents vengeance, instead of turning the other cheek!
6. Satan represents responsibility to the responsible, instead of concern for psychic vampires!
7. Satan represents man as just another animal, sometimes better, more often worse than those who walk on all-fours, who, because of his "divine spiritual development," has become the most vicious animal of all!
8. Satan represents all of the so-called sins, as they all lead to physical, mental, or emotional gratification!
9. Satan has been the best friend the church has ever had, as he has kept it in business all these years![11]

Members of the Church of Satan respond to a variety of attractions, which are analytically separable into six categories. These are hedonism, magic, diabolism, iconoclasm, millenarianism, and the

11. *The Satanic Bible*, p. 25. Satanic numerology relies primarily on nine and its multiples and much less so on thirteen.

charisma of High Priest LaVey. Although all members are probably somewhat attracted to each of these, emphases undoubtedly differ greatly from one member to the next. A brief discussion of each follows.

Hedonism is the philosophy of indulging physical, mental, and emotional desires. There is much specificity on sexual matters in this regard.[12] Satanists believe that any sexual act that does not hurt another against his or her will is acceptable. A distinction is drawn between freely chosen indulgence and compulsive acts. A "good" Satanist is expected to be free of compulsion. The hedonistic element of Satanism usually serves to ratify existing practices and to encourage and offer support for nascent hedonism in the life-styles of its adherents. In organized church activities, hedonism was manifested in the quarterly costume parties (which turned into orgies in the early history of the group), in the frequent casting of lust spells by individuals during the rituals, and in the use of naked young women *as* (not *on*) the altar of rituals.

The element *magic* includes both "greater magic," the ceremonial casting of spells and curses, and "lesser magic," the wily manipulation of the behavior of others. Effective greater magic requires a great deal of ritual knowledge, paraphernalia, and capability of performance. Although some members reported the performance of such rituals at home, the setting was usually the ritual chamber of the church headquarters. These rituals involved the use of an electric organ; bells and gongs; black and white candles in a red and black ritual chamber; elaborate robes, hoods, and masks; processionals and recessionals; and sometimes stunning visual and vocal effects. They frequently reached artistic peaks of musical-visual-vocal-kinesthetic integration and were appreciated by both participants and onlookers on an aesthetic level, regardless of the efficacy of the magic they were intended to carry out.[13] It is believed that ritual magic should be powerful psychodrama, that the ritual room should be an "intellectual decompression chamber."[14] Many members actually did report on the effectiveness of both greater and lesser magic, as performed both individually

12. LaVey's second published book, *The Compleat Witch*, is essentially a seduction manual for witches, based on a witches workshop for women only, which he taught at church headquarters in 1968–69.

13. This integration seems consciously patterned on Richard Wagner's concept of *Gesamtkunstwerk*. His music was much used both in rituals and as ambient background throughout the church headquarters, and Wagnerian themes recur frequently in Satanic writings and philosophy.

14. See *Satanic Bible*, pp. 119–20.

and in the group, and much of the talk at church functions was devoted to this subject. Presumably, those who did not find the magic efficacious did not remain around long enough to report it.

There are at least three ways in which this magic could have been working, according to both the official Church of Satan philosophy and the opinions of the members. First, members not only were learning *about* lesser magic but also were being tutored by LaVey in specific techniques of how to control situations to their own advantage. Second, the emotional intensity of greater magic was creating new confidence that they could recognize and then obtain their own desired goals, whether amorous, vengeful, financial, political, or whatever. Third, a sufficiently powerful ritual was deemed capable of implanting a suggestion in the mind of one on whom the magician wished to cast a spell. On several occasions telepathy was the only apparent explication for the successful working of a spell.

Diabolism is the attraction of Devil worship and the religiously forbidden or heretical. Most members of the Church of Satan view Satan as a symbol of worldly desire and opposition to conventional religious views, a representation of the concepts expounded in the "Nine Satanic Statements."[15] Despite the general attitude that the Devil is a symbol to be manipulated rather than a deity to be worshipped, some members do regard Devil worship and the performance of the "traditional" Black Mass blasphemies as an important part of Satanism; for them, the Church of Satan is serving as an inversionary sect, a topsy-turvy Christianity. During the period of my intensive study of the church, this subgroup of diabolists consisted almost entirely of lapsed communicants of the Russian Orthodox church, in whose theology the Devil plays a prominent part, and former seminarians from a variety of Christian religions. Diabolism in satanic rituals took the form of an invocation of the Four Crown Princes of Hell: Satan, Lucifer, Belial, and Leviathan, followed by a further selection from a crosscultural list of demons. Occasionally, the traditional Black Mass, an obscene parody of the Catholic Mass, was performed.

Iconoclasm is closely related both to diabolism and to charismatic authority. This iconoclasm seeks to free Satanists from the influence of institutions, customs, and values other than specifically religious

15. As LaVey put it in a 1968 study seminar, "Satan as a red devil is ingrained in the collective unconscious. The association can't be broken, so we might as well use it and exploit it as a positive symbol. It's just like Santa Claus as the spirit of generosity; we all think of Santa in a red suit with a white beard: no one sees him in a blue suit with sandals."

or spiritual ones. Thus, instead of a traditional Black Mass to free
the participants from the yoke of Christian slavery, a contempory
Black Mass would be directed at any current sacred cow of modern
society or at any institution or tradition from which the Satanist
seeks liberation. In such a ritual, for instance, a capsule of LSD was
stomped underfoot by LaVey. Iconoclasm is related on the other
hand to the "revolutionary" nature of charismatic authority, which
is not "bound to the existing order: 'It is written—but I say unto
you . . . !' "[16]

Interest in these first four elements has been facilitated by the
general relaxation in recent years of social taboos and even of legal
restrictions on the performance of magic and on sexual freedom.
With the clergy debating the "death of God" in many popular
media, surely heresy is not what it used to be; and a layman who
takes up Devil worship is not about to become an outcast. While it
is by no means true that nothing is sacred anymore, many things are
much less sacred to many people.

The fifth element of appeal is *millenarianism,* the belief in the
coming of a new age. Just as the Christian Bible concludes with the
millenarian Revelation of Saint John the Divine, so *The Satanic Bible* opens with the following prologue, sometimes read as part of
the rituals (note the Wagnerian imagery):

The gods of the right-hand path have bickered and quarrelled for an entire
age of earth. Each of these deities and their respective priests and ministers
have attempted to find wisdom in their own lies. The ice age of religious
thought can last but a limited time in this great scheme of human existence. The gods of wisdom-defiled have had their saga, and their millennium hath become a reality. . . . "Draweth near in the gloom the twilight
of the gods." The ravens of night have flown forth to summon Loki, who
hath set Valhalla aflame with the searing trident of the Inferno. The
twilight is done. A glow of new light is borne out of the night and Lucifer is
risen, once more to proclaim: "This is the age of Satan! Satan rules the
Earth!" The gods of the unjust are dead. This is the morning of magic, and
undefiled wisdom. The FLESH prevaileth and a great Church shall be
builded, consecrated in its name. No longer shall man's salvation be
dependent on his self-denial. And it will be known that the world of the
flesh and the living shall be the greatest preparation for any and all eternal
delights! REGIE SATANAS! AVE SATANAS! HAIL SATAN!

In an era of rapid social change, it is not surprising to find a belief
that an age is ending. The millenarianism of Satanism explains to its
adherents much of their confusion about this welter of change, especially in the religious and moral spheres, and promises the

16. Weber, *The Social Psychology of the World Religions,* p. 296.

dedicated and resourceful Satanist an important place in the new order.

By no means the least of the major elements of attraction to the Church of Satan is the *charismatic authority* of the High Priest and Magus of the Black Order, Anton Szandor LaVey. Charismatic authority "rests upon the belief in magical powers, revelations, and hero worship."[17] LaVey bases his authority on all three. Most active members of the church accept LaVey's magical abilities as demonstrated both by the tales he tells of his own magical workings and by what he has done for them. As for revelation, he cites his discovery of the magical "Law of the Trapezoid" and refers mysteriously to the "blinding flash" of his own satanic dawning.[18]

The high priest's colorful background enhances his image among his followers. He has been in succession teen-age musical prodigy, circus cage-boy, lion trainer, and calliope player, carnival magician, palmist, and hypnotist, burlesque-house organist, police and insurance-company photographer, cocktail organist, official city organist, and clinical hypnotist. All this was prior to his foundation of the Church of Satan on Walpurgisnacht 1966 (*1 Anno Satanis*). The subsequent publicity in local and national media, which has served to attract potential new members, along with his recent involvement in the motion-picture industry, has also had the function of enhancing his status as celebrity and hero. LaVey's appearance is impressive and imposing; his shaven head, piercing eyes, and commanding voice create a dramatic presence. This is emphasized during rituals by his vestments: a red-silk-lined black cape, black robe, and horned hood.

Max Weber states that the "charismatic leader gains and maintains authority solely by proving his strength in life . . . [and] that those who faithfully surrender to him must fare well."[19] Although being accepted as a charismatic sorcerer requires the successful performance of sorcery, the opposite seems also to be true. Both Claude Lévi-Strauss and Carlos Castaneda have pointed out that the consensual re-creation in magical terms of an event that is *potentially* definable as magic is what makes the event magical in

17. Ibid.

18. LaVey, "The Black Mass." The Law of the Trapezoid states that obtuse angles, and hence all trapezoidal forms, are magically harmful or dangerous. If this form and its power are recognized, however, it is no longer so dangerous and can even be used to advantage against those who are unaware of it (LaVey, Satanism Study Seminar). Thus, all to whom LaVey has taught this are benefited by his magical prowess and have a basis for charismatic trust in him.

19. *The Sociology of Charismatic Authority*, p. 249.

social fact.[20] It is by manipulating the will to believe, by carefully engineering "the process of validating special consensus," and thus creating "states of non-ordinary reality," that the charismatic sorcerer works.[21]

Charismatic power, then, builds up by accretive social construction, and magical *acts* soon become the very *nature* of the socially created "magician" in much the same way as deviant acts become the very nature of the socially created "deviant."[22] The same is undoubtedly true of other manifestations of charisma: for instance, belief engendered by earlier successful prophecy may encourage people to construe events so as to validate subsequent prophecies by the same person, who thus becomes a prophet. So prophecy itself may rest largely on the phenomenon of self-fulfilling prophecies.[23]

Thus, charisma is an aspect of a social relationship, and charismatic followership or attribution is as much at the heart of it as charismatic leadership or personality. This revisionist view is actually given support by Weber's own statement that charisma is a "quality of a person, regardless of whether this quality is actual, alleged, or presumed."[24] Further, charisma, the scent of sanctity, is the inverse of stigma, the odor of rejection.[25] The former is an extraordinarily enhanced identity, the latter, extraordinarily spoiled. Both are in some sense deviant, for charismatic authority challenges the existing order: it is nonordinary. The charismatic leader is one who leads others to redefine reality instead of redefining oneself as simply a deviant within the old reality. Both phenomena result from social labeling processes, involving in the one case a highly positive emotional charge and in the other a highly negative one. In the Western, Christian context, these polar types have been cast as sorcery and sainthood, the performance of magic and the working of miracles. The posthumous exoneration and later canonization of

20. Lévi-Strauss, *Structural Anthropology*, p. 162.

21. See Castaneda, *The Teachings of Don Juan*, pp. 231–71. (These page numbers are from the paperback edition of 1969.)

22. See Becker, *The Outsiders;* Erikson, "Notes on the Sociology of Deviance"; or Szasz, *The Manufacture of Madness*.

23. See Merton, *Social Theory and Social Structure*, pp. 421–36. Or, as Tolkien's wizard Gandalf said, "Surely you don't disbelieve the prophecies because you had a hand in bringing them about yourself?"

24. *Social Psychology of World Religions*, p. 295.

25. See Erving Goffman, *Stigma: Notes on the Management of Spoiled Identity.*

Joan of Arc is a good example of the historical reconstruction of stigma into charisma.[26]

Much of Anton LaVey's charisma is diabolical in nature, and he has been eminently successful in taking the stigma attached to the symbol of the Devil and, by dress, demeanor, and grooming, as well as by philosophy and ritual, turning it into a positive force for the attraction of publicity and followers. LaVey is familiar with and admires the works of sociologist Erving Goffman, and this, along with his comments on the Devil as a symbol, would indicate that the conversion of stigma to charisma is a deliberate undertaking. As the first of the above-ground Satanists, he has a treasury of stored stigma at his disposal, although he must share some of it with witches now publicly practicing the less-disapproved white magic.

MEMBERSHIP COMPOSITION AND RECRUITMENT

The Church of Satan claims to have seven thousand contributing members. While this many may have in fact joined and paid their "lifetime" membership fee ($13 to $25, depending on when they joined), only four or five hundred active members were still paying the $10 annual "active fee" and thus receiving the *Cloven Hoof* in 1971 when I was present while an issue was being mailed. (These fees, along with the $2.50 donation requested for attendance at classes and rituals at the headquarters, now rare, are an important source of income for the church. Church finances and personal finances for LaVey were never really separate; now he is receiving royalties for his books and fees for his work in the film industry.)

At the church headquarters in San Francisco during 1968–69, attendance at the rituals of the Central Grotto was usually about twenty to thirty from a pool of about fifty to sixty members at any one time. Regular weekly rituals are no longer held there; another grotto elsewhere in the city has since flourished and been disbanded after a political and personality dispute between the headquarters and the local leadership. Several other grottoes exist in California and in the Midwest and the East, and many members live in communities with too few members for the formation of a local group.

Those who attended the rituals at the Central Grotto were mostly

26. This entire process of substituting enhanced for spoiled identity is now being undertaken by a variety of stigmatized social groups—for instance, blacks ("black is beautiful"), women ("sisterhood is powerful"), and homosexuals ("gay is good").

middle-class white people in their forties, thirties, and late twenties, including many professionals. Frequently, new members attended regularly at first, only occasionally after a while, and finally, after a period of perhaps two to six months or longer, became completely inactive without ever formally withdrawing. On the other hand, there was always a much smaller group of members who attended nearly every week, on other occasions helped with various church tasks and responsibilities, and maintained their relationship with the group for long periods. The Central Grotto was often visited by out-of-town members who were traveling.

Membership enrollment almost always began by exposing the new member to the publicity the church has solicited and received. At first, much of this publicity appeared in nudist, "girlie," and pulp magazines, as well as the lurid weekly national tabloids. This produced an image of the church as primarily sexual in nature and resulted in a pool of new members with this in mind. Since 1968 there has been a change in emphasis of the formal functions of the church: respectability and modest demeanor have been emphasized, and group or public hedonism has been discouraged. There was also a successful effort to obtain publicity in the more respectable media; and extensive articles, several of them cover features, appeared in newsmagazines and pictorial weeklies and on nationally broadcast television news shows.

Despite the impression that the current revival in occultism is very largely a youth phenomenon, relatively few young persons were members of the Church of Satan during 1968–69. Of the over 140 different members observed in more or less regular attendance at the rituals, no more than 40 were younger than thirty, and many of these were in their late twenties. An attempt to missionize the Berkeley campus of the University of California in the spring and summer of 1968 produced little interest and few converts. From the data produced by the survey questionnaire (see chapter 13), it is clear that the absence of large numbers of young people in Satanism is not due to any ignorance of it, for 52.9 percent of the sample of Bay Area youth reported knowing about it. Of those who knew of it, however, only 2.0 percent reported being strongly attracted, 10.4 percent were mildly attracted, and 64.9 percent were "turned off." Fewer still—only 3.7 percent of those young people who knew about Satanism, or 2.0 percent of the total youth sample—reported having taken part in *any* satanic group. While these percentages may not be absolutely reliable, it is significant that, of the thirteen religious or semireligious groups for which data are available, Satanism ranks third in awareness among the youth sample (trailing only yoga groups and Synanon), but "turns off" the greatest numbers, is attractive to the fewest, and has the fewest actual participants. What accounts for this? Let us look again at the six categories of attraction discussed above.

Satanic hedonism, especially its sexual aspect, would certainly be attractive to young persons potentially interested in a new religion. Data on a sample of senior male college students indicate that 90 percent of those espousing one of the "new" religions are medium or high in sexual experimentation, and 75 percent are classified as high.[27] On the other hand, the Church of Satan's extremely negative attitude on drugs probably drives many young people seeking collective legitimation of their hedonism into the arms of other groups. Ninety-two percent of the "new" religion category in that sample are casual, serious, or hooked users of drugs; 48 percent are classified as serious or hooked.

Satanic magic is probably attractive to many young people, but their presence in relatively large numbers in other magical settings seems to indicate that their preferences in magic runs toward white rather than black magic, and to forms of witchcraft that are less organized, less canonical, and more craftlike and neotribal. These preferences are consistent with the altruistic and do-your-own-thing idealism of the counterculture. (Noncounterculture youths are unlikely to be involved in witchcraft or magic of any kind.)

The appeal of satanic diabolism to youth is probably undercut by the availability of certain popular figures as adequate identificational foci for the diabolical energies of the counterculture. Mick Jagger of the Rolling Stones rock group is the paramount example of this type. It is likely that some contemporary popular music is for many young people a phenomenological-experiential alternative to active involvement in the occult. More generally, the "new music" may be fulfilling wider functions of the "old religions" for the young, by providing a common symbol system that is appropriate to new life-styles and that can be experienced collectively and communally.

Both iconoclasm and millenarianism have undoubted appeal for contemporary youth, but apparently not often in the satanic context. Joining an institution organized along somewhat traditional lines does not seem a likely expression of iconoclasm by a genera-

27. Wuthnow and Glock, "Religious Loyalty, Defection, and Experimentation among College Youth," p. 168. The data here and below have been concentrated into fewer categories than are in the original.

tion that has vented much of its spleen against just such institutions. And the millennium either expected or vaguely wished for by those with millenarian tendencies is not usually the ego-glorifying, objectivist-Nietzschean-Wagnerian millennium offered by Satanism; more often it is either the traditional Christian variety of apocalypse or an ego-transcending development of group consciousness.[28] Moreover, as with diabolism, musical expression of millenarian themes is available. Bob Dylan's "The Times They Are A-Changin'" is perhaps the best-known and most powerful example of this kind.

LaVey's charisma is undoubtedly attractive to many young persons, but apparently not so much as that of competing heroes and gurus, from Mick Jagger to the Maharaj Ji. The law-and-order, generally right-wing, and patriotic nature of LaVey's charisma also fails to appeal to potential youthful converts. Ninety-five percent of the "new religion" subsample discussed above are described as radical in their political views, and 72 percent as both radical and activist.

For most young people, even for those who report some attraction to the philosophy and beliefs of Satanism, the negative aspects of the Church of Satan and the presence of alternative outlets are sufficient to keep them outside the organizational structure of the church. Even those few in the sample who are actually participating may include solitary, schismatic, and "acid" Satanists. It is important to remember that most of the analysis in chapter 13 is based on the "broader constituency" of all those in the sample reporting *attraction* to Satanism, whether they participated or not.[29]

SATANISM, SYMBOLISM, AND SHOWMANSHIP

LaVey seems to be well aware that one can be both a good showman and a good religionist, especially if one's religion is Satanism. "It's a Barnum-and-Bailey world," said the former circus hand in an interview. "Once you recognize that and start employing the

28. The latter theme is prevalent in the science fiction popular among the younger generation, especially in authors like Arthur C. Clark and Robert Heinlein.

29. This was necessitated by the small number (ten) of participating Satanists reached in the general sample. It was proposed that a small, stratified sample of Satanists be surveyed; but on philosophical grounds the Church of Satan refused to cooperate in the distribution of questionnaires: "Satanists do not submit to being tested or judged by others; they are themselves the judges" (LaVey, in an interview).

means of lesser magic, there's no telling what you'll stumble on. We don't discover anything. We fall upon what sits in our paths. It's like Menotti's opera, *The Medium:* you use what you believe to be trickery and then discover that that gives you powers beyond, whether you know them or not." LaVey is now concentrating on being a consultant to the film industry on matters diabolical. The Church of Satan is, according to him, but a small part of the much greater satanic movement. The mechanics of operating the church are now left to subordinates, and the high priest, though he still makes the major policy decisions, spends much of his time in a sourthern California residence and a retreat in one of the northern counties.

In one sense, LaVey has been in show business all along. He recognizes the theatrical nature of enthusiastic religion, and on occasion he has used the term "audience" rather than "congregation" to describe those who attended his rituals. His belief in the coming of the "Malpocalypse," or satanic millennium, is genuine and firmer than ever. His awareness of artifice and his conscious manipulation of belief are, within the satanic philosophies he propounds, no contradictions at all. Whereas in the past he had only the Church of Satan as a dramatic vehicle to advance the satanic movement and to glorify and gratify his ego (after all, the prime satanic raison d'etre), he now has Hollywood as well. He has his act together and is hitting the big time; and the international sales of *The Satanic Bible* have brought it to the very gates of St. Peter's. What is more, LaVey expects his followers to profit from his example, not by imitation, but by application: "One cherished child who can *create* will be more important than . . . fifty who can *believe.*"[30]

It seems to make little difference to the consciousness of Satanists that much of this may be "just pretend." Max Weber felt that the only crucial criterion of charisma is not that the leader's faith be true and unsullied, but that the trust of his followers be so, and that doubting the leader in such a manner is not "'edifying' to our minds."[31] This is true all the more for Satanism, whose adherents are constantly reminded that one of the magician's most powerful tools is his or her own strong imagination. Thus, the play functions ascribed by Marcello Truzzi to those peripherally involved in Satanism must apply as well to the "small but significant minority" at the center of the movement who take it seriously.[32] Here again, as

30. LaVey, *The Satanic Rituals*, p. 12 (italics in original).
31. *The Sociology of Charismatic Authority*, p. 246.
32. "The Occult Revival as Popular Culture," p. 29.

with psychedelic neo-Druidism, the boundaries between the playful
and the profound are blurred, for to take Satanism seriously means
to regard it, quite often, playfully.[33]

Thus, play functions and fantasy enactment are conscious for
many Satanists. Ideally, "the Satanist maintains a storehouse of
avowed fantasy gathered from all cultures and from all ages. With
this unfettered access to logic as well, he now becomes a powerful
adversary of Satan's past tormentors."[34] This is surely a statement of
symbolic consciousness, but for Satanists this consciousness is
perversely monotonic. It deals almost exclusively with manipulation, egotism, and power and very little with communication,
altruism, and love. This indeed may be at the heart of the failure of
the Church of Satan to attract the interest of significant numbers of
countercultural youths, and it also reveals the dark underside of the
movement, the "door to the abyss" opened by the grisly ritual mur-
ders reported to have been committed by fringe, solitary Satanists.

SATANISM AND THE FUTURE

There are a number of conflicts and contradictions in Satanism that
the Church of Satan must reconcile or transcend in order to ensure
its continued existence. First is the problem of espousing a policy of
indulgence and iconoclasm while trying to maintain discipline and
authority. A young minister of the church, who had earlier suggested that satanic symbols could be made the objects of denigra-
tion in a modern Black Mass, later challenged LaVey's magical
abilities and churchly authority and was disciplined so severely that
he resigned.

The philosophy of hedonism is at odds with the hard work and
study needed to learn and perform both greater and lesser magic
with the desire to make Satanists, Satanism, and the Church of
Satan respectable and acceptable to the public. Further, both the
hero worship necessary for the maintenance of charismatic authority, and Devil worship itself, create inappropriate attitudes for the
successful *mastery* of magic, and what is magically required by an

33. Several members have requested and received Satanic funeral rites. Were
they deadly serious or showmen to the death?

34. LaVey, *Satanic Rituals*, p. 27 (italics in original). See *The Satanic Bible* for a
description of canonical regalia and practice and the basic ritual forms; *The
Satanic Rituals* for the liturgies of rituals for special occasions; and the recording
The Satanic Mass for a staged but accurate performance of the basic ritual. The
flip side features LaVey reading, to musical accompaniment, "The Book of Satan,
or Infernal Diatribe" from *The Satanic Bible*.

individual may not be in the common interest of the group. It is significant that most of the magical workings or spells that LaVey regards as his most efficacious were performed either for his own benefit or as part of a practitioner-client relationship outside the formal structure of the church. Sorcery is still solitary and charismatic rather than communal and priestly. Thus, although there is a Church of Satan, it is still true that "*there is no Church of magic.*"[35]

Another conflict to be resolved lies in the need to maintain secrecy and the desire to foster lucrative publicity and the literary and cinematic career of the high priest. If the appeal of these ventures is largely the hidden and forbidden nature of their subject matter, their success will be self-limiting; for publicity, and favorable publicity at that, makes them both less hidden and less forbidden.

There has been a tendency for all such conflicts to be resolved eventually in favor of the long-dominant traditional value systems of post-Reformation Western culture. Thus, public hedonism has been phased out to enhance respectability, private hedonism has been tempered by the hard work required to produce enjoyment, the leader's authority and the group's iconography have been defended against iconoclasm, and the pursuit of knowledge has been placed above the excitement of bringing forth spirits. LaVey emphasizes that "one of the most important 'commandments' of Satanism is: *Satanism demands study—not worship!*"[36]

Thus, while retaining Protestantism's worldly interest in the value of work and discipline, Satanism no longer rejects the enjoyment of the mundane fruits of those labors. It is a final ratification of the spirit of capitalism, which Max Weber says became independent of the original Protestant ethic within a century of its inception. Satanism provides the religious legitimation for worldly hedonism in place of "worldly asceticism." It is a form of consciousness for which the expected increase in leisure will not be problematical: Satanists view their religion as one uniquely fitted to a wider social movement under way and in the meantime enjoy the proleptic benefits of a hedonistic millennium.

Rather than standing in stark opposition to traditional values, then, Satanism develops from them. In many ways, it is becoming another Protestant sect. Despite its thaumaturgical origins, it is a manipulationist sect. As described by Bryan Wilson, in *Religious Sects,*

35. Durkheim, *The Elementary Forms of the Religious Life*, p. 60 (italics in original).

36. *Satanic Rituals*, p. 19 (italics in original).

Manipulationist sects are secularized sects, for which the *means* to Salvation are religious: the goals are largely those of secular hedonism [p. 141].

Their deity is not a redeemer, but an abstract idea of great power, which men can be taught to apply for their own benefit in this world. . . . Worship is marginal [pp. 44–45].

What they provide for their votaries is less an alternative set of values of life, than the semi-esoteric means to the ends that are general to society. . . . Community is not an end in itself [p. 141].

As in mainstream Protestantism, each person is ultimately responsible for his or her own salvation, although in Satanism, as in other manipulationist sects,

salvation is largely seen as the ability to realize the good things of the world, and particularly long life, health, happiness, and a sense of superiority or even triumph. The sect provides short-cuts to attain these ends [p. 141].

It is also "self-consciously syncretistic" and calls upon a "more prestigious body of knowledge," namely that of social science (p. 143). In all these ways, and also in its rapid movement toward respectability, Satanism is like the other manipulationist sects described by Wilson: Christian Science from the nineteenth century, Scientology from the twentieth, and the contemporary Japanese Buddhist Soka Gakkai (imported to the United States as Nichiren Shoshu).

If there should develop the kind of super-producer, super-consumer, high-leisure society envisioned by futurists such as Alvin Toffler, Satanism would be ideally suited to it and should flourish. The Church of Satan headquarters, which has virtually ceased to be a location for ritual, might well develop into the center of a satanic show business empire like Hugh Hefner's *Playboy* media-entertainment-recreation conglomerate centered on philosophical hedonism. LaVey has referred on several occasions to the existence of plans for the continuation of authority after his death, and the now-advisory Council of the Nine Unknown Men (also known as the Order of the Trapezoid) could conceivably become a true ruling body as the "routinization of charisma" proceeds.[37]

On the other hand, Satanism, perhaps independently of the existence of the Church of Satan or any other institutional structure, may have a place as a particular symbol system within a polymorphous galaxy of such systems. As such, the monotonic nature of its ritual and mythic apparatus would serve specific needs without

37. See Weber, *Sociology of Charismatic Authority*, pp. 262–64.

presuming to constitute the *totality* of consciousness. Satanism, specifically, and the other witchcraft traditions generally recognize some basic factors of human existence, and one way or another they will have their place.[38]

38. Research expenses for this study were largely subvented by a generous grant from the Graduate Division of the University of California, Berkeley. The research was begun as a class project for Professor John Clausen and a tutorial project for Professor Robert Bellah. Subsequently, it was continued under the guidance of Professor Carl Werthman, as well as professors Bellah and Glock.

REFERENCES

Becker, Howard S. *The Outsiders.* New York: Free Press, 1963.

Bellah, Robert N. "No Direction Home: Religious Aspects of the American Crisis." In *Search for the Sacred: The New Spiritual Quest,* edited by Myron Bloy, Jr., pp. 64–81. New York: Seabury Press, 1972.

Castaneda, Carlos. *Journey to Ixtlan: The Lessons of Don Juan.* New York: Simon and Schuster, 1972.

———. *A Separate Reality: Further Conversations with Don Juan.* New York: Simon and Schuster, 1971.

———. *The Teachings of Don Juan: A Yaqui Way of Knowledge.* Berkeley and Los Angeles: University of California Press, 1968.

Durkheim, Emile. *The Elementary Forms of the Religious Life.* Translated from the 1915 edition by Joseph Ward Swain. New York: Free Press, 1965.

Erikson, Kai T. "Notes on the Sociology of Deviance." *Social Problems* 9 (Spring 1962): 307–14.

Felton, David. *Mindfuckers: A Source Book on the Rise of Acid Fascism in America.* San Francisco: Straight Arrow Press, 1972.

Goffman, Erving. *Behavior in Public Places.* New York: Free Press, 1963.

———. *The Presentation of Self in Everyday Life.* Garden City, N.Y. Doubleday, Anchor Books, 1959.

———. *Stigma: Notes on the Management of Spoiled Identity.* Englewood Cliffs, N.J.: Prentice-Hall, 1963.

Harner, Michael J. "The Role of Hallucinogenic Plants in European Witchcraft." In *Hallucinogens and Shamanism,* edited by Michael J. Harner, pp. 125–50. London, Oxford, and New York: Oxford University Press, 1973.

———. "Shamanism, Witchcraft, and Hallucinogens." Seminar presentation, Culture and Behavior Colloquium, Yale University, New Haven, Conn., February 28, 1967.

Hughes, Pennethorne. *Witchcraft.* London: Longmans, Green, 1952.

Jones, Ernest. *On the Nightmare.* London: Hogarth Press and Institute of Psycho-analysis, 1931.

LaVey, Anton Szandor. "The Black Mass." Lecture, San Francisco, May 23, 1968.

————. *The Compleat Witch; or, What to Do When Virtue Fails.* New York: Dodd, Mead, 1971.

————. *The Satanic Bible.* New York: Avon Books, 1969.

————. "The Satanic Mass." Record. Palo Alto, Cal.: Murgenstrumm Records.

————. *The Satanic Rituals.* New York: Avon Books, 1972.

————. Satanism Study Seminar. San Francisco, April 17, 1968.

Lévi-Strauss, Claude. *Structural Anthropology.* Translated in 1963 from the 1958 edition by Claire Jacobson and Brooke Grundfest Schoepf. Garden City, N.Y.: Doubleday, Anchor Books, 1967.

Mair, Lucy. *Witchcraft.* New York and Toronto: McGraw-Hill, World University Library, 1969.

Marwick, Max, ed. *Witchcraft and Sorcery: Selected Readings.* Baltimore: Penguin Books, 1970.

Merton, Robert K. *Social Theory and Social Structure.* Glencoe, Ill.: Free Press, 1957.

Siggins, Ian; Michael Harner; and Randall Alfred. "Witches, Demons, and Other Fly-by-Nights." Radio panel discussion. *Yale Reports,* transcript no. 532 (December 7). New Haven: Yale New Haven Educational Corporation, 1969.

Szasz, Thomas S. *The Manufacture of Madness: A Comparative Study of the Inquisition and the Mental Health Movement.* New York: Harper and Row, 1970.

Truzzi, Marcello. "The Occult Revival as Popular Culture: Some Random Observations on the Old and the Nouveau Witch." *Sociological Quarterly* 13 (winter 1972): 16–36.

Weber, Max. *The Social Psychology of the World Religions.* In *From Max Weber: Essays in Sociology;* translated from the 1922–23 edition, edited, and with an introduction by H.H. Gerth and C. Wright Mills, pp. 267–301. New York: Oxford University Press, Galaxy Books, 1958.

————. *The Sociology of Charismatic Authority.* In *From Max Weber: Essays in Sociology,* pp. 245–64.

Wilson, Bryan. *Religious Sects.* New York and Toronto: McGraw-Hill, World University Library, 1970.

Wuthnow, Robert, and Charles Y. Glock. "Religious Loyalty, Defection, and Experimentation among College Youth." *Journal for the Scientific Study of Religion* 12 (June 1973): 157–80.

PART IV

The Response of the Established Religions

The youth counterculture spawned, as we have been seeing, a variety of new religious movements and alternatives to them. In a study of religious consciousness, the question needed also to be addressed, we thought, concerning what impact the counterculture was having on established religions. The churches and synagogues were among the institutions about which youth were expressing disenchantment. What were the churches interpreting the disenchantment to mean? How were they affected by it? What, if anything, were they led to do as a result?

These questions were pursued most comprehensively in a study undertaken by Barbara Hargrove. She sought to discover how mainline Christian churches—Roman Catholic and Protestant —were relating to the counterculture at the two points where they came closest in contact with it—in campus ministry and at the parish level, in ministry to youth. At these points of contact and especially the first one, she finds that the churches, or perhaps more accurately their representatives, were struggling actively to find a way to minister creatively to countercultural youth, without sacrificing their own integrity but, at the same time, listening and responding to what youth were saying. Hargrove provides a vivid account of the encounter and of the consequences following from it; her chapter adds new and fresh insight into the church's abiding dilemma of how, except defensively, to deal with change.

Jim Wolfe approaches the matters at hand from a quite different tack. In his view, there was embodied in the counterculture a dream of new culture which had great potential for renewing and strengthening the churches. By and large, he finds that the dream was not understood by the churches and, consequently, not responded to. His chapter, in part, addresses the question of why this was so. He is also interested in the exceptions to the rule and in trying to understand how they came about and with what consequences for the churches involved. Wolfe pursues these themes adroitly through case analyses of three congregations whose experiences illuminate both why the churches generally failed to engage the counterculture and what might have happened had they been able to do so.

The chapters by Hargrove and Wolfe are concerned exclusively with the response of Christian churches to the counterculture. While we did not undertake similar studies of the response within Judaism, we did seize on an opportunity to investigate the consequences of involvement in the counterculture on identity among Jewish youth. Prior to the counterculture, considerable concern was already being expressed in the Jewish community about youth raised as Jews losing that identity as adolescents and adults. The counterculture aggravated these concerns. Tom Piazza has sought in his chapter to assess the justification for these fears and to learn how much, if at all, Jewish youth are attracted to new and alternative religions. Piazza's chapter is distinguished by being based on data collected from his subjects over a three-year time interval, thus enabling him to assess more than the immediate effects of countercultural involvement.

The counterculture and the dreams of new culture it espoused were not, it is evident from these reports, openly and widely embraced by established religion. On the contrary, the churches emerge as being more turned off than on by their experiences with the counterculture. Their posture, it seems likely, has been a stimulus to the growth of the new religions, although to what permanent damage to established religions it is still too early to say. As Jim Wolfe comments in his chapter, however, it would be a mistake on the basis of their general response to sell the churches short. For all of the opportunities lost, there remain signs that when the chips are really down the churches retain a capacity to respond creatively to events.

10

Church Student Ministries and the New Consciousness

BARBARA HARGROVE

Countercultural movements among the young in the 1960s presented a number of challenges to institutionalized religion. The frank religiosity of the counterculture awakened new hopes in churches that had nearly given in to a belief that secularization was reaching its logical conclusion in a completely areligious generation. And this new interest in religion did not become, as the revival of the fifties became, a renewal of interest in the church. Rather, young people were seeking religious experience in the mystical practices of the East, in esoteric cults, in psychedelic drugs. Or they were taking "Jesus trips," which spoke out in judgment against the deadness or the cultural captivity of the Christian church. Some combined radical religion with radical politics in ways sure to offend Middle American churchgoers. Others turned from social involvement to an inner quest, to the despair of activist church leaders.

Because there was this kind of ambivalence between radicalism and quietism in the religiosity of the counterculture—which was a mirror image of an often unrecognized ambivalence within the church—it was difficult for the churches to meet the challenge in any unified way. Missionaries in one guise or another were sent to the centers of the new culture, but if they were too obviously missionaries they were not accepted. If they were not so obvious, but more "into" the scene, they were often co-opted by the counterculture, which after all preached love for one's neighbor, peace on earth, enjoyment of life's simple pleasures rather than crass materialism—fine Christian virtues all. Others stayed, and are on hand yet, working with alternative institutions to serve new communities formed out of the wave of change. But it is hard to work out new alternatives in the context of loyalty to a traditional institution, so no real organizational form has developed within which these occasional ministries are regularized and bound to the institution.

It has never been easy for the church to deal with young people at that transitional period between childhood and adult status, particularly those youth who are separated from the rest of the society into educational communities. This has been recognized since the founding of the earliest student volunteer societies, whose criticisms of traditional religion (lack of missionary fervor, lack of concern for the poor and downtrodden) seem painfully familiar to the modern ear.[1] The voluntary movements, which developed by the last half of the nineteenth century into the YMCA and the YWCA, were followed by a response from the denominations in the form of campus ministries, which have been established by many denominations since the second decade of this century.[2] While the form of campus ministry has changed in the following decades, this is still the chief institutional form by which the church deals with youth during the years of "academic ghettoization."

Γ Since World War II the churches have been paying more attention to high school youth, recognizing that their school and peer identification have in many ways replaced family and religious ties as a primary focus of interest. In this context, specialized youth ministries have been developed in the denominations at national and district levels and often also at local congregational levels. These youth specialists, like the campus ministers, attempt to enter the somewhat separate world of the young in order to interpret the values and the programs of the church to that constituency.

Since the countercultural movements have been understood to be primarily youth movements, and since there is little evidence that churches have developed any other permanent organizational form to deal with the counterculture, it seems appropriate to look to youth and campus ministries in order to assess the impact on the churches of this movement toward cultural change.

This chapter is a report on a study undertaken to assess the experience of the churches in their youth and campus ministries. Like others in this volume, it is limited to the San Francisco Bay Area and to information gathered in 1972 and 1973. Since the experience

1. Underwood, ed., *The Church, the University, and Social Policy*, p. 53. (For publishing data on titles in the footnotes, see the references at the end of the chapter.)
2. Shedd, *The Church Follows Its Students*, pp. 30–62.

has been somewhat different in mainline Protestant, conservative sectarian, and Roman Catholic circles, these will be dealt with separately, with the Protestant mainline taken as the primary focus and point of comparison.

THE PROTESTANT MAINLINE

Early Protestant campus ministries attempted to bring to the students what the voluntary student Christian associations could not give them, the specific religious functions of providing a pastor and a church.[3] In so doing they gave recognition to what has been a continuing tension between town and gown within the churches, that the bulk of the college-age students could not be adequately integrated into local congregations in a university town. At first this was only a partial recognition, and the campus ministry was generally housed in a church of the denomination located close to the campus. Unless the congregation was made up predominantly of college people, this almost inevitably created tensions. Priorities were different for the parish and for the campus, and budget problems arose. In their meetings college students wanted to do things and talk about things that were deemed inappropriate within the sacred precincts of the church building. Ministers called to work with the university tended to be more liberal than parish ministers in their theological and social stances, regardless of the denominational tradition, and this brought a constant threat of conflict.[4]

National and district boards had early taken on much of the financial support of the campus ministry, since it seemed patently unfair to ask local congregations to support services to young people who came from and would return to other parishes. This financial freedom also allowed the campus ministry to be fairly free of direction from the local church, a situation that raised difficulties among local churchmen, who wanted more control over programs centered in their buildings and for which their neighbors tended to hold them responsible.

Meanwhile, many students were calling into question the activities and values of many local church members. In the 1930s the student religious associations were already involved nationally in pacifist activities, and were agitating against ROTC on campus, for racial equality, and against the unequal distribution of wealth in the country. They also were making use of the critical faculties in which the college was training them to question the theological assump-

3. Shedd, p. 30.   4. Underwood, p. 171.

tions of the churches and their authority structures. They became
less likely to seek out programs housed in a local church. It is not
surprising, then, that by the decade of the 1950s most mainline
denominations had begun to move their campus ministries to buildings near the campus which were neither churchlike in appearance
nor specifically tied to local congregations.

The 1950s were good years for campus ministries across the nation. The churches gained a legitimacy on campus and in the society at large that has seldom been equaled. The campuses were
overflowing and were still reflecting the seriousness of purpose
engendered by the influx of veterans under the GI Bill and the later
pursuit of excellence brought about by the post-Sputnik competition with Russian education. Churches were expansive in their outlook and had money to back that expansion, on campus as well as in
suburbia.

Many campus ministries became primarily teaching centers.
Students were no longer asking hard questions of the churches as a
prelude to leaving them; they were wanting answers so that they
could stay in without violating the intellectual values they were
learning in college. Campus ministers became teachers of religion.
Already attracted to the universities (else why choose to become a
campus minister?) and judged to be intellectually astute enough to
represent their denomination in working with students, they found
this role particularly fulfilling. Thus, in his 1966 study Phillip Hammond found a high percentage of campus ministers who would like
to be college teachers.[5] (Former Bay Area campus ministers con-
sulted for historical background for this study were found teaching
at a state college, a church college, and a seminary).

But teaching was by no means the only function of campus
ministry in those days. It was still well within its inheritance of
providing a "home away from home," fellowship with like-minded
students involved in familiar structures. As the decade of the sixties
approached, the student body began to reflect the post–World War
II mobility of the society; and campus ministries were often faced
with the need to provide structures where none had been familiar,
to offer as much of a home as young people may have felt they ever
had. Instead of "fellowship," the word became "community," and
the relationships often became much more intense. The need for
such social support also grew out of the experience of burgeoning
schools, overcrowded campuses, and the development of impersonal bureaucratic structures of expanding institutions.

5. *The Campus Clergyman.*

Furthermore, young people have always been harsh judges of those who would teach them ideals without acting them out, and campus ministers have always been pushed to be active in worthy causes. Many, then, became focal points around which social-action groups developed, mostly at this time bent on some kind of social reform.

A good description of one program of this period was given by a former campus minister at San Jose State:

We felt that we needed some sort of identity beyond that of any local church, so the first year we worked for finding some facilities of our own. We found a house, right next to one of the churches. It was a small house, and we bought it with conference money, and established a whole identity in that house, but used the facilities of the church for our evening meetings for the next few years. We became a fairly large student group: we were involved in student action. We had retreats. We had study groups. We started cooperating with other campus ministries on study programs, worship services at special seasons of the year, and all sorts of things. . . . We had a Tuesday noon luncheon, with about forty students coming, and women from local churches coming to serve the food . . . and having people from the campus or larger community in terms of social interest speaking. . . . it was always a student-oriented kind of group. Always they had student officers and student committees and this sort of thing, and it was their group—often at great conflict with the director, but it was their group. It seemed apparent to me always that if you really believed in that, that you had to let them do their kind of thing. . . . At times they didn't do what I wanted to, or what anyone else wanted them to, but what really happened is that there was a community there; and larger numbers of students who found their identity on campus, which is a commuter campus, in the identity of the campus ministry.

On other campuses, these communities often became residential groups, where students lived, ate, studied, and worshipped together. For example, Westminster House (Presbyterian) at Berkeley expanded from about ten women living in the facility to a coed "intentional community" of twenty-two to twenty-four students in the early 1960s. At that time, this was part of the ministry of one denomination among about twelve separate programs on the Berkeley campus. Patterns that were similar though not quite so extensive existed on the other state campuses and at Stanford.

Campus ministers became aware of the duplication of effort which prevented them from making the best use of their time and talents. While the kinds of cooperation on campus described in the quotation above were expanding, cooperative patterns developed by the major denominations to deal with general problems of expansion in the fifties came into play in the administration of campus ministries. United Ministries in Higher Education (UMHE) brought together administrative structures of the Presbyterians, Methodists, United Church of Christ, Disciples of Christ, Episcopalians, and American Baptists. Lutherans went together among themselves and, on the West Coast at least, offered cooperation with UMHE. By 1966 mainline Protestant campus ministries came under the aegis of UMHE (Methodists officially joined in 1969) with a staff of seventeen campus ministers and a total budget of $167,365 for the campuses at Berkeley, San Francisco State, San Jose State, and Stanford. It was expected that on each campus the UMHE ministers could form a team where some division of labor could occur, either in terms of special interests or of working with different parts of the campus community, such as undergraduates, graduate students, or faculty.

Thus in Berkeley the residential community at Westminster House became the primary responsibility of a Methodist campus minister, and the Presbyterians who organized it moved into working with graduate students and faculty. At Stanford, office space for all campus ministers was provided on campus. A campus Christian center was built at San Jose State, and UMHE and Lutheran ministers worked together there and at Ecumenical House at San Francisco State.

At least two weaknesses seem apparent in this move toward more efficient operation, one having to do with the internal style of campus ministry, the other with its relationship to sponsoring churches. Since the needs and expectations of campus ministry vary greatly over time and from one campus to the next, an individualistic style has been basic to the role of the campus minister. This militated against the concept of working as a team, not so much because of any unwillingness of the participants, but because each had his own view of how the work should be divided; and in most cases this was never resolved to everyone's full satisfaction. With regard to sponsoring churches, the ever-present tension between parish and college in their expectations of the role of the campus minister was increased by the imposition of an interdenominational agency between the two. Although this did provide greater latitude for activities on campus which no local congregation might wish to claim, it also constricted the channels through which such activity might be interpreted and defended. Every UMHE ministry was officially directed by a board composed of representatives of local churches of the cooperating denominations, but most members of such boards seemed to be working more out of a sense of personal support than serving as vital links to their congregations. Carefully wrought coalitions of faculty, local church people, students, and campus ministers based on a shared denominational identity were no longer really possible. Only the Lutherans remained denominationally identifiable.

Meanwhile, this internal restructuring was not going on in a vacuum. Even before the plan was put into operation, external events were changing the nature of the ministry. In Berkeley, the sort of intradenominational coalitions mentioned above were blown apart during the agitation of the Free Speech Movement of 1964. Campus ministers tended to take the side of the students, seeing the larger values of human liberation in their struggles. As a result, they tended to alienate many local church people, including some faculty; and though a valiant effort was made to interpret the action, that support has never been regained.

Hot on the heels of the FSM came the whole hippie phenomenon. As long as the flower children were centered in the Haight-Ashbury district in San Francisco, much of the church's attempt to minister to them did not need to be funneled through the campus ministry. But when they left the Haight-Ashbury many turned up on the streets of Berkeley, where the campus ministries attempted to deal with them. Faced with large numbers of hungry, homeless young people, one of the first acts of the UMHE ministry was to have the Briar Patch (the intentional community at Westminister House) open its doors as a "crash pad." However, the autonomous student government of the Briar Patch was not equipped to deal with the problems of displaced hippies; and the whole communal experiment collapsed in a whirlwind of people, dogs, dope, denominational disapproval, and general disorder.

In an effort to serve the street people of the growing counter-culture in the south campus area (which was also the location of most Berkeley campus ministry centers) campus ministers lent their support to a number of alternative institutions, including the Free Church. Over time the support became more and more indirect, as they recognized that street people and students, though alike in age and often in dress, were two separate constituencies. The campuses demanded their attention; the street people could not monopolize it. As a consequence, such ministries to the street people as the free-food program, the Berkeley Free Clinic, the Runaway Center, and others, while often assisted by volunteers from the campus centers, were housed in and became the responsibility of several local

churches willing to undertake the tasks. Many eventually developed secular means of support and were able to free themselves
from the churches, sometimes to the relief of both parties.

The time of greatest cooperation between students and street
people was the famous People's Park incident in 1969, when the
young people took over nearly a block of land in the south campus
area owned by the university and made a park of it. When the university enforced its claim with fences, the young people attempted
to storm the fences and reclaim the park. The national guard and
state and local forces were called in, tear gas was dispersed from
helicopters, and one young onlooker was shot and killed by a county
sheriff. People's Park became a symbol of resistance to the oppression of a dehumanized Establishment, most especially including the
Regents of the University of California. While most campus
ministers felt that they were supportive of the young people in this
effort, many participants felt that they were not sufficiently involved. Apparently, they drew fire from both sides for not providing
the guidance expected of them as (1) ministers to the young and
sympathizers with their causes or (2) representatives of values of established society among the disorderly young.

An ever-present factor in student unrest in the 1960s was the
Vietnam War. Campus ministers on all the campuses were involved
in carrying on a long tradition of pacifism in this context, and in the
process joined students in their exasperation with the militaristic activities of the nation. Their support of peace groups led them into
direct contact with various radical organizations and into negative
contact with those who tried to suppress them. One UMHE
minister who had been given the responsibility of ministering to the
radicals became so involved in their activities that he ran into trouble with the authorities and was eventually dismissed from his position, with an attendant diminution of support for UMHE from his
denomination. Others did not suffer such severe sanctions, but most
were deeply involved in radical antiwar activities. The University
Lutheran Chapel (Missouri Synod) at Berkeley was able to make a
singular contribution to that cause. As a congregation in their own
right, they voted to offer sanctuary to young men seeking to avoid
military duty, though not without creating some problems in their
conservative denomination. Other campus ministers were involved,
less directly, with the sanctuary program. Draft counseling became
a regular function of the campus ministry, replacing to some extent
the kind of personal counseling formerly done in the centers but

now largely taken over by student counseling services on the campuses.

Yet counseling services sponsored by the colleges had their drawbacks. Often the personal problems for which students sought help were brought about by the nature of the college itself, and seeking aid there appeared to the students to be the equivalent of asking succor of the enemy in a battle. Many sought help from one another. Their problems came, often indirectly, to the attention of the campus ministers. As with the draft evaders, campus ministers found themselves in an advocacy role on behalf of the young, frustrated by the unfeeling bureaucracies with which they had to deal.

It was in this context that Ecumenical House at San Francisco State became an off-campus headquarters for radical action during the 1968 strike at that college. College officials appealed to church officials to close down the center, but it remained a "liberated zone" they were unable to control. Campus ministers participated in demonstrations on campus and ran afoul of the police. (One was still involved in court action over this when interviewed in 1973.) At San Jose State similar advocacy roles were played, and one campus minister also capitalized on his freedom from college authorities to assist faculty groups seeking redress of grievances on that campus.

Campus ministers have always had something of a radical image, at least within religious circles; but in the 1960s they became radicalized in a special way. Called to minister on the campus to students and others whose lives were centered there, they came to believe that the very structure of the society and its institutions, including the university and often the church, were preventing the kind of human development into freedom which they defined as the chief goal of their ministry. For the most part—often for lack of clientele—they gave up their attempts to assist directly in the orderly religious and personal development of student members of their denominations and turned to work with those who, regardless of their ideological or religious position, were involved in attempts to restructure what they saw as an increasingly oppressive society.

Then came the 1970s, ushered in by the massive protests against the Cambodian invasion, which resulted in student deaths on at least two campuses in the country. The stakes were higher, and with the winding down of the Vietnam War and the draft, along with threats of economic recessions, the motivation for revolution was reduced. The hippie counterculture had left, instead of a joyous

convocation of flower children, the broken lives of those wasted by
drugs, lived out among the commercial activities of craftsmen who
were learning to become petty bourgeoisie by selling their wares on
Telegraph Avenue. Many of the true counterculture advocates had
gone to seek more natural surroundings removed from continual
confrontation with less experimental neighbors and their official
guardians. The radicals went underground, went straight, or
became religious in non-American, non-Protestant ways. The new
students who came to the campus were less active, less organized,
perhaps less hopeful. Some of the campus ministers also left, but
those who remained or replaced them were faced with a different
context of ministry.

Among the young, the quest had turned inward, to Eastern
religions, to the fundamentalist Protestantism that campus
ministers had early set out to help students grow beyond. Churches,
caught in the downturn of their own fortunes and alienated from
the radicalism of the campuses, withdrew support. In 1972, the Bay
Area UMHE budget had been reduced to $87,776 (its 1966 budget
was $167,365), and instead of seventeen ministers there were five.
Some talked of a time a few years hence when there would be no
campus ministry at all. Certainly the kind of campus ministry
developed in the 1950s and early sixties was dead, and the radical
activity that followed it was muted. Campus ministers continued to
seek to build coalitions between campus, church, and community,
but their authority to do so was often questioned. Many frankly
stated that they were in a period of limbo, trying to seek out new
strategies for action, trying to rebuild, to reassess, to make plans for
new beginnings. Individual denominations have begun to consider
once again sending separate campus ministers to students of their
own tradition; by 1973 part-time Canterbury appointments of the
Episcopal church were in operation at Berkeley and Stanford.

Some of the advocacy work is continuing, in quieter ways. A
broad coalition of campus ministers across the state cooperated to
provide a series of recommendations to a committee of the state
legislature working on a new master plan for higher education.
Coalitions with community groups have been effected, and
programs of child care, food distribution, and the like have been instituted with some input from campus ministries. But in most ways
the mainline Protestant campus ministries seem to suffer from a
peculiar crisis—they have no constituency. Students do not identify
with them; the radicals have used them and gone, and newer
students tend to find them obscure or frightening or irrelevant to

their more personal style. Churches have given up on them. Communities have little need to consult with them. In traditionally religious, or ritual, terms they are nearly defunct. The chapel at the center at San Jose State is rarely used—students seeking worship services are referred to the liturgies of the Catholic Newman Center down the street. The Lutheran Chapel at Berkeley can count it a fairly good Sunday when thirty people show up for worship, including the other two Lutheran campus ministers there. San Francisco State has never been equipped for formal worship in the center, but informal attempts are failing. Only Stanford, with its Memorial Chapel on campus and a university budget to bring in speakers of wide interest, has much going on in terms of traditional services. One of the executives of UMHE reports having helped so many people leave the campus ministry that he has become a recognized expert on mid-life career changes. Whatever its long-term effects, the youth counterculture of the 1960s and its radicalisms appear to have broken the back of traditional Protestant campus ministry.

THE SECTARIAN RESPONSE

Alongside the mainline Protestant campus ministries there have always been sectarian groups seeking to win the souls of college students to their own version of the gospel. Independent local congregations have been part of this effort, but the most notable groups working on campuses are nondenominational organizations developed specifically for this purpose, which are funded by donations from conservative congregations or individuals. Generally their approach has remained the same over the years, though particular organizations have come and gone. At the present time the most active in the Bay Area are Campus Crusade and Intervarsity Christian Fellowship—both of which have well-established nationwide organizations—and Navigators, which expanded from work with navy men to campus evangelism. All these groups deal with students as individuals rather than as members of churches or of social groups, seeking them out on campus and addressing them in terms of traditional evangelism. Their two chief aims are conversion and "discipling," a form of nurture through small-group support in prayer, Bible study, and training in evangelism for new converts. While there is some variation in their methods, in general these groups see themselves as working among the more "straight."

members of the student population, leaving the countercultural types to the Jesus people.

In general, the Jesus movement has not made heavy inroads into the student population in the Bay Area, though it is present in many forms. Perhaps the most notable activity is at Stanford, where the nearby Peninsula Bible Church is an active center. In addition to its many in-house programs, it has reached onto the campus with small-group Bible study and the like, to the extent that the activities are recognized within the structure of the chaplaincy and religious program of the university more than those of some campus evangelists of longer standing. There is also some cooperation between Campus Crusade and Intervarsity, on the one hand, and Berkeley's Christian World Liberation Front, on the other, on projects and programs often also involving evangelically oriented local church congregations. The wide publicity of the Jesus movement has made the other conservative campus groups appear a more legitimate part of the youth culture, and they are profiting from that.

All these groups vary from the mainline Protestant campus ministries in a number of significant ways. Their theology is literalistic, fundamentalist. They focus on the individual rather than the society. They tend to have a world view based on fixed verities, rather than the more open, fluid world view of the liberal campus ministers. The campus ministers are more likely to deal fully and sympathetically with problems students may be having as they look at their faith from new points of view presented by scientific, social scientific, or humanistic studies. But the sectarians can be more sure of their answers, pointing the young person confused by a complex world to the "One Way."

An important established sect in the area is the Church of Jesus Christ of Latter-day Saints—the Mormons. Although their first efforts were focused on their own institutions of higher learning, as a large part of their ministry to college students still is, they have followed their young people to the secular campuses. In student wards (congregations) and institutes of religion, the Latter-day Saints bring to students, as they do to all their people, a full round of activities, which can, along with classes, fully occupy the Mormon student. They stand in the position enjoyed by mainline Protestant campus ministries in an earlier time, maintaining the loyalty of their young, incorporating their growing intellectual sophistication into the pervasive framework of a theological and social system that is accepted as given. Social activities are frankly described as opening the possibility of courtship between believers, as well as providing healthy outlets for youthful enthusiasm and vigor. While liberal campus ministers expect to see only a miniscule fraction of the students whose religious preferences are of their denominations, and others have set out to save small numbers of the lost, the Mormons claim 75 percent or more participation of their students in campus-related services, classes, and social activities. They also report a small but steady stream of converts.

CATHOLIC CAMPUS MINISTRIES

Somewhere between the two Protestant extremes stand the Catholic campus ministries. Like the Mormons, Catholics have attempted to provide their own institutions of higher education and to encourage their young people to stay within their own religious world view by attending them. But the presence of Catholic students on secular campuses has been recognized and institutionally dealt with in this country since the establishment of the first Newman Club at the University of Pennsylvania in 1894.[6] As the name implies, at first these organizations were clubs whose main goal was to provide social contact with fellow Catholics on campuses where they were often small minorities. As numbers have expanded, Newman Centers have become headquarters for many activities—teaching, social action, worship, and the like—in many ways paralleling the development of the mainline Protestant centers.

Until the 1960s, Catholic students had the same kind of identification with Newman Centers on secular campuses, or the programs of the chaplains at Catholic colleges, as Mormon students do with their institutes and student wards. There was a sense of special identity wrapped in prescriptions of ritual obligation. But since Vatican II and the consequent reduction of both the sense of separateness and the rigidity of ritual obligation, students' responses to the campus ministry have changed.

There are large numbers of students on campus who identify themselves as Catholics, often in negative ways. Frequently the products of rote catechetical religious education, they are in rebellion against the narrowness of that training. They take for granted the superiority of the more secular education they are receiving at the college or university and judge the Catholic church harshly as an intellectual oppressor. Priests and nuns in campus ministry repeatedly tell of student outbursts of rage against the

6. Shedd, p. 60.

church. Changes in the church since Vatican II support the charges
of the disaffected young, and Catholic campus ministers find
themselves in a position of trying to mediate between rebels against
the older church and the post–Vatican II possibilities of that same
church.

Yet the contact and identifications are still there, and in many
ways the Catholic campus ministries of the 1970s seem similar to
those of the mainline Protestants in the fifties. The long history and
essentially broad tradition of Catholicism are aids in meeting the
present situation. The traditional emphasis on liturgy, enhanced by
recent changes toward more lay participation, fit well into much of
the contemporary emphasis on direct religious experience. There
has been a reaching back for traditions of Catholic mysticism in
response to the new interest in Eastern religions. Participation in
more informal folk masses is now being superseded in some places
by liturgies that are more meditative. Courses and discussions are
offered in some centers on such topics as Christian Zen and the use
of yoga in prayer and meditation.

The turn inward is most evident, of course, in the charismatic
movement among Catholics. In the Bay Area, this phenomenon is
centered at the University of San Francisco, where one of the
chaplains of that Jesuit institution has become unofficial chaplain to
the charismatics as well. A number of the Catholic campus
ministers in the Bay Area have participated in these charismatic activities, which include Saturday night services and classes, prayer
and training groups during the week, and a growing number of
groups seeking communal living places in the city where they may
practice the fellowship they have developed in religious meetings.
However, the impact of this movement may be greater among the
campus ministers than the students; in fact, some desire was expressed not to push students toward this kind of total commitment
during their searching undergraduate years.

Catholic campus ministers are not just involved in pietistic and
expressive forms of religious activity. They are as involved as the
Protestant campus ministers are in seeking social justice and more
often than not cooperate with them on such projects. They worked
on the Task Force for the Master Plan for Higher Education. They
are involved with urban ministries and with community action
among minorities and the poor, and have also been active in draft
counseling and other antiwar pursuits. Also, campus ministry has
become an accepted vocational field for nuns, who generally report
being accepted as equals by their priest colleagues and who give the

impression of being truly liberated women. Some are involved in women's caucuses on campus and in radical community organizations, as well as in more traditional social service and devotional groups.

The similarity of activities and goals of chaplains of Catholic colleges and universities of the area and those of campus ministers in Newman Centers on secular campuses has been recognized in the Bay Area Catholic Campus Ministers Association, which encompasses both groups. Chaplains are, of course, more involved in teaching and in planning organized activities sponsored by the institutions they serve. Some of these chaplains, as well as some of the Newman priests, are in charge of regular parishes. It is noteworthy that one of these campus parish priests was the only person surveyed who felt hampered in his campus ministry by the number of persons with whom he had to deal. At this center, four priests are serving a parish of some four thousand people, many of whom are university related—truly a phenomenal number in comparison with the empty Protestant centers!

Yet the Catholics are worried. Although a high percentage of Catholic students make at least some overtures toward the campus minister of their faith, the ministers suspect this may not last long. Students are still trained to ritual obligations that have been softened since Vatican II. Catholic students ten years from now may have no more firm commitment to institutional religious practice than Protestant students have now. They see many ways in which Catholic campus ministries may simply be following trends that hit the Protestants twenty years earlier and do not relish the idea that in another twenty they may be in the spot in which their Protestant colleagues now find themselves. Yet they cherish the greater voluntarism of the post—Vatican II church and hope that the present apparent increase of interest in things of the spirit may indicate a long-lasting trend. Meanwhile, they not only have high rates of contact with Catholic students, but find some Protestant students attending their liturgies in search of a sacredness the Protestants seem to have lost.

YOUTH MINISTRIES

The fears of the future expressed by Catholic campus ministers lead naturally into a consideration of the source of those fears, the young people who will be coming to the university in the future. What is the relationship of campus ministries to the programs of local

churches directed toward younger students? Why is it that Protestant students avoid campus ministers and their programs, that
Catholic campus ministers spend so much time dealing with hostility from students in their tradition, that sectarian groups deal so little with students who are mature in their faith, so much with new
converts? Why do we not find a logical progression of young people
in the church from childhood religious education through youth
programs to campus activities, as in the Mormon Church? Why are
young people so alienated from the church that they avoid its
programs, and in their stead seek out or invent new religious
movements?

⌈ While time limitations of this study prevented a truly systematic
survey of youth ministries in an attempt to answer these questions,
an impressionistic one was made. Interviews similar to those with
campus ministers were conducted with persons in each denomination who had responsibility for youth programs in the district
(synod, diocese, and the like) that included the Bay Area, and their
role in aiding local churches to minister to their youth was discussed. Each of these youth specialists was asked not only for a comprehensive view of the programs of his or her church in the area,
but also for recommendations of local churches whose youth
programs might be of interest. From these suggestions a list was
developed that contained at least two congregations and no more
than four from each major denomination, with at least one of these
from the metropolitan area around the bay and at least one from the
more distant suburbs down the peninsula or across the mountains of
the Coast Range.

Although generalizations from such a sample are perilous, some
patterns did seem to emerge. First, at least among liberal mainline
Protestant churches, youth programs were more available and
better attended in suburban than in urban areas. In many mainline
urban churches no special activities—church school or youth
groups—were offered for high school or older young people. Such
programs as these were focused on some special interest—a singing
group, drama productions, sports activities, or the like. One
minister proudly described the way in which his young people had
been integrated into the total structure of congregational committees and projects, but for most the lack of special youth groups
indicated no such integration but rather the absence of high school
youth from all church activities. And in some youth groups that did
exist, the level of secularism was high enough that several members
indicated obliquely what one said explicitly about his involvement,

"but not for *religious* purposes!" A high percentage of the urban churches seem to have lost contact with their young people before they reach high school age.

In suburban areas, where the youth population is high, a wide variety of youth programs could be found, many of them well attended. Some of these programs appeared to lead directly into the kinds of activities most valued by mainline campus ministers: young people were taken on "plunges" into the inner city, were attempting to understand current social problems, and the like. However, no evidence was found that any of these programs had made contact with the urban ministry of the campus ministers so that high school students might consider continuing these interests in cooperation with them as they moved on to college.

Many local congregations of mainline Protestant denominations are much more conservative than the denominational "party line" or campus ministries. Youth groups in these churches tended to be a part of a conservative religious milieu in which campus ministers of their denomination were held suspect. More of their members claimed to know campus ministers than those in more liberal programs, but further questioning revealed that these were generally representatives of one of the conservative sectarian groups on campus.

There are on the high school campus, as on the college campus, a number of those groups that deal exclusively with the young. Most prevalent in the Bay Area is Young Life, a group that focuses on the school as a basic social unit and appears to put much of its emphasis on providing Christian fellowship for its members. Campus Crusade also has its high school branches. Youth for Christ, while no longer highly evident at the college level, has reorganized as Campus Life and has made some headway in the high schools, particularly on the suburban side of the mountains. A number of other groups are also active among the high school set, shading from the traditional fundamentalist to the more expressive groups of the Jesus movement.

The place of Catholic young people in this picture is of interest. While traditional parish and diocesan programs can be found and the Catholic Youth Organization continues to offer special activities, new responses are emerging. Experimental liturgical programs are often well attended. Since the traditional exclusiveness of Catholicism has broken down, there has been some participation in the nondenominational groups, particularly in Young Life. One Catholic youth leader interviewed was the organizer of a Young

Life group that included about half Protestants and half young members of his Catholic parish. A priest reported that Young Life had been very strong at one of the Catholic prep schools in the area, but had been somewhat displaced by new groups that were charismatic and connected to the area Catholic charismatic movement.

If numbers and rates of activity are taken as the measure of success, the conservative Protestant local congregations have the most successful youth groups. One receives the impression that young people are flocking to them and eagerly participating in their fellowship, worship, and Bible study. A significant number of young people returning questionnaires from these groups listed their parents as members of more liberal mainline churches, an indication that the conservative programs are making direct inroads into the liberal camp.

Mormon Mutual Improvement Associations supplement traditional church youth activities with a program that is the near equivalent of a combination of Boy or Girl Scouts, Campfire, 4-H, sports clubs, sororities, and fraternities. Thus, at the high school level as well as the college, they reinforce their source of separateness with a full round of activities; and their young people remain involved.

SUMMARY AND ANALYSIS

The radical political activities of the 1960s and the counterculture that followed them were expressions of discontent with much of American society, and nowhere was that discontent more sharply focused than against the educational system, the institution with which proponents of these movements were most familiar. The form of their rebellion calls to mind the kinds of charges once leveled against the church during the eighteenth-century Enlightenment, out of which our modern educational system was born. This institution which was to free man from the bonds of slavery has become his oppressor; it constricts the range of his thinking; it cooperates with political power to oppress the poor; it denies full expression of man's abilities and denies gratification of important human needs.

Specific responses to political activism by the universities appeared to prove the point. The People's Park incident showed that the university cared more for property than for people. The intransigence of the administration at San Francisco State proved to the rebels that there was no concern for human values there. Responses at Stanford showed little concern for peace among nations or justice among peoples. And so on—in the eyes of the radicals a litany of failures to live up to values of fairness, equality, and individual worth which the universities had been teaching.

In the meantime, youth in another branch of the counterculture were reacting against the objectivity, rationality, and neutrality of the society, particularly its educational system. They were concerned with the dominance of the scientific method and its denial of the reality of any human experience that did not fit some rational paradigm. They sought new realities in the drug experience, in what they could learn of Eastern mysticism or American Indian lore, in a new style of living that was less manipulative of nature and more responsive to it. Broadly celebrated in the media and imitated by Madison Avenue, much of this counterculture has been given legitimacy as the style of youth in American society today.

Thus in the lives of many of the young in the country today there are two prime realities: the educational system with the university as its capstone; and the counterculture, which is its antithesis. Most find themselves marginal to both, seeking a synthesis, unsure of the sources of their identity or values.

The place of the church in this situation is also marginal. As the educational system is called into question, there are those who would reassert the lost dominance of religion over society in its place. For example, during the time of this study efforts were made to have the California Board of Education, or if necessary the legislature, require that public school science texts in the state include the Genesis account of creation along with evolutionary descriptions of the development of the earth and of man. This sort of return to a simpler world view is offered by the conservative churches, by most of the Jesus movement, and indeed by many aspects of the counterculture. But to deny the basis of pragmatic knowledge on which our society rests is to cut off more than would be desired by any but the most ardent back-to-nature counterculturists. Compromises have already been made in their world view which makes it acceptable only through strict compartmentalization of different aspects of one's life, always a precarious undertaking.

Another solution to marginality is to be removed from the scene and the choice into a separate social world. This is being done successfully only by the Mormons at the present time. If the Catholic experience is any guide, one may predict that this is possi-

ble only so long as a group is in a minority position and hence has
the cooperation of the rest of the society in defining itself as a
"peculiar people."

What, then, of those who identify with "majority religion," be it
Catholic or Protestant? For generations the liberal churches, including and often led by campus ministers, have been practicing
apologetics vis-a-vis the Enlightenment charges. They have been
concerned with showing that the church is not an oppressor, social
or intellectual, that it can be legitimate under the canons of scientific theory and humanistic studies. It may be seen as an effect of the
counterculture that they are now beginning to see that in so doing
they have been less critical of the universities and their values than
they might have been.

All the religious themes of the counterculture give to the
churches a sense that people are looking for something that they
should be able to provide. It seems to be more than the security of
conservative doctrine; it seems to challenge the long-held Western
assumption that religion is to be equated with beliefs. Religious *experience* is something that the rationalized modern church has
found difficult to handle.

Yet often the communal springs are stopped up, and the symbols
fail to communicate the common experience on which the validity
of any symbol must be based. The churches see the renewed interest in religion as a call to renewal, but are unsure of the nature of
that renewal. They are experimenting, often with the same sorts of
things the counterculture has tried. They try yoga and sensitivity
training as a means of moving toward religious experience. They
concern themselves with the possibilities of a Christian Zen. They
reexamine old theologies of the Holy Spirit and try to understand
the charismatic Christians without allowing them to tear the church
apart with a spiritual elitism.

Denominational campus ministries are no longer able to have
programs based on the kind of shared identity that is born out of
shared experience, which once was natural to their students—and
participating faculty. The counterculture emphasis on shared direct
religious experience indicates that this is a need young people
recognize and make the basis of their sense of community. Two-
thirds of the campus ministers and over 60 percent of the youth
specialists chose religious experience as the most, or one of the two
or three most, important dimensions of religion. Seventy-two percent of the local church youth leaders chose this dimension. Yet the
movement of youth away from the churches and into counter-

culture religious groups indicates that the established religious institutions have somehow lost the key to providing this important element. Churchmen remember with distaste past periods of emotional excess in religion. Yet they recognize that the basis of religious truth lies in the transcendent experience, and that often in the past this kind of experiential base has provided a platform from which people could get the psychological and social leverage to deal with the ambiguities of a time of change.

It cannot be left up to the campus ministers to meet such needs, for they lack contact with those who possess them. If it is the province of the local congregation, it cannot be relegated to its youth programs; in too many churches it is already too late to make contact there. If the churches cannot meet these specifically religious needs, we may be witnessing their death throes, for it has been their responsibility to provide the religious functions of the society; no other institutions share it. If indeed there is a basic need for religion in society, new institutions may arise to provide it, as the counterculture would indicate.

It is more likely, however, that some of the present experiments on campus and in the local church will develop into an answer for the current situation, even if they must become some kind of new Reformation. It is very likely that such an answer will include input from the counterculture, but the shape of that synthesis remains a mystery.[7]

7. This study was conducted through National Endowment for the Humanities Grant #F-72-391, Fellowship for Younger Humanists.

REFERENCES

Greeley, Andrew M. *Strangers in the House: Catholic Youth in America.* New York: Sheed & Ward, 1961.

Hammond, Phillip E. *The Campus Clergyman.* New York: Basic Books, 1966.

Horn, Henry F. *Lutherans in Campus Ministry.* Chicago: National Lutheran Campus Ministry, 1969.

Murphy, Laurence T., and John Whitney Evans, eds. *Perspectives for Campus Ministry.* Washington, D.C.: Division of Higher Education, United States Catholic Conference, 1973.

Shedd, Clarence P. *The Church Follows Its Students.* New Haven: Yale University Press, 1938.

Underwood, Kenneth, ed. *The Church, the University, and Social Policy.* Middletown, Conn.: Wesleyan University Press, 1969.

Wuthnow, Robert, and Charles Y. Glock. "Religious Loyalty, Defection, and Experimentation among College Youth." *Journal for the Scientific Study of Religion* 12 (June 1973).

Yankelovich, Daniel. *The Changing Values on Campus.* New York: Washington Square Press, 1972.

11

Three Congregations

JAMES WOLFE

The churches of the Bay Area did not embrace with open arms the dream of a new culture being espoused by the youth of the sixties. On the contrary, most local church congregations viewed the counterculture with suspicion and responded to it with suppressed and sometimes open hostility.

This was not the response of all Christian groups, of course. As we have seen, more evangelistic groups operating outside mainline Protestantism, such as the Jesus people, were open to positive encounter, as was the Charismatic Renewal Movement in the Roman Catholic church. However ineffectively, the mainline campus ministry, as Barbara Hargrove has just told us, also sought encounter. There were also some local congregations in the Bay Area who tried, albeit with mixed success, to respond creatively to what youth were saying about the ambiguities in American culture, social arrangements, and styles of life.

This chapter reports the results of a study of three such "deviant" congregations. The study was undertaken, initially, out of curiosity about what had led them to encounter when it was so much against the norm for Bay Area churches. Since the encounter led to such different outcomes for the three congregations, I also became interested in portraying and in trying to account for the differences. Doing so, I thought, might help to illuminate the larger question of what encourages and what inhibits institutional change and, in addition, round out the picture afforded us in the previous chapter of the counterculture's impact on mainline religion.

The study was carried out over the course of several years, primarily through participant observation and through interviews with congregational members and leaders. This report on the results of the study is divided into three parts: part 1 introduces the three congregations and examines the reasons for their openness to encounter; part 2 describes the ways in which the churches were and were not transformed by the encounter; and part 3 offers an interpretation of the transformations.

THE SOURCES OF ENCOUNTER

Given its national and international fame, there is no way to disguise the identity of one of the three congregations studied—Glide Memorial Methodist Church in San Francisco—and I have made no effort to try. It seems prudent that the other two congregations not be identified, not because anything particularly secret or negative is revealed about them, but simply because I feel that the congregations would rather have it that way.

Of the three churches, Glide was the most open to encounter. Indeed, it is probably fairer to describe Glide as an agent of the counterculture rather than as a congregation in engagement with it. Virtually from the very beginning of the youth movement, Glide was a party to it, offering it material support and spiritual encouragement. It was clearly unique among Bay Area congregations in these respects. No other congregation at so early a stage was doing more than pondering what its posture should be.

The roots of Glide's uniqueness lie in its history. Located in the economically depressed Tenderloin district of San Francisco, the church was founded in 1929 with a large endowment, including continuing revenue from the profits of a local hotel, bestowed on it by philanthropist Elizabeth Glide. The endowment enabled the building of a substantial sanctuary, an evangelistic center, and housing for women. The church was organized as a constituent congregation of the then Methodist Church South, later to become merged into the United Methodist church.

Over the course of most of its early history, Glide was a fairly typical urban parish with a considerable proportion of its membership coming from outside the immediate area. While its affluence enabled it to carry on a more extensive program than most comparable churches, the program was not distinguished by radical departures from the ordinary. Along with the church, philanthropist Glide also endowed an eleemosynary foundation. The foundation, under the congregation's control, made grants in and outside of California with some emphasis on Christian but, by and large, uncontroversial causes.

Judging only from its history through the fifties, Glide should have remained in the sixties as staid as other downtown San Francisco churches. Glide was not as dependent as other congregations on its constituency for support, but the endowment funds had not been used adventurously in the fifties; and there seemed little prospect, given congregational control, of a radical change in the sixties.

That a change did occur is a result essentially of the congregation's losing control of the foundation and its endowment to an independent board and to that board bringing in new leadership committed to making local rather than national and international use of the foundation's largesse. The change in structure was engineered by the Methodist bishop of San Francisco, Donald H. Tippett, in 1960. The change in program and orientation was inspired by Tippett but executed by Lewis Durham, who became director of the foundation in 1962.

In 1962 there was as yet no youth counterculture to encounter, but the changes instituted by Durham in 1962 set the stage for Glide being open to the encounter when the opportunity arose. Among Durham's first acts was the setting up of Glide Urban Center, an agency devoted to reorienting the foundation's resources to serving the people living within the vicinity of the church. These people were much younger and considerably poorer on the average than the regular constituency of the church. And they included many people already experimenting with alternative life-styles.

By virtue of the services it came to offer, the Glide Urban Center attracted considerable community interest and involvement; slowly, the clientele of the center began coming to church services as well. The result was the gradual transformation of the constituency of the church. Increasingly, the church became a haven for the kinds of people who were to be in the vanguard of the counterculture. By the time the counterculture became active, Glide was more than ready to welcome and to support it and had a new and sympathetic chief pastor, Cecil Williams, to lead the welcoming committee.

Unlike Glide, the other two churches in the inquiry are not highly endowed or did they experience the same kind of transformation in membership just prior to the onset of the counterculture. Both are upper middle class, predominantly white congregations associated with a mainline Protestant denomination. One of the two churches

—I shall call it St. John's—is theologically quite conservative; the other—Grace Church—is theologically more liberal but no more so than other Bay Area congregations that showed no disposition whatsoever to open encounter with the counterculture.

St. John's effort at encounter was a result mainly of there being no escape from doing so. Located in the vicinity of a Bay Area university that became a center of countercultural innovation, St. John's found itself surrounded by hordes of protesting students, destitute street people, heavy drug use, and occasional riots. The situation simply demanded a response.

It is clear, in retrospect, that the majority of St. John's constituency, including its senior pastor, was inclined to see the counterculture as more of a problem than an opportunity, as a plague rather than a potential leaven in society, and as needing redemption rather than providing it. The associate pastor, responsible for congregational outreach, was sympathetic to a positive response, however; and as a result of his personality and the presence of masses of people marching outside its doors, St. John's was persuaded to reach out to the "strange tribes" on its doorsteps, as it had throughout its history to "strange tribes" overseas.

Grace Church's engagement in encounter is more purely a result of pastoral leadership. There was certainly no demand from the congregation for it, and even the handful of youth in the church were indifferent. There were also no pressures from the community for encounter. The community population was upper middle class, staunchly Republican, and naturally prone to back the establishment. The location of the church also argued against encounter, being far removed from the turbulence that came to characterize university campuses and more urban settings in the Bay Area.

The pastor's success in overcoming these obstacles and winning the congregation to a positive response was helped, undoubtedly, by the church's being on the liberal rather than the conservative side of the theological spectrum. The more important key to his success, however, is in the manner, in both word and deed, of his interpretation of the counterculture. As I shall shortly report, he was able, as virtually no other Bay Area cleric, to bring about creative encounter by winning his congregation to selective acceptance of what youth were trying to say.

THE CONSEQUENCES OF ENCOUNTER

Just what the consequences would be of a church being transformed by countercultural encounter is not self-evident. Youth in the sixties were saying many things about life in America and about American culture and society. They were not saying these things in a highly articulate way, however, and certainly there was no clear, widely accepted vision of the whole. Still, there were many stimuli being thrown out to which a perceptive church might respond.

In my study, I was especially anxious to see how the three congregations responded to a set of stimuli that I judged to be at the core of youth's dream for a new culture. The stimuli relate to three levels of human experience: the inward, the interpersonal, and the institutional. At the inward level, the dream embodied visions of people at home on earth and enjoying life, being impulsive and creative, and being open to imagination and wonder. At the interpersonal level, the dream envisioned people telling each other how they feel, joining together with flexible bonds, and reaching across divisions. At the institutional level, the dream was of people speaking out for themselves, struggling for change, and resisting imposed authority.

This dream of a new culture stands in marked contrast to the cultural paradigm prevailing in most churches with its emphasis on industry, rationality, repression, propriety, individualism, ethnocentrism, meritocracy, privatism, and conformity. The old culture, the residue of the fantasies of past generations, remains potent in the churches, perhaps more so than in any other institution of American society. The resistance to new culture exhibited by the churches of the Bay Area may very well be a result of their being the chief remaining bastions of the old.

The grip of the old culture proved too strong to allow anything like a complete transformation to new culture to take place in any of the three congregations studied. Still, in only one of the churches did the old culture end up with a clear victory over the new.

THE INWARD LEVEL

Of the three congregations, Grace learned how to hang the loosest about playfulness, expressiveness, and cosmic awareness. Though many of its people still define themselves by their work roles (one of my contacts was such a "workaholic" that he would turn down jobs that didn't make him work overtime and, at home, would work around the house as the only means to relate to his family), there is a growing questioning of the Protestant work ethic and a recognition of the legitimacy of pleasure as an end in itself. The usual taboos against wine, laughter, and applause in church have disappeared. Wine is used to celebrate many occasions—the tragedy

and triumph of the Lord's Supper, the parting of good friends for a
new life in Oregon, the joy of a Sunday morning wedding with
dancing in the church courtyard. The high point now of the church
year is the annual Yule feast, an extravagant celebration of the
twelfth night of Christmas spiced with the wearing of Renaissance
clothes, the burning of a yule log, the display and eating of a boar's
head spiked with the drinking of wassail before, and wine during, a
sumptuous meal.

Worship has become pleasurable at Grace Church, often to the
surprise of members and visitors brought up in more solemn congregations. In the eyes of the pastor, Christian worship is a "Time
of joy, conviviality, and gaiety . . . an experience of holy mirth."
The church bulletin proclaims, "Worship to us is a festive drama, a
celebration designed to help us express our pleasure with Christ's
activity in the world." Film clips, excerpts from plays, multimedia
experiences render regular Sunday morning worship more vivid.
Music varies from traditional hymns, woodwind ensemble, recorder
trio, and classical productions with orchestra and choir to a folk-
rock group, a jazz trio, a Dixieland band, a folk-singing group, and
contemporary songs sung by the congregation (out of a self-created
cumulative songbook) to guitar accompaniment. The "Now Testament," which intervenes between the New Testament reading and
the sermon, is often a recording of a contemporary song with a
message, though it is more frequently a reading from a contemporary source including newspaper commentaries and Peanuts car-
toons. Mime, dance, and body movement have also been used in
worship. Such is the range of forms in worship at Grace that visitors
are warned in the bulletin not to expect the same fare from week
to week, and members who have stayed with the congregation
through these changes have learned to expect the unexpected.

For most members, the old supernatural God is dead. The pastor,
reacting in part against his fundamentalist background, is prone to
challenge people to grow by letting go, without guilt, of vestiges of
a God in whom they no longer believe. Jesus and the humanizing
forces he represents, however, are often on the pastor's lips, and the
search for a more adequate conception of the divine which will suit
the modern mind is taken seriously. A number dabble in astrology,
a fact recognized by the congregation's sponsoring a believers'
astrology contact group and also a weekend retreat on Christianity
and the occult. Yoga classes have also been conducted repeatedly
with some seeing their value mainly in terms of exercises and relaxation, but also with vectors of gaining peace of mind and receiving
and transmitting cosmic energy.

Glide Church is less into cosmic awareness than Grace but more into bodily expressiveness and almost on a par in playfulness. Glide has become noted for the expressiveness of its worship, its celebrative style derived, in part, from the youth culture and in part from Cecil Williams having his roots in the black church, where Sunday worship is more often an occasion for celebration. A light show on the front wall accompanies the loud sounds of a rock band. Banners festoon the side walls. Choruses are often repeated under Cecil Williams's direction, reaching a cresendo pitch. Applause routinely follows, raising a question for some visitors whether it really expresses what they feel. In a style characteristic of black preaching, Cecil solicits audience responsiveness to his sermon. Almost everyone, as instructed, puts arms around each other and sways during the offering. Traditional church strictures against expression and sensuality do not apply. At Grace there is a sense of being avant-garde and even naughty ("this church rated X," said a church ad). At Glide, openness to bodily expressiveness seems natural and to be taken for granted.

Glide Church tolerates any and every religious persuasion, which is to say that no religious position is central to its life. Explicit Christian symbols are absent inside its building, no sacraments are administered, and no profession of faith is required for membership. With the "Thoughts from Chairman Jesus" having largely disappeared from the program, only the songs, such as "Wade in the Water" and "Joshua Fit the Battle," turn the celebration back to its scriptural heritage. Although Cecil Williams will occasionally preach about the depths of the self or even about experience of nothingness, his answer to the current malaise tends to be phrased much more in terms of leftist revolutionary politics than in terms of a new inwardness. And revolutionary rhetoric tends to be taken over wholesale rather than reinterpreting it from a theological standpoint.

St. John's remains very restrained in its natural playfulness, bodily awareness, and cosmic consciousness. Its people were not "hip on hippies" to begin with; and while the church experienced a need to minister to them, it was soon evident that it didn't really know how. Even mild overtures produced congregational rows, as, for example, a gala, replete with garlanded statues of the Virgin Mary, held on the church's parking lot by a specialized ministry to the street people which counted St. John's among its initial supporters.

The congregation's worship service has remained more staid than celebrative, with none of the festivity that has come to characterize the other two churches. Organ and voice remain the only legitimate instruments, and sacraments are still performed infrequently and unmagically. The pastor preaches that the body is good, but all the bodies in the sanctuary sit still and let their minds take in what he says; there is no attempt to celebrate or express the body's goodness (and I received a quizzical look when I mentioned this being done at Grace Church). College student members are allowed to use guitars and sing more impassioned, though hardly gutsy, gospel songs in their post-church school hour. "Lord of the Dance" is even sung by request, but it is done sitting in a circle of chairs. The minister of music has introduced some new forms of expression —dance, modernistic music, slides, multimedia poetry, ambulatory Communion, kiss of peace—into a special series of experimental Sunday evening services, but doubts remain concerning how much from these side shows can be incorporated into the main Sunday morning service.

THE INTERPERSONAL LEVEL

None of the three churches has embraced all three of the interpersonal themes I have associated with the dream of new culture, partly because of the failure to try; but it is more a matter of not knowing what to do or of the obstacles' being greater than a congregations's capacity to surmount them.

Grace has achieved considerable success in creating an atmosphere of honest openness in interpersonal relations, as well as the kind of flexible joining together I shall call "familial community." Its efforts to break down class and ethnic barriers have been less successful; it remains a homogeneously upper-middle-class, largely white, Anglo-Saxon congregation.

At Grace, the pastor's call for people to open up to each other has been warmly responded to and the church has innovated a variety of ways to enable growth in interpersonal encounter. At weekend retreats of the church's governing body, which used to be all business, time is now taken to allow elders and deacons to explore the feelings they have about each other. Education for children includes an experimentally oriented course designed to encourage expression and the communication of anger, fear, and boredom as well as of love and joy and peace. Adult education now abounds with growth groups. A women's consciousness-raising group combined with a men's consciousness group to address the possibilities of family conflict as women abandon their stereotypic timidity, and assert themselves more openly. Those who have experienced divorce are encouraged to meet together to share their problems of adjustment, and those who have or have had cancer are exchanging experiences and anxieties in a "cancer club." The acme of personal self-revelation is the overnight marathon in which about a dozen people spend twelve hours opening up to each other. Amidst all of these opportunities, there is sensitivity that the pace of self-revelation must remain in the individual's control without the kind of pressure to "spill one's guts" that characterizes many encounter groups.

Disclosure of feelings at Grace takes place in an atmosphere of trust, so far as I could judge. There is a strong sense of community with constant reference being made to the church as a family. As a symbolic gesture to indicate that the church is just not a composite of families, the prior monopoly of married couples to serve as greeters has been broken. Such a traditional family experience as enjoying Thanksgiving together is now celebrated by members with and without families eating together at church. Weekend outings with the same kind of mix has also contributed to a sense of the church's being a familial community.

Grace Church's espousal of diversity and of dialogue has resulted in the recruitment of new members, primarily people who had not been attending church, but also in a loss of old members, more conservative in their outlook and unable to adjust to the changes taking place. The church's location in a virtually all-white middle-class enclave has frustrated efforts to transcend class, ethnic, and especially racial divisions which characterize the society at large. Black youth have occasionally participated in the church's youth programs, and several retreats have been held with youth from a black church in an effort to obtain broad exposure. Yet the church is still basically for the white, the more well-to-do, and the avant-garde liberal; and despite a desire not to be, it is likely to remain as exclusive as the hills in which it is located as long as neighborhood church patterning persists.

Glide Church reverses the pattern at Grace in its pluralism, but it does not directly offer much in the way of honest openness and familial community. Sermons are directed against being uptight and for setting yourself free; and Glide folk hang loose enough, but the congregation offers few avenues for personal communication at a deep level. The celebration provides an opportunity for self-expression in a group setting but not for self-revelation. The sex forum assaults conventional attitudes and occasions a sharing of personal insights, though there is not the easy opening up to one another that characterizes the atmosphere at Grace.

Simultaneous celebration with strangers on Sunday mornings does not breed community, even when togetherness is expressed by putting arms around one another and swaying during the offertory. Recognizing this, Glide's leaders have sought to develop a sense of community by encouraging worshippers to remain after celebration for a rap and an outing; but the efforts seem contrived, and few people remain regularly for the postcelebrative activities. Glide also serves as headquarters for the broader amorphous "community" to which it belongs, and the activities to which people are recruited—such as Counter Culture Village, Harrad West, work with prisoners, senior-citizen organizing—provide opportunity for solidarity. It is in such extensions of Glide's life that the greatest familial community is found.

Glide is by far the most pluralistic of the three congregations. Participants in its celebrations run about a third black and two-thirds white, plus a few Asians. Its inclusion of elements from both black and hippie-white experience has meant that neither group has had to jettison its style to participate. Many are the youth in jeans, but older people in suits also turn out. While Grace Church reached out to gay people by lending its hall for a gay women's dance and by including homosexuals among the "whole world in God's hands" in its singing and preaching, gay people are accepted as an integral part of the community at Glide. Cecil Williams has even performed gay marriages, lending the church's sanction to this form of "deviant" relationship. With much of its clientele not into family relations and not intending to enter them, there is no norm for how people should form close bonds operating at Glide. Nor is any uniformity of religious belief expected, not even confinement to some form of Christianity. Noting and symbolizing this, Rabbi Feinberg, Glide's "rabbi-in-residence" could say that, while he resisted the fundamentalist-Christian question, "Are you saved?" he did believe in Glide Church. However, Glide's pluralism at worship, while genuine enough, lacks something of an integral quality because of the ephemeral nature of the assemblage. With no center to unify its diverse elements—unless it is the fact of conglomeration itself or the charismatic personality of Cecil Williams—Glide Church is more of a crowd than an integrated congregation.

St. John's has experienced only the first hints of honest openness and familial community, and evidences very little by way of integral pluralism. Although a good majority of the college students answered a questionnaire item in favor of talking frankly with partners about sexual matters, their course in sexuality never got down to the nitty gritty; still, merely talking about sex at St. John's is a bow to openness. Without analyzing its social roots, loneliness is recognized as a problem for unattached college students; St. John's answer is Bible study groups in which room is left for personal communication as well as edification.

The students at St. John's strike me as nice kids, well-scrubbed and well-dressed, pious, moral, conventional, and uptight—a junior edition of their elders in the congregation. High school and college student congregants, with the permission of their elders, recently put on "For Heaven's Sake," a decade-old musical with an evangelistic message, after some controversy and minor cuts, despite some racy language and some mildly compromising scenes. But respectability is still clearly the norm, and any fudging in the direction of "telling it like it is" tends to require some secrecy or delicate negotiation.

The nuclear family and its ethos is dominant at St. John's. While there are attempts to make widows and students feel at home, family relatedness remains normative. Except for some Jesus people related to St. John's who live communally, almost everyone else abides by traditional family patterns or are prone to hide it if they don't.

Differences are tolerated but not encouraged at St. John's. A choir member and his wife do yoga during their quiet time; one college student raises radical questions. Still, although the pastor does not go so far as to enumerate specific rules for behavior, conservative Christianity is very much the norm. Orientals, including a new minister of Christian education, are in evidence and well accepted but not cherished for their distinctiveness. Blacks are virtually absent, as are the street people of the surrounding community. What diversity there is, is maintained by overlooking it and by developing enclaves insulated from each other rather than by espousing and embodying an integral pluralism.

THE INSTITUTIONAL LEVEL

Many Americans were uptight about the counterculture's advocacy of alternative life-styles. They were more bothered, however, by the new culture's advocacy of political change. Comparatively, the "flower children" seemed less of a threat than the hordes of youth mounting the barricades on the nation's campuses.

It was my expectation, consequently, to find more resistance in the three churches to the institutional themes I have associated with

new culture than with the inward and interpersonal themes.
Generally speaking, the expectation was confirmed but in a relative
rather than an absolute way. To varying degrees, all three churches
became more democratic, more politically sensitive, and more
politically involved as a result of their encounter with new culture.

Glide has become more revolutionary than Grace in its intentions
for society. Grace, however, outscores Glide and St. John's in how
far it has gone in democraticizing church government and in
developing a sense of personal responsibility among its members.
At Grace, considerable power is lodged in the church's governing
council by the polity of its denomination, but this power is now
delicately used. Council meetings are open and members are encouraged to attend and to participate. The council has delegated
much of its authority to committees which are empowered to act in
their own names without council approval. Both members and nonmembers of the congregation serve as committee members. Women
are well represented on the council and on committees; and despite
the paucity of members under twenty-five, there is one college-age
elder.

Grace encourages the presentation of political candidates and the
discussion of political issues at its postworship coffee hour. Several
members have spearheaded the Committee for Change, a nonpar-
tisan community organization that endorses political candidates
and ballot measures, and the congregation has accorded the committee access to its facilities and organs of publicity. The council
voted to make the church a "sanctuary"; and when an AWOL navy
airman who was seeking to become a conscientious objector took
advantage of the opportunity so offered, the church stood firm under navy pressure. In the end, it was the navy rather than the
church that agreed to compromise.

Committees of the congregation are encouraged to take advocacy
positions in their own names. A War/Peace Committee was active
in maintaining a peace table at coffee hour and holding programs
about peace; and the committee received congregational support to
send four busloads of its members and friends to a San Francisco
peace march. Ecology and Community Action committees also
flourished at the turn of the decade but have declined as the congregation's emphasis has shifted toward concern for its own internal
dynamics as a community and for the personal growth of its people.
Adult courses on black history and on community school problems
were very popular one year. But similar courses on minorities and
on youth culture failed to obtain minimal registration the following

year. Still believing social action to be a proper outlet for its ministry and seeking to find an appropriate role for itself, segments of the congregation have been active in supporting the farm workers' struggle and in sponsoring their own "internationalization" program, the latter spearheaded by a couple from the congregation who are working in Nigeria.

Grace generally upholds the Christian tradition but undogmatically. People are encouraged to take responsibility for their own theological views and to let them grow in dialogue with others. In an effort not to sanction loyalties alien to the church's own, the American flag had been eased out of the sanctuary; and celebrations have been devoted to the reinterpretation of the civil heritage in light of the church's faith. Sermons are called "Engaging the Ideas of our Teaching Elder" and are delivered out front rather than from on high—to indicate that they make no pretense of being authoritative—and they are sometimes replaced by small group discussions and feedback after a brief pastoral introduction. The right of the individual conscience, rather than any necessary agreement with a pacifist viewpoint, informed the congregation's resistance to the civil power in granting sanctuary. In the ecology area, members have taken personal responsibility by not only seeking political change but also by switching soaps and recycling their own cans and bottles. One lawyer in the congregation, who is particularly keen on not bowing to any institution, opened his own law practice at a considerable reduction in income; but most at Grace would not be that committed to their own personal independence. The basic mentality is reformist rather than revolutionary, and the impetus is largely to mitigate rather than to abolish the repressive authority of social institutions.

Glide is a good deal more committed to radical political involvement and to resistance to current political authority but has less participatory democracy, at least in structure, than Grace. Glide lacks the basic democracy of the congregational form and never has congregational business meetings. Although the board of the foundation that rules Glide has sought to make itself representative of the Glide community in its membership, the board has also been responsive to the recommendations of a program committee drawn from Glide people and has championed the causes of exploited minorities—blacks, other races, gays, women, prisoners, farm workers, youth, the aged. Although Cecil Williams has been active in these causes, especially in liberating political prisoners—attracting publicity as Angela Davis's spiritual adviser—social-action projects are not so much led from the top as sprung from the bottom. Glide staff and resources serve mainly as a catalyst for exploited people to organize themselves and recruit allies; for example, ex-convicts are very active in the SOS movement to aid ex-cons. With no visible symbols or restricting tradition, Glide serves as a kind of mecca for all kinds of third-world activism; its buildings have frequently been made available to various radical groups for rallies, including a memorial service led by antigovernment Vietnamese for one of their fallen comrades in the resistance. Following celebrations, rap tables are used to give information, raise funds, collect signatures, and solicit further action by such groups as the United Farm Workers, the Black Panthers, and ad hoc committees to free various political prisoners. When a portion of the Glide community gets together for a rap session following a celebration, there is such concern that every voice be heard that little leadership is exercised. As a result, decisions tend to be belabored, though sometimes action, such as a courthouse protest, eventuates. Although Glide has a minister to older persons, its primary thrust with old folks is not, as with most congregations, to provide consolation and entertainment but to organize them to seek their own betterment through political action, such as lobbying in the state capital.

Glide seeks to give people permission to be themselves and to think their own thoughts and do their own deeds. The right of every person to be somebody and to be free is frequently reiterated. However, the whole capitalist system and its structures with all their subjugating gradations is anathema to many Glide folks, and they are dedicated to bringing it down by any means necessary. There are limits imposed, consequently, on the direction that freedom of expression may take.

St. John's still exhibits little participatory democracy, political involvement, or personal responsibility. In keeping with its traditional polity, the church has a degree of direct democracy in having ministers, elders, and budgets voted on by the whole congregation; but most decisions are made, in the manner of a representative democracy, by the elected elders who compose the governing council. Even the congregational meetings tend to serve as a rubber stamp for decisions recommended by committees rather than being controversy-laden exercises in participatory democracy, and few in the congregation avail themselves of the opportunity to make their voices heard at open council meetings. Inability to influence current church policy or to get an elder elected who would represent them was a crucial factor in the drifting away of one enclave of more liberal-minded folk in the late sixties. Compared with the congregation, youth and women are underrepresented on the council; women also play subordinate roles, with Pauline sanction, in most of the congregations's families. Like most of established American society, St. John's remains under the control of the "white male club."

St. John's is in the business of religion, and the "evangelical" Gospel it propagates has little of the political cutting edge that the other two congregations have found in their interpretations of the Gospel. It has tended to be much more supportive of foreign missions with a religious conversion thrust than of national missions with a liberating thrust. The church seems to be largely unaware of the complicity of some missionaries with colonial power abroad; and when a missionary who had long had its support reversed this pattern by getting into liberation work under ecumenical auspices in Latin America, it dropped him. With what a now ex-associate minister called its "salt-water complex," the congregation is even less responsive to "third-world" movements at home. Although St. John's has shown some concern in its adult classes for racial minorities and has reached some minorities in its social service (for example, tutoring in schools), it has shown little taste for political activism of late. Except for the mid-sixties involvement of the minister for outreach and his tiny circle in such things as the formation of a "free church" and an attempt to get Saul Alinsky into the Bay Area, St. John's ended up sitting out the liberation struggles of the sixties and the early seventies. Sentiments against the war in Vietnam were fairly strong, especially in a forum on Nixon *versus* McGovern; but all the congregation did on the issue was pray for peace, the pastor backing down from a seminarian's suggestion that he pass a peace petition among his staff and let a peace table be set up in the narthex. One seminarian was hired to lead social-action—social-service concerns, but this led to no action controversial enough to make even the congregation's own newspaper; and the seminarian concluded, as he left to take a congregation of his own without being replaced at St. John's, that the congregation is better at self-justifying talk than at implementing action. Although concern for ecology was expressed in a sermon by an associate pastor, social issues are rarely mentioned from the pulpit, much less mobilized around. Whatever political involvement that does take place seems to arise more out of private initiative than out of public conscience, though at the time this study was made it seemed likely that a social-involvement center, adjoining a bookstore operated with the support of the congregation, would be established.

Without mounting any concerted resistance to established authorities, St. John's tends to legitimate the powers that be and to sanction the status quo, and it adheres to the authority of scripture in a way that neither invites radical interpretation of it nor encourages questioning of the conventions of society or the conduct of government from that basis. Unlike Grace and Glide, St. John's is not likely to "turn the world upside down" or to liberate its people into the kind of personal responsibility that recognizes a revolutionary Christ as the only Lord of one's conscience.

INTERPRETATION

The portraits of the three churches afford a glimpse of why the counterculture made so little impact on traditional churches and several visions of what might have ensued had the impact been greater. None of the churches responded typically to new culture, since all of them made some effort to encounter it. Yet, St. John's probably represents the kinds of constraints operative in the ordinary parish church which produce resistance to change even in the face of considerable counterpressure for it.

By virtue of being at the center of the blooming of new culture, St. John's had the greatest opportunity of the three churches to embrace it. Yet, as we have seen, it proved the least able to do so. St. John's was not ready for change, and in the end the congregation was capable of forestalling it. The church's roots were more embedded in old culture than were those of the other two churches. Well before the onset of the counterculture, St. John's was the most theologically and politically conservative, the most stifled by politeness and fear of conflict, the most oriented to the preservation of the nuclear family, the most committed to propriety in Sunday morning worship, and the most bureaucratic.

It succeeded in this mold in a university community because of the existence of an older, affluent, conservative subpopulation from which to draw membership. In addition, it had become *the* congregation for conservatively minded Protestant students at the university.

In a different setting, St. John's undoubtedly would not have attempted an encounter with a new culture. Certainly, its counterparts at nonuniversity locations in the Bay Area did not do so.

Forced by propinquity to make some response, St. John's sought essentially to convert the new culture back to the old rather than to open itself up to conversion to the new. Given its past history, this was not an unnatural posture for St. John's to have adopted. This strategy did not draw countercultural youth into the church in any sizable numbers. By standing firm, however, the church prevented a flight of its older members and it continued to attract those students whose theological and political views the church mirrored, of which there remained a substantial number.

Conceivably, St. John's might have been turned around if its leadership, as at Glide, had wanted to turn it around and had control of the congregational purse strings. In that case, however, the chances are that St. John's, like Glide, would have experienced a turnover rather than a transformation of its membership. Before accommodating to new culture, those into old culture would probably have ended up abandoning St. John's. Moreover, without the kind of resources available at Glide, St. John's once turned over to new culture would probably not have had the means to survive.

The alternative scenario afforded by Grace also was probably not in the cards for St. John's. Grace succeeded in its accommodation because it did not have the counterculture to deal with directly. There were no students on its doorsteps and no street people and their accompanying drug culture to contend with. Grace had only its own people to transform. I consider its doing so an exceptional achievement. However, given the same leadership, I am doubtful that the same transformation could have happened at St. John's. The old guard there might have been led to be more open with each other, but it is difficult to believe that they could have been more open with what they saw as the "rabble" on the church's doorsteps.

Of the three churches, Glide went the furthest in substituting new culture for old in the organizations of its ministry. Ironically, it was old culture money that made the transformation possible. The endowment, without the leadership, would not have led Glide in the direction it took; but the leadership would not have produced the transition alone either. It was the two factors in combination that enabled the unique congregation which Glide became.

Glide has not become a prototype for other congregations. This is not entirely because of a lack of interest in or sympathy for Glide's innovations. Glide's success in winning an urban constituency, which mainline Protestantism has been unable to reach ordinarily, has its admirers. Admiration has not turned to imitation, however, because the Glide model is not readily reproducible without a large injection of capital. Thus, Glide affords a demonstration that it is possible for a Protestant congregation to work effectively with the disinherited in society in other than the usual fundamentalist mode. The model Glide represents is unlikely to be repeated, however, unless it should come to inform mission churches which gain their primary support from denominations-at-large rather than from their own constituencies.

Of the three churches, Grace Church is my favorite as the portraits have undoubtedly made clear. This is because I like the adaptations that Grace has made to new culture. Grace has been transformed from a rather conventional congregation to a vital and alive one—a congregation that demonstrates the truth in the old saw that people who are helped themselves are made much more able thereby to help others. I like the openness at Grace, the feeling of community, and the joy that members express as they seek witness to their faith.

I like Grace also because it demonstrates that the possibility for creative renewal in the church remains alive. Unlike Glide, Grace was transformed to new culture, not turned over to it. While there was some turnover in membership, the changes at Grace were mostly the result of the same people becoming different rather than of one constituency replacing another. This kind of transformation is rare in any organization. That it can still happen in a church is a sign that the institution cannot be counted out in the future competition to inform the religious dimension in American life.

12

Jewish Identity and the Counterculture

THOMAS PIAZZA

In the past, the issue of Jewish identity was not as open as it is today to individual interpretation. Traditional Judaism was authoritative in defining social roles, patterns of behavior, and a system of belief for Jews. Even though the weight of this traditional authority had been declining for many years, the continuing latent and sometimes open hostility of the larger non-Jewish community served to restrain Jews from disengaging themselves from their culture and their religion.

These constraints are rapidly losing their force. The continuing decline of religious authority, a lower level of anti-Semitism, and the rising general affluence of Jews have provided the person of Jewish background with genuine options. One may choose to reaffirm his or her identity in a traditional way, redefine that identity in a personal way, or decide not to be Jewish at all. The Jewish community has come to recognize the increased openness and has become concerned about what it may imply for the future of American Judaism.

Within the context of this concern about the continued vitality of Judaism, it is not difficult to understand why the youth counterculture of the sixties was viewed with some alarm in Jewish circles. Many aspects of the movement were seen as a threat to Jewish identity. The counterculture's interest in nontraditional and Eastern religion was one focus of concern. More important, however, was the fear that the counterculture would lead to a disenchantment with Jewish culture and religious traditions and to a loss of personal identification with those traditions.

The validity of these concerns has not been explored systematically. It is evident that many Jewish young people were active participants in various countercultural movements, but how many were involved is not known. Furthermore, we have almost no idea what effect such participation had on their Jewish identity. This chapter explores these questions and reports the results of an investigation undertaken as part of the New Religious Consciousness project.

The investigation is based on a secondary analysis of a body of data collected originally for a different purpose but which, fortunately, lends itself to our interest.[1] The data are from a probability sample of approximately one thousand male students enrolled in the University of California, Berkeley, as freshmen in the 1970—71 academic year.[2] The sample included 139 students who said they were raised as Jews. In the fall of 1970, soon after arriving on campus to begin their freshmen year, these students were interviewed and also asked to fill out a questionnaire relating to their backgrounds, their aspirations, their politics, and especially their participation in a wide range of countercultural activities. They were also asked a few key questions about their sense of religious and cultural identity.

The same students were then reinterviewed two and one-half years later, just prior to their completing the junior year.[3] Essentially the same questions were asked as in their freshmen year. Of the original 139 Jewish students, 123 were reinterviewed on this second round.

Since the Jewish students at Berkeley are not representative of American Jewish youth, we cannot generalize conclusions based on

1. The data presented here are from a longitudinal study of "Changing Life Styles among University Males" being conducted by the independent, nonprofit Institute for Research in Social Behavior and currently supported by a grant from the National Institute of Drug Abuse (PHS Grant DA 0137). The author is indebted to Karen Landsman, who did preliminary research on these data.

2. The sampling ratio was less than 1:2. With special efforts made through careful interviewer training and unusually strict anonymity procedures to encourage student participation, a final response rate of slightly over 90 percent was obtained. See Dean I. Manheimer, Glen D. Mellinger, Robert Somers, and Marianne Kleman, "Technical and Ethical Considerations in Data Collection," *Drug Forum* 1 (July 1972): 323—33.

3. Of those originally interviewed, 87 percent returned a mail questionnaire at Time-2. Of that group, 86 percent were enrolled in some school when field work began in April 1973; 65 percent had been enrolled continuously at Berkeley. Note that all of the Time-2 respondents will be referred to as "Juniors" in order to simplify presentation of the data.

these data to the larger population. These data do have the advantage, however, of allowing us to examine what happens to Jewish identity over time and to determine what effect, if any, involvement in the counterculture may have had on identity. Moreover, it is probably of more than local interest to learn how a relatively elite group of young people faced the issue of their Jewish identity at a time and a place in which the challenges posed to it by the counterculture were at their height.

JEWISH IDENTITY BEFORE THE COLLEGE EXPERIENCE

To identify oneself as Jewish can have a variety of meanings. It is possible to identify with the Jewish religion, with the ethnic group, with Jewish culture, with Jewish organizations and causes, and according to scholars in other ways as well.[4] Identification in one sense may or may not be accompanied by identification in another. The majority of American Jews probably find some, but not all, of these dimensions relevant to their own identity. The concern of the Jewish community is less with identity's being expressed in any particular way as with its being expressed at all. What is wanted, essentially, is that persons of Jewish background continue to think of themselves as Jews and act in ways loyal to the Jewish community.

The data to be analyzed here were not collected to explore exhaustively the Jewish identity of the respondents. Nevertheless, information is available in two key areas, the religious and the ethnic dimensions. Looking first at the religious dimension, we see from table 12–1 that only 32 percent of the 139 students who said they had been raised in the Jewish faith or tradition identified their religion as Judaism at the time of their freshman year at college. About half said they had no religion at all or said they were agnostic, atheist, or humanist. Of the remaining 20 percent, 2 percent identified themselves with an Eastern religion or with mysticism, 6 percent said their religion was "my own," 1 percent (meaning one person) claimed conversion to Christianity, 9 percent said "other" without specifying what they meant, and 2 percent did not answer.

4. See, for example, Stephen Steinberg, "The Anatomy of Jewish Identification," in *Religion in Sociological Perspective*, ed. Charles Y. Glock (Belmont, Ca.: Wadsworth, 1973). See also Irwin D. Rinder, "Polarities in Jewish Identification: The Personality of Ideological Extremity" in *The Jews*, ed. Marshall Sklare (Glencoe, Ill.: Free Press, 1958); also Sidney Goldstein and Calvin Goldscheider, *Jewish Americans* (Englewood Cliffs, N.J.: Prentice-Hall, 1968), pp. 171–73.

Table 12–1

RELIGION BY RELIGIOUS BACKGROUND, BERKELEY FRESHMEN
(In percentages) [a]

| | Religious Background | | |
Present Religion	Jewish	Protestant	Catholic
Jewish	32	[b]	0
Protestant	0	36	0
Roman Catholic	0	[b]	53
No religion	14	13	8
Agnostic	23	26	16
Atheist	11	6	3
Humanist	1	0	1
Eastern or mystical	2	1	4
"My own"	6	4	5
Christian—unspecified	1	3	4
Polytheist	0	[b]	0
Deist	0	[b]	0
Other—unspecified	9	8	8
Undecided, No answer	2	2	1
(Number)	(139)	(373)	(200)

[a] Percentages are rounded and do not add exactly to 100 percent.
[b] Less than .5 percent.

A comparison of the students of Jewish background with those of Protestant and Roman Catholic backgrounds, also in table 12–1, reveals that the former were slightly less likely than those raised as Protestants (32 percent and 36 percent, respectively) and considerably less likely than those raised as Catholics (53 percent) to retain the religious identification of their childhood. Among all three groups, defection was primarily in the direction of abandoning religion altogether; only a minority opted for an alternative religion. This tendency for defectors to move completely away from religion was especially pronounced among those from Jewish and Protestant backgrounds.

Students were also asked whether they felt a sense of solidarity and identification with people of their religion. Of those raised as Jews, 25 out of the 32 percent who gave their religion as Judaism claimed such identification. An additional 14 percent of the students from Jewish backgrounds also gave this response, even though they had said that they belonged neither to the Jewish religion nor to any other religious group. A total of 39 percent, therefore, said they identified with people of the Jewish religion.

Compared with religious identification, the amount of ethnic identification was slightly less. In response to a question asking whether they felt a sense of solidarity and identification with people of their race or ethnic group, 34 percent of the freshmen raised as Jews responded affirmatively.

By combining this information on religious and ethnic identification, we sought to estimate the relative degree to which each student had, as a freshman, a positive sense of Jewish identity in the more general meaning of the term. It seems reasonable to assume that Jewish identity was strongest among those students who said that their current religion was Judaism and who also expressed a feeling of solidarity with people of the Jewish religion or ethnic group. Jewish identity would have been weakest among those who belonged to some other religious group or did not respond positively to any of the above-mentioned questions on identification. Among the remainder, who expressed at least some form of positive identification, the sense of Jewish identity was probably intermediate.

If the students of Jewish background are divided into groups by applying these criteria, 27 percent are classified as having a strong, or what I shall call a traditional, sense of Jewish identity. Another 23 percent receive intermediate scores and will be referred to as marginal. The remaining 50 percent are classified into the weakest identity group, here called indifferent.

It should be emphasized that these categories are only relative indicators of the strength of Jewish identification of these students, and that the labels assigned to each category are arbitrary. It should also be recognized that those who fell in the indifferent category may have identified themselves as Jewish on the basis of criteria other than those that the data enable us to apply. Still in all, it is evident that by the time they had begun their college careers, a substantial proportion of these young people did not have a strong feeling of solidarity with the tradition into which they were born.

The extent of this relative indifference raises the question of its source. An examination of the information available about the

Table 12–2

**BACKGROUND CHARACTERISTICS OF STUDENTS RAISED
AS JEWS BY FRESHMAN-YEAR IDENTITY CATEGORIES**
(in percentages)

	Traditional	Marginal	Indifferent
Religion important to mother	83	52	47
Religion important to father	67	57	32
Very close to father during high school	50	31	23
Very close to mother during high school	46	32	21
Family income $20,000 or over	39	57	71
Mother a college graduate	19	39	48
Father did postgraduate study	30	42	45
Mother liberal politically	26	43	54
Father liberal politically	43	33	59
Both parents born in U.S.	70	68	74
Two or more grandparents born outside U.S.	81	87	81
(Number)	(37)	(31)	(69)

backgrounds of these students indicates that the process of dis-
engagement, at least from the religious component of the tradition,
began not with this student generation but with the generation of
their parents and perhaps even before that. As can be seen in table
12–2, students in the indifferent category were considerably less
likely than those with a traditional sense of identity to have said that
religion was important to their parents. Forty-seven percent of the
indifferent and 83 percent of the traditional said that religion was
important to their mothers; 32 percent of the indifferent and 67 percent of the traditional said religion was important to their fathers.
Those students classified as marginal fell between the other two
categories—52 percent responding that religion was important to
their mothers and 57 percent considering it important to their
fathers.

The effect of one parent's religiosity reinforced that of the other.
Of those students who said that religion was important to both
parents, 43 percent were classified as traditional, compared with 7
percent of those with two nonreligious parents. Those with one
religious parent fell in between in the proportion traditional.

It should be kept in mind that this information about parents was
not obtained independently but was supplied by the students
themselves. There may have been a tendency for the students to interpret the religiosity of their parents in a manner consistent with

their own positions. Insofar as this was the case, the influence of parents' religious convictions on the Jewish identity of their children would not have been as strong in actuality as our data suggest. In all probability, however, that influence would still have been substantial.

Traditional students not only were more likely than the indifferent students to have had religious parents but also were likely to have said that they felt "very close" to their parents while they were in high school. For example, as can be seen in table 12—2, 50 percent of the traditional said that they felt very close to their fathers, compared with 31 percent of the marginal students and 23 percent of the indifferent. Having been very close to parents also reinforced the effect of having religious parents. Of those students who said that religion was important to their fathers and that they were very close to their fathers during high school, 63 percent were traditional and only 11 percent were indifferent. In the case of those for whom neither of the conditions was true, the figures were approximately reversed—13 percent traditional and 68 percent indifferent.

Once it is recognized that the Jewish identity of these students is strongly influenced by the religious environment in the home, we are led to ask why some of the parents are more religious than others. The data available on parents is very limited, but there are a few clues. As can be seen in table 12—2, the parents of the indifferent students were much more likely to have had a college education or better, to have a high income, and to be politically liberal. These figures suggest that a possible source of disidentification with Judaism as a religion on the part of the indifferent students' parents is their success in the larger community.

On the other hand, there is no relation to speak of between generation of family migration to the United States and student identity. Note in table 12—2 that all three identity groups were about equally likely to have parents or grandparents who were born outside the United States. Apparently, therefore, the decline in commitment to Jewish traditions among both parents and students was not simply a matter of successive generations becoming more assimilated.

Taken in sum, the data presented thus far show that as many as 50 percent of the students of Jewish background appear to be relatively indifferent toward their heritage by the time they enter college. The data also indicate that the family is an important socializing agent in this respect and that parental education and affluence contribute to reducing a sense of communal solidarity.

Still to be considered are factors outside of family background which may have influenced the identity of these students. Speculation that involvement in the counterculture may be a source of disidentification has tended to assume that the opportunity for such involvement comes primarily after, rather than before, entrance into college. When these students were beginning their college careers in the fall of 1970, however, the counterculture was already past its peak. These students' exposure to its more visible and exciting phase would have occurred while they were still in high school. If the counterculture had an effect on their sense of identity, that effect should be observable in the data collected at the beginning of their freshman year in college.

The youth counterculture, as has already been made abundantly evident in this volume, challenged traditional values and institutions in many different ways—in politics, religion, sexual morality, drug use, and general style of living. Jewish young people were not involved in countercultural religion to any great extent, judging from the present data and from other evidence collected by the New Religious Consciousness project. Nevertheless, elements of the counterculture other than the religious could have affected Jewish students' identity.

Students participating in the study were asked as freshmen about their support for a range of values and political positions associated with the counterculture and about their own participation in various activities of the youth movement. Table 12–3 presents a summary of their responses to these questions. The figures are given

Table 12–3

ACCEPTANCE OF COUNTERCULTURAL ATTITUDES AND BEHAVIOR BY FRESHMEN OF JEWISH AND NON-JEWISH BACKGROUNDS
(In percentages)

	Jewish Freshmen	Non-Jewish Freshmen	Total
Politics			
General Political Viewpoint			
Radical	17	6	8
Radical-Liberal	41	19	22
Liberal	20	23	22
Moderate	15	30	28
Conservative	0	12	10
Other responses	7	10	10
	100	100	100

Table 12–3 *(Continued)*

ACCEPTANCE OF COUNTERCULTURAL ATTITUDES AND BEHAVIOR BY FRESHMEN OF JEWISH AND NON-JEWISH BACKGROUNDS *(in percentages)*

	Jewish Freshmen	Non-Jewish Freshmen	Total
Pessimistic about future of American society	45	27	29
Say no hope for social justice within existing political system	16	11	12
Active in left-oriented political movements in past year [a]	36	14	17
Drug Use			
Ever used drugs	81	57	61
Used drugs in past two months	72	48	52
Used drugs other than marijuana in past six months	29	19	21
Life-style			
Say a couple should definitely live together before marriage	44	26	29
Lived with a girlfriend any time since entering college	7	6	6
Approve legalization of marijuana	80	68	69
Approve legalization of homosexual relations	84	66	68
Would like to try living in a commune	55	37	39
(Number)	(139)	(821)	(960)

[a] *Those who were active in political movements and whose general political viewpoint was radical or radical-liberal.*

separately for students of Jewish and non-Jewish backgrounds, as well as for the freshman sample as a whole.

Inspection of the total column in table 12–3 reveals that a substantial proportion of these male Berkeley freshmen were critical of established institutions and conventional morality even before they had become deeply involved in their college careers. Many had

THOMAS PIAZZA

already participated in activities associated with the counterculture, especially the use of drugs.

If we compare the columns for Jewish and non-Jewish freshmen, it is also apparent that students of Jewish background were consistently more likely than other students to support these positions or to have participated in these activities. Note, for example, that 58 percent of Jewish students classified themselves politically as either radical or radical-liberal, compared with 25 percent of non-Jewish students. Notice also that not a single Jewish freshman in the sample classified himself as conservative. The differences between the two groups were less pronounced on more specific issues relating to politics and life-style, with percentage point differences on this set of items ranging from 1 to 24 percent.

The stronger their ties to their Jewish backgrounds, however, the less likely Jewish freshmen were to have supported countercultural values or to have adopted countercultural life-styles. Table 12–4 presents the responses to these items for students in each of the three Jewish identity categories. Those classified as traditional were consistently less likely than the indifferent group to respond counterculturally to this set of questions, and the differences range

Table 12–4

ACCEPTANCE OF COUNTERCULTURAL ATTITUDES AND BEHAVIOR BY IDENTITY CATEGORIES OF JEWISH FRESHMEN
(in percentages)

	Traditional	Marginal	Indifferent
Politics			
General Political Viewpoint			
Radical	3	19	25
Radical-Liberal	46	33	40
Liberal	24	19	19
Moderate	27	19	7
Conservative	0	0	0
Other responses	0	10	9
	100	100	100
Pessimistic about future of American			
society	24	48	55
Say no hope for social justice within			
existing political system	3	7	26
Active in left-oriented political			
movements in past year. [a]	30	32	41

Table 12—4 *(Continued)*

***ACCEPTANCE OF COUNTERCULTURAL ATTITUDES AND BEHAVIOR
BY IDENTITY CATEGORIES OF JEWISH FRESHMEN
(in percentages)***

	Traditional	Marginal	Indifferent
Drug Use			
Ever used drugs	65	74	92
Used drugs in past two months	51	58	90
Used drugs other than marijuana			
in past six months	14	26	39
Life-style			
Say a couple should definitely			
live together before marriage	24	35	59
Lived with a girlfriend any time			
since entering college	3	7	10
Approve legalization of mari-			
juana	65	77	88
Approve legalization of homo-			
sexual relations	76	90	86
Would like to try living in a			
commune	41	55	62
(Number)	(37)	(31)	(69)

ª *Those who were active in political movements and whose general political
viewpoint was radical or radical-liberal.*

from 7 to 39 percentage points. Those classified as marginal fell
generally between the other two groups.

What is not revealed in table 12—4 is the causal sequence underlying the observed relations between involvement in the
counterculture and a weakening of Jewish identity. The process
could be one in which involvement in the counterculture was the
source of a weakening of identity. Or, the weakening of identity
could have occurred first and have been a stimulus to countercultural experimentation. A third possibility is that the relationship
was reciprocal, with loss of identity stimulating an interest in the
counterculture, which in turn reinforced the dispostion to disidentification. Or, there might be no causal connection between the two
at all, both rather having been the result of parental upbringing.
The data do not allow choosing precisely between these alternatives

Table 12−5

COMMITMENT TO A TRADITIONAL IDENTITY BY IMPORTANCE OF RELIGION TO PARENTS AND BY DRUG USE FOR FRESHMEN OF JEWISH BACKGROUND

	Identity classified as traditional among students who said:			
	Religion important to both parents % no.	*Religion important to one parent* % no.	*Religion important to neither parent* % no.	*Total* % no.
Drug use in previous two months				
Used drugs	32 (31)	19 (31)	6 (33)	19 (95)
Did not use drugs	63 (16)	55 (11)	10 (10)	46 (37)
Total	43 (47)	29 (42)	7 (43)	27 (132)

or deciding what combination of them may be determinate. It is possible, however, to explore whether the relationship between involvement in the counterculture and a weakening of Jewish ties existed independently of, or was a result of, parental influence.

Table 12−5 shows the joint effects of parental religiosity and of involvement in the counterculture on the identity of these Jewish freshmen. To indicate involvement in the counterculture, students have been divided according to whether or not they reported having used drugs in the last two months.

Looking across the rows of table 5, one can see that parental religiosity influenced identity regardless of whether the students had used drugs or not. Students with two religious parents were more likely to be traditional than those with only one religious parent. These latter students, in turn, were more often classified traditional than were students with two nonreligious parents. It is also true, as can be seen by examining the columns of table 12−5, that the relationship between involvement in the counterculture and a weakening of Jewish identity exists independently of the religiosity of the parents. It is interesting to note, however, that whether students used drugs or not seemed to make more of a difference to identity if the students came from homes where one or both parents were religious rather than from homes where neither parent was religious. In effect, among students in the latter group, there was already so much defection from a traditional identity as a result of parental influence that there was not much more that involvement in the counterculture could do.

In sum, these data suggest that there were grounds for the concern that involvement in the counterculture was having a negative impact on Jewish identity. The counterculture's influence, however, was to accelerate a process rather than to start one. The trend toward disidentification, it is clear, had begun before this generation of students.

Before turning to examine the effects of the college experience on Jewish identity, we might note that, while in general freshmen of Jewish background were more likely to be involved in the counterculture than non-Jewish youth, traditional Jewish freshmen were not. When the traditional Jewish freshmen are compared with non-Jewish freshmen (see the appropriate columns in tables 12–3 and 12–4), it is found that there was no consistent tendency for one group to favor countercultural values and activities more than the other. Thus, while these data confirm the widespread impression that youth of Jewish background were more likely to be active in the counterculture than youth of non-Jewish background, they do not support the additional assertion that it was something about these students' Jewishness that encouraged this activity. On the contrary, identifying oneself strongly as Jewish was a brake rather than a stimulus to countercultural experimentation.

THE EFFECTS OF THE COLLEGE EXPERIENCE

The discussion to this point has centered on the state of Jewish identity among youth of Jewish background at the time they entered college in 1970. The question I now wish to address is the effect of the Berkeley college experience on that sense of identity.

Ordinarily, our expectation in approaching this issue would be that the college experience will be found to weaken rather than to strengthen Jewish identity. Although not all studies have found that religious commitment declines during the college years, that is the predominant finding. In the present instance, a factor that might upset ordinary expectations is the general decline in the elan of the counterculture that occurred during the time our sample was at college—1970 to 1974. It is conceivable that those students who rejected their traditions while the counterculture was at its height might have reembraced them while it was waning.

Table 12–6 compares how students of Jewish, Protestant, and Roman Catholic backgrounds identified themselves religiously as freshmen and as juniors. The table reveals a further erosion of identification on the part of students of Protestant and Roman Catholic

Table 12−6

**RELIGIOUS IDENTIFICATION OF STUDENTS OF JEWISH, PROTESTANT,
AND ROMAN CATHOLIC BACKGROUNDS AS FRESHMEN AND AS JUNIORS
(In percentages)**

Religious Background	Present Religion					
	As raised	None [a]	Eastern/ mystical	Other [b]	Total	Number
Jewish						
Freshman year	33	49	2	16	100	(123) [d]
Junior year	33	55	4	8	100	(123)
Change	0	+6	+2	−8		
Protestant						
Freshman year	38	44	c	18	100	(325) [d]
Junior year	25	52	3	20	100	(325)
Change	−13	+8	+3	+2		
Roman Catholic						
Freshman year	53	26	2	19	100	(167) [d]
Junior year	43	39	3	15	100	(167)
Change	−10	+13	+1	−4		

a *Includes agnostics, atheists, and humanists, as well as those who say "no religion."*

b *Includes the small religious categories (except Eastern or mystical), the nonresponders, and those few persons who belong to Protestant, Catholic, or Jewish religions without being raised in them.*

c *Less than .5 percent.*

d *For purposes of this comparison, only those freshmen are included who also responded in the junior year. Table 1 gives figures based on the full sample of freshmen.*

backgrounds with the religious traditions in which they were raised. Among students of Jewish background, however, as many identified themselves religiously as Jews in their junior year as had done so at the beginning of their freshmen year. The only net changes are a 6 percent increase in the "none" category, a 2 percent increase in the number of those identifying with Eastern and mystical religions, and a corresponding 8 percent reduction in the "other" category. By the junior year proportionately more students of Jewish background identify themselves with the religious tradition in which they were raised than do students from Protestant backgrounds. Students of Roman Catholic background are the most likely to retain their religious identification, but even among that group the identifying students have fallen into the minority.

Table 12–7

**LEVEL OF JEWISH IDENTITY AMONG STUDENTS OF
JEWISH BACKGROUND AS FRESHMEN AND AS JUNIORS
(In percentages)** a

| | Freshman Year | | | |
	Traditional	Marginal	Indifferent	Total
Junior Year				
Traditional	16	4	1	21
Marginal	7	10	12	29
Indifferent	4	9	37	50
Total	27	23	50	100

a *This table is based only on the results obtained from 123 students
who responded both as freshmen and as juniors.*

In addition to the question on current religious affiliation, the
questions about identification with people of the students' religious
and ethnic groups were also repeated in the junior-year survey. On
these measures there was a net decline in both types of identification among students of Jewish background. Identification with people of the Jewish religion declined from 39 to 30 percent between
the freshman and junior years, and ethnic identification went from
34 to 26 percent.

Using the same criteria as with the freshman responses, we combined the junior-year data on current religion, religious identification, and ethnic identification into a summary measure of Jewish
identity. A comparison of the identity scores of those Jewish students for whom we have comparable data in both years is given in
table 12–7. This table shows that a majority fall into the same identity category as juniors as they did in their freshman year. Sixteen
percent are classified as traditional in both years, 10 percent as
marginal, and 37 percent as indifferent. Out of the remaining 37
percent, 20 percent showed a weakening in the level of identity,
and 17 percent demonstrated a more positive identity. In only 5
percent of the cases, however, was there a shift from one extreme to
the other. Four percent moved from the traditional to the indifferent category, and 1 percent in the reverse direction.

The principal conclusion to be drawn from table 12–7 is that the
identity levels of the Jewish students have changed remarkably little during their college years. Indeed, the best predictor of junior-

year identity we could find in these data is freshman-year identity. It is also worthy of note that the changes that did occur in the level of identity were not all in the same direction. The college experience encouraged some students to move toward rather than away from traditional identification.

The relative stability of Jewish identity during the college years is paralleled by relative stability in political orientation as well. As can be seen in table 12–8, the proportion of Jewish students who consider themselves radical is the same in both years, and all across the political spectrum there is very little net change from one time period to the next. Similarly, the proportions expressing pessimism about the future of American society and saying that there is no hope for social justice within the existing political system remained at roughly the same levels over the college years. There was, however, a substantial drop—from 33 percent to 20 percent—in the proportion of students of Jewish background who report being *active* in the more radical political movements.

Among non-Jewish students there was a slight shift toward the Left in political viewpoint during the college years. As freshman, 25 percent classified themselves as radical or radical-liberal; by their

Table 12–8

ACCEPTANCE OF COUNTERCULTURAL ATTITUDES AND BEHAVIOR BY JEWISH AND NON-JEWISH STUDENTS IN THEIR FRESHMAN AND IN THEIR JUNIOR YEARS   (In percentages)

	Jewish Students			Non-Jewish Students		
	Freshmen	Juniors	Change	Freshmen	Juniors	Change
Politics						
General Political Viewpoint						
Radical	16	16	0	6	10	+4
Radical-Liberal	41	43	+2	19	22	+3
Liberal	23	19	−4	23	23	0
Moderate	13	8	−5	31	23	−8
Conservative	0	3	+3	11	11	0
Other responses	7	11	+4	10	11	+1
	100	100		100	100	
Pessimistic about future of American society	46	40	−6	25	28	+3
Say no hope for social justice within existing political system	15	19	+4	10	17	+7
Active in left-oriented political movements in past year [a]	33	20	−13	13	8	−5

Table 12–8 *(Continued)*

**ACCEPTANCE OF COUNTERCULTURAL ATTITUDES AND BEHAVIOR BY
JEWISH AND NON-JEWISH STUDENTS IN THEIR FRESHMAN AND
IN THEIR JUNIOR YEARS** *(in percentages)*

	Jewish Students			Non-Jewish Students		
	Freshmen	Juniors	Change	Freshmen	Juniors	Change
Drug Use						
Ever used drugs	80	92	+12	56	75	+19
Used drugs in past two months	71	68	−3	47	50	+3
Used drugs other than mari-						
juana in past six months	28	27	−1	17	22	+5
Life-style						
Say a couple should definitely						
live together before marriage	44	64	+20	24	40	+16
Lived with a girlfriend any						
time in past two years	7	33	+26	5	22	+17
Approve legalization of mari-						
juana	80	95	+15	67	82	+15
Approve legalization of homo-						
sexual relations	86	93	+7	66	82	+16
Would like to try living in a						
commune	55	48	−7	36	37	+1
(Number)	(123)[b]	(123)		(711)[b]	(711)	

  a *Those who were active in political movements and whose general political viewpoint was radical or radical-liberal.*
  b *Freshmen who also responded in the junior year. Table 12-3 gives figures based on the full sample of freshmen.*

junior year 32 percent did so. The proportion saying that there is no hope for social justice within the existing political system also increased, from 10 to 17 percent. Although students of Jewish background were more liberal politically than the other students in both years, the differences between the two groups diminished over time. In the freshman year, for example, 80 percent of the Jewish students classified themselves radical, radical-liberal, or liberal, compared with 48 percent of the other students—a difference of 32 percent. The comparable figures in the junior year are 78 percent and 55 percent, a difference of 23 percent.

These figures on the political attitudes of the students are in marked contrast to the decline in political activism occurring during this period. The campus may have become more peaceful, but the political attitudes of these students were no less liberal and radical in 1973 than they were at the height of the activist period. The figures also suggest that the basic political orientation of most students is established before they ever come to college.

There was also very little net change in the proportion of students using drugs at the two time periods (see table 12—8). Although the percentage of students who had tried drugs increased among both Jewish and non-Jewish students, the proportion actually using them at the time each survey was taken did not change very much. As was the case with political attitudes, the difference in rate of drug use between students of Jewish and non-Jewish backgrounds diminished over the college years.

Much more change is in evidence if we look at the life-style issues included in table 12—8. Both Jewish and non-Jewish students were substantially more likely as juniors than as freshmen to advocate that couples should definitely live together before marriage and also to have lived with a girlfriend themselves in the previous two years. Among both groups the number of students approving legalization of marijuana and of homosexual relations between consenting adults also increased, and they were in the overwhelming majority by the senior year. It should be noted finally that enthusiasm for communal living did not increase, and among the Jewish students such interest even declined.

Taken as a whole, the figures in table 12—8 are in accord with other findings of the New Religious Consciousness project to the effect that the end of the more visible and active phase of the youth counterculture did not signal a rejection of all that it stood for. Political activism clearly was no longer as widespread as it had been in the sixties. In other respects, however, the countercultural positions, judging from the number of students supporting them, were either holding their own or were gaining recruits during the early seventies; and these patterns were roughly similar for students of Jewish and non-Jewish backgrounds.

A final question to be considered is the relationship between acceptance of countercultural values or behavior and changes in Jewish identity. No clear-cut relationship emerged. Those students whose identity shifted in the traditional direction during college did not, as might be expected, become more conservative on matters such as those included in table 12—8. In the junior-year survey such students in fact are more likely than those who remained marginal or indifferent to consider themselves radical, to have used drugs in the two months prior to the survey, and to express interest in living in a commune. There is not enough evidence to conclude that the counterculture was a factor in strengthening their Jewish identity, but it apparently was no hindrance either.[5]

Those students whose identity shifted away from the traditional and toward the indifferent category give no indication that involvement in the counterculture influenced the change. Their responses to the questions included in table 12–8 are generally similar to those of students who remained either traditional or marginal. Given the small number of cases and the absence of data to test alternative theories, we cannot explore further what did produce the changes in identity that occurred. The data do suggest strongly, however, that factors other than the counterculture were responsible.

CONCLUSIONS

The thrust of the evidence, consequently, is that the youth counterculture was not a major source of disidentification for college students of Jewish backgrounds. Although a substantial proportion of these students appear to be relatively indifferent toward their Jewish heritage, the data indicate that, generally, the indifference existed before the students ever enrolled in college. The counterculture may have had some effect on Jewish identity while the students were in high school, but the primary source of their identification as Jews, or lack thereof, is family socialization. Insofar as there may be a crisis of Jewish identity, its roots lie further back than this generation of students.

It is impossible with these data to say whether or to what extent the observed disidentification would be reversed if, for example, the incidence of anti-Semitism in America were to increase or if the threat to Israel's survival should become more acute. Barring unforeseen developments, however, it is clear that the present level of identification of these students is very salient in determining the degree of their support for Israel. Judging from the responses to a question asked at the junior level about relative support for the then-clear United States policy of favoring Israel over the Arab countries in the Middle Eastern conflict, the Jewish community can count on greater support from students of Jewish background,

5. On the potentially positive effects of the counterculture, see Albert S. Axelrad, "Encountering the Jewish Radical: The Challenge for Campus Rabbis and Student Groups," in *The New Jews*, ed. James A. Sleeper and Alan L. Mintz (New York: Vintage Books, 1971).

Table 12—9

POSITION ON PRO-ISRAEL POLICY, JUNIOR YEAR
(in percentages)

	Identity Categories [a]			All Jews	Non-Jews
	Traditional	Marginal	Indifferent		
Opinion on U.S. policy which favors Israel in Middle East conflict					
Strongly approve	76	37	24	38	7
Approve with reservations	24	43	41	38	27
Undecided	0	14	27	18	37
Disapprove	0	6	8	6	19
Strongly disapprove	0	0	0	0	10
	100	100	100	100	100
(Number)	(25)	(35)	(63)	(123)	(709)

a *Based on responses to the junior-year survey.*

whatever their level of Jewish identity, than from non-Jewish students. At the same time, as table 12—9 indicates, the level of support is greater among those whose identity is traditional than among those who are marginal or indifferent. The question of Jewish identity, therefore, is not simply a matter of religious or cultural preference. The issue is a critical one for the Jewish community, and it is one that warrants continued study as events unfold.

Part V

The Survey

*So far, our examination of new religious consciousness has pro-
ceeded, with the major exception of Tom Piazza's chapter, in a
qualitative fashion. This has been entirely appropriate to our quest
to learn about the beliefs and practices of different religious
movements, to identify and to come to understand their symbol
systems, and to obtain a feeling for the religious experiences they
are capable of invoking. A qualitative approach has also been
suitable to inquiry into the organizational structure and polity of
these movements and to gaining some initial insight into the
character and extent of their appeal. By their nature, however,
qualitative procedures alone can only take us so far in satisfying
curiosity about these movements. To learn, among other things,
about the strength of these movements, their sizes, the sources of
their recruitment, the amount and character of attention they are
commanding in the general community, qualitative means need
to be complemented by quantitative ones.*

*In the original research design of our project, we had in mind
two approaches to get answers to these quantitative questions. We
planned a survey of the general population of the Bay Area to
enable us to judge the impact the new religions were making on
the population at large. We also intended to conduct mini-surveys
of the members of the movements that were the subjects of
ethnographic study in order to produce enough cases of adherents
to these movements to allow comparing them with youth in the
general population.*

*The general population survey was executed with, if anything,
more than the usual dispatch. Respondents, by and large, were
highly interested in the subject of the survey and very little
difficulty was experienced, once an interview was under way, in
completing it.*

*Our resources did not permit conducting the planned mini-
surveys by personal interviews as was done in the general population survey, nor did we anticipate that personal interviews would
be necessary. Given the rapport investigators had established with
the groups they were studying, it seemed entirely reasonable to
suppose that a procedure calling for the self-administration of a
questionnaire would suffice. To this end, we transformed the interview version of the research instrument into a questionnaire
suitable for group administration.*

*To our surprise and regret, our strategy didn't work. Filling out
questionnaires, it turns out, is part of old rather than new consciousness, and we experienced considerable resistance in virtually
all of the groups in which administration of the questionnaire was
tried. (The exception, interestingly enough, was that Barbara
Hargrove secured good cooperation from participants in the
Protestant youth groups to whom she administered the questionnaire.) The resistance was not absolute, of course, and in all
settings some questionnaires were filled out, but neither in enough
quantity nor of an adequate enough cross section to warrant being
used except in a qualitative way.*

*Fortunately, the damage done was not total. Contrary to our
fears, enough interest and participation was expressed by respondents to the general population survey in most of the groups in
which we were especially interested to enable their responses to be
analyzed for the purposes we had in mind.*

*For this volume, we have asked Robert Wuthnow, who was
responsible for the design and execution of the general population
survey, to prepare the special chapter that follows on those survey
results bearing on the impact of the new religions on the general
population. Wuthnow has also written a more extensive report on
the results of the survey, which will be published as a separate
volume by the University of California Press under the title
The Consciousness Reformation.*

13

The New Religions in Social Context

ROBERT WUTHNOW

THE NEW RELIGIONS: TRIVIAL OR PROFOUND?

The foregoing chapters give evidence of the great variety of new religious movements that have appeared in recent years. These movements have obviously provided meaningful ways for some people to express their religious sentiments. But do they represent an important new thrust in American religion? or are they simply an interesting, but minor, development?

I shall consider this question from three perspectives. First, how many people are currently experimenting with these new movements? Other things being equal, the significance of these movements depends greatly on their size. Even though they may espouse extremely profound insights, if they cannot appeal to a somewhat broad audience, their impact on American society is likely to be relatively inconsequential. Second, are these movements, whatever their size, reinforcing values that augur change for American society? For example, do they nourish commitments to political change? or do they foster political apathy? Do people who subscribe to them pursue unconventional life-styles? or do they differ from other people only in their religious commitments? The foregoing chapters suggest that at least some of these movements reinforce values that are markedly different from those that most Americans espouse. This chapter examines this question in somewhat more systematic detail. And third, are these movements appealing to "bellwether" or to "backwater" segments of the population? Some kinds of people (for example, college-educated people) are likely to become both more numerous and more influential in the future than they are today. Other kinds of people (for example, grade-school-educated people) are likely to become less numerous and less influential. Thus, to judge the long-range effect of these movements, it is useful to consider which kinds of people are most attracted to them.

The data on which this chapter is based are from a sample of one thousand persons age sixteen and over, living in the San Francisco Bay Area. The sample is a three-stage random sample drawn to represent the population of the five counties that make up the San Francisco-Oakland Standard Metropolitan Statistical Area. The data were collected by professional interviewers in the spring and summer of 1973.[1] One purpose of this survey was to ascertain how many people have taken part in or are attracted to the movements discussed in this volume. In addition, numerous questions were asked which allow a determination of what these people are like compared with the average Bay Area resident.

The inquiry focuses on thirteen contemporary religious and quasi-religious movements. All of these movements have been highly publicized. Six have been the focus of previous chapters in this volume. For purposes of simplifying the discussion, I shall speak of these groups under three headings. Those that are offshoots of distinctly non-Western or non-Christian traditions will be termed *Countercultural;* those that are of Western origin but are essentially neutral to the Christian tradition will be termed *Personal Growth* movements; and those that represent relatively new Christian groups will be termed *Neo-Christian.*[2] The following movements are in each category:

Countercultural: Zen Buddhism, Transcendental Meditation (TM), yoga groups, Hare Krishna, Satanism. *Personal Growth:* Erhard Seminars Training *(est)*, Scientology, Synanon. *Neo-Christian:* Christian World Liberation Front (CWLF), Children of God, groups that speak in tongues, Jews for Jesus, Campus Crusade for Christ.

1. Further details of the study, including a copy of the interview schedule, are presented in Robert Wuthnow, *The Consciousness Reformation.* (Berkeley and Los Angeles, University of California Press, 1976).

2. Besides the present volume, the following provide useful background information on these movements: Peter Rowley, *New Gods in America* (New York: David McKay, 1971); Jacob Needleman, *The New Religions* (Garden City, N.Y.: Doubleday, 1970); Ronald Enroth, Edward Erickson, and C. Breckinridge Peters, *The Jesus People* (Grand Rapids, Mich.: Eerdmans Publishing Company, 1972).

HOW MANY ARE INVOLVED OR ATTRACTED?

For any social movement to grow and to perpetuate itself, it must recruit members. To recruit members it must first make itself known. Among those who learn about it, a significant number must also become attracted rather than repulsed. The potential impact of a social movement, other things being equal, is likely to be stronger, therefore, if large numbers of people have *heard* of it than if only a few have, if a lot more people are *attracted* to it than are turned off by it, and if at least a significant number of those who hear about it also decide to *take part* in its activities. These are by no means the only criteria by which the relative impact of social movements can be judged, but they do afford a minimum basis for such an assessment. Table 13–1 reports how the thirteen movements with which this inquiry is concerned compare with respect to these criteria.

The numbers who have heard of each movement and the proportions who claim to know a lot about each one would probably be disappointing to anyone committed to these movements. On the average, only one in four knows even a little about each movement and only 3 percent claim to know a lot about each one.

The average, however, masks important differences between the movements. Two—Synanon and yoga groups—were known to about one of every two persons surveyed. Synanon also has the highest proportion who know a lot about it (8 percent). The Countercultural groups are on the whole the mostly widely known, with about one in three persons knowning something about them. Of these, yoga is best known, then Hare Krishna (although only 1 percent claim to know a lot about it), and then Satanism. Approximately equal proportions—three in ten—know at least a little about Transcendental Meditation (TM) and Zen. Of the Personal Growth movements Synanon is the most well known. Scientology is familiar to only about one in four. And Erhard Seminars Training *(est)* is the least familiar of all the groups. Only 6 percent know anything about it.

Perhaps the most surprising finding is that none of the Neo-Christian groups is widely known. For example, only 15 percent know anything about the Children of God, in spite of the widespread press coverage this group has received. Groups that speak in tongues are familiar to only one in four, even though such groups have existed both before and beyond the immediate counterculture. Campus Crusade, despite an international organization, is

Table 13–1

KNOWLEDGE OF, ATTRACTION TO, AND PARTICIPATION IN NEW RELIGIOUS AND QUASI-RELIGIOUS MOVEMENTS
(In percentages)

	Countercultural					Personal growth				Neo-Christian			
	TM	Hare Krishna	Zen	Yoga	Satanism	Scientology	Synanon	est	CWLF	Campus Crusade	Jews for Jesus	Children of God	Tongues
Knowledge of each group													
Know a lot	4	1	3	4	3	2	8	1	1	4	1	2	6
Know a little	28	38	27	45	34	22	44	5	11	16	21	13	21
Know nothing	68	61	70	51	63	76	48	94	88	80	78	85	74
(Number)	(1.000)	(1.000)	(1.000)	(1.000)	(1.000)	(1.000)	(1.000)	(1.000)	(1.000)	(1.000)	(1.000)	(1.000)	(1.000)
Attraction to each group (among those who have heard of it)													
Strongly attracted	10	1	8	9	2	3	7	17	4	9	8	13	10
Mildly attracted	29	12	32	34	8	22	40	37	31	30	21	24	15
Turned off	12	44	11	10	66	37	13	16	19	26	24	22	40
Nothing either way	49	43	49	47	24	38	40	30	46	35	47	42	34
(Number)	(323)	(388)	(303)	(483)	(368)	(233)	(523)	(60)	(113)	(195)	(215)	(149)	(262)

Table 13–1 (Continued)

KNOWLEDGE OF, ATTRACTION TO, AND PARTICIPATION IN NEW RELIGIOUS AND QUASI-RELIGIOUS MOVEMENTS
(In percentages)

	Countercultural					Personal growth			Neo-Christian				
	TM	Hare Krishna	Zen	Yoga	Satanism	Scientology	Synanon	est	CWLF	Campus Crusade	Jews for Jesus	Christian of God	Tongues
Ever taken part in each group													
Among those who have heard of it	16	4	8	16	3	5	6	24	6	15	4	6	23
(Number)	(323)	(388)	(303)	(483)	(368)	(233)	(523)	(60)	(113)	(195)	(215)	(149)	(262)
In total sample	5.3	1.6	2.6	7.9	.9	1.1	3.1	1.5	.6	2.9	.9	1.0	6.0
(Number)	(1.000)	(1.000)	(1.000)	(1.000)	(1.000)	(1.000)	(1.000)	(1.000)	(1.000)	(1.000)	(1.000)	(1.000)	(1.000)

known to only one in five, as is Jews for Jesus. And the Christian
World Liberation Front (CWLF), unique by comparison since it is
a strictly local group, is known to about one in eight.

In part, these differences reflect the fact that some of the groups
asked about are specific local groups, such as CWLF and *est*, while
others are national or international groups or even categories of
groups, such as yoga and tongues groups. Most of the differences,
nevertheless, are fairly consistent with what might be expected
simply from the publicity that each group has received. Synanon,
for example, has been widely publicized in the Bay Area, as has
Satanism. Hare Krishna and TM have also frequently received mass
media coverage. The strategy of other less-well-known groups, such
as *est* and CWLF, in contrast, has been to grow by word of mouth
rather than from mass publicity.

Attraction, versus repulsion or indifference, among those who
have heard of each group affords another way to assess its impact.
By this indication, *est* has made the greatest impact, at least in
terms of those who are strongly attracted to it (17 percent). Children of God ranks next with 13 percent, perhaps surprising in view of
the characteristically unfavorable press it has received. TM and
tongues groups are tied for third. In general, however, none of the
groups has managed to elicit much strong attraction from their
publics.

When the proportions who are at least mildly attracted are added, the picture changes somewhat. Synanon ranks as equally attractive with *est*, with approximately half of those who know anything
about each of them being favorably impressed. Yoga and Zen stand
second highest, attracting about 40 percent of their publics. Children of God, TM, CWLF, and Campus Crusade all rank somewhat
lower, although each has managed to make a favorable impression
on over a third of its public.

To gain a more precise picture of the relative appeal of the
movements, we must also consider those turned off by them. This is
especially important since the tendency for those most committed
to particular movements is often to count only converts and not
those who have become repulsed along the way. Satanism has
created the most negative impression of all the groups. Nearly two-
thirds are turned off by it. Hare Krishna has repulsed almost half of
those familiar with it, and groups that speak in tongues have turned
off nearly as many (40 percent). Scientology has also created a
slightly more negative than positive balance of opinion, and Campus Crusade, Jews for Jesus, and Children of God hold only narrowly favorable margins.

When the proportions turned off are subtracted from the proportions attracted, *est* still enjoys the most favorable balance, with 38 percent more being positive than negative. Synanon, in second place, still ranks high, and yoga groups are third. Zen also has a significant positive balance, as does TM and, to a lesser extent, CWLF.

Feelings toward many of the groups are more often "nothing either way" than either attraction or repulsion. To some movements, such indifference has been seen as worse even than repulsion. By this standard, those with the best records are Satanism, *est*, Scientology, and groups that speak in tongues. Each has left no more than about a third indifferent. From another perspective, however, indifference is better than negative opinion, for it constitutes a more likely body of potential converts. By this standard, those in the best positions are TM, Zen, yoga, Jews for Jesus, and CWLF, all with approximately half indifferent publics.

Table 13–1 also shows how many people have ever taken part in each movement, both as a percentage of those who know anything about it and as a percentage of the total sample. Merely "taking part," of course, can range from the most minimal or distant participation to active, current, full-time involvement. Also, some people may have fabricated their answers to show themselves as being more experienced than they really are. Therefore, the figures do not necessarily provide an accurate estimate of the absolute numbers of participants in these movements; but they do provide a reasonable estimate of the relative extent of participation in the different movements. In the total sample yoga, tongues groups, and TM have attracted the largest number of participants—each with over 5 percent. Relatively, Zen and Campus Crusade are also among the leaders. None of the groups, however, has attracted participation from more than a minute proportion of the population.

Looking at participation only among those who have heard of each group, we see that *est* and tongues groups have been most successful—both with over 20 percent of their publics having taken part. TM, yoga groups, and Campus Crusade have done nearly as well, each eliciting actual participation from about one of every six who have heard of it. Probably because of widespread publicity in the mass media, Satanism, Hare Krishna, and Jews for Jesus have induced the smallest proportions of their publics to take part.

On all the various criteria, several of the groups, particularly yoga, TM, and Synanon, show themselves to be relatively strong. It is clear, however, that for many of the groups the data give different assessments, depending on which figures are cited. Any summary evaluation of the impact of each group is likely to depend to a large degree on the value judgments of the person making the appraisal and on his initial expectiations about what the group's impact *should* be. For example, one reader can point to the fact that *est* is known to only 6 percent of the sample, while another can counter with the fact that it attracts over half of those who know about it.

If the impact of each group is subject to differing interpretations, more consensus can probably be secured about the impact the groups have made as a whole. On this score, the groups show a widespread impact (see table 13—2). Nearly four out of every five persons claim to know a little about at least one of these movements, over half claim to know something about at least three of them, and about one person in every three claims to know something about five or more of them. More than half the population is currently attracted to at least one of them and about a third is attracted to at least two of them. Actual participation is much less common, of course; yet, one out of every five persons claims to have taken part in at least one of these groups. Eleven percent of the people interviewed also said they had taken part in other groups similar to these. Mentioned were groups such as Nichiren Shoshu, Aikido, Resurrection City, Meher Baba, and Divine Light.

The general impression conveyed by these figures may be discouraging to someone who had hoped that such groups would bring about a veritable transformation of American society. In terms of the sheer numbers who have become at least mildly attracted to these groups, the results are clearly less discouraging. At minimum, it does not appear likely that they will either be crushed by negative opinion or wither away from indifference. Each movement has secured for itself a considerable degree of social and cultural space in which to function.

VALUES AND LIFE-STYLES
OF THE RELIGIOUS EXPERIMENTERS

Much of the interest that has been expressed in recent religious and quasi-religious movements has been stimulated by the belief that these movements, however small, may be nourishing values and life-styles that augur change for American society. What this change may be is not entirely clear. It is not known whether some or all of these movements are reinforcing truly "countercultural" values in general or whether they reflect nothing more than unrest in the area of religion.

Table 13–2

**EXTENT OF KNOWLEDGE OF, ATTRACTION TO,
AND PARTICIPATION IN NEW GROUPS**

	Percentages who know about, are attracted to, or have taken part in each number of groups		
Number of groups	Know at least a little about	Attracted to	Taken part in
None	21	48	79
At least			
1	79	52	21
2	66	30	8
3	55	18	3
4	45	10	2
5	35	4	1
6	26	2	*
7	20	1	*
8	14	1	0
9	4	0	0
10	6	*	*
11	4	*	0
12	1	0	0
13	*	*	0
(Number)	(1,000)	(1,000)	(1,000)

*Less than .5 percent.

Measures of at least four kinds of values and activities are available in these data with which to compare the constituencies of each movement, both with each other and with the general Bay Area population. Each of these values and activities has been identified by observers of the so-called counterculture as representing either disaffection with the conventional or a form of experimentation with alternatives to the conventional. They have to do with radical political change, alternative life-styles, drug use, and introspective values.

The desire for major political change, together with a variety of visible attempts to bring it about, has been one of the hallmarks of the recent counterculture. The relationship of contemporary religious and quasi-religious movements to this unrest has been perceived differently by different observers. Some have claimed

Table 13-3

RADICAL POLITICS AND ATTRACTION TO RELIGIOUS MOVEMENTS

		Countercultural movements		Personal-growth movements		Neo-Christian movements	
Tolerance toward an avowed revolutionary							
Zen	1.4		*est*	1.4			
TM	1.4						
Satanism	1.4						
Hare Krishna	1.2		Scientology	1.2			
			Synanon	1.2			
Yoga	1.1						
					Tongues	1.0	
					CWLF	1.0	
					Children of God	1.0	
					Campus Crusade	.8	
					Jews for Jesus	.8	
Taken part in demonstrations or marches							
TM	2.5						
			est	2.3			
Zen	2.1						
Satanism	2.1						
Yoga	1.9		Scientology	1.4			
Hare Krishna	1.4		Synanon	1.4			
					CWLF	1.1	
					Jews for Jesus	1.0	
					Tongues	.9	
					Children of God	.8	
					Campus Crusade	.7	

that the two have been integrally related, reinforcing one another; others have seen them as competing alternatives. While we cannot wholly resolve these disputes with the present data, especially with respect to processes from one to the other over time, we can determine whether attraction to new religious movements and a desire for political change tend to go together, tend to be independent of one another, or tend to be negatively associated.

Table 13-3 shows how those who are attracted to each movement compare with each other and with the total sample with respect to two questions about radical political activity. The groups are arranged according to how likely their adherents are to engage in or support each kind of radical political activity. The number to the right of each group tells how many times more or less likely its adherents are than the total Bay Area sample to accept each item. For example, 1.9 means 1.9 times more likely than the total sample; .8 means only .8 times as likely.[3]

The question reported in the top half of the table is a story-type question which asks for feelings regarding radical political activity.

Betty Wilson thinks of herself as a "revolutionary." She is working to overthrow the U.S. government, but she has not broken any laws. Which of these answers best expresses your feelings about her?

1. She should be arrested immediately.
2. The FBI should tap her telephone to get evidence against her.
3. The police should keep their eyes on her.
4. She should be treated like anyone else since she hasn't broken any laws.
5. Personally, I'm in favor of what she's trying to do, even if she does break a few laws.

The last two responses are used as a basis for comparing the constituency of each movement with the general sample. In the bottom half of the table, activities rather than attitudes are compared. The question used asks whether respondents have ever "taken part in demonstrations or marches, not just watched."

The data reveal, first, that over half of the movements score significantly above the sample norm on both items.[4] Second, they show that those movements we have called Countercultural and Personal Growth tend to be the ones highest and most consistently above the norm, while the Neo-Christian groups typically fall near or below the norm. Tolerance for radical political activity is highest among those attracted to Zen, *est*, TM, and Satanism and lowest for Jews for Jesus and Campus Crusade. Participation in demonstrations is also highest for the same four groups (Zen, *est*, TM, and Satanism) and is lowest for Campus Crusade and the Children of God.

These data do not tell whether people first develop an interest in radical politics and then an interest in Countercultural religious

3. These figures are computed simply by dividing the percentage of those attracted to each group (mildly or strongly) who answer a question in a certain way by the percentage of the total sample who answer the same question in the same way.
4. In the total sample 57 percent are tolerant of Betty Wilson and 17 percent have taken part in demonstrations.

movements and Personal Growth movements or whether the
process is in the opposite direction. They do reveal that interest in
radical political change and in these kinds of movements tend to go
together. The one kind of interest does not, as some have suggested,
produce either disinterest in or disapproval of the other. The numbers who are attracted to Countercultural religious movements and
to Personal Growth movements is perhaps too small at present to
suggest that their attitudes are of much significance to the overall
political climate of American society. Were their numbers to grow,
however, these data suggest that experimentation with radical
politics would probably also be nourished. In this sense, these
movements are of significance beyond what they imply for the
character of religion itself. They appear to augur change in politics
as well. The Neo-Christian movements, in contrast, do not seem to
go together with such changes; if anything, they appear to dis-
courage them.

The second set of values on which we can compare these
movements concerns alternative life-styles. Many commentators on
contemporary culture have noted that unrest is in evidence not only
regarding political arrangements but also in domestic areas, such as
marriage, childrearing, sex roles, and sexual practices. The extent to
which this is true in the Bay Area is evidenced by the two questions
regarding living arrangements examined in table 13–4. Over half
the total sample (55 percent) say they mostly approve of "an unmarried couple living together," and nearly half (46 percent) say
they mostly approve of "more freedom for homosexuals."

Do the new religious movements appeal to and reinforce this ferment in living arrangements or not? Table 13–4 suggests that they
do as far as the Countercultural and Personal Growth movements
are concerned; they do not as far as the Neo-Christian movements
are concerned. In addition, the Countercultural groups appear to be
somewhat more strongly associated with an inclination for alternative life-styles than are the Personal Growth movements. TM,
Zen, yoga, Satanism, and Hare Krishna are all considerably more
likely than the average to express approval on both items. Scientology, *est*, and Synanon are somewhat more likely than the average, but the differences are not as large as for the Countercultural
groups. None of the Neo-Christian groups are more likely than the
average to express approval; in general, they are below average.

Again it is impossible to say which kind of attitude is more likely
to develop first and then lead to the other—attraction to religious
groups or interest in alternative living arrangements. Nevertheless,

Table 13–4

ALTERNATIVE LIFE-STYLES AND ATTRACTION TO RELIGIOUS MOVEMENTS

Countercultural movements		Personal-growth movements		Neo-Christian movements	
Mostly favor an unmarried couple living together					
TM	1.5				
Zen	1.5				
Yoga	1.5				
Satanism	1.4	Scientology	1.4		
Hare Krishna	1.2	Synanon	1.2		
		est	1.2		
				CWLF	1.0
				Tongues	.9
				Children of God	.8
				Jews for Jesus	.6
				Campus Crusade	.5
Mostly favor more freedom for homosexuals					
TM	1.8				
Zen	1.7				
Yoga	1.7				
Hare Krishna	1.5				
Satanism	1.5				
		Scientology	1.3		
		Synanon	1.3		
		est	1.2		
				CWLF	.8
				Tongues	.8
				Jews for Jesus	.7
				Campus Crusade	.6
				Children of God	.6

the data clearly indicate that being attracted to these groups, at least the Countercultural and Personal Growth groups, goes hand in hand with being interested in unconventional living arrangements as well.

The third area in which the movements can be compared is drug use, widely perceived as a key countercultural phenomenon, both as a form of protest against laws prohibiting it and as an avenue to

Table 13—5

DRUGS AND ATTRACTION TO RELIGIOUS MOVEMENTS

Countercultural movements		Personal-growth movements		Neo-Christian movements	
Ever experienced being "high" on drugs					
Satanism	2.1				
TM	2.1				
Yoga	1.8				
Zen	1.7	*est*	1.7		
		Scientology	1.7		
Hare Krishna	1.6				
				Tongues	1.4
		Synanon	1.3		
				CWLF	1.2
				Children of God	1.1
				Jews for Jesus	.9
				Campus Crusade	.9
Mostly favor legalizing the use of marijuana					
TM	1.9				
Zen	1.7				
Yoga	1.7				
Hare Krishna	1.6				
Satanism	1.5	Scientology	1.5		
		est	1.5		
		Synanon	1.3		
				CWLF	1.2
				Children of God	1.0
				Tongues	.9
				Jews for Jesus	.8
				Campus Crusade	.6

nonrational, experiential states of consciousness. The two items at our disposal for examining drug use and attitudes toward it are, having ever experienced being "high" on drugs—27 percent say they have—and being mostly in favor of legalizing the use of marijuana, which 41 percent say they are. Table 13—5 reports the results.

The Countercultural groups are again associated with a significantly higher than average propensity to experiment with drugs.

The Personal Growth movements are also above the norm, but not to the same degree. Of the Neo-Christian groups, only CWLF is consistently associated with above-average drug experimentation. The overall pattern, then, is much the same as that already seen with regard to radical politics and alternative living arrangements. Although the Neo-Christian movements do not appear to reinforce unconventional activities, all of the other movements do.

Although the last area in which the groups can be compared—an introspective or inward orientation—is not generically a sign of

Table 13–6

INTROSPECTION AND ATTRACTION TO RELIGIOUS MOVEMENTS

Countercultural movements		Personal-growth movements		Neo-Christian movements	
Value spending time getting to know your inner self					
TM	1.9				
Satanism	1.8				
		Scientology	1.7		
		est	1.7		
Zen .	1.6				
Hare Krishna	1.6				
Yoga	1.5				
				Tongues	1.4
				CWLF	1.3
				Children of God	1.1
		Synanon	1.0	Jews for Jesus	1.0
				Campus Crusade	1.0
Practice meditation using special techniques					
Hare Krishna	3.4				
TM	3.1				
Zen	2.6				
Yoga	2.3				
				Tongues	2.1
		Scientology	2.0	CWLF	2.0
				Children of God	1.7
Satanism	1.6			Campus Crusade	1.6
		est	1.4		
		Synanon	1.4		
				Jews for Jesus	1.1

cultural ferment or change, observers have often associated the two in recent years, since an interest in inward experiential knowledge has been seen as a reaction against the historically dominant objective, rational-scientific world view of the West. The two measures available for examining this dimension are concerned with valuing it (placing great or fair importance on "spending a lot of time getting to know your inner self") and with actually pursuing it by practicing meditation "using definite techniques such as sitting or breathing or thinking in special ways"[5] (see table 13–6).

In general, people attracted to any of the religious groups are as likely or more likely to espouse introspective values as the average person in the Bay Area. The Countercultural movements are more likely than the other movements to be associated with these values. All five of the Countercultural movements score considerably above average on the value of knowing the inner self, and all but Satanism are considerably more likely than the average to practice meditation. Of the Personal Growth groups Scientology and *est* are consistently more likely than the average to espouse introspection as a value and to practice meditation, although not to the extent that the Countercultural groups are. The Neo-Christian groups vary somewhat in the extent to which they are associated with introspection. Groups that speak in tongues and CWLF are both relatively likely to score high on introspection. On the whole, the Neo-Christian groups do not score as highly as the Countercultural groups. To the extent that introspection represents a new kind of value in American culture, the Countercultural movements, therefore, appear to be the main groups of those examined here that are nourishing these values.

To summarize briefly, we have learned that the Countercultural movements especially, and to a slightly less extent the Personal Growth movements, are compatible with, and probably reinforce, values and life-styles that contrast sharply with more conventional American values and life-styles. This is as true with respect to radical politics as it is to novel living arrangements, drug use, and meditation. Attraction to these movements appears to be but one part of a more general attraction to unconventional life-styles and social arrangements.

Thus far, the data have revealed little about what is distinctive about the Neo-Christian groups. People who are attracted to these

5. In the total sample 33 percent attach great importance to spending time getting to know one's inner self and 7 percent practice meditation using special techniques.

Table 13−7

CONVENTIONAL RELIGIOUS BELIEF AND
ATTRACTION TO RELIGIOUS MOVEMENTS

Countercultural movements		Personal-growth movements		Neo-Christian movements	
God strong influence on my life					
				Tongues	1.4
				Jews for Jesus	1.4
				Campus Crusade	1.4
				CWLF	1.2
				Children of God	1.1
		Scientology	1.0		
Hare Krishna	.9	*est*	.9		
		Synanon	.9		
Satanism	.8				
Yoga	.8				
TM	.8				
Zen	.6				
Value taking part in church or synagogue					
				Campus Crusade	1.9
				Tongues	1.8
				CWLF	1.7
				Jews for Jesus	1.6
				Children of God	1.3
Hare Krishna	.9				
		Synanon	.8		
		Scientology	.8		
Yoga	.6				
TM	.6				
Zen	.6				
Satanism	.6				
		est	.5		

groups are generally no more likely than the average to be interested in unconventional values and life-styles. We might ask, therefore, what are the distinctive characteristics of these people?

The most reasonable answer seems to be that they are simply committed very strongly to Christian beliefs and values and are attracted to these Neo-Christian groups as ways of possibly revitalizing Christianity (see table 13—7). All of the Neo-Christian groups are significantly above average, for example, in believing that their lives are strongly influenced by God or some other supernatural force.[6] Other data (not shown in the table) reveal that the constituencies of the Neo-Christian movements are consistently above average on belief in God, in the importance of following God's will, in creation, in life after death, and in prayer.

These results suggest that the Neo-Christian groups may, if anything, encourage a return to traditional Christian beliefs and values. The data also suggest that this return may include a return to the established churches as well. Although much has been made of the antagonism between these movements and the churches, the data in table 13—7 show that those who are attracted to these movements are also significantly more likely than the average to attach importance to taking part in church or synagogue. However, while the Neo-Christian groups appear to be a force in favor of traditional religious commitments, the Countercultural groups appear to be a force just as strong, if not stronger, away from these commitments. On all the items concerning traditional Christian beliefs and commitment to the established churches, those attracted to the Countercultural movements are considerably less likely than the average to express support.

If these movements were to grow, it seems highly likely that the Countercultural and perhaps the Personal Growth movements would foster experimentation with a whole range of unconventional life-styles and commitments. There remains the question, How likely is it that these groups will come to play a more important role in American culture?

The future significance of these religious movements depends on many factors, about most of which we have no data. The resourcefulness of the leaders of these movements, the capacity of the established churches to meet people's religious needs, the extent to which ideas from other sources, such as science, come to inform the culture—all are factors that would have to be considered in any overall attempt to predict how significant these movements will be in the future. One important factor about which we do have some data, though, is what the constituencies of these movements are like. Are they people who are likely to play an increasing role in shaping American culture in the future? Or are they people whose role is going to diminish as time goes by? In brief, are they "bellwether" or "backwater" types of people?

6. In the total sample 54 percent believe God has a strong influence on their lives and 38 percent value taking part in church or synagogue.

THE RELIGIOUS EXPERIMENTERS:
BELLWETHER OR BACKWATER?

Virtually all accounts of contemporary religious movements have described them as youth phenomena. People over thirty have been said to be scarce either as members or as supporters of these groups. Any such "generation gap" always arouses suspicion that some profound changes may be taking place. Today's young people, as the adage has it, are tomorrow's leaders. And if they are committed to activities that are different from those of their elders, these activities are likely to become more and more important as time goes by. One possible sign of the future strength of these movements, therefore, is the extent to which they are more common among the young than among the old.

Table 13–8 shows the relations between age and attraction to the thirteen new religious movements. Under each of the four age categories shown, those groups are listed that overselect people from that age category at least 20 percent more often than would be expected by chance. The table shows that in general virtually all the groups overselect young people rather than older people. The Countercultural movements tend to overselect persons aged 16 to 20 and persons aged 21 to 30. The Personal Growth movements appear to appeal to a somewhat older audience, overselecting most-

Table 13–8

AGE AND ATTRACTION TO RELIGIOUS MOVEMENTS

	Groups overselected by at least 20 percent within each age category			
	Age 16 to 20	Age 21 to 30	Age 31 to 50	Over age 50
Countercultural movements	Hare Krishna Yoga Satanism	TM Zen Satanism		
Personal-growth movements		Scientology Synanon	est	
Neo-Christian movements	Campus Crusade CWLF Children of God Jews for Jesus Tongues	Tongues		Campus Crusade Jews for Jesus

ly persons between 21 and 30 with *est* overselecting from persons aged 31 to 50. The Neo-Christian groups seem to overselect mostly among the young (aged 16 to 20), although Campus Crusade and Jews for Jesus also overselect among those over age 50.

Data also confirm that it is chiefly the young who participate actively in these groups. Too few people in the sample have taken part in each group to make reliable comparisons for each of the thirteen groups separately. It is interesting to compare those who have taken part in at least one of the Countercultural groups, in at least one of the Personal Growth groups, and in at least one of the Neo-Christian groups. These comparisons show again that all three kinds of participants are more likely to be young than would be expected by chance. For instance, the Countercultural participants are 1.8 times more likely than the total sample to be age 30 or younger, and the Personal Growth and Neo-Christian participants are 1.3 times more likely than the average to be under 30.

These results suggest two possible conclusions regarding the future prospects of the new religious movements. The first is that these movements will probably continue at least at their present strength for some time. The argument underlying this conclusion can be stated as follows: Young people are basically a bellwether group. Their youthfulness gives them many years to practice their particular commitments and to persuade others to adopt them. Older people, in contrast, are a backwater group. Time is running out for them and for their ways of life. If the new religious groups were appealing mostly to old people, we might assume that these groups would soon disappear as new generations come along. Since these movements appeal mostly to young people, however, we can expect them to be of significance for a longer time. The other conclusion that might be drawn from these results is that these movements are probably just youthful experiments that will soon be abandoned as these youth become more mature. This, too, is a plausible conclusion. Before we examine it, there is another characteristic of the people who are attracted to these movements that bears examining, namely, their educational level.

Most observers of the recent counterculture have noted the prevalence of the better educated within its ranks. This is of significance for two reasons. One is that the better educated typically have more influence in shaping the overall character of the culture than do the uneducated, suggesting that the social experiments of the counterculture may come to have more of an impact on American culture than their numbers alone would suggest. Second, the educated are a significant group because their numbers have grown steadily over the years. If social experimenters tend to be recruited from the ranks of the educated, their numbers are likely to increase in the future as more and more people become better educated.

Previous research has tended to suggest that young people who experiment with the new Eastern religions are generally more intellectually sophisticated than the average.[7] It has been less clear whether those experimenting with Jesus groups and other new religious or quasi-religious groups are better educated and more highly sophisticated than the average or whether they may be among the relatively disadvantaged.

Table 13—9 indicates that those who are attracted to the Countercultural movements, with the exception of those who are attracted to Hare Krishna, tend to be above average in terms of educational level.[8] Leaving out those too young to have attended college, Zen, Satanism, TM, and yoga are all considerably more likely to appeal to people with at least some college education than would be expected by chance. The Personal Growth movements are somewhat ambiguous with respect to educational level. Only Synanon is distinctly more likely than the average to overselect educated people. The Neo-Christian groups are also somewhat ambig-

7. See, for example, Robert Wuthnow and Charles Y. Glock, "Religious Loyalty, Defection, and Experimentation among College Youth," *Journal for the Scientific Study of Religion* 12 (June 1973):157—80.

8. In the total sample age 23 and older, 51 percent have at least some college education.

Table 13—9

RESPONDENT'S EDUCATION (AGE 23 AND OLDER)

Countercultural movements		Personal-growth movements		Neo-Christian movements	
Zen	1.6				
Satanism	1.5				
TM	1.4	Synanon	1.4		
Yoga	1.4				
		Scientology	1.2	Tongues	1.2
Hare Krishna	1.1	*est*	1.1	Campus Crusade	1.1
				Jews for Jesus	1.1
				CWLF	1.0
				Children of God	.4

uous. For the most part they appeal to educated people about as much as would be expected by chance, although Children of God are much less likely than the average to appeal to the better educated.

These data suggest that as far as the future prospects for these groups are concerned, the Countercultural movements are strongest in the sense of appealing to people who are both more likely to be influential than the average and likely to become more numerous in the future. This conclusion is also indicated by other questions having to do with educational level and intellectual sophistication. For example, the Countercultural groups are more likely than any of the other groups to come from better-educated backgrounds and to express interest in intellectual activities such as reading books and going to concerts and plays.

The data give somewhat different conclusions with regard to those who have actually taken part in these movements. On this score, all three kinds of movements seem to recruit from the relatively better educated: participants in each of the three kinds of movements are 1.6 times more likely than would be expected by chance to be college graduates. The other items having to do with educational level and cognitive sophistication also show this pattern.

To summarize, all of the new religious and quasi-religious groups appear to be somewhat stronger than their numbers would indicate, by virtue of the fact that those who take part in them tend to be among the better educated and, as a result, are the kind of people whose numbers and whose influence will probably become greater in the future. In addition, the Countercultural groups appear to be on somewhat stronger ground than the others, since those to whom they *appeal*, but who do not necessarily take part, are also among the better educated.

The characteristics examined thus far pose a somewhat optimistic outlook for these religious movements. However, there is another aspect to consider: the possibility that these groups are currently appealing to people who are at a particular stage in their personal development and who will perhaps abandon their interest in these groups as they become more mature. This possibility is suggested especially by the prevalence of the young among the supporters of these groups.

A widely held theory of counterculture, indeed, of behavior in general that deviates from the conventional, is that it arises among those who are experiencing problems or frustrations in their lives.

Table 13–10

**MARITAL STATUS AND MARGINALITY
TO THE LABOR FORCE**

Countercultural movements		Personal-growth movements		Neo-Christian movements	
Never married					
TM	1.7				
Yoga	1.7				
Zen	1.5				
Hare Krishna	1.5				
Satanism	1.4	Scientology	1.4	Tongues	1.4
				CWLF	1.4
				Children of God	1.3
				Jews for Jesus	1.2
		est	1.1		
		Synanon	1.0		
				Campus Crusade	8
Working only part time or looking for work					
				Children of God	1.9
Zen	1.7				
Yoga	1.7				
TM	1.6				
Hare Krishna	1.4				
		Scientology	1.2	Tongues	1.2
				Jews for Jesus	1.2
		Synanon	1.1	CWLF	1.1
				Campus Crusade	.9
Satanism	.8	*est*	.8		

An explanation for the prevalence of youth among the counter-cultural experimenters, therefore, is that they are experiencing frustrations because of not being able to get married and have a family, or not having a job yet, not being a stable member of the community, not feeling comfortable with their career plans or their sex lives, and so forth. This explanation suggests, moreover, that as young people mature and resolve these problems their interest in countercultural activities will subside.

The Bay Area data lend considerable support to the notion that those who are attracted to the new religions, especially to the Countercultural groups, are experiencing the kinds of frustrations

Table 13–11

GEOGRAPHICAL MOBILITY AND SUBJECTIVE DISCONTENT

Countercultural movements		Personal-growth movements		Neo-Christian movements	
Moved at least twice in last two years					
		est	1.7		
TM	1.6				
Zen	1.6				
Satanism	1.6				
Hare Krishna	1.6				
Yoga	1.5				
		Scientology	1.4	Children of God	1.4
				CWLF	1.2
		Synanon	1.1	Tongues	1.1
				Campus Crusade	.9
				Jews for Jesus	.6
High scores on subjective discontent index					
Satanism	1.4				
TM	1.3				
Yoga	1.2				
Zen	1.2				
		Scientology	1.1	Children of God	1.1
		est	1.1		
		Synanon	1.1		
				Tongues	1.0
Hare Krishna	.9			Jews for Jesus	.9
				Campus Crusade	.8
				CWLF	.7

that are common to young people. Table 13–10, for example, shows that people who are attracted to the Countercultural movements are substantially more likely than would be expected by chance to be single and to be employed only part time or looking for work.[9] And table 13–11 shows that these people also tend to be geographically unsettled and subjectively dissatisfied about such

9. In the total sample 26 percent have never been married and 16 percent are either working only part time or looking for work.

things as their work plans and their sex lives.[10] These tables also show that all the groups are generally more rather than less likely than the average to appeal to people with these characteristics; with the exception of the Countercultural groups, these differences are small enough that they might be due simply to chance.

The data on actual participants in the three kinds of movements suggest even more clearly that these groups appeal to those who are in the midst of the kinds of problems that young people tend to face (see table 13–12). And again it appears that the Countercultural movements are especially likely to recruit from among these types of people.

This evidence suggests—although further analysis beyond that which the present data can provide would obviously be needed to say for certain—that the present religious experimenters may gradually lose their interest in these groups as they grow older, get married, take jobs, settle down, and so on. New cohorts of young people may come to take their places, but the scope of these groups would always remain limited to the relatively small minority who at any one time are passing through these youth-related situations.

10. In the total sample 16 percent have moved at least twice within the past two years and 59 percent received high scores on the subjective discontent index. The subjective discontent index was constructed by giving scores of 1 for each of the

Table 13–12

CHARACTERISTICS OF PARTICIPANTS

	Countercultural movements	Personal-growth movements	Neo-Christian movements
Never married	2.0	1.2	1.3
Looking for a job or working part time	2.2	1.5	1.7
Moved twice or more in last two years	1.7	1.8	1.3
Bothered about work or work plans	1.4	1.4	.9
Bothered about sex life	1.5	1.1	1.0

CONCLUSIONS

Of the thirteen new religious movements we have been able to examine, none is profound in terms of sheer size. By even the most
minimal standards of participation or simply feelings of attraction,
none of these groups has appealed to more than a minute fraction of
the Bay Area population. If national data were available, this fraction would undoubtedly be even smaller. Taken all together,
however, these movements are clearly a noteworthy new force in
American religion. A sizable minority is currently both aware of and
attracted to at least one or more of these groups.

In terms of the values and life-styles they represent, these
movements also seem to be worthy of serious attention. Especially
those groups we have called Countercultural appear to be part of a
larger shift away from traditional religious commitments and
toward some new, yet undefined, mode of religious expression.
They are not simply a reflection of religious unrest, however, but
are part of a broader wave of experimentation with countercultural
life-styles and social arrangements.

It is not possible to say what the recent counterculture might
have been like without these new religious movements, especially
those of Eastern origin. It might have produced the same amount of
social unrest that it did. Yet, from all that is known about the importance of religion to any culture, it seems reasonable to suggest that
the recent social unrest and experimentation has at least been
nourished and legitimated in significant ways by these new religious
movements. However trivial the numbers, those who have become
involved with these groups appear to have developed life-styles and
attitudes that are decidedly different from those that have been
more common to American culture in the past.

The future of these movements, judging from the present data, is
uncertain. On the one hand, they have garnered most of their support from the better educated and more intellectually aware. If
there is something about these movements that is more compatible
with the modern intellectual climate than traditional religion has

following problems about which people were bothered a lot, scores of 2 for
problems bothering people somewhat, scores of 3 for problems of past but not immediate worry, and scores of 4 for problems having never been experienced. The
problems listed were loneliness, money problems, problems with health, problems
with work or work plans, problems with sex life, wondering about the meaning
and purpose of life, and the death of a loved one. The scores for each item were
averaged, yielding an index ranging from 1 to 4. An examination of cutting points
indicated that for present purposes the index could be dichotomized between 3
and 4.

been, they may prosper well into the future, especially as more and more people become educated. On the other hand, they seem to appeal most to young people who are still at an unsettled stage in their lives. As these young people mature and become more settled, they may abandon these groups. Thus, the appeal of these groups would be limited to new cohorts at similar stages in their life cycles.

In either case, it seems likely that there will continue to be at least some for whom these religious groups provide meaningful ways to express their religious sentiments. Just as new religious groups have developed in the past in response to the needs of new ethnic minorities, the urban dispossessed, and those on the agrarian frontiers, so these movements may continue to find a responsive chord among the young, the educated, and those interested in more general forms of cultural and societal transformation.

Part VI

Historical Perspective

*There are many possible ways in which to place the cultural up-
heaval of the late 1960s and early 1970s in historical perspective.
Nothing under the sun is ever new, at least not completely new,
and the historically informed have been quick to point out that
what we have just lived through is "not new," that something
"just like it" was to be found in the early Franciscan movement or
the German Youth Movement before World War I. We have never
argued for absolute uniqueness and have from the beginning of
our research been aware of the many threads that tied what we
were studying to the past. The question is, however, which
historical reference points will help illuminate our material more
than others?*

Sydney E. Ahlstrom in his monumental A Religious History of
the American People *has spoken of the 1960s as the end of the
Puritan epoch in America. It might be instructive to compare our
period with the sixteenth and seventeenth centuries when the
Puritan epoch was just beginning. Then too there was much
cultural turmoil and much turning away from established
authorities in church and state. Then too there were many competing groups each purporting to convey the light. Or we might
reach much further back, to the waning centuries of the Roman
Empire. Then too a heavily successful technical military empire
was in trouble because it had lost the loyalty of its best citizens
and could no longer deal adequately with its practical problems.
Then too there was an invasion of religions from the East,
suggesting an inward turn and a withdrawal from the practical
concerns of this world.*

*While these comparisons and others might indeed prove instruc-
tive, Linda Pritchard has chosen a period considerably more recent
and closer to home, our own nineteenth-century religious history.*

The "Great Awakening" phenomenon is endemic in America, and it is probable that, however atypical, our period is another example of it. Like all good historical comparisons, Pritchard's description is illuminating for the differences from as well as the similarities to our material. The great virtue of her chapter is that it helps to place the new religious consciousness of the last ten years in the context of a long history of religious consciousness in America. It is impossible to jump completely out of one's tradition; and it is clear that, for better or for worse, most of what we studied, however exotic, is still indelibly American. Even if we have become "post-American" or "post-Puritan," it is still, we would suggest, in a most American and Puritan way.

14

Religious Change in Ninteenth-Century America

LINDA K. PRITCHARD

And the final effect of Revivals was a hope watching for the morning, which remains in the life of the nation, side by side, nay identical with, the great hope of Socialism.[1]

The complex interaction of religion and society must be analyzed in order to understand the rise of new religious consciousness during any particular time period. One form of religious expression must be related to another and the entire spectrum of religious institutions and ideology must be linked to the society as a whole. Unfortunately, most standard historical and contemporary accounts of religious change examine individual religious groups without analyzing the social context out of which they emerged. While the organization, leadership, and theology of new religious groups can partially illuminate religious change, an analysis of broader social and economic developments must inform the examination of particular new religious expressions.

Since the current flourishing of new religious sects is by no means unique in American history, a historical perspective of religious transformation provides an opportunity to analyze the relationship between religion and social change. Only in retrospect is it possible to reconstruct the dynamic process of religious change. This essay examines the religious upheaval that occurred between 1820 and 1860—known as the Second Great Awakening—from the vantage point of the larger society. It has been chosen as a case study because rapid social and economic shifts in American society during

1. John Humphrey Noyes, *History of American Socialisms*, with a New Introduction by Mark Holloway (New York: Dover Publications, 1966), pp. 25–26.

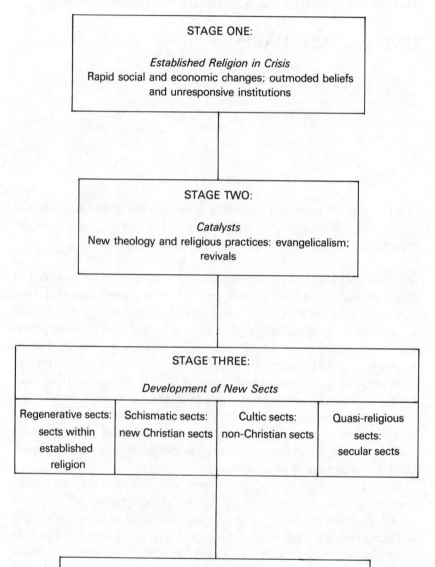

FIGURE 14-1
Stages of Religious Transformation, 1820-1860

STAGE ONE:

Established Religion in Crisis
Rapid social and economic changes; outmoded beliefs
and unresponsive institutions

STAGE TWO:

Catalysts
New theology and religious practices: evangelicalism;
revivals

STAGE THREE:

Development of New Sects

| Regenerative sects: sects within established religion | Schismatic sects: new Christian sects | Cultic sects: non-Christian sects | Quasi-religious sects: secular sects |

STAGE FOUR:

Creation of a New Established Religion
New beliefs and sects and former established religion: new
established religion

this time gave rise to a significant period of religious uncertainty, schism, and reorganization.[2]

The process of religious transformation between 1820 and 1860 will be examined in four stages. In Stage One, social and economic changes undermined established religion, that is, religion as it was constituted prior to the Second Great Awakening. In Stage Two, new theological perspectives and religious practices, emerging out of the specific social changes of the period, began to challenge established religion. In Stage Three, a host of new sects developed in response to the new social structure. In Stage Four, the religious upheaval culminated in the development of a new established religion which realigned religion and society. Figure 14–1 is a diagram of these stages.

STAGE ONE: ESTABLISHED RELIGION IN CRISIS

As major demographic shifts, rapid urbanization, westward expansion, unprecedented advances in transportation and communication, and industrial development transformed American society between 1820 and 1860, the fabric of most people's lives— workplace, residence, family life, and religion—changed dramatically. According to the U.S. census, the total population of the United States grew from nine to thirty-one million people, including five million immigrants who came primarily from Germany and Ireland. The railroad, canal system, and telegraph directly facilitated urbanization and economic specialization. While the total population increased by 344 percent, the proportion of people living in towns and cities larger than 2,500 people increased by 797 percent. The exchange of cash crops for manufactured goods replaced self-sufficient farming. Capital investments, the volume

2. Other accounts of this period in American religious history include Sydney Ahlstrom, *A Religious History of the American People* (New Haven: Yale University Press, 1972), chaps. 24–40; William W. Sweet, *The Story of Religion in America* (New York: Harper & Brothers, 1950), chaps. 12–14; Timothy Smith, *Revivalism and Reform* (New York: Abingdon Press, 1967); and William McLoughlin, *Modern Revivalism* (New York: Ronald Press, 1959), chaps. 1–3. Whitney Cross, *The Burned Over District* (New York: Harper Torchbooks, 1950); and Lee Benson, *The Concept of Jacksonian Democracy* (Princeton, N.J.: Princeton University Press, 1961) provide a detailed analysis of upstate New York. For an account of the communitarian societies which were organized at this time, see Noyes, *History of American Socialisms* and Charles Nordhoff, *The Communistic Societies of the United States*, with a New Introduction by Mark Holloway (New York: Dover Publications, 1966.)

Table 14-1

RANGE OF PROTESTANT RELIGION, 1800-1860

Reactionary	Established Religion	Reformist	New Sects	Cults
Hopkinsonians Andover	Congregational ◄─►	Nathanial Taylor Yale	*Conversionist* United Brethren (1800)	astrology
Old School Princeton	◄─ Presbyterian ─►	New School (1838-1868) Auburn Yale	Evangelical Association (1803)	phrenology
			Cumberland Presbyterian (1810)	mesmerism
"hardshelled"	◄─ Baptist ─►	American Baptist Home Mission Society	Disciples of Christ:	homeopathic medicine
Seventh Day		Free-Will Baptists	O'Kelley's (1792)	
Six Principle		Christian Connection	Stonites (1804)	
antimission			Campbellites (1809)	Grahamism
Dunkers			Wesleyan Methodist (1844)	
			Free Methodist (1860)	vegetarianism
			Methodist Protestant (1830)	
Anglo-Catholic ◄─	Episcopal ─►	Low Church		agrarianism
General Council	◄─ Lutheran ─►	General Synod	*Adventist* Millerites (1843)	"radical" reform
Buffalo Synod			Adventists	
Missouri Synod			Seventh-Day Adventists	
Norwegian Evangelical			Mormons (1823)	
Augustana				

Table 14–1 (Continued)

RANGE OF PROTESTANT RELIGION, 1800-1860

Reactionary	Established Religion	Reformist	New Sects	Cults
Hicksites ←→	Quaker ←→	Guerneyites		
(little) ←→	Methodist ←→	General Conference		
			Gnostic	
			Spiritualists	
			Universalists	
Mercersburg ←→	German Reformed ←→	Free Synod (1822)	New Thought	
John Nevin		Winebrunner Baptist (1823)	Swedenborgians	
Philip Schaff				
			Communitarian	
recent immigrants ←→	Dutch Reformed ←→	pietist tradition	Fourier—Brook Farm	
	Moravian		Owenite—New Harmony	
	Mennonite		Noyes—Oneida	
			Universalist—Hopedale	
			pietist—Amana Zoar	
Scotch-Irish ←→	Associate, Associate Reform ←→	(little)		
immigrants				
Harvard ←→	Unitarian ←→	Transcendentalists		
(none) ←→	Communities ←→	(renewed interest after		
	Shakers (1787)	revival seasons)		
	Rappites (1805)			

and total value of manufactured goods, and the size of the labor force grew rapidly. By 1860 the United States was clearly an economically advanced nation.[3] When established religion did not effectively cope with these social and economic changes, new religious beliefs and structures replaced outmoded Protestant theologies and unwieldy institutions and created a new established religion that could deal more fully with a reordered society.

On the eve of the Second Great Awakening, denominationalism was the core of established religion. While the range of American denominations was broader than it had ever been, a few orthodox Protestant denominations still controlled the country. The Presbyterian and Congregational bodies commanded the largest number of members, while Baptist, Anglican, Lutheran, German and Dutch Reformed, and Quaker denominations were the next largest religious groups.[4] (See table 14—1).

Historical creeds and theologies provided the religious authority for most of these denominations. Calvinism, which stressed predestination, was the predominant theology for Presbyterians, Congregationalists, the Reformed, and most Baptists. For members of these denominations, an omnipotent God determined who went to heaven or hell, leaving individuals with no control over their own salvation. The Augsburg Confession was the foundation of the Lutheran denomination, while the Westminister Confession anchored the Anglican church. Both of these creeds emphasized strict adherence to traditional practices.

Members achieved a good standing in their denomination if they upheld the historical beliefs and participated in the denominational rituals. In those denominations that required personal encounters with Jesus, such conversion experiences routinely occurred at an early age. Children generally assumed the denominational affiliation of their parents. While denominational rites ranged from high-church liturgies to simple services, each denomination required some kind of ritual observance at specified times in a member's life. Birth, baptism, marriage, and death were especially important life-cycle events.

3. Figures cited in George Rogers Taylor, *The Transportation Revolution, 1815—1860* (New York: Harper Torchbooks, 1951), pp. 384—98. For a more detailed account of the growth and development of the United States, see Douglass C. North, *The Economic Growth of the United States, 1790—1860* (New York: W.W. Norton, 1961).

4. Edwin Scott Gaustad, *Historical Atlas of Religion in America* (New York: Harper & Row, 1962), pp. 4, 43, 44.

Although the structure of each denomination varied significantly by historical tradition, most denominations utilized a tight bureaucratic organization and explicit decision-making procedures. Elaborate administrative networks usually linked individual congregations to a regional or national denominational body. Trained clergy, educated in denominational facilities, governed each denomination. In order to protect traditional orthodoxy, denominations imposed rigorous standards of scholarship on ministerial candidates in areas of systematic theology, Hebrew and Greek, Bible exegesis, church history, and homilectics. For well-educated ministers, job opportunities ranged from parish posts to highly specialized positions within the denominational bureaucracy.

It is not possible at this time to define precisely the relationship between socioeconomic changes and religion during this period. Historians know little about the composition of the religious groups that arose during the Second Great Awakening. They have asked a few questions about the age, sex, class, education, ethnicity, mobility, social status, political affiliation, or former religious identification of the members of various religious bodies. Furthermore, no theory adequately explains the sudden disruption of established religion and explosion of new religious groups during this period of extensive social turmoil. Sociologists of religion generally attribute the rise of new religious sects to conditions that prevent a small minority of people from fulfilling their personal needs within established religion. While marginal groups, those who were forced to stand outside the mainstream of society, like blacks, women, and young people, did join and lead sects in large numbers,[5] it was the groups who participated most fully in the social changes of the period that transformed religion in America. Recent evidence suggests that people affected by urbanization, geographical relocation, and changes in job structures were more likely than others to be sympathetic to new religious groups. During the Second Great Awakening, the construction of new religious groups occurred primarily because of the changing religious needs of a significant proportion of the population.[6]

5. See Linda K. Pritchard, "*The Woman's Bible*: Women and Religion in Historical Context," paper presented at the American Academy of Religion, November 1973; E. Franklin Frazier, *The Negro Church in America* (New York: Schocken Books, 1964); and Joseph Kett, "Growing Up in Rural New England," in Tamara Haraven (ed.), *Anonymous Americans* (Englewood Cliffs, N.Y.: Prentice-Hall, 1971), pp. 1—16.

6. The pioneering efforts in this attempt include Cross, *The Burned Over District*, chaps. 2—5; T. Scott Miyakawa, *Protestants and Pioneers* (Chicago:

STAGE TWO: CATALYST

Evangelicalism was the major religious response to the socioeconomic changes of the period. Although evangelicalism previously
existed as a minor religious trend, under the impact of the particular
nineteenth-century social and economic changes, it became a major
religious expression in American religion. The theology of evangelicalism gave individuals a much greater role in obtaining salvation
than traditional Protestant theologies, especially Calvinism, allowed. Nathaniel Taylor, the leading advocate of evangelicalism,
argued that salvation was "man's own act" rather than God's.[7] Individuals no longer had to wait for God; they could initiate their
own conversion. This shift from waiting to searching for salvation
produced new religious priorities. Instead of correct belief or
regular ritual observance, the most important religious act became
a direct personal conversion to Jesus.

Massive revivals, led by unorthodox ministers called either revivalists or evangelists, carried evangelical religion throughout the
country. Revivals were religious meetings of indefinite duration
where "sinners" could uncover their wicked hearts and confront
their God. Several denominations usually sponsored revivals in
small towns and cities, where agents advertised the forthcoming
event to the community and arranged the necessary facilities.
While revivals had been previously viewed as "gifts" from God,
they were now purposefully organized events which maximized the
possibility of religious conversion. "A Revival of Religion is not a
Miracle," insisted one revivalist. "It consists entirely of the right
use of the powers of nature . . . or the right use of means."[8]

A new breed of clergy conducted revivals in most parts of the
United States. Although critics felt that revivalists were inauthentic
ministers, "actually quite lost to the church,"[9] most revivalists were
simply itinerant ministers who traveled around the country leading

University of Chicago Press, 1964); Robert W. Doherty, *The Hicksite Separation*
(New Brunswick, N.J.: Rutgers University Press, 1967); and Robert W. Doherty,
"Social Bases of the Presbyterian Schism of 1837–38: The Philadelphia Case,"
Journal of Social History 2 (fall 1968): 69–79.

7. Nathaniel W. Taylor, "Concio ad Clerum: A Sermon, 1828," in Sidney
Ahlstrom (ed.), *Theology in America* (New York: Bobbs-Merrill, 1967), p. 217.

8. Charles Grandison Finney, *Lectures on Revivals of Religion,* ed. William
McLoughlin (Cambridge: Belknap Press of Harvard University Press, 1960),
pp. 12–13.

9. Charles Hodge, "Systematic Theology," in Ahlstrom (ed.), *Theology in
America*, pp. 261–62.

revivals. Although some evangelists were converted laymen without formal religious training, for the most part they were as well educated as other denominational ministers. Most began their career of exhortation in their own parish and left their congregation only after they had secured a reputation as a successful preacher. Interdenominational and denominational mission agencies frequently hired revivalists to carry religion to specific parts of the country, especially pioneer areas of the West.

Although styles of preaching and organizing revivals differed enormously, evangelists attempted to convert every unregenerated soul who attended their revivals. They preached the utter depravity of each individual and the willingness of God to administer grace to everyone who begged forgiveness. Employing special revival techniques, or "new measures," revivalists worked to create an emotionally charged atmosphere where conversion experiences would routinely occur. The number of people converted determined a revivalist's success, or as one evangelist put it, "the amount of a minister's success in winning souls *(other things being equal)* invariably decided the amount of wisdom he had exercised in the discharge of his office."[10]

Although hundreds of revivalists emerged during the Second Great Awakening, Charles Grandison Finney conducted the most successful revivals. Models of clarity and efficiency, Finney's revivals embodied his own compelling personality and innovative revival techniques. A contemporary describes him at the famous series of revivals in Troy, New York in 1827, where "his great eyes (were) rolling around the congregation and his arms flying about in the air like those of a windmill. One evening he described hell and the devil and the long procession of sinners being swept down the rapids, about to make the awful plunge into the burning depths of liquid fire below, and the rejoicing hosts in the inferno coming up to meet them with the shouts of the devils echoing through the vaulted arches."[11]

The fiery Finney believed that his first task was to get the attention of the sinner, because "there are so many exciting subjects constantly brought before the public mind, such a running to and fro, so many that cry 'Lo here' and 'Lo there,' that the church cannot maintain her ground, cannot command attention, without exciting

10. Finney, *Lectures on Revivals of Religion*, pp. 194–95.

11. Elizabeth Cady Stanton, *Eighty Years and More* (New York: European Publishing Company, 1898), p. 42.

preaching, and sufficient novelty in measures, to get a public ear."[12]
In order to create the appropriate atmosphere for the sinner to feel
God's presence and repent, Finney utilized extemporaneous
preaching and daily prayer meetings. In addition, he introduced
novel techniques like the "anxious bench" and the "anxious room."
They enabled him to devote his full attention to potential converts
by segregating people who were obviously nearing a religious
climax from the rest of the audience. But in the final analysis, Finney knew that, "as sure as the effect of a measure becomes stereo-
typed, it ceases to gain attention, and then you must try something
new."[13]

By offering evangelicalism as an alternative to established
religion, revivalists such as Charles Finney triggered widespread
ideological confrontation and denominational schism. They polar-
ized denominations into competing old- and new-school factions,
where the new school embraced the new revival measures and the
old school rejected them. The ensuing battles resulted in divisions
at every denominational level, from parish churches to the highest
administrative bodies. In the process people shed anachronistic
beliefs and founded a myriad of new religious sects throughout the
country.

STAGE THREE: DEVELOPMENT OF NEW SECTS

Although the relationship between sectarian development and social change is not yet clear, the creation of new religious sects both
substantially expanded the religious spectrum and facilitated the
realignment of religion and society. The unstable social and
economic environment, ripe for new ideologies and movements,
produced an enormous variety of new sects, and conversion to the
"new" became the religious standard of the day. Providing more
meaningful religious experiences than established religion, the new
sects promoted the realignment between religion and the emerging
social structure.[14]

12. Finney, *Lectures on Revivals of Religion*, pp. 10, 272. See also his lectures,
"What a Revival of Religion Is," "How to Preach the Gospel," and "How to
Promote a Revival," in the same volume.

13. Ibid., p. 181.

14. In 1911 Ernst Troeltsch opened a confusing discussion about types of
religious organization when he published *The Social Teachings of the Christian
Churches*, vol. 1 (Harper Torchbooks, 1960). Recently, Allan W. Eister summarized and critiqued the subsequent literature in "H. Richard Niebuhr and the
Paradox of Religious Organization: A Radical Critique," in Charles Y. Glock and

Depending on specific historical circumstances, the organization, belief system, and ultimate success of each new sect varied considerably. While some sects relied on strong institutions, specialized leadership, and centralized decision making, others exhibited fluid boundaries and few formal structures. Beliefs ranged from reactionary interpretations of Christianity to secular ideologies. Although many sects required their members to conform rigidly to prescribed beliefs and standards of behavior, others required nothing more than a superficial interest in a particular religious explanation. Some sects maintained an indifferent, even hostile, relationship to the outside world, while others explicitly sought to accommodate themselves to the larger society.

Nevertheless, in order to examine the relationship between certain types of sects and the general process of sectarian development, the new sects can be classified into four categories based on their distance from the standard beliefs and structures of established religion.[15] From within established religion, *regenerative sects* attempted to modify traditional denominational beliefs and forms. *Schismatic sects*, advocating radical transformations in Christian beliefs, permanently separated from their former denominational affiliates; while *cultic sects*, substituting their own religious alternative for Christianity, arose independent from established religion. Finally, *quasi-religious sects* repudiated religion altogether and replaced it with explicitly political beliefs and structures. Table 14—2 delineates representative groups for each type of sect.

Regenerative Sects

During the battle for denominational control, old- and new-school supporters separated into old- and new-school regenerative sects. From within established religion, as well-defined factions or short-lived splinter groups, they attempted to reshape the contours of established religion in either an old- or a new-school direction. Numerous denominational divisions, shifting constituencies, and leaders who misrepresented their factions, however, make it ex-

---

Phillip Hammond (eds.), *Beyond the Classics? Essays in the Scientific Study of Religion* (New York: Harper and Row, Harper Torchbooks, 1973), pp. 355—408. For the purposes of this essay, a sect is any new religious movement that emerged during the Second Great Awakening.

15. For other classifications of sects, see Bryan R. Wilson, *Sociology of Religion* (Baltimore: Penguin Books, 1969), pp. 361—83; and Charles Y. Glock, "On the Origin and Evolution of Religious Groups," in Charles Y. Glock (ed.), *Religion in Sociological Perspective* (Belmont, Calif.: Wadsworth, 1973), pp. 207—20.

Table 14–2

NEW SECTS, 1820–1860

Regenerative Sects	Schismatic Sects	Cultic Sects	Quasi-Religious Sects
Old School			
Presbyterian old school	Missouri Synod (1847)	Mormon church	Owenism
Congregational old school	Norwegian Evangelical Synod (1853)	Spiritualism	(New Harmony, 1825)
Antimission Baptist	United Presbyterian Church of	Swedenborgianism	Fourierism
Anglo-Catholic Episcopal	North America (1858)	Mesmerism	(Brook Farm, 1841)
Lutheran General Council	Church of the United Brethren (1800)	phrenology	Oneida Society
Mercersburg German Reformed	Evangelical Association (1803)	homeopathy	abolitionism
Quaker Hicksite	Cumberland Presbyterian church (1810)	Grahamism	agrarian reform
	Methodist Protestant church (1830)	astrology	
	Free Methodist church (1860)		
New School			
Presbyterian new school	Free Synod (1827)		
Congregational new school	Disciples of Christ (1832)		
American Baptist Home Mission	Winebrunner Baptist (1823)		
Society	Millerites (1842)		
Low Church Episcopal	(Former schismatic sects)		
Lutheran General Synod	Unitarian		
Methodist Episcopal Church	Universalist		

Table 14-2 (Continued)

NEW SECTS, 1820-1860

Regenerative Sects	Schismatic Sects	Cultic Sects	Quasi-Religious Sects
Quaker Guerneyite	Mennonite		
	Moravian		
	Shaker		
	Rappite		
	Seventh Day Baptist		
	Six Principle Baptist		
	Dunker Baptist		
	Free Will Baptist		
	Christian Connection		

tremely difficult to characterize regenerative sects broadly. Never-theless, by 1860, although the old school successfully retained a significant following in most denominations, the new school clearly had established itself as the major religious force in America.

Fearful of the potential demise of denominationalism, the old school opposed the new measures of evangelicalism and attempted to recapture its own unique denominational beliefs and practices. According to one historian, by applying strict traditional standards to ministerial training, doctrinal belief, and ritual observance, "the old school clung to the ideal of an organic Christian society guided by the spiritual leadership of the clergy."[16] Regular participation in specific denominational rites, not a revival conversion experience, continued to be the route to salvation

Although the new school believed that the old school was the vestige of an antiquated religious system, in fact, the old school program corresponded to a significant demographic change within the country. For the most part, the membership base of the old school consisted of recent immigrants from Europe who feared the dilution or "Americanization" of their denominational standards. Demanding purity in theology and ritual, immigrants pushed their denomination in a decidedly old-school direction. In most de-nominations, the size and strength of the old school depended on the number of first and second generation immigrants in that denomination.

The old-school development in the major Lutheran denomina-tion, the Evangelical Lutheran Church in America, provides a par-ticularly good illustration of the interplay between immigration and old schoolism. The Pennsylvania Synod, composed primarily of first and second generation Germans, was the most consistently old-school synod in the denomination. In order to maintain denomina-tional standards, the synod required its clergy to preach both in German and English and required that "whosoever applied into our ministerium, must know so much of the Greek language, as to be able to read the New Testament in that language without difficulty; if possible know so much Hebrew, as to translate the more easy parts of the Old Testament, he must likewise give sufficient proof of his acquaintance with the most important branches of theology; viz. Exegesis, Dogmatik, Morality, Church History, Apologetik, and Homiletik."[17] When the new school, led by Samuel Schmucker,

16. McLoughlin, introduction to Finney, *Lectures on Revivals of Religion*, p. xi.

17. *Minutes of the German Evangelical Lutheran Synod of Pennsylvania* (Sum-nytown: Enos Benner, 1834), p. 8. See also *Verhandlungen der Deutsch*

attempted to expel certain "popish" tendencies from the Augsburg Confession, the Pennsylvania Synod replied that since Schmucker's *Definite Platform* "professes to be an improvement on the Augsburg Confession—the venerable, common, confession of the entire Lutheran Church, in the old world and the new—and in view of the fact that as the oldest Evangelical Lutheran Synod in this country, we feel it our duty to publicly bear testimony to the faith of our Fathers, in opposition to every innovating attempt to lay violent hands on the ancient foundations of faith."[18] Finally, in 1862, the Pennsylvania Synod and other "Representatives from various Evangelical Lutheran Synods in the U.S. and Canada accepting the Unaltered Augsburg Confession" withdrew from the new-school General Synod and founded the old-school General Council.

In the case of the Presbyterian, U.S.A. denomination, Scotch-Irish immigrants were the most vigorous proponents of traditional beliefs and practices. One contemporary observer wrote about a congregation in which the "old Scotch Presbyterians were opposed to all innovations that would afford their people paths of flowerey ease on the road to Heaven" to the extent that "the introduction of stoves, a violincello, Wesley's hymns, and a choir split the church in twain."[19] In 1838 the old-school expelled the strongly new-school Presbyterians and synods from the Presbyterian General Assembly, and the denomination remained split into two nearly equal parts until 1868.

At the same time that the old school attempted to combat a constant stream of heresies, it also struggled to restyle orthodoxy in light of contemporary realities. The Mercersburg theology, created by John Nevin and Philip Schaff, successfully reinstated the mystery and "real presence" of the Eucharist in German Reformed ceremonies. In addition, the Anglo-Catholic movement, influenced by the Tractarians in England, endeavored to put new life into the Reformation doctrine and liturgy of the Protestant Episcopal church.

Although the influx of European immigrants reinvigorated traditional religion in America, in the final analysis, the old school failed to protect established religion from evangelical contamina-

Evangelisch-Lutherische Synode von Pennsylvanien und benachbarten Staaten (Allentown, Pa.: Carl L. Huetter, 1819.)

18. *Minutes of the 109th Annual Session of the German Evangelical Lutheran Ministerium of Pennsylvania and Adjacent States* (Sumnytown: Enos Benner, 1856), p. 27.

19. Stanton, *Eighty Years and More*, p. 25.

tion. Despite the sharp indictment by the old school of "sectarian spirit," with one leader ranking it with heresy as "unchurchly and anti-sacramental,"[20] in fact, the old school fostered denominational divisions. Purging new-school factions and withdrawing from overwhelmingly new-school denominations only encouraged additional sectarian development. While the emerging old-school sects were highly traditional, they could not protect religious innovation in other types of sects.

By effectively promoting evangelicalism within established religion between 1820 and 1860, the new school became the most important sectarian tendency of the nineteenth century. Thousands of converted "sinners," located both inside and outside established religion, joined new-school sects. As a result, new-school sects grew at a faster rate than old-school sects, and the Methodists, the only completely new-school group, emerged as the largest denomination in the country.[21] In addition, the new school developed vital interdenominational missionary agencies and social reform organizations.

The Methodists, the most successful new-school group, were at the forefront of saving souls west of the Allegheny mountains. In Kentucky and Tennessee, the Methodists, along with the Baptists and a few new-school Presbyterians, organized the famous Cane Ridge revivals of 1801. These revivals significantly increased Baptist and Methodist membership in Kentucky, so that by 1820, the state census reported 21,000 Baptists and Methodists and only 3,700 Presbyterians.[22] Although the Baptists were equally as successful as the Methodists in converting new members, the Methodists gained a competitive edge by replacing traditional parishes with an innovative system of circuits and preaching stations in order to utilize effectively their small number of trained clergy. As a result, by 1860 the U.S. census showed that the Methodists had nearly three times as many churches and the Baptists had twice as many as the combined number of Presbyterian and Congregational churches.[23]

Although many Lutherans staunchly resisted evangelicalism

20. John Nevin, *The Mystical Presence*, in Ahlstrom (ed.), *Theology in America*, p. 408.

21. *Statistics of the United States (including mortality, property, &c.,) in 1860*; comp. from the original returns and being the final exhibit of the eighth census, under the direction of the secretary of the interior (Washington: Government Printing Office, 1866), pp. 497–501.

22. Reported in Sweet, *The Story of Religion in America*, p. 214.

23. *Statistics of the United States in 1860*, pp. 497–501.

throughout the century, the main thrust of the denomination was in a decidedly new-school direction. By the 1840s, entire synods incorporated evangelicalism into their practices. The strongly new school Lutheran Synod of Miami in Ohio, for example, passed a resolution in 1849 stating that "protracted meetings, revivals of religion, prayer meetings, religious conferences, and Sabbath Schools, are in accordance with the teachings of the Bible, and upon which depends in a great measure, the prosperity of our Lutheran Zion."[24]

The Presbyterian new school, under the leadership of Charles Finney, achieved most of its successes in the upper Mohawk Valley of New York. This area became known as the "burned-over district" after several intense revivals swept through the region. Auburn Theological Seminary, located in the heart of this area, trained new-school leaders for the entire country. After the old school ousted the new school from the denomination in 1838, the new school quickly organized the Presbyterian, U.S.A., New School, a parallel Presbyterian denomination based on evangelicalism. By 1868, when the warring camps finally reunited, the new school had forced the old school to accept a moderate brand of evangelicalism into the denomination.

In addition to internal difficulties, old- and new-school sects faced the geographical problem of a scattered constituency.[25] As a result of the nation's acquisition of new territory during this period, one denomination reported that "there are thousands of members of our church, scattered over the broad prairies as sheep having no shepherd, and fall prey to the destroyers," including rum, popery, and heathenism.[26] Based on their commitment to evangelicalism, the new school developed missionary and social reform programs designed to reach the scattered population.

Although the old school eventually established its own mission agencies within each denomination, the new school developed more efficient interdenominational missionary organizations in response to the challenge of the heathen West. In order to reach Catholics, Mormons, and other religious "heretics," as well as un-

24. *Minutes of the Sixth Convention of the Evangelical Lutheran Church of Miami* (Dayton, Ohio: Printed at the Daily Journal Office, 1849), p. 18.

25. The Roman Catholic church also posed a threat to both old and new schools. Due to the heavy European immigration in this period, the number of Catholic churches grew faster than those of any other denomination. Much of the mission and social reform activity was directed toward the Catholics, resulting in the most virulent anti-Catholic sentiment of any period in American history.

26. *Minutes of the Eleventh Annual Convention of the Evangelical Lutheran Synod of Miami* (Springfield, Ohio: Evangelical Lutheran Office, 1854), p. 5.

churched Protestants, the new school created an elaborate web of national, state, and local interdenominational mission agencies. Some of the prominent national organizations included the American Bible Society, the American Home Mission Society, the American Tract Society, and the American Sunday School Union.

Although nearly all new-school groups paid lip service to this interdenominational cooperation, in fact, each denomination was primarily concerned about saving its own population.[27] The competition among denominations for converts was so acute that in one case the members of a Methodist church in Cincinnati promptly abducted and beat a local Lutheran minister when he called Methodism "the false prophet of the day."[28] The Methodists earned a particularly bad reputation for actively recruiting members of other denominations and refused to participate in joint efforts altogether. In addition, most interdenominational agencies were funded by new-school Congregationalists and Presbyterians, such as the Tappans of New York City, and the literature and personnel reflected this denominational bias.

Although social reform movements frequently functioned as denominational recruiting arenas, both the old school and new school also participated in reform programs such as temperance, sabbatarianism, nativism, women's rights, and abolitionism in order to control certain kinds of "unsocial" behavior. While some issues, like women's rights, appealed solely to new-school groups, most reforms attracted shifting coalitions of old- and new-school sects. Depending on their constituency, the sects carefully selected their reform issues and proposed various solutions to the social "problems." Anti-Catholic movements, for example, generated support from a broad range of groups; but nativism, temperance, and sabbatarianism, aimed directly at recent immigrants, failed in sects with a significant immigrant population.[29]

While the old school and the new school advocated the same side of many reform issues, tactical considerations often separated the

27. See Miyakawa, *Protestants and Pioneers*; Ahlstrom, *A Religious History of the American People*, chaps. 26, 27; and Donald Scott, "Watchmen of the Walls of Zion: Evangelicals and American Society, 1800–1860" (unpublished Ph.D dissertation, University of Wisconsin, 1968).

28. *Proceedings of the Fourth Session of the Evangelical Lutheran Synod of Miami* (Baltimore: Evangelical Lutheran Church, 1847), pp. 39–40.

29. See Paul Kleppner, *The Cross of Culture* (New York: Free Press, 1970); Frederick C. Luebke, *Immigrants and Politics* (Lincoln, Neb.: University of Nebraska Press, 1969); and Joseph Gusfield, *Symbolic Crusade* (Urbana, Ill.: University of Illinois Press, 1963).

two. In the case of slavery, for example, where the old school was at least as active in antislavery activities as the new school,[30] they disagreed about how and when to free the slaves and the position of blacks in society after emancipation. In addition, the new school created large interdenominational agencies, structurally similiar to their missionary organizations, including the American Anti-Slavery Society and the American Temperance Society, in order to promote specific reforms. The old school, fearing the erosion of their denominational beliefs, refused to join these agencies, even the American Society for Promoting the Observance of the Seventh Commandment, which fought prostitution.

Even within the new school, controversies raged over the best strategy to rid the world of sin. Since converting individuals to Jesus, the new school's main priority, could not proceed fast enough to reform the entire society, opinions differed over whether to continue to convert individual sinners, legislate their behavior, or attack the social causes of sin. As one historian explains the dilemma, "inspiration came to individuals, and each person charted his own course. Disregarding any established authority or institutions, ultraists concerned themselves with single souls, theirs and others, their standard of piety and morality absolutely fixed by personal holiness. But their objectives—rooting out sin, converting the world, and bringing forth the millennium—could be approached only by concerted energies."[31]

Although the new school put together a religious formula for a broad cross section of society, ironically, its success eventually undermined American Protestantism. The old school correctly perceived that evangelical theology, by encouraging denominational conflict and schism, would open the floodgates for new religious movements. As one old-school leader put it, "if every man is at liberty to exalt his own intuitions, as men are accustomed to call their strong convictions, we should have as many theologies in the world as there are thinkers."[32] Religion spun off in numerous di-

30. For a discussion of abolitionism within the Quaker denomination, see Doherty, *The Hicksite Separation;* among Presbyterians, see Linda K. Pritchard, "Ministers: A Comparative Framework" (unpublished manuscript, Department of History Library, University of Pittsburgh, 1970); and within the Presbyterian Covenanter denomination, see David Ray Wilcox, "The Reformed Presbyterian Church and the Anti-Slavery Movement" (unpublished M.A. thesis, Geneva College, 1948).

31. Cross, *The Burned Over District,* p. 206.

32. Charles Hodge, *Systematic Theology,* in Ahlstrom (ed.), *Theology in America,* pp. 261–62.

rections, and a variety of new Christian and non-Christian sects emerged out of the Second Great Awakening.

Schismatic Sects

Schismatic sects were splinter groups that broke off from established religion to form permanent independent institutions. These Christian sects originated within established religion during the theological and political controversies triggered by the Second Great Awakening. Although schismatic sects shared some of the same positions on the religious issues of the day with old- and new-school regenerative sects, schismatic sects offered a broader critique of established religion and designed more consistent religious alternatives than regenerative sects. Their stridency and unwillingness to compromise with either secular or denominational structures led schismatic sects to organize their own groups.

While most of the schismatic sects founded in the mid-nineteenth century spun off from the new school, several came out of the old-school experience. Some European immigrants, for whom any contact with American religion compromised traditional denominational theology and ritual, founded separate, more conservative old-school sects. The Lutheran Missouri Synod, for example, which remains extremely conservative even today, originated in 1847 during a period of heavy German immigration to the Midwest. Norwegian immigrants organized the Norwegian Evangelical Synod in 1853, and foreign-born Swedes founded the Augustana Synod in 1860. The Associate Presbyterian and Associate Reformed Presbyterian denominations, composed of immigrants from Scotland who settled around Pittsburgh early in the century, merged to form the conservative United Presbyterian Church of North America in 1858.

Most of the schismatic sects to emerge between 1820 and 1860, however, were highly evangelical. Using personal salvation as the initial indicator of perfectionism, they believed that a narrow "fundamental" interpretation of the Bible and stringent standards of behavior would bring about a sinless world. Early in the century, dissident evangelicals left the Mennonite and Presbyterian denominations to form the Evangelical Association and the Cumberland Presbyterian church, and former Lutherans and German Reformed members came together in the church of the United Brethren. The Methodist Episcopal church, dividing three times during this period, spawned the Methodist Protestants in 1830, the Wesleyan Methodists in 1844, and the Free Methodists in 1860.

Other Methodist and Presbyterian evangelicals united in 1832 to found the Disciples of Christ. Finally, local "union" churches, informally organized congregations of mostly discontented Presbyterians and Congregationalists, proliferated throughout the Second Great Awakening.

However, the millennial Millerite movement most fully embodied the evangelical spirit of the period. According to William Miller, a nineteenth-century Baptist preacher, the Second Coming of Jesus was to occur between March 21, 1843, and March 21, 1844. Both positive signs, like revivalist successes, and negative ones, like the "seducing" beliefs of Shakerism and Roman Catholicism, pointed to the impending event. Miller's prophecy spread rapidly, especially in the "burned-over" district of New York; and by the end of 1843, there were well over fifty thousand believers and another million who were "skeptically expectant."[33] Even though the world did not end at the appointed time, several sects emerged out of Millerism, including the Seventh-Day Adventists.

The presence of schismatic sects that had originated during earlier historical periods added yet another dimension to the nineteenth-century religious spectrum. Although not usually evangelical themselves, these former schismatic sects offered antebellum spiritual wanderers proven routes to salvation. German, Dutch, and Russian sects, including the Rappites, Mennonites, and Moravians, arrived early in colonial America seeking religious toleration for their schismatic beliefs. Somewhat later, in 1776, Mother Ann Lee brought the Shakers, or "shaking Quakers," to this country. These communities became places where, as one leader stated, "some practical application could be made of the fresh views of philosophy and life."[34] The twenty Shaker "families" and the German colonies of New Harmony, Amana, and Zoar swelled with uprooted religious zealots after periods of intense revivalism.[35]

The Unitarians and Universalists are examples of earlier schismatic sects that did not begin to grow significantly until the Second

33. Cross, *The Burned Over District*, p. 287.

34. Elizabeth P. Peabody, "The Original Ideal of Brook Farm," in Noyes, *The History of American Socialisms*, pp. 109–13.

35. Elder Frederick Evans of the Shaker community in Mount Lebanon, New York, regarded religious revivals as the "hot beds of Shakerism" because his community "always gain[ed] members after a revival in any part of the country." Quoted in Nordhoff, *The Communistic Societies of the United States*, p. 158. See also Henri Desroche, *The American Shakers: From Neo-Christianity to Presocialism* (Amherst, Mass.: University of Massachusetts Press, 1971), pp. 101–8.

Great Awakening discredited the traditional Protestant preoccupation with original sin. Believing that "it is the purpose of God,
through grace revealed in our Lord Jesus Christ, to save every
member of the human race from sin,"[36] the Universalists attracted
followers for whom predestination had lost all meaning. According
to the Unitarians, even Jesus was unnecessary since men and
women controlled their own salvation. Both of these religious sects
believed that the kingdom of God would be ushered in by social
reform activities promoting "moral behavior," not by dramatic conversion experiences brought about by revivals.

Cultic Sects

Cultic sects developed religious alternatives for people who broke
from the Christian mainstream during the Second Great Awakening. Most cultic sects were based on the discovery and implementation of universal laws of nature. Utilizing a prescientific method,
including the use of empirical data, nonliteral interpretation or
"higher criticism" of the Bible, and new classifications of physical
and psychic phenomena, cultic sects described the world in a variety of new ways.

In terms of strength and longevity, the Mormons were the most
important cultic sect to come out of this period. Like the Presbyterian new school and the Millerite movement, they originated in the
burned-over district of upstate New York. In 1823 the angel Moroni
revealed divine commandments to Joseph Smith. Their translation
into the Book of Mormon disclosed that, contrary to Christian
belief, the Son of God had not yet come to earth but was due at any
time. Smith led his followers from New York to Utah in various
stages to prepare for the impending millennium. During this
pilgrimage, the Mormons encountered bitter abuse for their practice of polygamy and submitted to the highly authoritarian
leadership of Smith and, following his death, Brigham Young. The
combination in early Mormonism of persecution, autocratic rule,
and physical isolation laid the foundation for the contemporary
Mormon church.

Other cultic sects to emerge out of the turmoil of the Second
Great Awakening proved to be less cohesive and more ephemeral
than the Mormons. Creating and maintaining religious institutions
based on a vague scientism was difficult. Most people supplemented
rather than replaced other belief systems with selective cultic
beliefs and practices. Because most cultic sects maintained no ex-

36. Ahlstrom, *A Religious History of the American People*, p. 482.

clusive membership requirements, people could accept cultic tenets that fit their own notions about the world and still remain within other religious groups. Although most cultic sects failed to develop strong institutions, they were important because they significantly enlarged the spectrum of religion in America.

Spiritualism, the cultic sect that focused on supernatural revelation and departed spirits, began in Rochester, New York, when the Fox sisters communicated with their departed relatives in 1848. By 1855, at the height of the organized Spiritualist movement in the United States, there were over a million and a half believers and 150 practicing mediums.[37] For most of these people, however, spiritualism was primarily a bridge to further religious experimentation. According to one historian, "few, in any case, remained active spiritualists very long. . . . this was probably a further step on the path to religious modernism of some variety. Its scientific manner, social awareness, Biblical and historical criticism, and eager attention to current speculation must have tended to obliterate any remnants of literal-mindedness and orthodoxy embedded in its converts."[38] Despite the popularity of these tenets, Spiritualist congregations numbered only seventeen in 1860.[39]

In contrast to spiritualism's supernatural analysis, Swedenborgianism produced "natural laws" to explain the world. Based on the ideas of Emanuel Swedenborg, an eighteenth-century Swedish philosopher, this nineteenth-century cultic sect embodied his "universal understanding" and his ideas about sex and marriage, spiritual healing, and "animal magnetism." New Thought churches, based on Swedenborgian beliefs, usually dissolved within a short time; but participants in movements that relied on a "scientific" understanding of the world, including Unitarians, spiritualists, socialists, and some new-school advocates, utilitized Swedenborg's views.

Mesmerism, phrenology, homeopathy, and dietary prescriptions provided additional cultic alternatives to established religion. The goals of these cults included psychic and physical healing and the discovery of unknown truths. Their reliance on supernatural explanations kept them closely related to spiritualism and Swedenborgianism. Since extraordinary experiences were highly valued, one historian reports that "persons acknowledged insane were even sought after for leadership into higher inspiration."[40] For the most

37. Cross, *The Burned Over District*, p. 349.
38. Ibid., p. 348.
39. *Statistics of the United States in 1860*, p. 500.
40. Cross, *The Burned Over District*, p. 203.

part, itinerant lecturers, appearing irregularly and infrequently in any location, promoted these cults. Additional information was circulated by personal communication, independent tracts, and isolated articles in religious periodicals.

Mesmerism, introduced by F.A. Mesmer, an Austrian physician, advanced ideas about psychic healing based on the astrological, electrical, and magnetic forces of the earth and stars. An apprentice cobbler, Andrew Jackson Davis, dubbed the "Poughkeepsie Seer," became the most famous proponent of mesmerism in this country after he was hypnotized in the 1850s. Phrenology, the practice of reading a person's skull to determine character and intelligence, reached epidemic proportions in the 1840s along the Erie Canal in New York. Homeopathy, according to one practioner, "held that disease was, essentially, a dynamic aberration of the spirit."[41] As the forerunner of the Christian Science sect in the later nineteenth century, homeopathic medicine employed natural herbs, spiritual healing, and dietary prescriptions. Additional cultic movements centered around dietary fads. Eating "organic" foods was thought to align one's body with the forces in the universe. The graham cracker, created by Sylvester Graham, became a popular health food of the period.

Quasi-Religious Sects

Secular ideologies, especially political ones, replaced religious theologies for some people caught up in the turmoil of the Second Great Awakening. Quasi-religious sects, based on these secular ideologies, offered the most radical alternatives to established religion during the nineteenth century.[42]

Socialist ideologies supplied the foundation for the most significant quasi-religious sects of the period. Although some religious sects had previously adapted communistic living arrangements for pragmatic purposes, it was not until the nineteenth century that sectarian groups utilized explicitly socialist doctrines. Abandoning reliance on the promise of a better world after death, socialism translated the contemporary dissatisfaction with society into a

41. Ahlstrom, A Religious History of the American People, p. 486.

42. For a discussion of functional equivalents to traditional religion, see Peter L. Berger and Thomas Luckmann, The Social Construction of Reality (Garden City, N.Y.: Doubleday, 1966); Thomas Luckmann, Invisible Religion (London: Collier-Macmillan, 1967); and Robert Bellah, "Civil Religion in America," in William McLoughlin and Robert Bellah (eds.), Religion in America (Boston: Beacon Press, 1966).

movement to change this world. Socialist sects attempted to replace a stratified, unequal society with programs to redistribute equally the ownership and control of the means of production to the entire society. For the most part, socialists organized small-scale communist societies which they hoped would act as models for the larger society. Although the formulas differed somewhat, each community designed belief systems and life-styles that were radically different from the prevailing social standards of private property, familial arrangements, and government.

Disciples of two famous European socialists, Robert Owen in England and Charles Fourier in France, brought socialism to this country between 1825 and 1855. They primarily organized communitarian societies based on the thriving Owenite or Fourier experiments in Europe. Although many small local communities were founded during the Second Great Awakening, only the most successful cases have been documented. A.J. MacDonald, a follower of Owen who took it upon himself to report on all communitarian sects, recorded only twelve Owenite societies and thirty-four Fourier phalanxes.[43] Although none were religious by nineteenth-century standards, one early historian of socialism argues that "all communes under consideration have as their bond of union some form of religious belief. . . . For the commune to exist harmoniously, it must be composed of persons who are of one mind upon some question which to them shall appear so important as to take the place of religion, if it is not essentially religious." In one case "communism" appeared to be the religion of the community.[44]

New Harmony, founded in 1825, was the first and most famous Owenite community. Robert Owen purchased 30,000 acres in Indiana from the Rappites, a German schismatic sect that was moving to western Pennsylvania. Because of his educational theories and his beliefs about free thinking and idealism, Owen eventually drew 900 followers into New Harmony.[45] Within eighteen months after its organization, however, disagreements and jealousies disrupted the society.

Brook Farm, founded in 1841 by a group of Unitarians known as Transcendentalists, became a successful Fourier society within two years. Fourier's principles of productive labor, art, and science, in addition to certain "social and religious affectations," attracted 115

43. Noyes, *History of American Socialisms*, pp. 10–20.

44. Nordhoff, The Communistic Societies of the United States, pp. 387, 339. See also Noyes, *History of American Socialisms*, p. 280.

45. Noyes, *History of American Socialisms*, pp. 15, 58.

wealthy intellectuals from the Boston area. Brook Farm, sometimes referred to as "the newness," "the renaissance," and "the revival," survived until 1846.[46]

An independent socialist, John Humphrey Noyes, founded the most successful quasi-religious sect in 1847, the Oneida society. A revival convert himself, Noyes believed that socialism, through the revitalization of Christianity, would usher in the kingdom of God on earth. "The question for the future is," according to Noyes, "Will Revivals go forward into Socialism, or will the Socialists go forward into Revivalism? . . . If the churches can not be put into this work, we do not see how Socialism on a large scale is going to be propagated."[47] Oneida promised its participants a sinless life based on communal living and Christian love, a liberal "Social Science" method, a self-evaluation process known as "Mutual Criticism," and a nontraditional marriage standard. Forced out of Putney, Vermont, because of this "complex marriage" practice, looking suspiciously like free love to the townspeople, the society moved to a permanent site just outside Oneida, New York, in 1848, where it flourished for three decades.

A variety of loosely organized radical reform movements, including immediate abolitionism and agrarian reform, also embodied socialism. William Lloyd Garrison challenged the legitimacy of contemporary social institutions by demanding the immediate emancipation of all slaves. Although Garrison himself was more of an anarchist than a socialist, he did recommend alternative forms of social organization to his followers. Socialist land-reform movements were also popular during the Second Great Awakening. George Evans, along with New York City labor radicals, led the fight to distribute western lands on a free and equitable basis in anticipation of the homestead programs. Additional groups, like the Oberlin perfectionist colony founded by Charles Finney, flirted with an ill-defined Christian socialism.[48]

Summary

Thus, four types of new sects emerged in Stage Three to provide alternatives to established religion. The sects in each successive

46. Ibid., pp. 15, 512–63; and Ahlstrom, *A Religious History of the American People*, p. 500.

47. Noyes, *History of American Socialisms*, p. 656.

48. Cross, *The Burned Over District*, pp. 326–27; and Larry Gara, "Who Was an Abolitionist?" in Martin Duberman (ed.), *The Anti-Slavery Vanguard* (Princeton, N.J.: Princeton University Press, 1965).

type replaced traditional orthodoxy with increasingly unconventional doctrines. Old and new school regenerative sects created new religious options inside established religion. Schismatic sects, unwilling to compromise with established religion, split from their parent bodies to proclaim their own Christian truths. Non-Christian religious alternatives, previously alien to established religion, originated in cultic sects. Quasi-religious sects departed furthest from established religion by substituting secular ideologies for religious ones.

But in the final analysis, individual people created new models of religion, recreated society itself, based on their own perceptions of reality. Not all people participated, and many traveled only a short distance away from established religion. Once the process of religious innovation started, however, it was difficult to turn back. As one religious wanderer acknowledged to another, "you have been led, as I have, to unexpected results. In attacking one weak spot of the current system, you have found that there were a good many others in the near neighborhood, till at last it became difficult to tell what was not rotten."[49] A few adventurers moved through all the types of sects, continually searching for the ultimate panacea, the perfect society, the Universal Truth.

James Boyle, an "evangelist," is an example of a person whose personal development paralleled the larger pattern of religious change during the Second Great Awakening. In less than twenty years, Boyle journeyed through nearly every conceivable new religious movement of the period. Born a Catholic in Ontario, Canada, James Boyle worked as a Methodist minister in the Northwest as a young man. In 1825, he took a pastorate, under the sponsorship of the American Home Mission Society, at Watkins Glen, New York. He alternated parish work with itinerant evangelizing for the new-school Presbyterians until 1832, when he left for New England to take over a "free church" at the request of John Humphrey Noyes. In 1834 Boyle and Noyes published the *Perfectionist* magazine in New York City, until Noyes' "complex marriage" ideas estranged Boyle. Theophilus Gates, the "Battle Axe" holiness leader in Philadelphia, then attracted Boyle for a short time; but he finally went to work in a machine shop in Newark, New Jersey, until 1838. At the same time, he traveled the countryside as an agent for the Ohio Anti-Slavery Society. He later became a lecturer on socialism in New England and in 1842 joined

49. Cross, *The Burned Over District*, p. 282.

the Northampton Fourier community. In 1844 he studied phrenology and medicine as a Methodist Protestant minister. Finally he became a Swedenborgian and worked closely with Andrew Jackson Davis in faith healing.[50]

STAGE FOUR: CREATION OF A
"NEW" ESTABLISHED RELIGION

As religion caught up with the structural transformations in society, the schismatic impulse to create new forms of religion diminished. Although no exact date marked the demise of the Second Great Awakening, by 1860 a new established religion based on the realignment of religion and society had replaced the former established religion. This new established religion integrated selected new beliefs and new sects into the framework of American denominationalism instead of creating an entirely new system. Until social change again triggered religious reorganization, stability rather than change characterized religion in America.

Evangelicalism emerged as the dominant theology in the new established religion. In an increasingly complex society, people preferred to work out their own salvation instead of deferring to the whim of God. Although the precise interconnections between religious and social change during this period have not yet been established, evangelicalism and other new ideologies offered more appropriate explanations for the new social order than theologies offered by the former established religion.

The practice of evangelicalism, however, was somewhat moderated because both traditional denominations and new sects needed to build permanent institutions. Instead of the conversion of sinners, the main priority of religious groups became ministering to the continuous needs of their members. The number of revivals dwindled; and when they did occur, they functioned to revitalize church members rather than save new souls. Consequently, highly stylized revivals organized by church leaders for their own members replaced spontaneous outbreaks of religious fervor.

While schismatic, cultic, and quasi-religious sects erected independent religious structures, regenerative sects rebuilt denominational institutions. Faced with the advances of the other new sects, the old school and the new school worked together to bind up denominational wounds and bring denominations more in line with the new social structure. They united their denominations around a

50. Ibid., pp. 189–90.

blend of inherited and contemporary theology and ritual. Either conciliatory leaders replaced a generation of firebrands or former radicals significantly modified their extreme views. By the end of the Second Great Awakening, for example, Charles Finney publicly denounced the "irresponsible" use of his new revival techniques. While neither the old school nor the new won a total vindication of its religious position, most denominations definitely moved in a new-school direction. Although the new school had to give up much of its interdenominational emphasis, denominations added many new-school reforms, such as evangelical theology, new conversion techniques, and innovative missionary programs, to their traditional concerns. The incorporation of new beliefs and practices placed traditional denominations in a strongly competitive position with the new sects.

Most old- and new-school factions merged by 1870. The last partition of the Methodist Episcopal church occurred in 1860, while the old school and the new school reassembled in the Presbyterian church, U.S.A., in 1869. Horace Bushnell, a prominent parish minister, united his Congregational denomination around an elaborate Christian education program, while preoccupation with parish members mediated the previous controversies in the Quaker, Episcopal, and German Reformed denominations. The continuation of the massive old-school Lutheran immigration, however, prevented the merger of the new-school General Synod and the old-school General Council in the Lutheran church until early in the twentieth century.

The survival of the other types of new sects depended on their ability to develop strong institutions. For the most part, successful sects immediately codified beliefs, organized supporters into congregations, and built permanent edifices. Ministers, with administrative rather than charismatic qualifications, educated parish members in sectarian doctrine and ritual. Members were expected to abide by prescribed beliefs and strict standards of behavior, and most sects made special provisions for the children of church members to be brought up within the sect. Rituals marked important cradle-to-grave events for all members. In many cases, elaborate bureaucracies developed when individual congregations came together in regional and national associations.

Schismatic sects, with parent denominations providing the organizational model, tended to survive longer than most other sects that emerged during the Second Great Awakening. Several continue to be important religious groups today. Although only

seventy Adventist churches existed in 1860, the Seventh-Day
Adventists, under the leadership of Ellen Harmon White, became
an important religious body by the early twentieth century. In addition, the Disciples of Christ, which had but 4 percent of the total
number of churches in the country by 1860, is a major religious
denomination today.[51]

For the most part, cultic sects failed to develop permanent institutions. Only a handful of Spiritualist and New Thought Swedenborgian churches have survived to the present. A few cultic beliefs,
such as dietary prescriptions, have persisted in some traditional
denominations and sects. The exceptional Mormons, however, did
turn inward and established a strong sectarian organization. By
1900 they were the tenth largest religious body in the country.[52]

With the exception of the Oneida Society, which lasted for about
fifty years, most quasi-religious sects simply faded away. John
Humphrey Noyes sadly reported that all of the Owen and Fourier
communities died young, most before they were two years old.[53]
Abolitionism ended with the Emancipation Proclamation in 1863,
and at no time did agrarianism ever develop much of a membership
base. Many members of shattered quasi-religious sects eventually
dropped out of organized religion altogether.

The final configuration of the new established religion reflected
the dynamic process of religious change during the Second Great
Awakening. While most religious groups expanded between 1820
and 1860, evangelical denominations and new sects grew much
faster than more traditional denominations. The number of Methodist churches increased sevenfold, a rate twice as rapid as in any
other denomination, and the number of Baptist churches quadru-
pled. As a result, the Methodists and Baptists deposed the previous
denominational leaders. In 1860 the Methodists controlled 38 percent and the Baptists had 23 percent of the total number of
churches in this country, while the Presbyterians accounted for only
12 percent; and the Lutherans, Episcopalians, and Congregationalists each had less than 5 percent of all churches. The non-Christian alternatives offered by the Mormons, Universalists, Unitarians,
Spiritualists, and Swedenborgians rounded out the enlarged spectrum of religion in America.[54]

51. *Statistics of the United States in 1860*, p. 497.
52. Gaustad, *Historical Atlas of Religion in America*, p. 44.
53. Noyes, *History of American Socialisms*, p. 20.
54. Gaustad, *Historical Atlas of Religion in America*, p. 43.

The creation of a new established religion completed the realignment of religion and society during the mid-nineteenth century. As economic and demographic changes altered the social structure, concurrent new religious impulses emerged to challenge the traditional religious underpinnings of American society. Bitter controversies over evangelicalism resulted in a shake up of the former established religion and the formation of a broad range of new religious groups. While the new sects varied tremendously, each one provided an alternative to traditional denominations. As conventional denominations picked up some of the religious innovations and the new sects produced permanent institutions, a new established religion emerged to serve the needs of a society better than the former established religion. Specific historical conditions prevented a total break from the past, so that the new established religion continued to embody many traditional Protestant doctrines and beliefs. The new established religion defined religion in America until subsequent social change triggered another period of religious reorganization.

Over a century after the Second Great Awakening, another spiritual upheaval challenges established religion.[55] While no single episode marks the beginning of the upheaval, controversial events in the late 1950s and early 1960s severely divided established religion. As one contemporary observer noted, "the ministers and laity alike have shown an increasingly widespread tendency to regard local church structures as irrelevant, or as extremely unadaptable to the most urgent needs of the times, or even as an impediment to social action."[56] By the early 1970s, religious rebels began to explore a bewildering array of new religious sects. However, since the outcome of the current "awakening" is by no means certain, it is impossible to examine the contemporary religious upheaval in the same depth as the Second Great Awakening. Any analysis of the relationship between religious and societal change remains incomplete until the conclusion of the current religious reorganization. Caught in the middle of the dynamic

55. By now, of course, Catholicism and Judaism have become part of established religion.

56. Sidney Ahlstrom, "The Radical Turn in Theology and Ethics: Why It Occurred in the 1960s," *Annals of the American Academy of Political and Social Sciences* 387 (January 1970): 5. See also Harvey Cox, *The Secular City* (Toronto: Macmillan, 1965); Peter Berger, *The Noise of Solemn Assemblies* (Garden City, N.J.: Doubleday, 1961); and Luckmann, *Invisible Religion*.

process, the dazzling new religious alternatives obscure the larger context of religious change.

In addition, it is problematic to extrapolate insights from a particular historical study to the contemporary period. Nonetheless, the analysis of the Second Great Awakening, which viewed religious change specifically in terms of process, offers a fruitful approach to examining the "new" religious consciousness. While the four stages of religious transformation previously outlined may not entirely apply today, they can help to focus the present discussion of religious change.

The larger social context of the current crisis in established religion is even more difficult to characterize today than during the Second Great Awakening. It seems likely that a number of trends in the postindustrial society—specifically certain demographic shifts and technological innovations, the restructuring of the occupational hierarchy, and new patterns of geographic mobility—underlie the current religious upheaval. By drastically altering the nature of American society, these social structural changes have undermined established religion.

No single theology has replaced nineteenth-century evangelicalism as the catalyst for sectarian development. Rather than theological differences, the established religion of the twentieth century divides primarily over political and social controversies that emerged outside of religious institutions. The civil rights movement beginning in the late 1950s and the subsequent movement against the Vietnam War forced established religion first to confront and then to act on the disparity between its ideology and the reality of American life. At the same time, life-style issues such as marijuana usage, communal living, and other individual liberties divided the country. The countercultural ideology, which developed out of the attempt to resolve these social and political questions, threatened the integrity of established religion.

These questions provoked bitter internal struggles in every major religious institution in the country.[57] Factions within these bodies tended to divide along old- and new-school lines. Old-school adherents staunchly defended traditional doctrines and denominational differences, and new-school proponents encouraged reforms. Such opposing religious orientations led to differing solutions to specific social problems. While the old school continued its

57. Charles Y. Glock and Rodney Stark, *Religion and Society in Tension* (Chicago: Rand McNally, 1965), chap. 5; and Jeffrey K. Hadden, *The Gathering Storm in the Churches* (Garden City, N.J.: Anchor Books, 1970).

traditional activities, the new school created modern-day mission outposts in the colleges, the drug culture, and the inner city and promoted social reform programs that focused on racism, sexism, and environmental pollution. Controversies raged within the Roman Catholic church, for example, over the introduction of the folk mass, the participation of priests in civil rights and antiwar activities, and the development of outreach programs in the urban parishes.

As in the Second Great Awakening, the crisis in religion has led not only to tensions within religious bodies but to the development of new sects. Some of these sects are emerging from within established religion itself. So far, the splitting off of the old-school National Presbyterian church from the Southern Presbyterian denomination is the only official Protestant denominational division that has occurred, but the oldschool Lutheran Missouri Synod is trying zealously to purge the new-school Seminex faction from its ranks. Several sects, as well, have arisen out of American Judaism, including the Jews for Jesus and the Hasidim.

Both Christian and non-Christian sects have originated outside established religion. Although the Jesus groups, especially the Children of God, are the most visible new Christian sects, revitalized fundamentalist sects such as the 700 Club, faith-healing sects, and snake-handling sects continue to grow. Non-Christian sects are considerably more numerous today than they were during the nineteenth century. Transcendental Meditation, Hare Krishna, the Maharaj Ji, and other groups are directly influenced by Eastern religions. The diverse human-potential movement, including *est* and Scientology, investigate the powers of the mind. Astrology, herbal medicine, dietary prescriptions, and Rolfing are concerned with the functioning of the human body and its relationship to natural and supernatural forces.

Reflecting the roots of the current religious upheaval, important new sects have grown directly out of the social and political controversies of the period. Although not religious in the traditional sense of the word, they replace "otherworldly" theologies with competing secular ideologies that advocate changing this world.[58] Diverse political explanations for the current social and economic crises have contributed to the formation of new groups and organizations that are attempting to fundamentally change the ex-

58. See Berger and Luckmann, *The Social Construction of Reality;* and Luckmann, *Invisible Religion.* See also the essay on the New Left included in this volume.

isting social and economic system. The civil rights, antiwar, and women's liberation movements of the sixties generated new visions of society as well as the establishment of socialist organizations, originating primarily from the New Left. In response to these movements and the overall direction of society, reactionary forces such as the National Rifle Association, the KKK, and the Wallacites are consolidating their power. At the same time, groups advocating personal solutions to systemic problems have emerged from divisions within society. For example, environmental concerns gave rise to ecology groups such as the Sierra Club; and the youth and drug culture produced half-way houses and groups such as Synanon.

It is too early to determine the outcome of the contemporary upsurge of new religious consciousness. However, it seems possible that a new established religion, with expanded religious alternatives that conform to the social structure, will develop in America. As in the nineteenth century, some contemporary observers assume this process of religious change will result in the eventual secularization of American society. Certainly the religious focus is shifting today. New conceptions of religion and new definitions of "god" and "faith" are replacing older ones. As alternative realities create alternative world views, it seems more likely that we are witnessing a new phase in the history of American religion than its demise.[59]

59. A generous Research Training Fellowship from the Social Science Research Council allowed me to study the sociology of religion at the University of California, Berkeley, in 1972–73. Members of the New Religious Consciousness project, especially Charles Glock, made this visit both profitable and enjoyable. In addition, special thanks go to Nora Faires and Maurine Greenwald, Department of History, University of Pittsburgh, who offered invaluable assistance and support in drafting this paper.

Part VII
Conclusions

15

*New Religious Consciousness and the
Crisis in Modernity*

ROBERT N. BELLAH

Our research project is a response to the cultural and political upheaval of the 1960s. We have been concerned to understand the
deepest meaning of that upheaval, that is to say its religious dimension, and to interpret that meaning in the context of modern
American history. As it turned out our project got under way in
early 1971, just when the upheaval in its most dramatic forms had
passed. We ended up studying the successor movements to the
counterculture rather than the counterculture in its effervescent
stage. But if we are to put our findings in the broadest possible context—and that is what I intend to do in this chapter—then we must
begin with the developments in the 1960s that lie immediately
behind our study and with the nature of the society in which those
developments occurred.

The disturbances and outbursts in America in the 1960s were
hardly unique in modern history. Indeed, in a century where
irrationalities and horrors of all sorts—mass executions, mass im-
prisonments, wars of annihilation, revolutions, rebellions, and
depressions—have been common, the events of that decade in
America might even be overlooked. But it is precisely the
significance of that decade that the irrationalities and horrors of
modern history were borne in upon Americans so seriously that for
the first time mass disaffection from the common understandings of
American culture and society began to occur. Far more serious than
any of the startling events of the decade was the massive erosion of
the legitimacy of American institutions—business, government,
education, the churches, the family—that set in particularly among
young people and that continues, if public opinion polls are to be

believed, in the 1970s even when overt protest has become less frequent.

The erosion of the legitimacy of established institutions among certain sectors of the populations of many European countries—particularly the working class and the intellectuals—began at least a hundred years ago. In many of the newer third-world countries the nation-state and modern institutions have not yet gained enough legitimacy to begin the process of erosion. But in America, in spite of a civil war, major social and religious movements, and minor disturbances of occasionally violent intensity, the fundamental legitimacy of the established order had never before been questioned on such a scale. This is in part because that order was itself a revolutionary order, the result of one of the few successful revolutions in the modern world. The messianic hope generated by the successful revolution and nurtured by the defeat of slavery in the Civil War for long made it possible to overlook or minimize the extent to which the society failed to achieve its own ideals. The promise of early fulfillment, which seemed so tangible in America, operated to mute our native critics and prevent mass disaffection, at least for a long time. But in the decade of the sixties for many, not only of the deprived but of the most privileged, that promise had begun to run out.

By way of background we may consider those interpretations of reality in America that had been most successful in providing meaning and generating loyalty up until the sixties: biblical religion and utilitarian individualism. The self-understanding of the original colonists was that they were "God's new Israel," a nation under God. (From this point of view the addition of the phrase "under God" to the pledge of allegiance in the 1950s was an indication of the erosion of the tradition, not because it was an innovation but because it arose from the need to make explicit what had for generations been taken for granted.) In New England this understanding was expressed in the biblical symbol of a covenant signifying a special relationship between God and the people. American society was to be one of exemplary obedience to God's laws and subject to the grace and judgment of the Lord. The notion of Americans as an elect people with exemplary significance for the world was not abandoned but enhanced during the revolution and the period of constructing the new nation. It was dramatically reaffirmed by Lincoln in the Civil War and continued to be expressed in the twentieth century in the thought of men like William Jennings Bryan and Woodrow Wilson. This biblical aspect of the national self-understanding was strongly social and collective, even though it contained an element of voluntarism from its Protestant roots. Its highest conception of reality was an objective absolute God as revealed in scriptures, and its conception of morality was also based on objective revelation.[1]

A second underlying interpretation of reality that has been enormously influential in American history, utilitarian individualism, was never wholly compatible with the biblical tradition, complex as the relations of attraction and repulsion between the two were. This tradition was rooted ultimately in the sophistic, skeptical, and hedonistic strands of ancient Greek philosophy but took its modern form initially in the theoretical writings of Thomas Hobbes. It became popular in America mainly through the somewhat softer and less consistent version of John Locke and his followers, a version deliberately designed to obscure the contrast with biblical religion. In its consistent original Hobbesian form, utilitarianism grew out of an effort to apply the methods of science to the understanding of man and was both atheistic and deterministic. While the commonsense Lockian version that has been the most pervasive current of American thought has not been fully conscious of these implications, the relation between utilitarianism and Anglo-American social science has been close and continuous from Hobbes and Locke to the classical economists of the eighteenth and early nineteenth centuries to the social Darwinists of the late nineteenth century and finally to such influential present-day sociologists as George Homans.

Whereas the central term for understanding individual motivation in the biblical tradition was "conscience," the central term in the utilitarian tradition was "interest." The biblical understanding of national life was based on the notion of community with charity for all the members, a community supported by public and private virtue. The utilitarian tradition believed in a neutral state in which individuals would be allowed to pursue the maximization of their self-interest, and the product would be public and private prosperity. The harshness of these contrasts was obscured, though never obliterated, by several considerations. The biblical tradition prom-

1. See Robert N. Bellah, *The Broken Covenant: American Civil Religion in Time of Trial* (New York: Seabury Press, 1975), for an analysis of the role of biblical religion in the formation of American society and also for the relations between biblical religion and utilitarian individualism. Two related essays are "Reflections on Reality in America," *Radical Religion* 1, no. 3 (1974); and "Religion and Polity in America," *Andover Newton Quarterly* 15, no. 2 (1974).

ised earthly rewards as well as heavenly for virtuous actions. The
utilitarian tradition required self-restraint and "morality," if not as
ends then as means. But the most pervasive mechanism for the har-
monization of the two traditions was the corruption of the biblical
tradition by utilitarian individualism, so that religion itself finally
became for many a means for the maximization of self-interest with
no effective link to virtue, charity, or community. A purely private
pietism emphasizing only individual rewards that grew up in the
nineteenth century and took many forms in the twentieth, from
Norman Vincent Peale to Reverend Ike, was the expression of that
corruption.[2]

The increasing dominance of utilitarian individualism was expressed not only in the corruption of religion but also in the rising
prestige of science, technology, and bureaucratic organization. The
scientific instrumentalism that was already prominent in Hobbes
became the central tenet of the most typical late American
philosophy, pragmatism. The tradition of utilitarian individualism
expressed no interest in shared values or ends, since it considered
the only significant end to be individual interest maximization, and
individual ends are essentially random. Utilitarianism tended
therefore to concentrate solely on the rationalization of means, on
technical reason. As a result the rationalization of means became an
end in itself. This is illustrated in the story about an American
farmer who was asked why he worked so hard. To raise more corn,
was his reply. But why do you want to do that? To make more
money. What for? To buy more land. Why? To raise more corn.
And so on ad infinitum. While utilitarian individualism had no interest in society as an end in itself, it was certainly not unaware of
the importance of society. Society like everything else was to be
used instrumentally. The key term was organization, the instrumental use of social relationships. "Effective organization" was as much
a hallmark of the American ethos as technological inventiveness.

The central value for utilitarian individualism was freedom, a
term that could also be used to obscure the gap between the
utilitarian and the bibical traditions, since it is a central biblical
term as well. But for biblical religion, freedom meant liberation
from the consequences of sin, freedom to do the right, and was
almost equivalent to virtue. For utilitarianism, it meant the freedom to pursue one's own ends. Everything was to be subordinate to

2. An excellent treatment of the deep inner cleavage in American culture is
Wilson Carey McWilliams, *The Idea of Fraternity in America* (Berkeley and Los
Angeles: University of California Press, 1973).

that: nature, social relations, even personal feelings. The exclusive concentration on means rendered that final end of freedom so devoid of content that it became illusory and the rationalization of means a kind of treadmill that was in fact the opposite of freedom.

That part of the biblical tradition that remained uncorrupted or only minimally corrupted found itself deeply uneasy with the dominant utilitarian ethos. Fundamentalism in America is not simply an expression of backward yokels. Even Bryan's opposition to evolution was in part an opposition to the social Darwinism that he saw as undermining all humane values in America. But that opposition remained largely inchoate, in part because it could not penetrate the facade of biblical symbols which the society never abandoned even when it betrayed them.

It was this dual set of fundamental understandings that the eruption of the 1960s fundamentally challenged. It is important to remember that the events of the sixties were preceded and prepared for by a new articulation of Christian symbolism in the later fifties in the life and work of Martin Luther King. King stood not only for the actualization of that central and ambiguous value of freedom for those who had never fully experienced even its most formal benefits. Even more significantly he stood for the actualization of the Christian imperative of love. For him society was not to be used manipulatively for individual ends. Even in a bitter struggle one's actions were to express that fundamental love, that oneness of all men in the sight of God, that is deeper than any self-interest. It was that conception, so close to America's expressed biblical values and so far from its utilitarian practice that, together with militant activism, was so profoundly unsettling.

We are accustomed to think of the "costs" of modernization in the developing nations: the disrupted traditions, the breakup of families and villages, the impact of vast economic and social forces that can neither be understood nor adapted to in terms of inherited wisdom and ways of living. Because it is our tradition that invented modernization we have thought that we were somehow immune to the costs or that because the process was, with us, so slow and so gradual, we had successfully absorbed the strains of modernization. What the sixties showed us was that in America, too, the costs have been high and the strains by no means wholly absorbed. In that decade, at least among a significant proportion of the educated young of a whole generation, occurred the repudiation of the tradition of utilitarian individualism (even though it often persisted unconsciously even among those doing the repudiating) and the biblical tradition too, especially as it was seen, in part realistically, as linked to utilitarianism. Let us examine the critique.

The criticisms of American society that developed in the sixties were diverse and not always coherent one with another. What follows is more an interpretation than a description. In many different forms there was a new consciousness of the question of ends. The continuous expansion of wealth and power, which is what the rationalization of means meant in practice, did not seem so self-evidently good. There were of course some sharp questions about the unequal distribution of wealth and power, but beyond that was the question whether the quality of life was a simple function of wealth and power, or whether the endless accumulation of wealth and power was not destroying the quality and meaning of life, ecologically and sociologically. If the rationalization of means, the concern for pure instrumentalism, was no longer self-evidently meaningful, then those things that had been subordinated, dominated, and exploited for the sake of rationalizing means took on a new significance. Nature, social relations, and personal feelings could now be treated as ends rather than means, could be liberated from the repressive control of technical reason.

Among those who shared this general analysis there was a division between those who placed emphasis on overthrowing the present system as a necessary precondition for the realization of a more human society and those who emphasized the present embodiment of a new style of life "in the pores," so to speak, of the old society. The contrast was not absolute, as the effort to create politically "liberated zones" in certain communities such as Berkeley and Ann Arbor indicates. And for a time in the late sixties opposition to the Vietnam War, seen as an example of technical reason gone mad, took precedence over everything else. Yet there was a contrast between those mainly oriented to political action (still, in a way, oriented to means rather than ends, though it was the means to overthrow the existing system) and those mainly concerned with the actual creation of alternative patterns of living. The difference between demonstrations and sit-ins on the one hand and love-ins, be-ins, and rock festivals on the other illustrates the contrast. Political activists shared some of the personal characteristics of those they fought—they were "uptight," repressed, dominated by time and work. The cultural experimenters, represented most vividly, perhaps, by the "love, peace, groovy" flower children of the middle sixties, believed in harmony with man and nature and the enjoyment of the present moment through drugs, music, or meditation. In either case there was a sharp opposition to the dominant American ethos of utilitarian instrumentalism oriented to personal success. There was also a deep ambivalence to the biblical tradition, to which I will return.

The question of why the old order began to lose its legitimacy just when it did is not one we have felt equipped to answer. Clearly in the sixties there was a conjuncture of dissatisfactions that did not all have the same meaning. The protests of racial minorities, middle-class youth, and women had different causes and different goals. In spite of all the unsolved problems, the crisis was brought on by the success of the society as much as by its failures. That education and affluence did not bring happiness or fulfillment was perhaps as important as the fact that the society did not seem to be able to solve the problem of racism and poverty. The outbreak of a particularly vicious and meaningless little war in Asia that stymied America's leadership both militarily and politically for years on end acted as a catalyst but did not cause the crisis. The deepest cause, no matter what particular factors contributed to the actual timing, was, in my opinion, the inability of utilitarian individualism to provide a meaningful pattern of personal and social existence, especially when its alliance with biblical religion began to sag because biblical religion itself had been gutted in the process. I would thus interpret the crisis of the sixties above all as a crisis of meaning, a religious crisis, with major political, social, and cultural consequences to be sure.

Religious upheaval is not new in American history. Time and time again, after a period of spiritual dryness, there has been an outbreak of the spirit. Linda Pritchard's chapter has described such a case in the Second Great Awakening of the nineteenth century. But the religious crisis was in more ways a contrast to the great awakenings of the eighteenth and nineteenth centuries than a continuation of them. By all the measures of conventional religiosity the early 1950s had been a period of religious revival, but the revival of the fifties proved to be as artificial as the cold-war atmosphere that may have fostered it. The sixties saw a continuous drop in church attendance and a declining belief in the importance of religion, as measured by national polls. It is true that conservative and fundamentalist churches continued to grow and that the major losses were in the mainline Protestant denominations and in the Catholic church after the full consequences of Vatican II began to sink in. But in terms of American culture the latter had long been more important than the conservative wing. Although clergy and laity of many denominations played an important part in the events of the sixties, the churches as such were not the locale of the major changes, even the religious ones.

Indeed, it was easier for many in the biblical tradition to relate to the political than to the religious aspect of the developing counter-culture. The demand for social justice fitted closely with the prophetic teachings of Judaism and Christianity. The struggle for racial equality and later the struggle against the Vietnam War drew many leaders from the churches and synagogues, even though the membership as a whole remained passive. But in spite of the leadership of Martin Luther King and the martyrdom of divinity students in the civil rights movement and in spite of the leadership of the Berrigans and William Sloan Coffin in the peace movement, those movements as a whole remained indifferent if not hostile to religion. By the end of the sixties those churchmen who had given everything to the political struggle found themselves without in-fluence and without a following, as the chapter by Barbara Har-grove documents for our area. For most of the political activists the churches remained too closely identified with the established powers to gain much sympathy or interest. As dogmatic Marxism gained greater influence among the activists during the decade, ideological antireligion increased as well.

But the churches were even less well prepared to cope with the new spiritually of the sixties. The demand for immediate, powerful, and deep religious experience, which was part of the turn away from future-oriented instrumentalism toward present meaning and fulfillment, could on the whole not be met by the religious bodies. The major Protestant churches in the course of generations of defensive struggle against secular rationalism had taken on some of the color of the enemy. Moralism and verbalism and the almost complete absence of ecstatic experience characterized the middle-class Protestant churches. The more intense religiosity of black and lower-class churches remained largely unavailable to the white middle-class members of the counterculture. The Catholic church with its great sacramental tradition might be imagined to have been a more hospitable home for the new movement, but such was not the case. Older Catholicism had its own defensiveness which took the form of scholastic intellectualism and legalistic moralism. Nor did Vatican II really improve things. The Catholic church finally decided to recognize the value of the modern world just when American young people were beginning to find it valueless. As if all this were not enough, the biblical arrogance toward nature and the

Christian hostility toward the impulse life were both alien to the new spiritual mood. Thus the religion of the counterculture was by and large not biblical. It drew from many sources including the American Indian. But its deepest influences came from Asia.

In many ways Asian spirituality provided a more thorough contrast to the rejected utilitarian individualism than did biblical religion. To external achievement it posed inner experience; to the exploitation of nature, harmony with nature; to impersonal organization, an intense relation to a guru. Mahayana Buddhism, particularly in the form of Zen, provided the most pervasive religious influence on the counterculture; but elements from Taoism, Hinduism, and Sufism were also influential. What drug experiences, interpreted in oriental religious terms, as Timothy Leary and Richard Alpert did quite early, and meditation experiences, often taken up when drug use was found to have too many negative consequences, showed was the illusoriness of worldly striving. Careerism and status seeking, the sacrifice of present fulfillment for some ever-receding future goal, no longer seemed worthwhile. There was a turn away not only from utilitarian individualism but from the whole apparatus of industrial society. The new ethos preferred handicrafts and farming to business and industry, and small face-to-face communities to impersonal bureaucracy and the isolated nuclear family. Simplicity and naturalness in food and clothing were the ideal, even though conspicuous consumption and one-upmanship ("Oh, you don't use natural salt, I see") made their inevitable appearance.

Thus, the limits were pushed far beyond what any previous great awakening had seen: toward socialism in one direction, toward mysticism in the other. But perhaps the major meaning of the sixties was not anything positive at all. Neither the political movement nor the counterculture survived the decade. Important successor movements did survive and they have been the focus of our study, but the major meaning of the sixties was purely negative: the erosion of the legitimacy of the American way of life. On the surface what seems to have been most drastically undermined was utilitarian individualism, for the erosion of the biblical tradition seemed only to continue what had been a long-term trend. The actual situation was more complicated. Utilitarian individualism had perhaps never before been so divested of its ideological and religious facade, never before recognized in all its naked destructiveness. And yet that very exposure could become an ironic victory. If all moral restraints are illegitimate, then why should I believe in religion and morality? If those who win in American society are the big crooks and those who lose do so only because they are little crooks, why should I not try to be a big crook rather than a little one? In this way the unmasking of utilitarian individualism led to the very condition from which Hobbes sought to save us—the war of all against all. Always before, the biblical side of the American tradition has been able to bring antinomian and anarchic tendencies under some kind of control, and perhaps that is still possible today. Certainly the fragile structures of the counterculture were not able to do so. But out of the shattered hopes of the sixties there has emerged a cynical privatism, a narrowing of sympathy and concern to the smallest possible circle, that is truly frightening. What has happened to Richard Nixon should not obscure for us the meaning of his overwhelming victory in 1972. It was the victory of cynical privatism.

In this rather gloomy period of American history, and the mood of the youth culture in the period of our study has been predominantly gloomy—not the hope for massive change that characterized the sixties but the anxious concern for survival, physical and moral—the successor movements of the early seventies take on a special interest. We may ask whether any of them have been able to take up and preserve the positive seeds of the sixties so that under more favorable circumstances they may grow and fructify once again. Some of the successor movements clearly do not have that potential. The Weathermen and the Symbionese Liberation Army on the one hand, the Krishna Consciousness Society and the Divine Light Mission on the other, are parodies of the broader political and religious movements that they represent, too narrow and in some cases too self-destructive to contribute to the future solution of our problems. About others there may be more hope.

To some extent the successor movements, especially the explicitly religious ones, have been survival units in a quite literal sense. They have provided a stable social setting and a coherent set of symbols for young people disoriented by the drug culture or disillusioned with radical politics. What Synanon claims to have done for hardcore drug users, religious groups—from Zen Buddhists to Jesus people—have done for ex-hippies. Gregory Johnson's chapter points out this function explicitly for the Krishna Consciousness Society, which grew up amidst the disintegration of Haight-Ashbury as a hippie utopia. The rescue-mission aspect of the successor movements has had quite tangible results. In many instances reconciliation with parents has been facilitated by the more stable life-style and the religious ideology of acceptance rather than confrontation. A new, more positive orientation toward occupational roles has often developed. In some cases, such as followers of Meher Baba, this has meant a return to school and the resumption of a normal middle-class career pattern.[3] For others, such as resident devotees of the San Francisco Zen Center or ashram residents of the 3HO movement, jobs are seen largely as means to subsistence, having little value in themselves. While the attitude toward work in terms of punctuality, thoroughness, and politeness is, from the employer's point of view, positive, the religious devotee has no inner commitment to the job nor does he look forward to any advancement. In terms of intelligence and education the job holder is frequently "overqualified" for the position he holds, but this causes no personal distress because of the meaning the job has for him. For many of these groups the ideal solution would be economic self-sufficiency, so that members would not have to leave the community at all; but few are able to attain this. As in monastic orders some full-time devotees can be supported frugally by the gifts of sympathizers, but they are exceptions. Many of the groups also insist on a stable sexual life, in some instances celibate but more usually monogamous, with sexual relations being confined to marriage. Such norms are found not only among Jesus people but in the oriental groups as well.

These features of stability should not be interpreted as simple adaptation to the established society, though in some cases that may occur. Donald Stone indicates that the human-potential movement may serve such an adaptive function, and perhaps Synanon as Ofshe describes it also does to a certain extent. But for the more explicitly religious groups, stable patterns of personal living and occupation do not mean acceptance of the established order. Our survey found that sympathizers of the oriental religions tend to be as critical of American society as political radicals, far more critical than the norm. While the survey shows that people sympathetic to the Jesus movement are less critical of American society, the Christian World Liberation Front, the Berkeley group studied by Donald Heinz, is atypical in being quite critical. All of these movements share a very negative image of established society as sunk in materialism and heading for disaster. Many of them have intense millennial expectations, viewing the present society as in the last

3. See the interesting study of Thomas Robbins and Dick Anthony, "Getting Straight with Meher Baba," *Journal for the Scientific Study of Religion* 11, no. 2 (1972).

stage of degradation before the dawning of a new era. 3HO people
speak of the Aquarian age which is about to replace the dying Piscean age. Krishna Consciousness people speak of the present as the
last stage of the materialistic Kali Yuga and on the verge of a new
age of peace and happiness. More traditionally biblical expectations
of the millennium are common among Jesus people. All of these
groups, well behaved as they are, have withdrawn fundamentally
from contemporary American society, see it as corrupt and illegitimate, and place their hope in a radically different vision. We
should remember that early Christians too were well behaved
—Paul advised them to remain in their jobs and their marriages
—yet by withholding any deep commitment to the Roman Empire
they helped to bring it down and to form a society of very different
type.

An important dimension of variation among the groups we have
studied is the degree of openness or closure toward the outside
world. This is similar to Bryan Wilson's contrast between conversionist and introversionist sects. However, some groups with tightly
controlled boundaries—that is, specific and demanding requirements for membership—are also highly conversionist, as in the case
of Krishna Consciousness and Jesus movements. Nonetheless, open
boundaries are undoubtedly more conducive to rapid expansion.
Transcendental Meditation, which claims not to be a religion and
has few doctrinal requirements, has attracted hundreds of thousands, even though many quickly abandon the practice. The Krishna Consciousness movement on the other hand has remained quite
small, Johnson estimating no more than three or four thousand
members. Recently this movement has shown distinct introversionist tendencies in sending hundreds of its followers permanently to
India.

Some of the more interesting movements show a range of
possibilities or a change over time on the dimension of openness
and closure. Zen Buddhism is one of the most pervasive influences
on the entire range of countercultural developments. Philip
Kapleau's *Three Pillars of Zen* was for a time a kind of bible of the
counterculture, influencing thousands who had only the most casual
acquaintance with Zen meditation. Alan Watts, one of the most influential countercultural gurus, preached essentially a modified
Zen, as does Gary Snyder. The influence of Zen on everything from
psychotherapy to aesthetics has been major. Yet full-time membership in a Zen monastery or center is an extremely demanding enterprise, leading in some cases to vows of chastity and poverty. The

history of the San Francisco Zen Center from the late 1950s to the present (1975) shows a continuous movement from general intellectual and cultural interest in Zen to high and demanding standards of practice.[4] Of course Zen, perhaps more than any other movement of oriental origin, exercises an influence out of all proportion to the number of its full-time devotees. Just for that reason it represents clearly the tension between general cultural influence and a tightly organized in-group that is to be found in many other movements. 3HO has undergone a shift comparable to the Zen Center in moving away from general yoga practice to the specific beliefs and rituals of Sikhism. A slight tendency in the opposite direction is to be found in the Christian World Liberation Front, which has sacrificed some of its "forever family" community for more active ministries, especially in the cultural field with its publications and courses. Political groups probably show something of the same spectrum of openness and closedness, but they have not been at the center of our study.

On the whole the human-potential groups are open compared with the religious groups, having few requirements for participation, though abstention from drugs and alcohol and avoidance of aggressive behavior may be required of participants during the actual period of training. Acceptance of certain frames of reference ("I am perfect just as I am") may be a prerequisite if the training is to make sense, but these views are not seen as doctrinal requirements. In general, the human-potential groups and groups like Transcendental Meditation that are very similar to them may be seen as cults rather than as sects, in that they are not usually membership groups, except temporarily. Their leaders may be charismatic, but are seen more as healers and teachers than as organizational leaders.

Both our survey and our qualitative observations indicate that sympathizers of the human-potential movement are less alienated from American society than followers of oriental religions or political radicals. They are, nonetheless, more critical than the norm, and many of their beliefs contrast sharply with established American ideology. A tension exists within the movement over the issue of latent utilitarianism. If the techniques of the human-potential movement are to be used for personal and business success (the training-group movement out of which the human-potential

4. My information on the San Francisco Zen Center comes mainly from a Ph.D. dissertation by David Wise. ("Zen Buddhist Subculture in San Francisco," Department of Sociology, University of California, Berkeley, 1971).

movement in part derives had tendencies in that direction), then it
is no different from the mind cures and positive thinking of the most
debased kinds of utilitarian religion in America. But for some in the
movement the whole idea of success is viewed negatively, and the
training is seen in part as a way of gaining liberation from that goal.
The high evaluation of bodily awareness and intrapsychic experience as well as nonmanipulative interpersonal relations place
much of the movement in tension with the more usual orientations
of American utilitarian individualism. Here as elsewhere in our field
of research we have found that utilitarian individualism is a hydra-
headed monster that tends to survive just where it is most attacked.

We have already considered some of the common themes of the
counterculture of the sixties. We may now consider how they have
survived and been elaborated in the successor movements.
Immediate experience rather than doctrinal belief continues to be
central among all the religious movements, including the Jesus
movements, and in the human-potential movement as well.
Knowledge in the sense of direct firsthand encounter has so much
higher standing than abstract argument based on logic that one
could almost speak of anti-intellectualism in many groups. Yet it
would be a mistake to interpret this tendency as rampant irrationalism. Even though science is viewed ambivalently and the
dangers of scientific progress are consciously feared by many in our
groups, science as such is not rejected. There is a belief that much of
what is experienced could be scientifically validated. Indeed, the
human-potential groups (and Transcendental Meditation) believe
that their teachings are in accord with science broadly understood.
The study of the physiology of the brain during meditation is seen
not as a threat but as a support for religious practice. Since reality
inheres in the actual experience, explanatory schemes, theological
or scientific, are secondary, though scientific explanations tend to be
preferred to theological ones because of the general prestige of
science. At a deeper level the lack of interest in critical reflective
reason may be a form of anti-intellectualism, but the conscious
irrationalism of groups such as the romantic German youth movement is quite missing. Similarly, there is a complete absence of
primordial loyalties and hatreds based on race, ethnic group, or
even, usually, religion.

In spite of the primacy of experience, belief is not entirely missing. In some groups, as we have already seen in the case of 3HO,
the stress on doctrine may be increasing. The early phase of the
New Left was heavily experiential: Unless you had placed your

body on the line you could not understand the reality of American society. Consciousness raising in racial and women's groups continues to emphasize the experiential aspect of oppression and the struggle against it. But New Left groups became increasingly doctrinal toward the end of the 1960s and remain today more oriented to doctrine than experience in comparison with religious and human-potential groups.

A central belief shared by the oriental religions and diffused widely outside them is important because of its sharp contrast with established American views. This is the belief in the unity of all being. Our separate selves, according to Buddhism, Hinduism, and their offshoots, are not ultimately real. Philosophical Hinduism and Mahayana Buddhism reject dualism. For them ultimately there is no difference between myself and yourself, and this river and that mountain. We are all one and the conflict between us is therefore illusory.

While such beliefs are diametrically opposed to utilitarian individualism, for whom the individual is the ultimate ontological reality, there are elements in the Christian tradition to which they are not entirely opposed. Christian theology also felt the unity of being and the necessity to love all beings. The New Testament spoke of the church as one body of which we are all members. But Christianity has tended to maintain the ultimate dualism of creator and creation which the oriental religions would obliterate. Christian mystics have at times made statements (viewed as heretical) expressing the ultimate unity of God and man, and in a mediated form the unity of God and man through Christ is an orthodox belief. Still, American Christianity has seldom emphasized the aspect of the Christian tradition that stressed the unity rather than the distinction between the divine and the human, so that the oriental teachings stand out as sharply divergent.

Much of the countercultural criticism of American society is related to the belief in nondualism. If man and nature, men and women, white and black, rich and poor are really one, then there is no basis for the exploitation of the latter by the former. The ordination of women by Zen Buddhists and 3HO, even though not warranted in the earlier traditions, shows how their American followers interpret the fundamental beliefs. It is significant that from the basis of nondualism conclusions similar to those of Marxism can be reached. But because the theoretical basis is fundamental unity rather than fundamental opposition, the criticism of existing society is nonhostile, nonconfrontational, and often nonpolitical. Nonetheless, the effort to construct a witness community based on unity and identity rather than opposition and oppression can itself have critical consequences in a society based on opposite principles.

Another feature of oriental religions that has been widely influential is their view of dogma and symbol. Believing, as many of them do, that the fundamental truth, the truth of nondualism, is one, they also accept many beliefs and symbols as appropriate for different groups or different levels of spiritual insight. Dogmatism has by no means been missing in the oriental religions and has been traditionally more important than many of their American followers probably realize. But in relation to Christianity and biblical religions generally, the contrast holds. Belief in certain doctrinal or historical statements (Jesus is the Son of God, Christ rose from the tomb on the third day) has been so central in Western religion that it has been hard for Westerners to imagine religions for whom literal belief in such statements is unimportant. But the impact of oriental religion coincides with a long history of the criticism of religion in the West in which particular beliefs have been rendered questionable, but the significance of religion and myth in human action has been reaffirmed. Postcritical Western religion was therefore ready for a positive response to Asian religions in a way different from any earlier period. Paul Tillich's response to Zen Buddhism late in his life is an example of this. Thomas Merton's final immersion in Buddhism is an even better one. Such tendencies, however, are not to be found in the Christian World Liberation Front or other Jesus movements.

But in many of the oriental groups and certainly in the human-potential movement there has been a willingness to find meaning in a wide variety of symbols and practices without regarding them literally or exclusively. The danger here as elsewhere is that postcritical religion can become purely utilitarian. This can happen if one fails to see that any religious symbol or practice, however relative and partial, is an effort to express or attain the truth about ultimate reality. If such symbols and practices become mere techniques for "self-realization", then once again we see utilitarian individualism reborn from its own ashes.

Our study began with the thought that the new religious consciousness that seemed to be developing among young people in the San Francisco Bay Area might be some harbinger, some straw in the wind, that would tell us of changes to come in American culture and society. We were aware that studies of American religion based on

national samples could tell us mainly about what was widely believed in the present and perhaps also in the past, since religious
views change relatively slowly. Such samples, however, could not
easily pick up what was incipient, especially what was radically new
and as yet confined to only small groups. Even our Bay Area sample, weighted as it was to youth, picked up only a tiny handful of
those deeply committed to new forms of religion, although it did
lead us to believe that the new groups had gotten a hearing and
some sympathy from a significant minority. Our qualitative studies
of particular groups, based on participant-observation field studies,
have told us a great deal about them.

But to assess what we have discovered with respect to possible
future trends remains terribly hazardous. The future will certainly
not be determined mainly by the groups we studied. What role they
can play will depend very largely on other developments in the
society as a whole. Thus, in trying to assess the possible meaning
and role of our groups in the future I would like to outline three
possible scenarios for American society as a whole: liberal, traditional authoritarian, and revolutionary.

The future that most people seem to expect and that the
futurologists describe with their projections is very much like the
present society only more so. This is what I call the liberal scenario.
American society would continue as in the past to devote itself to
the accumulation of wealth and power. The mindless rationalization of means and the lack of concern with ends would only increase
as biblical religion and morality continue to erode. Utilitarian individualism, with less biblical restraint or facade than ever before,
would continue as the dominant ideology. Its economic form,
capitalism, its political form, bureaucracy, and its ideological form,
scientism, would each increasingly dominate its respective sphere.
Among the elite, scientism—the idolization of technical reason
alone—would provide some coherent meaning after traditional
religion and morality had gone. But technical reason would hardly
be a sufficient surrogate religion for the masses. No longer accepting
the society as legitimate in any ideal terms, the masses would have
to be brought to acquiesce grudgingly by a combination of coercion
and material reward. In such a society one could see a certain role
for oriental religious groups and the human-potential movement—perhaps even for a small radical political fringe. All of these
could be allowed within limits to operate and provide the possibility
of expressing the frustration and rage that the system generates but
in a way such that the individuals concerned are cooled out and the

system itself is not threatened. The utilitarian individualism that is latent in all the countercultural successor movements, political and religious, makes this a real possibility. This scenario depicts the society as heading, mildly and gradually, into something like Aldous Huxley's *Brave New World*.

Lately, however, questions have been raised as to the viability of this direction of development. Perhaps there are inner contradictions that will lead to a drastic breakdown in the foreseeable future. Robert Heilbroner has recently predicted such a collapse, largely as a result of ecological catastrophe.[5] But Heilbroner also envisages the possibility that tensions between the rich and the poor nations could bring disaster sooner than would ecological attrition. Even since Heilbroner wrote, the proliferation of atomic weapon capacity in India and the Middle East has strengthened this possibility. Another distinct possibility is worldwide economic collapse bringing social convulsions in train. No matter how the breakdown of the "modernization" syndrome might occur, Heilbroner envisages a relapse into traditional authoritarianism as the most likely result—providing, that is, that the worst outcome, total destruction of life on the planet, is avoided. Simpler, poorer, and less free societies might be all that humans would be capable of in the wake of a global catastrophe. The social and personal coherence that the modernizing societies never attained might be supplied by the rigid myths and rituals of a new hierarchical authoritarian society. To put it in terms of the present discussion, the collapse of subjective reason, which is what technical reason ultimately is, would bring in its wake a revival of objective reason in a particularly closed and reified form.[6] Technical reason, because it is concerned not with truth or reality but only with results, not with what is but only with what works, is ultimately completely subjective. That its domineering manipulative attitude to reality in the service of the subject leads ultimately to the destruction of any true subjectivity is only one of its many ironies. But a new traditional authoritarianism would set up some single orthodox version of what truth and reality are and enforce agreement. Some historically relative creed, belief, and ritual would be asserted as identical with objective reality itself.

    5. Robert Heilbroner, *An Inquiry into the Human Prospect* (New York: W.W. Norton, 1974).

    6. The contrast between subjective and objective reason has been developed by members of the Frankfurt School. See, for example, Max Horkheimer, *The Eclipse of Reason* (London: Oxford University Press, 1947; Seabury Paperback, 1974).

In this way social and personal coherence would be achieved, but ultimately at the expense of any real objectivity.

If a relapse into traditional authoritarianism is a distinct possibility in America, and I believe it is, we might ask what are the likely candidates for the job of supplying the new orthodoxy. Perhaps the most likely system would be right-wing Protestant fundamentalism. We already have a good example of such a regime in Afrikaner-dominated South Africa.[7] Conservative Protestant fundamentalism has a large and, by some measures, growing following in America. It has the religious and moral absolutism that a traditional authoritarianism would require, and it is hard to see any close rival on the American scene today. The Catholic church, which might at an earlier period have been a candidate for such a role, is certainly not, in its post-Vatican II disarray. Some of the more authoritarian of our Asian religions might provide a sufficiently doctrinaire model, but their small following in comparison with Protestant fundamentalism virtually rules them out. The future for most of the groups we have studied, all but the Jesus movements, would be bleak indeed under such a neo-traditional authoritarianism. It is doubtful if even a group as open as the Christian World Liberation Front could survive. Neo-authoritarian regimes are hard on nonconformity in every sphere. The new Chilean government, for example, not only sets standards of dress and hair style but also persecutes oriental religions.

There remains a third alternative, however improbable. It is this that I am calling revolutionary, not in the sense that it would be inaugurated by a bloody uprising, which I do not think likely, but because it would bring fundamental structural change, socially and culturally. It is to this rather unlikely outcome that most of the groups we have studied, at least the most flexible and open of them, would have most to contribute. Such a new order would involve, as in the case of traditional authoritarianism, an abrupt shift away from the exclusive dominance of technical reason; but it would not involve the adoption of a reified objective reason either. In accord with its concern for ends rather than means alone, such a revolutionary culture would have a firm commitment to the quest for ultimate reality. Priorities would shift away from endless accumulation of wealth and power to a greater concern for harmony

7. See Dunbar Moodie, *The Rise of Afrikanerdom* (Berkeley and Los Angeles: University of California Press, 1974), for an excellent analysis of Afrikaner civil religion and its Dutch Calvinist dimension.

with nature and between human beings. Perhaps a much simpler material life, simpler, that is, compared to present middle-class American standards, would result; but it would not be accompanied by an abandonment of free inquiry or free speech. Science, which would ultimately have to be shackled in a traditional authoritarian regime, would continue to be pursued in the revolutionary culture, but it would not be idolized as in the liberal model. In all these respects the values, attitudes, and beliefs of the oriental religious groups, the human-potential movement, and even a group like the Christian World Liberation Front, as well as the more flexible of the radical political groups, would be consonant with the new regime and its needs. Indeed, many of the present activities of such groups could be seen as experiments leading to the possibility of such a new alternative. Neither safety valve nor persecuted minority, the new groups would be, under such an option, the vanguard of a new age.

Such an outcome would accord most closely with the millennial expectations which we have seen are rife among the new groups. Even if an enormous amount of thought and planning were devoted to such an alternative, thought and planning that the small strug- gling groups we have been studying are quite incapable at the moment of supplying, the revolutionary alternative seems quite utopian. Perhaps only a major shift in the established biblical religions, a shift away from their uneasy alliance with utilitarian in- dividualism and toward a profound reappropriation of their own religious roots and an openness to the needs of the contemporary world, would provide the mass base for a successful effort to es- tablish the revolutionary alternative. To be politically effective such a shift would have to lead to a revitalization of the revolutionary spirit of the young republic, so that America would once again at- tract the hope and love of its citizens. This outcome too at present seems quite utopian. It may be, however, that only the implementa- tion of a utopian vision, a holistic reason that unites subjectivity and objectivity, will make human life in the twenty-first century worth living.

16

Consciousness Among Contemporary Youth:
An Interpretation

CHARLES Y. GLOCK

From the foregoing chapters it is evident that there is widespread exploration among youth of alternative ways of interpreting their worlds and living their lives. Consciousness exploration and experimentation seem very much the order of the day. Such has happened before, as Linda Pritchard makes clear in her historical contribution to this volume. And, if the past and present are any predictors of the future, there will be times again characterized by a lack of satisfaction with the everyday.

That such periods are repeated in history does not inhibit curiosity about them. Judging from the past, they can and often do occur, with very little permanent effect on the course of human events. It is also true, however, that watershed periods of human history have all been marked by radical changes in consciousness. Consequently, finding oneself in the midst of a period of consciousness raising, it is difficult not to wonder about its more abiding meaning and significance.

Partly because the time perspective is too short, the wondering cannot be done precisely. We are still probably more in the midst of the youth counterculture than beyond it. More distance is needed for adequate perspective. Being sure about the meaning of what is taking place is also made difficult by the paucity of data. The "snapshot" afforded by the research undertaken to produce this volume is better than no data at all. Yet, static data hardly suffices to answer the question of what short- and long-term effects a phenomenon might have. Under the circumstances, any assessment must necessarily be speculative. Still, speculation at this juncture can constitute theory to be tested by the subsequent course of events. It is in this spirit that the present chapter is written.

Simply stated, the thesis to be advanced and elaborated on is that the youth counterculture of the sixties was not the initiator of any significant change in American society. Rather, it will be argued that it was a highly visible sign of fundamental changes already under way. During the period of its ascendency, the youth counterculture probably accelerated the process of this fundamental change, although the subsequent response may have inhibited it. Whether a stimulant or a brake on change, what happened in the sixties was a surfacing of a mode of consciousness—or perhaps more accurately, of a way of understanding the world—which had been diffusing quietly to ever-increasing numbers of Americans for decades.

That the surfacing took place when it did rather than later is the result of the chance coalescence of a number of predisposing factors, which will be specified later, with America's involvement in the Vietnam War playing a necessary, although not sufficient, part. The war effectively triggered what had been a much more latent disenchantment with the status quo in American life. Neither the war, however, nor the events of the youth rebellion produced either a clear articulation of the underlying process of change at work or a clear vision of what the alternatives to the status quo might be. It is also doubtful, as I shall try to demonstrate later, that the alternatives would have become clear had the processes of change been correctly understood. In any case, the absence of clear and agreed upon alternatives meant that with the effective end, as far as American youth were concerned, of the triggering event, the war, the open rebellion came to an end. The quiet revolution continues, however, once again at a slower pace.

The sixties have already been characterized in a variety of ways: as the making of a counterculture, as the greening of America, as the coming of age of the Spock generation, as the apex of a long process of student rebellion, and so forth. None of these characterizations seems eminently viable now that they can be looked at in retrospect, although at the time of their appearance they were for many the last word in accounting for what was going on.

The benefit of additional hindsight does not equip one to be omniscient about what took place in the sixties, of course, and my lenses may well be blurred by the thesis I wish to develop. The thesis, however, leads to the judgment that the two things of central importance about the youth counterculture were the all-encompassing character of its protest and the widespread experimentation with, but lack of consensus about, alternatives. Not just one or several aspects of American life were being questioned—if we add up all that was being protested we find that nearly everything American was found wanting. Politics, religion, the mass media, education, business and industry, the family—all were targets of the counterculture. Nothing "sacred" was spared.

At the same time, no comprehensive alternative model was articulated, at least not one around which the counterculture coalesced. Yet, in a piecemeal fashion, a remarkably wide range of alternatives to conventional institutions, life-styles, values, mores, and folkways were proposed and experimented with. What was going on was not only countercultural, it was multicountercultural.

Disenchantment with cultural, social, and political arrangements accompanied by proposals for and experimentation with alternatives is not unique to the sixties, of course. Protest has been an abiding, if undulating, characteristic of American society since its founding, and probably no nation has been the source of so many or so wide a variety of counterproposals about how society should be organized and how individuals ought to live. Protest in the past has been generally more reformist than revolutionary, and where revolutionary, it has operated from a very small base. Historians will disagree, perhaps, and point, for example, to the Civil War period as a time when a substantial number of Americans stood ready to abandon their country, or to the 1930s and 1940s when there was support for a thoroughgoing upturning of existing governmental structures and social arrangements on a Marxist model. In both these instances, however, the disenchantment was much more sharply focused and narrowly political than it was in the sixties, and there existed a reasonable degree of consensus around a single solution rather than advocacy of and experimentation with a great variety. The sixties, I am suggesting, were characterized by a crisis in consciousness unique in American history.

Since the sixties, the call for a radical upturning of existing political and social arrangements has been considerably muted. There remains nevertheless a residue of disenchantment with the conventional accompanied by an openness and, among a sizable minority, an active search for alternatives. Interestingly, the alternatives most actively pursued, as our volume makes clear, are those rooted in revolutionizing not society but the self.

Just what produced the youth counterculture of the sixties? Why did it lose its momentum when it did? What is signified by the crisis in consciousness that followed in its wake? What does it all portend for the future? Judging from the literature, there is agreement about some of the variables at work. Urbanization, for one, the rapid increase over the last decades in the education level of the population, the growing affluence of the society, the spread of the mass media, the population explosion, and the resulting increase in population density. All of these reflect changes of major moment whose effects, it is widely agreed, are hardly conducive to a stable society. Yet, to point to one or a combination of such factors as the causes of the youth rebellion and as leading to its manifest demise and latent continuity leaves the phenomenon largely unexplained. It needs also to be made clear just how the effects were produced: by what process does urbanization, increased education, the population explosion, and so forth make for widespread disenchantment with the everyday and produce an accompanying drive for alternatives?

The intervening variable, I shall here argue, is a cognitive one having to do with the way the world is apprehended and with whether or not and in what way that apprehension shapes and gives meaning to existence. The counterculture was grounded in a "new" cognition, recently emerging in American society and still not fully formed—a cognition affording a way to comprehend the world, but unlike its American predecessors, not one given to shaping and finding meaning in the world. The "new" cognition inspired the disenchantment associated with the counterculture and produced, at the same time, the crisis in consciousness that continues to be the counterculture's legacy. What then is the new cognition and whence did it come?

To answer these questions, it is necessary to specify beforehand the old cognitions, the ways of viewing the world that have been dominant in America's past, and to show how they both shaped the character of American life and gave meaning to it.

The way of viewing the world I wish to assert was dominant in America's past, and which is perhaps, indeed probably, dominant today, is one that conceives of human beings as essentially in control of what happens to them in this world and, if they believe in it, the next. In its earliest formulation, this view included a conception of God as having granted mankind this control—"God created human beings in his own image but then left them free to choose for or against him." As time went on, the idea that human beings were in control gained ascendency, so that it became the operating assumption, whether God was believed in or not.

An additional and related assumption is the idea that human beings can be held responsible for their behavior. The two follow logically on one another. If human beings are responsible, then they must be free; if they are free, then they must be responsible. Thus, being in control of their destinies, individuals could also be held to account for how they exercised that control.

Of course these assumptions were not explicit. Americans were not going around proclaiming themselves masters of their fate and responsible for their actions. Implicitly, however, as they lived their daily lives, these were (and for most, probably still are) their operating assumptions, the ones that guided most judgments made about their own behavior and the behavior of others. They were also the operating assumptions from which they responded to their environment.

This is not the place to trace historically the origins of this world view. Max Weber sees its source in the ideas of Calvin and the ascetic branches of Protestantism. It appears also to have some links to Arminianism, to the theological view that how human beings comport themselves in this life can influence their fate in the next—clearly a view that would ascribe freedom and responsibility to humankind. Whatever its origins, a world view that conceives of individuals as in control of their lives had a pervasive influence in shaping American culture and the social arrangements that emerged out of the American Revolution. The view also became a ground both for justifying cultural values and social structures and for making it meaningful to live in conformity with them.

The major cultural impact of the imagery was the high regard it afforded individual achievement. Achievement became the hallmark of individuals living their lives responsibly. Contrariwise, the failure to achieve was a sign of a person's not acting responsibly, or at least, not responsibly enough. What constituted achievement was also shaped by the imagery. Achievement came to mean acquisition—of money, goods, power, and prestige for oneself rather than, say, doing good for others; the latter would have been contrary to the assumption that individuals had the capacity to care for themselves.

This individualistic world view influenced social arrangements to the extent that they were constructed to be consistent with it. In all the major institutions of the society, it was a governing principle in how they were organized to allow individual behavior to be judged and rewarded (or punished) as if that behavior were determined entirely by the individual. The law, with its emphasis on individual accountability, was grounded in this principle, as was social welfare with its view that "charity was to be pursued out of Christian duty, not of any merit in the poor." The educational system, in its emphasis on achievement, took it for granted that individuals were free and must assume responsibility. Business and industry made the same assumptions about the performance of its employees.

Built into the world view was also a rationalization of the kind of society it had wrought. Thus, it was reasonable that criminals be punished, because they had the option not to be; and that the poor live with their poverty, since it is their choice; and that students be failed in school, because they could have made it had they only tried; and that employees be fired, because it was up to them how they performed their jobs. The world view was also an element, although not the only one, in rationalizing the second-class citizenship accorded black Americans: "Blacks could be as success-ful as anyone else if only they would try."

The imagery also served to give purpose to life and to make it meaningful. There were goals set forth and paths to their achieve-ment and, built into the assumptions, the incentive to try. The rewards for most were less than the ideology promised. Yet, today's failure might always be transcended by tomorrow's triumph, and to cease trying was to admit only of a flaw in oneself.

This is not to say that the world view made no acknowledgment that individuals are differently endowed and, therefore, unequal in their ability to guide their destinies. The primary response that such recognition evoked, however, was that it was somehow in the power of individuals to make up for their deficiencies. How far one ran in the race of life, consequently, tended to be judged on the assump-tion that everyone began on the same starting line. It was how far one ran, not where one started, that counted.

Both at the nation's founding and throughout its history, a sec-ond mode of consciousness has coexisted with the one just de-scribed. This second mode was considerably less informing of American culture and social arrangements than the first. At a sec-ondary level, however, it has been an important force in main-taining stability in the society and in containing the potential for protest latent in the individualistic world view. For those absorbed by it, it has also been a source of meaning and purpose in their lives.

The principal agent of control in this second view is not humankind but God. It is God who has created the world and all that it is made up of, and it is God who decides what is and what is not to be in this world ahd the next. This view is much more otherwordly than the first view and endows human beings with considerably less influence in determing their fate. Persons are enjoined to lead their lives according to God's commandments; but God remains in control, and it is he who decides, or who in fact may have already decided, what each person's destiny is to be.

This view is in conflict theologically with the first one, and it obviously has different implications for practical conduct. A society organized around its precepts would certainly not place high regard on individual achievement. Yet, in a society so organized, persons conceiving of God as in control are disposed to go along. This is partly because social arrangements are thought to be God's doing; and even if they appear unfair, it is understood that God must have some reasons for making them so and, in the world to come, will make up for the unfairness. In addition, since social arrangements are ordained by God, it follows that individuals should perform without complaint the roles to which God has assigned them. A life lived from the perspective of this world view is made meaningful by the knowledge of God's concern and purposeful by God's instruction to do his will. There are rewards also from feeling that one is among the elect even though that is not absolutely sure.

Once again, this is not the place to go into the history of the imagery. Suffice to say, it is akin to the imagery that informed social life in the Middle Ages, given new impetus by Luther's theology, with its emphasis on salvation by grace, and Calvin's doctrine of predestination. The main thrust of the theology of American fundamentalism is consistent with it and, if contemporary evidence is any judge, the world view was (and is) also represented to varying degrees among the membership of all Christian denominations, including the Roman Catholic.

It has been possible for the two world views to coexist alongside each other throughout American history because the supernatural did not effectively challenge the social arrangements inspired by the individualistic view; on the contrary, it supported them. Also making for accommodation, if not compatibility, was the fact that, although the conceptions of God and his creation and purposes for man are different, both world views acknowledge God and his ultimate dominion over the world.

These modes of consciousness survive today. Indeed, as was suggested earlier, the individualistic mode is probably still the dominant one in the country as a whole. In the San Francisco Bay Area, the individualistic world view commands support from about 25 percent of the population—at least, that proportion chose to say that their own will power was the single most important influence in their lives. The supernatural view has less support—16 percent acknowledge God or some other supernatural force to be the most important influence on their lives. And once again the chances are that the figures would be higher for the country as a whole.

Also, it is evident from the Bay Area survey that how the question on world view is asked influences how much support various alternatives attract. Thus, while 25 percent say their life is governed by their own will power, 46 percent strongly agree that, "whenever I fail, I have no one to blame but myself"; and 37 percent strongly agree that, "if one works hard enough, he can do anything he wants to." Similarly, while 16 percent acknowledge God as control agent, 23 percent agree that God influences history, and 25 percent strongly agree that "poverty is due to God giving people different abilities so that the work of the world will get done."

The varying estimates of support for the two world views suggest that it will take research other than ours to develop a wholly reliable and valid way to measure them. Still, for present purposes, the figures afford evidence that the world views that have been described remain viable and operative for some substantial proportion of the population.

The burden of the argument being presented is not so much that these modes of consciousness survive today but that they were dominant in America's past. For the present, their dominance must remain an assertion, made reasonable, we hope, by what has been said about them thus far, but requiring further demonstration through harder evidence than is now at hand.

During the period of the alleged dominance of the two world views—judged to be undoubtedly until the turn of the century, probably until the 1930s and 1940s, and more than likely still today—protest was not absent from the American scene. These modes of consciousness, for all the support they gave to existing social arrangements, were not able to contain all dissent. The protest, however, came from within rather than outside of the prevailing imagery, and most of it came from those making the individualistic rather than the supernatural assumptions. What was essentially protested was that social arrangements were not living up to the imagery, that impediments in the form of slavery, bigotry—especially against Roman Catholics and immigrants— monopoly control of industry, and low wages were unwarranted constraints on the inherent rights of human beings to pursue their own destinies. The thrust of the protest, consequently, was not to upturn the society to conform to a different world view but to reform it to conform to the espoused imagery.

Protest emerged much less from those immersed in a super-natural mode of consciousness, and not because they were neces-sarily more content with the way things were. On the contrary, the world was wicked and full of sin. But the only path to social regeneration was through God, and if human beings could do anything it would be through winning everyone to him. When, rarely, protest did emerge from persons holding to this mode of con-sciousness, it tended to be around an issue thought to represent a direct affront to God, such as businesses remaining open on Sundays or the drinking of alcoholic beverages being too openly and widely countenanced.

The youth rebellion of the 1960s was not entirely uninformed by the modes of consciousness just described. Indeed, a considerable part of the outrage of youth was grounded in a perceived discrepan-cy between principles espousing the right of human beings to fulfill themselves and practices abridging that right. Also present, although at a lower key and a distinctly secondary level, was a con-ception of a nation turned too far from the God of its creation. By and large, however, the youth counterculture was more denying than confirming of old world views. Its informing power came from a way of comprehending the world basically at odds with in-dividualistic and supernatural modes of consciousness. This alter-native world view was not new to the counterculture. It had been slowly diffusing, albeit in an inchoate form, through the American population over a number of decades.

The new cognition has its inspiration from science, including the social sciences. The sciences do not contribute a fully articulated world view, but one which, even in its unfolding state, comes in conflict with supernatural and individual modes of consciousness. The sciences, and here I refer especially to the social sciences, effec-tively deny that human destiny is entirely either in man's or in God's control. The possibility that both may be control agents is not closed out; but that they function as either of the old imageries would have it is not accepted. Insofar as they exert an influence, the sciences tell us, they do so in interaction with other forces— biological, psychological, sociological, anthropological, genetical —all of which have some influence in shaping human and social events.

What the sciences do not now know and conceivably may never know is the precise character of the mix. Where heredity begins and environment ends in influencing the course of human life, for example, is not known now, and the chances are it will never be known. By virtue of the uncertainty, the sciences substitute a highly ambiguous world view for the relatively unambiguous, if their assumptions are accepted, earlier ones. An ambiguity of special significance for this discussion has to do with when individuals may be judged responsible for their behavior and when not. The assumption that the responsibility always lies with the individual is denied, but the sciences are unable to say when and when not, either in general terms or in particular instances. In every instance, what appears to be an event or individual behavior governed by human beings' acting out of free choice may in fact not be so governed, but science cannot say for sure.

The effect of a scientific world view is to undermine the underlying assumptions of the old imageries, the cultural values and social arrangements informed by them, and the inherent ability of these world views to give life meaning and purpose. At the same time, by virtue of its uncertainty and ambiguity, a scientific world view offers no clear alternative formula either for organizing society or for living one's life. What, for example, are the grounds for social organization if the boundaries between freedom and determinism cannot be established? What are human beings to live for if they cannot distinguish between what is decided for them and what they decide for themselves? As a consequence of its ambiguity in these respects, a scientific world view, as it diffuses and becomes the lens from which increasing numbers of people view their worlds, has the potential for creating crises both for the society and for individuals.

Since no one has made a study of the diffusion of a scientific world view, it is impossible to say when the process began and at what pace it has proceeded. Nor is it possible to describe the various guises in which it is manifested among those who have absorbed it. It is probably a reasonable conclusion that what is being diffused is not a highly sophisticated view or one that is uniform and consistent. The sciences themselves, and especially the social sciences, are not agreed on any single causal model, and it is hardly likely that such a model is being diffused to the general public.

But, for its effects to be felt, it is not necessary that a scientifically inspired world view be highly sophisticated and coherent. Effects will follow as long as it is recognized that there are variables at work—whether they be genetic, biological, sociological, psychological—which function to shape, mold, and change human behavior and human institutions over and above the individual's ability to choose.

The effects of the diffusion of a scientific world view were being experienced in the United States well before the sixties, most dramatically in changing attitudes toward the poor and in changing white perceptions of blacks and blacks' perceptions of themselves. Less dramatically, the effects were also being felt in the courts of the land, in its educational institutions, in the churches, in business and industry—indeed in all facets of American life. Such ideas as "the poor are poor because they choose to be poor," "blacks could be as well off as whites if only they would try," "punishment ought to fit the crime," "up or out", did not go entirely unchallenged in an era when individualism was dominant—mostly, however, because compassionate people were not willing to countenance the implications then because the ideas themselves were judged false. Confronted from a scientific perspective, however, all of these ideas become suspect: "What causes poverty may not be known precisely but it is patently false to believe that it is the result of individual choice." "Whether it is white racism or latent social forces or historical processes that have produced oppression of the blacks in the United States, it is ridiculous to think that blacks ever had the option to be as successful materially in the United States as whites." "Individuals commit crime to be sure, but it does not follow necessarily that the fault is theirs; the guilt may very well rest with society."

Criticism of existing social arrangements emanating from a public opinion and from an elite more and more informed by a scientific world view, however dimly perceived, brought with it a call for social reform. The call had been quietly sounding throughout much of the early part of the century, though not loud enough to be heard and responded to. It was not until the late 1930s and 1940s that a scientific perspective had diffused sufficiently to have much clout. Beginning at about that time, rather serious efforts began to be made in the United States to deal with neglected social problems, most especially the problems of poverty and the secondary status afforded black citizens, and to do so in the light of the new knowledge coming from the social sciences.

By and large, these efforts at social reform delivered much less than was promised. This was partly because the new cognition was ambiguous about what effective reform would constitute. For example, what ought the dividing line be between individuals being helped and being called on to help themselves? Reform efforts also suffered because policy makers failed to respond to the call, implicit in a scientific world view, for a reconsideration of the bases for distributing societal rewards. In effect, what is the justification, when it is made evident that individuals are not in control of their own destinies, to base a societal reward and punishment system on the assumption that they are in control?

The failure to respond is due probably to the fact that the implication is not recognized, as well as to a reluctance to recognize it. In any case, although the matter of taking account in social policy of differences in endowment has since surfaced, social reform efforts in the fifties ended up being more informed by an individualistic mode of consciousness than by a scientific one. Thus, for example, programs to relieve poverty were directed much more toward getting "poor people to the point where they can help themselves" than to changing social arrangements so that societal rewards would be distributed according to a principle such as "from each according to his abilities and to each according to his needs."

By the time of the sixties many Americans whose hopes and aspirations had been raised had become bitterly frustrated when things were not made considerably better for them. To their ranks were added many, more affluent, Americans made sensitive to the inequities of the society by their growing exposure to what the sciences were learning and saying about it. Thus, at the time of the outbreak of the youth rebellion there existed a widespread disenchantment with a social system that had failed to fulfill the hopes of a better society, which the alternative world view had nurtured.

The open rebellion that followed is not to be understood wholly as a result of a clash of world views, of course. An alternative world view was a necessary ingredient, it is being argued here, and an ingredient that had a powerful influence on shaping the character of the protest. It is evident, however, that the youth counterculture would not have happened nearly as early as it did without the triggering effect of the Vietnam War. It was necessary, too, that a leadership should emerge to organize the protest. The state of relative affluence in the society, affording the resources to protest, was also a conditioning factor.

That the outbreak occurred principally among college youth was also no accident. They were the most affected by the Vietnam War. They had the "leisure" to protest, and the wherewithal; this was not a rebellion of the poor. And they were the most exposed part of the citizenry to the altered world view being provided by the sciences; majors in the social sciences were prominent in their leadership.

Although the participants were unaware of it, the youth counterculture, once launched, quickly came to reflect both the power of a scientific world view to expose the myths of old world views and its failure to contribute an alternative myth as a substitute for the old ones. The counterculture was clear and united in its stand that the old myths and the social arrangements and ways of life they had fostered were no longer viable and acceptable. It was unable to come up with an agreed on substitute to fill the void it created, although it insisted in a kind of desperation that the void be filled.

In the absence of a vision to be derived from a scientific understanding of the world, nearly everything that afforded even a slight promise of answers to the question of meaning were subject to being tried and experimented with. Old ideas were brought out, dusted off, and made available either in their original or in amended forms. Ideas were also imported from abroad and entered in the competition. New, or seemingly new, solutions were also part of the variety from which choices might be made.

Some of the proposed alternatives called for a transformation of society. Marxism in many guises and Maoism were the most prominent of these. Communes organized around other and varying world views constituted another kind of societal solution. More frequently, the alternatives were characterized by solutions grounded in transformation of self. Here the sciences, most notably psychology, were the inspiration for some of the movements spawned by the counterculture. Religion—Eastern and Western—the occult, astrology, drugs, and extrasensory perception, were the sources of other alternative realities. Some of the things tried worked for those who tried them, but there was no solution on which there was enough agreement to form a mass base for revolution, symbolic or real.

The time, in effect, was not ripe for a confrontation of world views, as yet unevenly matched. The old world views simply had too much going for them, in the number of their adherents and in their control of existing social arrangements, to be effectively challenged. The new cognition was, at best, still a weak adversary ideologically; and its adherents, while vocal and visible, were small in number and without effective control of a base of power.

The youth counterculture ended its more visible phase, a movement ahead of its time, more a foreshadowing of things to come than a signaling of their arrival. The crisis in consciousness presaged will not, it seems now evident, come quickly to pass, at least not for the majority of the population. Yet, unless something entirely unforeseen occurs, the further diffusion of a world view informed by the sciences seems inevitable.

What this will mean for the future will depend a great deal on whether the sciences are able, out of new discoveries, to identify a life purpose to which individuals can commit themselves and around which a new social order can be built. If they can, there will be a period of struggle and conflict before the society is transformed in a scientific model. It is unlikely that in the process the old modes of consciousness will have the vitality to withstand the takeover.

Should the sciences fail to incorporate into their world view a way to make life meaningful, as seems more likely, the scenario for the future is likely to resemble, only writ large, what the society experienced in miniature in the sixties. There will again be disenchantment with the way things are, and a lack of consensus about what would be a viable alternative; only this time, because the eroding power of the diffusion of a scientific perspective will have had its effect, the old world views will not have prevailed. In their place, there will be competition from a variety of alternative myths seeking to fill the gap in meaning left by the sciences.

It now seems doubtful that any single alternative vision can come to prevail, since it would have to be compatible with or supersede a scientific comprehension of the world. The crucial question, then, will be whether a society, other than a dictatorship, can result where disconsensus rather than relative consensus prevails about what constitutes a meaningful life, and where, presumably, many people will have found no answer to the question of meaning at all.

Viewed from the perspective of what has been happening in America in the seventies, a scenario for the future such as the one just described seems hardly in the cards. The campuses are now quiet. There is no violent protest on the streets. The sixties' decline in church membership appears to have been arrested. The nation seems ready to return to "normalcy," to the old modes of consciousness and the kind of society they wrought. Perhaps.

The position advocated here is that the end of the open rebellion did not mark the end of the process of which it is a part. All that has gone before in this volume is testimony that the search for alternative realities continues.

ABOUT THE CONTRIBUTORS

RANDALL H. ALFRED

Randall H. Alfred, who describes himself as a "nondirective shaman," received his A.B., *magna cum laude*, in Culture and Behavior in 1967 from Yale University, where he was elected to Phi Beta Kappa. He has continued his studies in sociology at the University of California, Berkeley, on a Woodrow Wilson Fellowship and received an M.A. in 1968. From 1969 to 1971, he was Instructor of Sociology at Southampton College of Long Island University in New York, where he also served on the counseling staff. He is now writing science-fiction stories, poetry, double-dactyl verse, and a book on consciousness, value change, and the environmental crisis. He is active in conservation and other political organizations.

ROBERT N. BELLAH

Robert N. Bellah is Ford Professor of Sociology and Comparative Studies in the Department of Sociology at the University of California, Berkeley. He is the author of *Beyond Belief, The Broken Covenant,* and other books and articles. He is currently preoccupied with the role of religion in the history of the American republic.

CHARLES Y. GLOCK

Charles Y. Glock is Professor of Sociology at the University of California and also Director of the Research Program in Religion and Society at the university's Survey Research Center. He is committed to the proposition that how the religious questions of life are answered has a central bearing on how social life is organized, and he has devoted a major part of his research career to tracing out the connections. Next on his agenda is a monograph on racial prejudice, after which he plans to turn to further work on reality structuring and social organization.

BARBARA HARGROVE

Newly appointed to the faculty of Yale University's School of Divinity, Barbara Hargrove came to work with the research team during the 1972–73 academic year under a grant from the National Endowment for the Humanities. She styles herself as a "retread" scholar, since she interrupted her education in the middle of her undergraduate years to become a farm housewife and the mother of four children. She is, then, a product of both the campus of the 1940s and that of the 1960s. Her interest in the young stems both from the recency of some of her undergraduate years and contacts made through her children and their friends. Similarly, her interest in religion ranges from participation in traditional church activities to contact with many of the less customary activities of the campus of the 1960s. She is the author of a text in the sociology of religion, *Reformation of the Holy*.

DONALD HEINZ

Donald Heinz's forthcoming monograph, *Jesus in Berkeley*, is his doctoral dissertation for the program in Religion and Society at the Graduate Theological Union in Berkeley. After spending two years as a participant-observer for his dissertation research, he led a project for the National Council of Churches on Religious Signals in Culture and Counterculture and recently has begun a study of religious and social values in alternative family styles for the Center for Ethics and Society of the Lutheran Church in America. He is a Lutheran clergyman, a church musician, a therapist, a carpenter-gardener, and an active participant in a family of five. His current research interests are new religious consciousness, intentional communities, and the evangelical revival. He is now Visiting Assistant Professor of Religious Studies at California State University at Chico.

GREGORY JOHNSON

Gregory Johnson is Assistant Professor of Sociology at the University of Massachusetts at Boston. He did his graduate work in the Department of Social Relations at Harvard University, where he received his M.A. and Ph.D. His primary research interests include the study of youth and adolescence and the study of therapeutic communities. At present, he is engaged in a study of a therapeutic community for former drug addicts in San Francisco, California.

RALPH LANE, JR.

Ralph Lane, Jr., Professor of Sociology at the University of San Francisco and Adjunct Professor at the Graduate Theological Union, has monitored over the years the myriad changes in the Roman Catholic church in the United States. He has shared his observations from time to time with his colleagues, chiefly in the pages of *Sociological Analysis*, the journal of the Association for the Sociology of Religion, of which he was president in 1970–71. In recent years, whether in despair or not, he has turned his research attention more and more to the social organization of nonhuman primates.

JEANNE MESSER

Jeanne Messer, contributor of the material on Divine Light Mission, was not an original member of the research team but was a devotee of Guru Maharaj Ji who agreed to write a contribution as the Divine Light movement gained in size and notoriety and seemed an essential topic for this volume.

Mrs. Messer has an A.B. in sociology from the University of California at Berkeley and is presently Administrative Director for the Institute for Research in Social Behavior, Berkeley. Her primary occupational interest is in problems of contemporary social research design (especially survey) in the face of rising costs, increased concern with the protection of human subjects, and increasingly elusive foci of research, including the problems of studying "consciousness" raised in this volume. With her husband and young son, she is a member of a large household of devotees and is engrossed in the problems and rewards of group living and the expansion of her sense of "family".

RICHARD OFSHE

Richard Ofshe is Associate Professor of Sociology at the University of California at Berkeley. He received his Ph.D in sociology from Stanford University in 1968 and has been on the faculty of U.C. Berkeley since 1967. His research interests center around issues of social structure and social choice (co-author of *Utility and Choice in Social Interaction* and editor of *Interpersonal Behavior in Small Groups*) with particular focus on the transmission of social pressure at the institutional level to the level of interpersonal behavior.

THOMAS PIAZZA

Thomas Piazza escaped from a Benedictine monastery a few years ago and has been engaged in varied pursuits ever since. After spending some time as business manager of a college, he came to Berkeley to continue studies in sociology at the University of California. His interest in Judaism goes back several years to a time when he studied Hebrew and visited Israel. He once taught a course in Jewish culture at a university in Argentina. At the moment he is working on a book on American mythology.

LINDA K. PRITCHARD

Linda K. Pritchard is pursuing a doctorate in history at the University of Pittsburgh. In her thesis she is seeking to sort out the interplay between theological factors and social and economic ones in the emergence of the Second Great Awakening. She was recruited to the religious consciousness project during a visit to Berkeley to see whether or not it might be helpful for a historian of religion to have some exposure to sociology. Through her participation in the project she demonstrated more how much the sociology of religion needs to be informed by history.

DONALD STONE

Donald Stone is a graduate student in sociology at University of California, Berkeley. His chapter grows out of three years' participation and observation in a number of encounter, body, and consciousness-raising groups in the San Francisco Bay Area. Interviews with participants from groups mentioned in this chapter, notably from *est*, are the basis of a forthcoming monograph on the religious and political implications of the Human Potential movement, "Enlightenment American-style."

ALAN TOBEY

Alan Tobey has pursued an interest in American culture and its changes through formal education at the Massachusetts Institute of Technology, Lutheran Theological Seminary, and the Graduate Theological Union; and less formally, through participation in most of the causes, disciplines, fads, and entertainments of the recent counterculture. His present academic task is the development of a sociology of consciousness; otherwise, he is busy at such pursuits as winemaking, yoga and meditation, Renaissance music, and herbal medicine.

JIM WOLFE

Jim Wolfe is a poet, composer, minister, cherry picker, and house painter. As an advocate of civil rights, he worked in the Hough ghetto of Cleveland before undertaking graduate work in religion and society at the Graduate Theological Union in Berkeley, and he recently worked with six suburban Bay Area congregations in their attempts to understand and counteract white racism. As a proponent of the new culture, Jim has been on the staff of Montclair Presbyterian Church and contributed to the planning and execution of experimental worship services at First Presbyterian Church; he has also taught new religious consciousness to ministers at the Advanced Pastoral Studies center of San Francisco Theological Seminary. He has taught at the G.T.U., at Holy Names College in Oakland, California, and at the University of British Columbia in Vancouver. He plans to write books on new culture values and on the religious peace movement, as well as stretching the present chapter on the impact of the new culture on Protestant congregations into a book.

ROBERT WUTHNOW

Robert Wuthnow is Assistant Professor of Sociology at the University of Arizona. While at the Survey Research Center, he served as Project Director for the survey phase of the religious consciousness project. An analysis of the relations between different forms of consciousness and contemporary social unrest, based on this survey, is presented in his forthcoming monograph, *The Consciousness Reformation*. Wuthnow is also co-author of *Adolescent Prejudice*, and his articles have been published in such journals as *Psychology Today, Journal for the Scientific Study of Religion,* and *Review of Religious Research.*

INDEX

Abolitionism: as quasi-religious sect, 308; during Second Great Awakening, 314, 315; and socialism, 322

Achievement: as value, 357

Adventists: sects, 300

Afrikaners: fundamentalism among, 351

Age: of 3HO members, 13, 22; of Maharaj Ji, 52; of DLM devotees, 62; of Synanon residents, 124; of Church of Satan members, 193, 194; and attraction to new religions, 285 −286; and participation in new religions, 286

Agrarian reform, 300, 308; and socialism, 322

Ahlstrom, Sydney E., 295

Aikido: classes at 3H Solstice, 17; concept of God in, 102; described, 102n; participation in, 274

Alameda County Sheriff's Deputies, 83

Alcohol: in Hare Krishna, 39, 49; in DLM, 64, 65; in Synanon, 116, 121, 129; in Church of Satan, 186; at Grace Church, 231−232; in Human Potential movement, 345

Alcoholics Anonymous: Synanon evolved from, 117

Algiers, Algeria: Leary and Cleaver in, 78

Alinsky, Saul, 241

Allende, President, 90

Alpert, Richard, 341

American Anti-Slavery Society, 315

American Baptist Home Mission Society, 300, 308, 314

American Bible Society, 314

American Indians. See Native Americans

American Society for Promoting the Observance of the Seventh Commandment, 315

American Sunday School Union: as missionaries, 314

American Temperance Society, 315

American Tract Society, 314

And It Is Divine, 64, 66, 67

Anglicans. See Episcopalians

Anglo-Catholic Episcopalians, 300, 308

Anglo-Catholic movement, 311

Ann Arbor, Michigan: CCR at, 163, 172; as "liberated zone," 338

Antimission Baptists, 300, 308

Antinomianism: in Human Potential movement, 113; among Synanon residents, 132

Aquarian Age, 5, 6, 11, 13, 26, 27, 344

Arica Training: as part of Human Potential movement, 93, 97; as Eastern discipline adapted to West, 96; described, 97n; numbers trained, 100

Arjun, Guru: in Sikh scriptures, 12

"Armed defense," 86

Arminianism, 357

Ashrams: 3HO, 7−8, 13, 17, 19, 23; DLM, 62−67 *passim*

Assagioli, Robert: on Psychosynthesis, 101

Associate Reform, 301

Association for Humanistic Psychology, 98

Aston, Judith, 109n

Astrology: in 3HO, 17; as part of occult revival, 180; and witchcraft, 181; and Church of Satan, 186; as sect (1820 −1860), 300, 308, 329; in Mesmerism, 320; provides alternative world view, 365

Auburn Theological Seminary, 313

Augsburg Confession, 301, 311

Augustana Synod: organized by immigrants, 316

Authoritarianism: as future scenario, 350−351

Authority: in DLM ashrams, 64; in Human Potential movement, 74, 113, 114; in Synanon, 135, 136; in Church of Satan, 183, 184, 197, 198, 199, 200; in traditional Protestant denominations, 303, in Mormon church, 318. *See also* Charismatic leadership; Hierarchy; Leadership

Baez, Joan, 79

Baptists: sects (1800−1860), 300, 312; historical dominance, 302; theology, 302; growth, 326

and politics, 90, 145, 149, 150, 153, 160, 276, 343; defined, 140; finances, 144; numbers in family, 144; leadership, 144–145, 159; communal living in, 144, 153, 160; activities, 144, 153, 157; meaning of Jesus in, 140, 145, 148–157; as church, 145, 153, 159, 160; cultural conditions at start of, 146–147; "third way," 151, 159; Dwight House, 157; image of homecoming in, 157–158; cooperation with other groups, 216; openness in, 345; future in authoritarian society, 351. *See also* Neo-Christian movements

Churches. *See* Campus ministries; Established religions

Church of Jesus Christ of the Latter-day Saints. *See* Mormons

Church of Satan: as institution, 183; research design, 183–185; leadership, 184, 197, 198, 199, 200; magic in, 185; attitudes toward occult, 185–187; drug use condemned, 186–187, 195; philosophy, 187; attractions of membership, 187–194, 195; membership and recruitment, 193, 194–195; finances, 194; contradictions in, 198–199; secrecy in, 199; as manipulationist sect, 199–200. *See also* Satanism

Church of the Fountainhead, 183

Civil Rights Movement: joined politics and religion, 78; FSM as offspring of, 79, 83; effect on established religion, 328, 329

Cleaver, Eldridge, 78, 81

Clothing: of 3HO members, 6, 9, 13, 14, 17, 18, 29; in Hare Krishna, 31, 38, 39; of DLM devotees, 62; standards enforced by Chilean regime, 351

Cloven Hoof: as Church of Satan newsletter, 184; denigrated white witchcraft, 185

Coffin, William Sloan, 340

Columbus, Ohio: Hare Krishna in, 33

Communal living: in 3HO, 7, 8, 27; in Hare Krishna, 45, 46; in DLM, 64–65; united political and religious radicals, 80; in Synanon, 128, 129–130; in CWLF, 144, 153, 160; in CCR precursors, 174; in CCR, 177, 218; in campus ministries, 209, 210,

211; and Jewish students, 253, 255, 261, 262; and non-Jewish students, 253, 261, 262; in 19th century communitarian sects, 320, 322

Communism: Catholic response to, 174; as religion, 321

Communist Party: weakness of, 83

Communitarian sects, 301, 320–322

Communities, intentional: two-person relationships in, 46

Community service. *See* Social action

Congregationalists: sects (1800–1860), 300, 308, 317; as dominant denomination, 302; theology, 302; as missionaries, 314; factions reunited, 325; decline of, 326

Countercultural movements: listed, 268; knowledge of in general population, 269, 270, 272; attraction to, 270, 272–273, 285, 286; participation in, 271, 273, 278, 286, 288; and politics, 276, 277, 278; and life-style, 278–279; and drug use, 280–281; introspection in, 281, 282; and conventional religious belief, 283, 284; education in, 287, 288; and marriage, 289, 290; and employment, 289, 290, 291; and discontent, 290, 291; and geographical mobility, 290, 291; impact of, 292

Counterculture: Asian influence, 1, 2, 7, 205, 223, 341, 347–348; Native American influence, 3, 223, 341; 3HO devotees' background in, 21–22; Hare Krishna opposed to, 43, 49; failure of exemplified by Haight-Ashbury, 48; drug use, 77, 105, 275, 279–280, 341; politics, 81, 178–179, 205, 275–276, 277–278; new religions, 139–140, 175, 292; presents alternatives, 146–147, 149, 275, 355; Jesus in, 147, 151, 152, 153–154; importance of experience in, 151; Catholic lay groups in, 174; and discontent, 175, 275, 287–291, 355; magic in, 195; music in, 195, 196; Satanism's lack of appeal to, 195–196, 198; effect on established religions, 203–204, 205, 206, 223–225, 227–244, 328; missionaries to, 205–206; introspections in, 205, 281–282; and campus ministries, 211–215 *passim;* dream of, 231; Berkeley students' identifica-

DATE			
NOV. 1 8 1988			
FEB. 2 4 1989			